THE STORM CLOUDS CLEAR
OVER CHINA

THE STORM CLOUDS

EDITED AND COMPILED,

WITH AN INTRODUCTION AND NOTES, BY

Sidney H. Chang and Ramon H. Myers

CLEAR OVER CHINA

岑山春
外孫雨
孫卿霽
原主
涯

THE MEMOIR OF
Ch'en Li-fu WITHDRAWN
1900–1993

The landscape painting on the title page is
by Sun Lu-ch'ing. It is inscribed by her
husband, Ch'en Li-fu: "Mountains after the
spring rain — for Hsiao-jung, our grandchild"

Hoover Institution Press Publication No. 419

First printing, 1994
00 99 98 97 96 95 94   9 8 7 6 5 4 3 2 1
Simultaneous first paperback printing, 1994
00 99 98 97 96 95 94   9 8 7 6 5 4 3 2 1

Manufactured in the United States of America

The paper used in this publication meets the minimum requirements
of American National Standard for Information Sciences—Permanence
of Paper for Printed Library Materials, ANSI Z39.48–1984. ∞

Library of Congress Cataloging-in-Publication Data
Ch'en, Li-fu, 1900–
    The storm clouds clear over China : the memoir of Ch'en Li-fu,
1900–1993 / edited, compiled, and with an introduction and notes by
Sidney H. Chang and Ramon H. Myers.
        p.   cm. — (Studies in economic, social, and political change,
the Republic of China)
    Includes bibliographical references and index.
    ISBN 0-8179-9271-5 (alk. paper). — ISBN 0-8179-9272-3 (pbk. :
alk. paper)
        1. Ch'en, Li-fu, 1900– . 2. Statesmen—China—Biography.
3. Statesmen—Taiwan—Biography. I. Chang, Hsu-hsin. II. Myers,
Ramon Hawley, 1929– . III. Title. IV. Series.
DS777.5366.C644A3   1994
951.05'092—dc20   93-23214
                                                            CIP

340029

*To the memory of those who
sacrificed for the common good of
the Chinese national revolution*

Contents

                 Spring 1945–Winter 1949

CHAPTER NINE   The Hopeful Years   218
                 1950–1993

                 Notes   257

                 Glossary   301

                 Selected Bibliography   323

                 Index   349

Editors' Note

AFTER MANY YEARS OF WRITING and rewriting, we at last have the memoir of Ch'en Li-fu. Timothy Tung did a preliminary English translation of some of the original eleven-hundred-page handwritten Chinese manuscript. We then edited that manuscript down to seven hundred pages, carefully checking the original Chinese writing of Ch'en against Tung's translation. Ch'en Li-fu also gave ten oral interviews, averaging two to three hours each, in the fall of 1991 and in the summer of 1992 when we were in Taipei. Questions and answers related to the various chapters of the manuscript were tape-recorded, which added two hundred pages of transcriptions to the Chinese original. From the summer of 1992 to the end of that year, we corresponded with Ch'en. All this information was integrated into the final product, along with notes, bibliography, and glossary. In addition, we verified the facts and events recorded in the memoirs and the tapes through such sources as *U.S. Military Reports: China 1911–1941*, *U.S. State Department Confidential Central Files: China Internal Affairs 1945–1949*, and other publications of the State Department, notably *U.S. Foreign Relations*, 1927–1951. The rich collections of the Stanford University libraries, the Columbia University libraries, the various libraries of the University of California at Berkeley, and the Henry Madden Library of California State University, Fresno, provided more information.

At California State University, Fresno, several colleagues contributed to our endeavor. We wish to express our gratitude to the following: the typing expertise and other assistance of Geri Simmons and Anita L. Ramirez; the professional assistance rendered by Interlibrary Loan Assistant Jean M. Tempesta and Government Documents Librarian Olivia Estrada of the Henry Madden Library; the photographic reproductions provided by Randy Dotta-Dovidio, Instructional Media Center; the moral, spiritual, and logistical support of Peter Klassen, dean of the School of Social Sciences, John Kendall, chairman, Robert Smetherman, member of the history department, the University Research Awards Review Committee, and the Research Committee of the School of Social Sciences. We also appreciate the sabbatical and research leaves granted by our home institutions.

We also owe much to the support and interest of Yao-tung Chao of the China Steel Corporation; Donald Jordan of Ohio University; David Yu, attorney-at-law with Orro and Reno, Concord, New Hampshire; C.C.Y. Inc., of Oakland, California; Daniel Pao-hsi Chao of Tunghai University; Ts'ai Ling of the Hoover Institution; Yu-sheng Chang of the Pacific Cultural Foundation; and Chou Chung-fei of the Shanghai Academy of Social Sciences Institute of World Economy. We were greatly assisted in obtaining information and documents by Martin Heijdra of Princeton University's Gest Oriental Library; Cheng-hua Wang of the National Chengchi University's history department; Tsui-hua Yang of the Institute of Modern Chinese History of Academia Sinica; Jui-lin Lu and Taijing Li of Fu Hsing Kang College; Lung-t'ien Ku of National Taiwan University; Jan-chih Hsieh and Ho-ching P'eng of Chinese Culture University; Yun-han Li of the Kuomintang Historical Archives; Yu-lin Hau, member of the Control Yuan; Paul Shih-chen Cheng of the Institute for Information Industry; Tien-shan Wang of the Association of Overseas Chinese in the United States from Szechuan Province; Ta-chung Pu of *Chung-kuo shih-pao*; and Ts'an-hua T'ang of the Chinese Consolidated Benevolent Association of New England in Boston. We also acknowledge the encouragement of T'ien-kou Chow, Leonard Gerald Pardue, and Chung-ning Chang. For their tireless proofreading and painstaking corrections, we thank Elaine Pardue Chang, Margaret Plucinsky, and Marcy Kuenstler Curtiss.

The photographs are from Ch'en Li-fu's personal collection. In romanizing Chinese names and terms, we used the Wade-Giles system except in limited examples of a preferred personal romanization.

Author's Note

Owing to advanced scientific and technological innovations, we all now live in a "global village" of great complexity. Nothing can be accomplished by one person. Many friends and colleagues generously gave me their help. They copied my Chinese version, searched and researched libraries and archives, and provided thoughtful suggestions. In completing my *Memoir* for English-language readers, I have been touched by the patience and long days of exhaustive research of my two editors, Sidney H. Chang and Ramon H. Myers. I also want to thank the editorial staff of the Hoover Institution Press for their assistance. For the preliminary translation of some of my *Memoir* from Chinese into English, I appreciate Timothy Tung's efforts. I also want to thank the Taipei Pacific Cultural Foundation for a research grant that made possible the typing of the preliminary draft of the English translation.

Introduction

MARSHALL PÉTAIN ONCE SAID that "to write one's memoirs is to speak ill of everybody except oneself."[1] Does the memoir make for a true, reliable history, or is it a self-serving account to interpret history in a particular way? How do we judge the authenticity of the memoir, especially when the author was at the center of great events? By what standards can we judge a memoir to be true and credible? These are questions worth pondering when we read the personal account of how Ch'en Li-fu (now ninety-four years old) served Chiang Kai-shek for twenty-five years and moved in the highest circles of power within the Chinese Nationalist party (Kuomintang, or KMT) and the government of the Republic of China (ROC).

Ch'en begins by apologetically confessing that he never wanted to write about his life and that only the constant urging of his friends and colleagues forced him to reconsider. In fact, Ch'en expresses considerable personal pain when recalling the bitter experiences he suffered. Like so many whose lives have intersected with twentieth-century Chinese history, Ch'en hopes that his recollections will help future historians get the facts right about China's tragic fate. But many have advanced that argument to justify their efforts to make sense of history.

What makes Ch'en's account significant, at least to us, is his candor about personal mistakes and his charity of feelings toward those great men he observed and with whom he interacted. When evaluating the weaknesses and strengths of Chiang Kai-shek, for example, Ch'en never hides that Chiang had a fierce temper, thirsted for power, and made policy mistakes that contributed in complex ways to the defeat of the KMT and the ROC government in 1949. Yet Ch'en argues that Chiang was the only leader the KMT and the ROC government had after the death of Sun Yat-sen and that, if not for the conflation of certain events, Chiang and the ROC government might have unified China and created a different China than did the Communist party and its leader, Mao Tse-tung.

But who is Ch'en Li-fu? Ch'en Li-fu (Tsu-yen) was born on August 21, 1900, in Wu-hsin County of Chekiang Province, the youngest surviving son, along with four others (two elder sisters and two elder brothers, the elder of whom, Kuo-fu, was eight years Li-fu's senior) of ten children. Li-fu grew up in a tightly knit, loving family. His father had passed the special provincial imperial examinations to earn the *kung-sheng* degree, but he later went into business. His second uncle, Ch'en Ch'i-mei (Ying-shih), was a right-hand man of Sun Yat-sen and led the Shanghai Uprising in early November 1911, only to be assassinated by Yüan Shih-k'ai's agents on May 18, 1916.[2] That Ch'en's family had close ties with leading Chinese revolutionaries undoubtedly impressed him but did not dampen his desire to study mining and engineering. Li-fu majored in engineering at Peiyang University in Tientsin and in 1925 earned an M.A. degree in mining engineering at the University of Pittsburgh, writing a thesis about mechanizing and electrifying the Chinese mining industry.

Ch'en's brother Kuo-fu introduced him to Chiang Kai-shek on January 9, 1926, and Ch'en Li-fu accepted Chiang's offer to become his private secretary. He worked for several years in that capacity, later becoming secretary-general of the KMT, then minister of education, and finally a troubleshooter for Chiang Kai-shek until 1950, when he decided to leave political life and retire to the United States. After a checkered career of managing a newspaper, operating a chicken farm, and working at various jobs, he returned in 1970 to Taiwan, where he currently lives as this book is being published.

Ch'en's memoir reveals little of his interior world, nor does it offer personal ruminations about the key individuals who played a role in his life. Instead, the reader will find simple, matter-of-fact descriptions of the key people and main events in that critical period of China's history when the KMT and the Chinese Communist party (CCP) were locked in a fierce struggle. Ch'en's strong character, great confidence, and courage were products of a happy childhood and strong family relations. Ch'en never approved of the anti-Confucian rhetoric of the May Fourth literature, and as a strong nationalist he also valued such Confucian values as loyalty and self-cultivation to improve one's moral character. In his youth he rejected Marxism and admired American private enterprise management and engineering, which instilled in him a penchant for applying the scientific approach to solving problems. Without arrogance he speaks honestly and sincerely of others he knew well. Tenacious and tough in performing his duties, he was incredibly loyal to those he served. Ch'en's greatest regret was not working as a mining engineer; his single-minded purpose and ingenuity would have undoubtedly made him a successful one.

We learn little about Ch'en's family and personal life, especially his relations with his wife and other family members. Ch'en's memoir does, however, offer unusual evidence and insights to help us better understand certain events and how they influenced twentieth-century Chinese history. To highlight these extraordinary events, we need some historical context.

In the first decade of this century, student and military revolutionaries plotted to overthrow the Ch'ing monarchy, finally succeeding in 1911 but then failing to build a political center strong enough to preserve the young republic and keep China unified. Within five years, China had divided into regional power centers dominated by military commanders who waged war with one another. As China disintegrated into warlordism in the late teens, revolutionaries such as Sun Yat-sen established the Chinese Kuomintang (KMT) in 1919, and Li Ta-chao and others formed the CCP. Although these two parties briefly cooperated to destroy the regional warlords, attacking and defeating them in the eastern coastal provinces between September 1926 and March 1927, mistrust and treachery thoroughly undermined their cooperation. Thus on April 12, 1927, Chiang Kai-shek, leader of the KMT, ordered that the CCP be exterminated. Ch'en Li-fu helped organize the purge of the CCP in Shanghai, readily using the underworld gangs of that city in his mission. The CCP survived, however, and from then on both parties struggled to destroy each other and unify China. The next twenty-two years were a time of nation-building by the KMT; then came war with Japan, followed by civil war and the defeat of the KMT, culminating in the establishment of two separate Chinese states, the People's Republic of China (PRC) on the mainland and the ROC on Taiwan.

For the next thirty years, the CCP and its leader, Mao Tse-tung, isolated the PRC from most of the world, particularly the modern capitalist states, and embarked on radical societal reforms. Mao and the CCP not only created the greatest bureaucratic state in Chinese history but entirely reorganized village and city life, destroying the old society and integrating families into collective organizations. Anyone criticizing or opposing the new collective order was imprisoned or relegated to being a citizen with few rights. Meanwhile, the CCP leaders quarreled over how China should be developed; their struggles became so severe that in 1966 the party divided, plunging the country into chaos for more than a decade.

In 1978, after the death of Mao, the CCP's power holders, led by Teng Hsiao-p'ing, agreed that ideas, technology, and investment from the West were needed in the PRC. The expanding Western influence gradually loosened collective controls to allow families greater choice and more freedom. Freedom became associated with a rising economic boom, and people soon began enjoying material comforts. These developments gave rise to tensions between the new forms of individual expression and demands and the old habits and behaviors of socialist collective life. These tensions came to a head in the late spring of 1989, when, in public demonstrations in Beijing and other large cities, the people demanded that the CCP further relax its controls over society. These demonstrations were ruthlessly suppressed by the CCP and the armed forces. By 1993, however, the economy again boomed and talk of reforms seemed more permanent.

The island of Taiwan, under Japanese colonial rule since 1895, had, by the end of World War II, acquired roads, harbors, and railroads along with a small modern industrial base and a well-developed agricultural sector. After the island reverted to ROC rule on October 25, 1945, the ROC government in Nanking sent officials and KMT leaders to Taiwan to establish a provincial government similar to the one on the mainland. Their efforts failed, and on February 28, 1947, a great rebellion broke out in the cities, with people demanding a greater voice in the ROC's governance of the island. Although the central government suppressed the rebellion, killing thousands of Taiwanese, many elite fled overseas to establish a nationalist Taiwanese independence movement dedicated to ending KMT rule over the island.

Overwhelming numbers of communist troops were preparing to invade from Fukien when the ROC government and KMT party retreated to Taiwan in 1949. Their refuge became more secure in the summer of 1950 when North Korea invaded South Korea and the United States assigned its Seventh Fleet to the Taiwan Strait to deter communist attacks on Taiwan. Because the United States was now committed to keeping the Pacific Asian states from falling into the orbit of communist rule, the ROC government on Taiwan began receiving U.S. military and economic aid.

Challenged by the communist threat and the Taiwanese revolutionary movement, the KMT leadership realized that it could not survive unless it successfully modernized and democratized Taiwan. For the next forty years the KMT encouraged the traditional Chinese family and its organizations through land reform, local elections, free primary education, and so on. By the mid 1980s Taiwan's largely urban society possessed advanced manufacturing and service sectors that generated high per-capita income, provided high employment, and guaranteed price stability. In 1986 the KMT's paramount leader, Chiang Ching-kuo, confident of the country's economic prosperity and social stability, initiated political reforms that produced a free press, allowed competing political parties, and expanded national elections. Even the cold war between the PRC and the ROC began to change. In 1987 the ROC government decided to allow individuals to visit relatives in the PRC. The PRC approved, and within five years a booming trade and people exchange were taking place across the Taiwan Strait. A new era of cooperation between the regimes had begun.

Although the KMT and the CCP held opposing visions of how China should be modernized, both parties shared a Leninist-style method of governing in which a powerful leader and a small committee dominated the membership, who in turn controlled the levers of power in society. Many Chinese elite disliked both parties and tried to challenge them by creating a third party. That effort failed, and the KMT and the CCP continued to occupy center stage. To this day, however, no high KMT or CCP leader had published a detailed memoir, so we know little about the thinking and behavior of top leaders and how they influenced historical events. Therefore, the memoir of Ch'en Li-fu, Chiang Kai-shek's personal secretary and confidant for more than a quarter century, marks a historic breakthrough.

Ch'en never informs us why, after working so hard to become a mining engineer, he accepted Chiang Kai-shek's offer to be his secretary. We do know that Ch'en had rejected the radicalism of the May Fourth, 1919, movement and that Marxist writings had never persuaded him. But, like many young, educated people of his generation, he wanted to save China from becoming weak, poor, and humiliated by foreign powers. Nationalistic sentiments strongly burned within him, and Ch'en also believed in Sun Yat-sen's Three Principles of the People and vigorously endorsed Confucian values and institutions such as the family as necessary for revitalizing Chinese society. But as to why Ch'en suddenly decided to abandon a career of mining engineering for the life of a revolutionary, we can only speculate that Ch'en identified with his family, which had played a great role in the unfinished 1911 revolution, and must have felt morally obligated to his elder brother, Kuo-fu, who instead of educating himself had dedicated his entire life to the cause of revolution. Li-fu constantly refers to his elder brother with great affection and feeling, without revealing what views they must have shared or what anxieties they must have suffered.

When Ch'en Li-fu joined the Nationalist cause in Canton, the KMT, then allied with the CCP, was struggling to maintain its revolutionary base in Kwangtung Province and prepare for its military expedition to defeat the northern warlords. Ch'en, ignorant of politics and the sinister conspiracies being hatched between members of the KMT and the CCP, was convinced by one major incident of CCP treachery, which turned him into an ardent anti-Communist quite willing to use any means to destroy them before they destroyed him and the KMT.

Late on the night of March 18, 1926, Hu Kung-mien, a member of the CCP's Central Executive Committee, visited Chiang Kai-shek at his residence to warn him of a communist plot on his life. On March 20, Li Chih-lung, the communist captain of the gunboat *Chung-shan*, weighed anchor and sailed to the middle of the Huang-p'u River with guns ready to fire on Chiang's residence. On that same day, the wife of Wang Ching-wei, a famous revolutionary colleague of Sun's, called Chiang's residence several times inquiring as to his whereabouts; Chiang had, however, gone into hiding, and the CCP's plot to assassinate him failed. Chiang immediately asked the Russian advisers to leave Canton and arrested Wu T'ieh-cheng, police commissioner of Canton, and several others, but he did not incarcerate or execute those military commanders who Chiang believed had been involved in the conspiracy, such as Teng Yen-ta, whose loyalty and services Chiang hoped to win. Thus Chiang Kai-shek continued cooperating with the CCP so as to use its personnel and organizational skills for the Northern Expedition.

According to Ch'en, whose description of the day-to-day events of this incident makes it as memorable to the reader as it was to the young secretary, Chiang never forgot the duplicity of the CCP and those KMT leaders like Wang Ching-wei who were responsible for the attempt to murder him. But this episode also profoundly influenced Ch'en Li-fu, for he now recognized Chiang's political skills. From then on, Chiang Kai-shek bided his time until the opportunity came to destroy the CCP's power and eradicate it from Chinese society. Like Chiang Kai-shek, Ch'en Li-fu never again trusted the Communists.

The next year, Chiang Kai-shek's National Revolutionary Army advanced northward from Kwangtung Province, eventually occupying Shanghai on March 21, 1927, and Nanking three days later. Meanwhile, information continued to accumulate, informing Chiang and those around him that the CCP still intended to split the KMT leadership and seize power in the provinces and cities under the National Revolutionary Army's control. For these reasons, then, only three weeks after occupying Shanghai, the KMT, both in Shanghai and in other cities, began arresting and executing Communists on a massive scale. Lacking lists of the CCP members who controlled the labor unions and the student associations, Ch'en Li-fu ordered that members of the KMT, as well as Shanghai's famed underground Green Gang and the Shanghai police, attack anyone they believed to be Communists. Li-fu takes full responsibility for the events that followed, arguing that "we were in a battle to the death." Ch'en does not apologize for using Shanghai's Green Gang but argues that the KMT never controlled that group, although some of its members belonged to the KMT. The Green Gang, like the Triad societies in Kwangtung and the secret societies in other provincial cities, engaged in both illegal and legitimate activities, including providing community services that public officials were unable to, such as maintaining public order and protecting businesspeople. The purge of the Communists in Shanghai set the stage for bitter conflict in the years to come and deepened the mistrust in each party of the other's intentions and activities.

Shortly after the ROC's new government was formally established in Nanking on April 18, 1927, Chiang Kai-shek decided to create new organizations to eliminate the communist threat once and for all. He asked Ch'en Li-fu to organize an Investigation Section under the KMT's Organization Department to monitor the Communists' activities and take punitive measures to destroy them. Awed by the responsibility of his assignment and not sure how to proceed, Ch'en sought advice from Tai Chi-t'ao, a party elder and confidant of Chiang Kai-shek. Tai counseled him to be just and kind, careful to select good personnel and to act without selfishness or "things will go wrong and you will have trouble." Borrowing organizational methods from the USSR and the United States in 1927, Ch'en established a new party intelligence and security organ to remove the Communists from political life.

To form this unit, Ch'en selected educated party members with specialized training in the sciences. The unit first operated in the large east-central cities, where the Communists were most active, but later moved to the provinces of south and central China to build up a network of reliable informants on CCP activities. About a year later, Ch'en Li-fu learned that Chiang Kai-shek had also appointed Tai Li, another young party member, to run the Military Bureau of Investigation and Statistics for the same purpose as Ch'en's organization. Thus we see that Chiang preferred keeping some of his trusted officials ignorant of one another's activities, loyal only to the top leader, rather than developing a team-type organization. On May 4, 1935, Chiang asked Ch'en to head the Combined Reporting on Investigation and Statistics Unit and made Tai Li director of a unit concerned with monitoring communist activities in the military. According to the memoir, Ch'en's activities in 1927–1928 encouraged some sixteen thousand persons to leave the CCP; these people were not punished and were allowed to join the KMT.

With the CCP shattered and KMT power in the ascendant, Chiang and others set about reorganizing the KMT and reconstructing the country. But just as ideology and personal ambition for power had split the CCP-KMT coalition, so ideological differences and the struggle for political power sowed discord among KMT leaders and prevented that party from winning substantive popular support between 1928 and 1937.

Ch'en's memoir presents a fresh interpretation of why the Nationalist government was unable to expand its influence and win greater popular support in the cities and villages of east-central China and beyond. On March 28, 1929, Ch'en Li-fu, only twenty-nine, became the first secretary-general of the KMT's Central Executive Committee and was privileged to attend its weekly meetings and listen to the opinions of the committee's powerful leaders. According to Ch'en, a major debate now came to a head in the party's leadership: should the party continue to rely on political tutelage, with the KMT having absolute power, or should it move to establish a constitutional government and allow political parties to compete? (Sun Yat-sen argued late in his life that the young 1911 republic had disintegrated because political tutelage had not been extended long enough to allow the ruling party and government to launch the land-to-the-tiller program, build railroads, and so forth, as well as establish county elections and educate people at the subcounty level to govern their affairs and reorganize economic and civil life. Sun believed that the party should postpone moving to a constitutional government and national party elections until firm foundations had been laid.) But in 1930 others believed differently. Wang Ching-wei urged Chiang Kai-shek to consider constitutional government, and Chiang endorsed this suggestion. Hu Han-min, however, disagreed, arguing that the move was premature and that Sun's strategy should be followed.

As the ideological debate raged, the struggle for power also heated up. Chiang Kai-shek, already chairman of the National Government Council, had assumed the presidency of the Executive Yüan on November 24, 1930, after T'an Yen-k'ai died. Moreover, Chiang had become the commander in chief of the military forces. Chiang resented Hu's opposition and feared that others would rally behind Hu. Ch'en's memoir sheds much light on the ideological debate and power struggle at this moment of leadership crisis.

Hu Han-min, a senior KMT member from Kwangtung Province who held enormous power and prestige, had been touted as one of Sun's closest disciples. He also was arrogant and overly critical of his colleagues, often speaking ill of them behind their backs. In March 1931, Chiang lost patience and ordered Hu's house arrest. According to Ch'en, however, Hu was also principled, loyal, and clearly understood Sun's doctrine and policies. Ch'en courageously spoke up on Hu's behalf, but Chiang proved unyielding. Chiang's fatal decision deeply divided the KMT and produced rebellions first in Kwangtung and later in Fukien. These rebellions diverted party and government resources away from the urgent task of economic reconstruction and reforming *hsien* (county) governance, activities that might have enabled the KMT and the ROC government to undertake a land-to-the-tiller program, improve economic welfare, and win the support of the people in the cities and villages of east-central China and elsewhere.

To make matters worse, the Kwangtung rebellion occurred just as the Communists were expanding guerrilla activities in Kiangsi, Fukien, and elsewhere. In addition, various politicians, furious with Chiang's attempts to expand his power, demanded that Chiang resign his posts. The final blow to Chiang and the KMT came on September 18, 1931, when the Japanese Kwantung Army contrived to blow up a section of the South Manchurian Railway in northeast China and blamed the incident on the Chinese, providing justification for Japanese troops to sweep over Manchuria and annex that area under a Chinese puppet regime subservient to the Kwantung Army.

The division in the KMT and rising opposition to party and ROC government policies greatly weakened the legitimacy of both party and government, and neither recovered from these enormous setbacks. Moreover, the greatly weakened party and government were never able to coordinate economic and political reform so as to improve local welfare and increase popular support for their cause. Constant factional and personal bickering in the KMT affected ROC governance as well. The 1930–1931 ideological debate and power struggle marked a major watershed in that the legitimacy and the capacities of the KMT and the ROC government declined thereafter.

Ch'en's memoir also indicates that certain individuals were responsible for serious mistakes in ROC foreign policy-making. For instance, the ROC's inability to form an alliance with Japan eventually encouraged Japan to attack China in 1937. As early as 1935, Ch'en Li-fu, on his own initiative, consulted with Tai Chi-t'ao and later with Wang Ching-wei, then president of the Executive Yüan and minister of foreign affairs, about a long-term Japanese strategy. He proposed that Wang send an envoy to Japan to convince officials there that the Soviet Union only wanted to provoke Japan into attacking China and that China wanted to cooperate with Japan to oppose Soviet imperialism. Unpersuaded by Ch'en's line of reasoning, Wang Ching-wei countered that Japan planned to expand westward and that Ch'en's idea was not feasible. Ch'en believes that China thus lost a golden opportunity to form a new alliance against Soviet communism.

Chiang seems to have formulated his own ideas about international alliances. Few senior KMT leaders, let alone Ch'en, were consulted by Chiang. For example, Ch'en reveals that the establishment of an independent Outer Mongolia after World War II was a decision Chiang made on his own. Ch'en seems never to have discussed foreign policy with Chiang Kai-shek but merely to have served his leader. Eager to mend ties with the Soviet Union as late as December 1935, Chiang hoped that the Soviet Union might yet agree to a peace pact with China. He started Ch'en Li-fu and Chang Ch'ung off on a secret mission to the Soviet Union to negotiate such a pact, but after arriving in Europe and waiting for several months, moving from one hotel to another to avoid recognition, the two officials finally returned home empty-handed. The ROC government's ineffective foreign policy never gave China time to build its defenses.

Even after Japan had invaded China and occupied Shanghai and Nanking, Ch'en attempted another diplomatic initiative. While in Hankow awaiting a possible Japanese attack, the German ambassador, Oskar P. Trautmann, visited Ch'en, who immediately proposed that Germany urge Japan to withdraw from China and "advance northward" while Germany "advanced castward." Ch'en also suggested that Japan, Germany, and China form a secret agreement to defeat the Soviet Union and then liberate the colonies of the world. In this way, the British Empire would disappear and Sun's Principle of Nationalism (*min-tsu chu-i*) could be realized. Ch'en believed that the Soviet Union only wanted to provoke a war between Japan and China to reduce any threat on its eastern flank and that Moscow assisted China during the Sino-Japanese War to encourage both sides to fight each other.

Whereas the ROC's leaders' inability to agree on domestic and foreign policies doomed Sun's Three Principles of the People building a united China, the ambitions and machinations of powerful KMT leaders undermined party unity and purpose. A shining example of such hubris was Wang Ching-wei's inability to cooperate and serve Chiang Kai-shek loyally.

Wang Ching-wei's defection to the Japanese did not surprise Ch'en Li'fu, whose networks had informed him that Wang might break with the KMT and whose personal assessment of Wang had long prepared him for his betrayal. Ch'en had observed Wang Ching-wei for more than a decade and judged him to be ambitious and vain, goaded by his wife, Ch'en P'i-chun, who lusted for power and prestige. On November 1, 1935, high KMT officials, including Wang Ching-wei, were being photographed to commemorate the start of the party's Sixth Plenary Session of the Central Executive Committee at the Fourth Party Congress, when an assassin wounded Wang in the back. Chiang ordered Ch'en to capture the guilty parties; within five days Ch'en's investigation team arrested Ho Pu-kuang, Chang Ming-yin, and others who confessed to plotting to kill Wang. The conspirators were furious with Wang Ching-wei because he had used them in his rise to power and then abandoned them, as he had so many others. After Japan invaded China, Wang despaired over China's inability to stop the Japanese war machine; not long after, he fled, first to Vietnam and then to Japan to become the paramount puppet leader of the Japanese-occupied areas. Wang's puppet regime, however, continued to maintain contact with Chiang Kai-shek during the war years. Wang's betrayal also induced several high-ranking KMT members such as Ting Mo-tsun, the head of the Third Division of Chinese intelligence, to defect to the Japanese. Those former KMT members gave valuable information to the Japanese police, who proceeded to arrest many national government agents in Shanghai and other Japanese-occupied areas.

Ch'en, then, stresses that policy mistakes by powerful individuals in high places were responsible for the KMT's failure to legitimize its power, win greater popular support, and prevent further Japanese expansion into China between 1928 and 1937. He downplays the pathological political and social patterns—inept party-government management, loss of revolutionary spirit, rampant corruption, and political repression—that scholars like Lloyd Eastman have argued were responsible for weakening KMT revolutionary legitimacy and power between 1928 and 1937.[3] Certainly these same pathological political and social patterns prevailed in Taiwan under KMT rule in the 1950s and 1960s, yet they never prevented the KMT from promoting modern economic growth, stable urban development, and gradual democratization. Perhaps the leadership mistakes identified by Ch'en and the sociopolitical patterns identified by Eastman interconnected and combined in complex ways to weaken the KMT regime's rule on the mainland but not in Taiwan. Could geographic size, as John King Fairbank has argued, explain the contrasting political developmental performances? Or must we search for a more complex analysis to explain the differences? More studies of KMT political history are needed to resolve this puzzle; Ch'en's account introduces new evidence and at least a partial explanation for why the KMT-dominated political center on the mainland failed but that on Taiwan succeeded.

Ch'en's account never hints that KMT legitimacy and power were to be anything but revitalized and expanded after Japan's surrender on August 15, 1945. Indeed, as John K. Fairbank points out, "The Nationalist armed forces were at least twice the size of the CCP's and moreover had the advantage of American equipment and supplies plus the assistance of the U.S. Navy in transporting troops and the U.S. Marines in the Tianjin-Beijing Area."[4] If KMT military superiority greatly exceeded that of the CCP, why did the KMT regime collapse only four years later?

First, as Eastman has argued, KMT organizational capabilities greatly declined during the wartime period and simply were not adequate to meet the postwar challenges of defeating the CCP's combined civil and military forces and eliciting sufficient popular support.[5] Second, the disastrous KMT takeover of the Japanese-controlled coastal provinces between late August and October 1945 alienated the intellectuals and local people; thus the Nationalist regime was unable to control postwar inflation, revive the war-weary economy, or defeat communist forces in the field.[6]

In autumn 1945, however, according to Ch'en's memoir, the ROC regime was strong enough to rebuild mainland China and defeat the CPP, had not three major leadership mistakes—military, economic, and political—set in motion forces that irreversibly strengthened CCP military power. First, Generals Ho Ying-ch'in and Chen Cheng's tactical errors in the late summer of 1945 enabled communist guerrilla forces to seize much of north and northwest China and extend their control over the countryside. The Communists then began to project sufficient military power to cut the transportation and communication links with the Nationalist-controlled cities, thereby making urban inflation worse and separating the cities from their rural hinterlands.

In the fall of 1945 General Ho ignored Ch'en's suggestion of using Japanese troops to protect the railroad lines from Nanking and Pu-k'ou in east-central China to Tientsin in the north so that Chinese-trained troops could speedily link up with Nationalist guerrillas in the northern provinces. In that way, the central government could have quickly controlled the north China countryside. Instead, General Ho insisted on sending his troops to Shanghai and then on (by sea) to Tientsin, delaying their arrival in the North by several months and giving the communist forces time to expand their rural power base. General Chen Cheng also refused to integrate the north China guerrilla forces into his ROC military command. (Ch'en Li-fu hints that General Chen Cheng's erroneous decision might have been influenced by Liu Fei, a communist spy in the upper echelon of the military and close enough to General Chen Cheng to discuss these military matters.) The same attitude prevailed in Manchuria, where Nationalist commanders refused to use Chinese troops that had been controlled by the Japanese military on the grounds that they were traitors. The Communists naturally welcomed them, thus expanding their ranks to near-equivalence with the Nationalist military forces. According to Ch'en Li-fu, these erroneous military judgments made it easy for the communist forces to seize control over the countryside and begin their strategy of surrounding the major cities of north and northeast China.

Mistaken economic policies also fueled inflation and intensified the economic grievances of local people and the intelligentsia toward the KMT and the central government. During the war the coastal provinces under Japanese control had used Japanese military scrip and the currency of the Chinese puppet government headed by Wang Ching-wei. After August 1945, T. V. Soong insisted on a currency exchange ratio of one yuan of ROC currency to two hundred yuan of puppet currency. As government officials, their families, and troops returned to the coastal provinces in late 1945, their currency had greater purchasing power over local goods and services priced in the old puppet currency. A major transfer of wealth from local people to returnees quickly took place. This process generated enormous criticism of the ROC government's unjust economic policy, and the central government lost the support of the people in the coastal provinces, who had enthusiastically welcomed its officials after VJ-day. (According to Ch'en, Chiang and his close confidants agreed to Soong's disastrous financial policies.)

These economic grievances worsened when Soong refused to redeem fully the gold deposit certificates that were sold in the war years, allowing only 60 percent of the original value of the certificates to be repaid to their holders. Ch'en Li-fu explained to Chiang Kai-shek that Soong's financial policy cheated the people and destroyed the credibility of the government, but Chiang refused to listen and supported Soong. Soong also did not allow the U.S. dollar deposit certificates, purchased in large quantity by patriotic overseas Chinese, to mature to their full value. Instead, he repurchased those certificates at far less than their maturity value, thus angering the overseas Chinese community. Ch'en states that Soong's assistant, Chi Chao-ting, was a communist agent and that after the civil war, Mao's regime gave Chi a high post in the government, rewarding him for the financial disasters he helped perpetrate while working under Soong.

The third error was made in late 1945 by Chiang Kai-shek when he agreed that President Truman could send General George C. Marshall to China to negotiate a truce between the KMT and the CCP. According to Ch'en, this disastrous decision only made relations worse between the United States and the ROC, but certainly no more than if Chiang had declined the American president's attempt to mediate in a civil war that had raged for over a quarter of a century. That decision gave the CCP time to consolidate its troop strength in north and northeast China, infiltrate the ROC government and military with its spies, and sow discord and dissension in cities under ROC control. Ch'en urged Chiang to reject the Marshall visit, arguing that if any foreign power should mediate the Chinese civil war, it should be the Soviet Union; the USSR had long backed the Chinese Communists, and exposing those efforts would hold it up to world ridicule. The CCP also wanted more time to build up its forces and intended to use Marshall's mediation efforts as a means to that end. Finally, Marshall, a world-famous military leader, had been given an impossible task, which meant the KMT leadership would ultimately be blamed for his failure. Ch'en failed to persuade Chiang, but recent scholarship supports Ch'en's argument.[7]

By 1946, Ch'en Li-fu had served Chiang for two decades as personal secretary, confidant, and loyal official. Ch'en had modernized Chiang's filing system to improve the flow, use, and preservation of KMT documents and had pioneered the use of radio between the staff commands of military units, first between Shanghai and Nanking and later when the Northern Expedition tried to recover Beijing. Every assignment Chiang gave Ch'en was performed brilliantly and efficiently. Chiang valued Ch'en's uncompromising loyalty and courageous honesty in speaking up when he thought Chiang was wrong. Many cowered in Chiang's presence because of his fierce temper but not Ch'en Li-fu. After just a few months as Chiang's private secretary, Ch'en told Chiang that if he ever lost his temper with him again, he would quit. Chiang never again became angry in Ch'en's presence, and the two men became extremely close.

Ch'en even influenced the destiny of his boss. In early 1926 the KMT party leadership convinced Chiang Kai-shek to visit the Soviet Union. On the way to the boat dock, Ch'en asked Chiang to reconsider making the trip on the grounds that he could lose his power base in Canton. Although by then at the dock and waiting to board ship, Chiang ordered his driver to return to his residence.

The memoir also notes poignant moments. On July 6, 1928, after the Northern Expedition, Chiang Kai-shek, Ch'en Li-fu, and other KMT leaders and military commanders assembled at the P'i Yun temple outside Beijing to commemorate the defeat of the northern warlords and conduct a funeral for Sun Yat-sen. When Chiang saw Sun's body, he began to weep like a son grieving for his father. He muttered a short speech, promising to reduce China's military forces and rebuild the nation; the service abruptly ended. Ch'en never saw Chiang cry again.

As a close confidant of both Sun Yat-sen and the commander of China's military forces, Ch'en firmly believed that Chiang Kai-shek was the most suitable person to lead the country in those decades. But Ch'en does not hesitate to expose Chiang's character flaws. Chiang insisted on total personal loyalty and rewarded it with promotion and good career assignments. The memoir suggests that he lacked vision and, like most leaders of the time, did not understand the difficulties of state-building. He could not assemble the best administrators and encourage them to work together. He had neither a clear domestic developmental strategy nor an appropriate foreign policy strategy. Many of the people Chiang picked as high officials were excessively ambitious and incapable of working together as a team. Chiang's penchant for bureaucratization produced unnecessary infighting and distrust: witness Ch'en Li-fu's astonishment when he learned that an intelligence unit similar to his own had been created under Tai Li.

Once Chiang trusted an adviser or official, he would not replace that person even if that person's policies damaged the party and government. Those Chiang handpicked, he stubbornly defended even when they performed poorly. Thus, he never dismissed the officials who had made the ill-advised decisions and policies immediately after Japan's defeat in 1945. The KMT's inability to form an effective administrative team was a fundamental defect Chiang never corrected. As the years passed, Ch'en Li-fu's loyalty to his commander in chief was sorely tested. Yet Ch'en continued to serve Chiang faithfully as a loyal, dedicated Confucian official, accepting each assignment without complaint and performing to the best of his abilities.

By 1946, manifestations of ROC government decay had become evident everywhere; by 1947 tensions between Chiang and Ch'en had begun to surface. In 1947, to demonstrate a more genuine political democracy, the KMT assigned a quota of seats in the National Assembly to the Youth and the National Socialist parties. The KMT, however, had trouble persuading the elected KMT delegates to give up their seats to the other two parties.

When the enraged delegates told others about this arrangement, they also became angry. At that time Chiang Kai-shek asked Ch'en to return to the party's Organization Department to manage the election. Although agreeing to seat the Youth and Socialist parties, Ch'en realized that the KMT was violating the principle of democratic election. Therefore, he appealed to the party's secretary-general to change the election law, but his request was denied.

Chiang, having alienated many National Assembly KMT delegates, was warned by Ch'en that Li Tsung-jen might have enough votes to become vice-president and that Chiang should ask Li Tsung-jen not to run. Chiang refused, publicly declaring that he did not want the presidency and offering it to Hu Shih, a non-KMT member who shocked Chiang by accepting. Many KMT National Assembly delegates, now concerned that the highest position in the government might go to a non-KMT member, voted for Chiang, who easily won. But then, instead of announcing his preferred vice-president, Chiang recklessly declared the vice-presidential election open. Four candidates immediately put their names forward: Yu Yü-jen, Sun Fo, Cheng Chien, and Li Tsung-jen. The National Assembly elected Li vice-president, angering Chiang.

At this time Li Tsung-jen's Kwangsi troops were in Honan, and communist forces were moving southward from Tsinan in Shantung. Rather than send his troops to fight the Communists, Li, who had always disliked Chiang, held them back. After a huge battle at Hsuchow-Pangfu, the defeated ROC forces retreated south of the Yangtze River, leaving the northern provinces under CCP control. Li's Kwangsi troops crossed the Yangtze and returned to Kiangsi without ever having fired a shot.

Ch'en sees a causal connection between the voting irregularity of the first National Assembly election, which set the stage for the assembly's election of the president and vice-president, and the worsening personal relations between President Chiang and Vice-President Li. Li's refusal to permit his Kwangsi troops to fight the Communists helped produce a crucial military defeat at Hsuchow-Pangfu. Setting this process in motion, Ch'en believes, was his decision to deny the elected KMT candidates their rightful seats in the first National Assembly.

The ROC presence in China came to a speedy end. On January 21, 1949, Chiang Kai-shek stepped down as president of the ROC and went into seclusion. Ch'en resigned his post the next day. Leading officials like Chang Chih-chung and Shao Li-tzu defected to the Communists. The acting president, Li Tsung-jen, schemed to place his closest friends like Chu Cheng in leading government posts. Because Kwangtung Province had become indefensible, part of the government and military moved to Chungking; the rest retreated to Taiwan. Ch'en Li-fu wired Chiang, now in Taiwan, that

Chungking could not be defended. Yet Chiang insisted on flying there to make a last-ditch stand, where he was joined by Ch'en. By November 1949, military commanders in Szechwan had become untrustworthy; everywhere they were defecting to the Communists. Chiang finally decided to return to Taiwan, ordering Premier Yen Hsi-shan and Ch'en Li-fu to follow on another military plane. Ice on their plane's wings forced a return to Chengtu, where mechanics discovered that Yen's gold bars had made the plane too heavy to fly. Yen ordered some bodyguards to remain behind, and the plane flew to Taiwan. Ch'en's life as a revolutionary was now at an end.

In late 1949 Ch'en urged Chiang to draw up a reform plan for the KMT and informed Chiang that he and his brother would take the blame for the party's failures and leave political life. Chiang then asked Ch'en to assemble a committee of nine party faithful to draft such a plan. Soon after, Chiang convened a meeting of top party leaders, but Ch'en, who was unable to participate, later learned that Chiang had flown into a rage when someone suggested that the KMT cadres should "reform the KMT in a democratic way" and that Chiang should be responsive to that. Chiang reportedly said, "If you do not trust me to do the reform, you go ahead and be Ch'en Li-fu's followers."

Whatever he said, Ch'en now believed that Chiang suspected that he and his brother were conspiring against him. This, then, was the pretext for Ch'en to leave Taiwan and go to the United States to take up a new life.

Ch'en lived abroad during much of the next two decades. In those years the KMT rebuilt its leadership and membership from scratch. Sun's ideas of redistributing land to the tiller, educating the people in Confucian values, and establishing democracy first at the grass roots and gradually expanding it to elect the leaders at the top slowly took root in Taiwan. Chiang Kai-shek proved to be a driving force behind these reforms, but his son and successor, Chiang Ching-kuo, deserves perhaps even more credit. According to Ch'en Li-fu, Chiang Ching-kuo recruited talented leaders, especially Taiwanese, gave the KMT a new vision of its destiny, and began democratizing the polity in 1986–1987. By the 1990s the ROC's new prosperity, social stability, and expanded democracy gave it a vitality and force that greatly influenced mainland China. Ch'en is optimistic that the Chinese people are now rejecting communism and that in the future a new China, borrowing heavily from the Taiwan experience, will emerge.

In 1990, Ch'en Li-fu publicly proposed that the ROC government offer the PRC government between five and ten billion U.S. dollars in economic aid if that leadership would jettison communism. Ch'en's offer was coolly ignored. As the twentieth century comes to an end, Ch'en Li-fu is still optimistic that the Chinese in the PRC will rediscover their Confucian roots and, rejecting both capitalism and socialism, begin to develop a Chinese-style modernization, perhaps along the lines achieved on Taiwan under ROC governance. He believes that the reunification of China and Taiwan will occur because of the strength of the Chinece culture; only that culture will bring all the Chinese people together. As the two Chinese societies under PRC and ROC rule become more economically integrated, the more dynamic of the two, Taiwan, has already profoundly influenced the way the Chinese elite and ordinary people of the mainland view their present life and want to change it. Having failed to establish a prosperous and democratic society on the mainland, Ch'en Li-fu and those of his generation still living have much to regret, but their hopes have been realized on the island of Taiwan.

The editors' detailed notes inform readers about particular persons, institutions, and events mentioned in the memoirs. This information often confirms the insights or views of Ch'en Li-fu about the people and events taking place around him, thus giving veracity to the memoir. For others writing about life in twentieth-century China, the Ch'en memoir will serve as a credible building block for interpreting how the KMT-CCP conflict doomed China to tragedy and suffering and which party bears the greater responsibility for that tragedy. For the first time in this century, we see signs of hope that China and its people will eventually achieve peace, prosperity, and human freedom.

THE STORM CLOUDS CLEAR
OVER CHINA

CHAPTER ONE

Early Years

1900–1925

A Brief Introduction

IN THE PAST, MANY PEOPLE TOLD ME I should write my memoirs, but I could not make up my mind to do so until recently, for I thought my life and work during the past decades were not as I intended and planned. I studied mining engineering in China before I went abroad for graduate study. My interest was in science and engineering, for at that time China was a weak nation, and I believed that only science and modernization could make China prosperous and strong. My faith in science and industrialization as China's only salvation inspired my return to China. On my return to China in 1925, I made up my mind to devote myself to China's reconstruction by working as an engineer.

I did not expect that I would start a new career in politics right after returning from abroad. It is painful for anyone to give up one's lifelong interest and ambition. I was consoled, however, by the thought that it was valuable to follow Chiang Kai-shek and dedicate myself to our national revolution. For this, I became a member of the Kuomintang; I rendered my services to overthrowing the warlords, unifying China, defeating the Japanese invaders, and winning the second Sino-Japanese War. I worked to help abrogate the unequal treaties with foreign nations, to build China—from the position of a semicolony—into one of the Five Powers in the world, to lay the foundation for constitutional government, and to prevent communism from conquering China and spreading to the rest of Asia. I could modestly contribute to these achievements only because I followed Chiang's lead. For exactly twenty-five years, I worked at his side as an assistant. I participated in many confidential and important policy-making decisions. Because of these considerations, I had no plan to write my memoirs.

Unfortunately, Chiang suddenly found himself on the verge of complete defeat after having scored great achievements. That depressed me, because all the effort and time I had devoted to completing the national revolution had now come to nothing.

Saddened by the outcome of our anticommunist struggle, I took the blame for the defeat in 1949, and from 1950 to 1969, I raised chickens, developed an egg business, and manufactured peppery chili sauce in the United States. In 1970, upon Chiang's request, I returned to the Republic of China on Taiwan and worked with him until his passing in 1976. I continued to support his son Chiang Ching-kuo. I participated in Taiwan's "economic miracle" and the Kuomintang's democratization. I observed and played a role in Taiwan's presidential election of 1990.

I am approaching one hundred years of age, and so I have decided to take the advice of my friends and faithfully record my activities in this century. My only purpose in writing my memoirs is to bear witness to history and try to explain some historical events. I participated in many of the great events that took place in China during the past century. If possible, I want to provide some authentic materials for understanding the history of the Republic of China.

In writing my memoirs, I recall past events with a heavy heart. I cared little about my political career. I had wanted to be an engineer. Maybe I made the wrong choice in my life. But I want to point out that as a follower of Chiang I ardently and faithfully did my job. I shall give a clear, honest, and detailed account of those years, based on my memory.

My Family

I was born on August 21, 1900, in the Prefecture of Huchou, now the county of Wuhsin, Chekiang Province. My original family home had been in Chengchou, Honan Province, before my ancestors moved to the southeast, first to Anhwei Province and then further on, until a branch of them settled in Wuhsin at the end of the Ming dynasty, circa A.D. 1600, where it became a prominent family.

At the end of the Ch'ing dynasty, when the T'ai-p'ing Rebellion of the 1850s and 1860s ravaged the area, my family's financial situation suffered a disastrous decline. Fortunately, my grandfather Tin-yu had succeeded in his business dealings and was able to improve the family's living conditions.

His eldest son, my father, Ch'i-yeh, styled Ch'in-shih, earned a *kung-sheng* degree in the Ch'ing dynasty, began his career as a private school-teacher, and later became a successful businessman. As a result of his enthu-siasm for helping others, he was elected the president of my home county

Three generations of my family. Photo taken at my home village in Wushan, Chekiang
Province, in 1915. Rear row, from right to left: third uncle Ai-shih (with baby Han-fu in
arms), father, Ch'in-shih, second uncle Ying-shih (Ch'i-mai), second aunt Yao, Grandmother
Yang, third aunt Huang. Front row, from right to left: Li-fu (at age of fourteen), elder
brother, Kuo-fu, cousin Heng-fu, cousin Tseng-chih, eldest sister Shun-fu, second elder
sister Chin-fu.

Chamber of Commerce and later a representative to the First National
Congress of 1948. My parents had ten sons and daughters, but five died
before reaching three years of age. On the male line, only my eldest brother,
Tsu-t'ao, styled Kuo-fu, and I, the fifth child, Tsu-yen by name and Li-fu
by style, survived. Kuo-fu was eight years my senior and passed away in
Taipei on August 25, 1951, at the age of sixty. The remaining three were my
elder sisters. My father remarried after my mother passed away. My step-
mother gave me two half brothers and one half sister.

When my mother died on February 17, 1910, I was only ten years old.[1]
My mother's life was mainly work with little pleasure. I still remember that
she was strict with our discipline and carefully cultivated our good habits.
Every evening after dinner, she sat with us and told stories of famous
historical figures. She was well-versed in Chinese classics and educated us

My father, Ch'in-shih, at ninety.

in the Confucian and Mencian doctrines of benevolence and forbearance. She taught me to read *The Four Books* and *I-Ching* [*Book of Changes*]. Through my mother's teaching and guidance I fell in love with Confucian learning, which has had profound influence on my life.

For sentimental reasons, I wish to add that my mother was from a prominent family in Wuhsin. My elder uncle on my mother's side managed a silk factory in Shanghai, and he inspired me to be interested in engineering. My father owned a pawnshop about four miles from our home. Poor transport and his busy schedule kept him away from home. I had two famous uncles on my father's side who were close to each other. One of the two uncles was the noted Ch'i-mei, styled Ying-shih, who first apprenticed himself to my father's pawnshop. He later led the 1911 revolution[2] in Shang-hai and assisted Sun Yat-sen in establishing the republic. As a member of T'ung-meng-hui, he briefly served (from April 2 to June 29, 1912) as the minister of industry and commerce in T'ang Shao-i's cabinet. More than once, he suggested to Sun Yat-sen that Shanghai was vitally important to the success of the revolution in the Lower Yangtze provinces. During the second revolution, on July 18, 1913, he became the commander in chief of the Shanghai Anti-Yüan Army and he virtually declared the independence of Shanghai from Yüan's control. After Yüan Shih-k'ai dissolved the Kuo-mintang on November 4, 1913, Uncle Ch'i-mei continued to be active in the revolutionary camp in Japan and in northern China, and this led him to initiate the Shao-ho Gunboat Insurrection of December 5, 1915, in Shanghai to oppose Yüan. Yüan Shih-k'ai, in return, ordered Ch'i-mei's assassination on May 18, 1916. After that unfortunate event, his wife lived with my family until her passing. Today I am ninety-four years of age and I still vividly remember Uncle Ch'i-mei's enthusiastic discussions of politics and revolutionary thoughts with my mother.

My third uncle on my father's side, Ch'i-ts'ai, styled Ai-shih, was born in 1880. He graduated from the Japanese Shimbu Gakko in 1902, a military school in Tokyo; he later founded a military school in Hunan Province. After the establishment of the National government in 1927, he was chief comptroller and a national policy adviser to the president of the Republic of China. From 1931 to 1946, he held other important posts, mainly in banking circles. He died on August 7, 1954.

My elder brother, Kuo-fu, neither drank nor smoked and had no interest in movies. He enjoyed a simple life. Without much formal education in his youth, he loved books and reading was his only hobby. He would buy only books, even if spending his last dollar. He enjoyed browsing in bookstores, especially secondhand bookstores. Although I enjoyed reading, I had other interests as well, such as movies and sports. I recall that in my childhood I hardly ever argued with Kuo-fu. We were extremely close, perhaps because my brother was eight years my senior and, as an elder brother usually does, he took me under his wing. When we later worked together in the Kuomintang headquarters, we always discussed party affairs. We sometimes had different opinions, but we learned to respect each other's views. Although my brother was emotional and I controlled my temper, we usually held the same views on most problems, especially our outlooks on life. In poor health, he often fell ill, but he never stopped working or giving lectures until his illness forced him to stay in bed. Even on his sickbed, he still studied with a book in hand. He often remarked that the most important weapon to fight sickness was to forget that you were ill. He was always glad to help promising young men go to college or go abroad for advanced studies. His greatest regret in life was to be denied a higher education.

School in Huchou

My mother started to teach me before I went to school at the age of seven. My mother always taught me to be honest. When I was sent to study at an old-fashioned private school run by a local schoolmaster, Shen Jo-chen, I had learned several hundred Chinese characters. The first textbook Shen assigned was a primer entitled *Lesser Learning* [*Hsiao-hsüeh*]. It described

My local schoolmaster and childhood
teacher, Shen Jo-chen.

manners and morals, being written in short sentences and composed of four
character sentences that rhymed. I later read *Young Learning* [*Yu-hsüeh*]; *The
Four Books*; and *The Five Classics*.

Each student had his textbook depending on his grade, some studying
the *Analects of Confucius, Lun-yü,* and others *Mencius, Meng-tzu.* Most textbooks were Chinese classics, but a few were new, published by the Commercial Press. To an outsider, this method seems confusing and inconve-
nient. Some educators, however, claim this teaching method was ideal
because each student was treated as an individual and could develop according to his aptitude without conforming to some standard. To encourage
students to study hard, Teacher Shen allowed those who came to school
early to leave early in the afternoon and kept those who had not done well
in school until dark. Every afternoon after class, his students could leave
after taking attendance and returning their corrected exercise books. The
homework that Shen assigned was to be memorized. My ability to memorize
proved useful in my future work. In 1948, for example, I knew the names
of at least two-thirds of all the elected National Assembly representatives—
who numbered more than two thousand—when I saw them. Even today,
my memory is almost as good as ever.

Another person I recall was Nanny Chung, who nursed me. She ran a
grocery store just across the street from my school. I always chatted with

her while waiting for my two sisters to return from school. A gentle old lady, Nanny Chung was very nice to me. Whenever I was home, she would bring me fresh eggs because she believed them to be most nourishing. Each New Year's Day, if I happened to be in Huchou, I visited her.

When I was a child, my mother, Teacher Shen, and Nanny Chung were most important in my life.

Life in Shanghai

At the invitation of my second uncle, Ch'i-mei, who had liberated Shanghai from Manchu rule on September 14, 1911, my whole family visited Shanghai in 1911. This was the first turning point of my life. Except for my father, who remained in Huchou, my grandmother, second aunt, and brothers and sisters visited Shanghai in a jubilant mood. My third uncle's family also arrived from Peking. Everybody was joyful and curious about this cosmopolitan city. Had the revolutionary uprising been unsuccessful in Shanghai, I would have had no opportunity to come to this metropolis, where I later received a modern education.

We stayed in a house in the British Settlement near the race course. I was impressed by the boulevards, Western-style houses, and automobiles. But I was strongly repulsed by the insolent attitude of the British toward our people and, in particular, by the Sikh policemen who often beat Chinese coolies without provocation. Most outrageous was the sign at the gate of a public park saying "No Chinese and dogs are allowed." These humiliations caused our people great pain and later became the driving force for my joining the Kuomintang and devoting myself to the cause of the national revolution.

Before I could officially enroll in a Shanghai school for further education, I first had to take English lessons, which I never received in Huchou. There was a special school in Shanghai for Huchou children, sponsored by Huchou people. After a few months of studying English in evening school, I was admitted to Nanyang Railway and Mining School [Nanyang lu-k'ung hsüeh-hsiao]. I still remember the name of the principal of that school, Lin Chao-hsi, a Christian who was very fond of speaking English. My teacher, Shen Chieh-sheng, was a good teacher, and we became so close that later he served as my personal secretary for more than ten years.

There were more than 100,000 Huchou natives living in Shanghai. Most of them lived in the British Settlement and engaged either in the silk business or in educational and cultural work. Huchou was famous for its raw silk, silk goods, fish, writing brushes, feather fans, and bamboo products and was close to Shanghai, Soochow, and Wuhsi. Three steamship companies provided daily round-trip services to Shanghai and carried Huchou products. Many Huchou natives owned silk mills in Shanghai and sent their children to Shanghai for further education. They not only opened their own schools but managed theaters and charity organizations such as the Huchou Society.

I started my formal four-year school at Nanyang Railway and Mining School in 1913. My grades in mathematics, chemistry, and physics were consistently excellent, and I received a certificate of merit for seven of the eight terms. I cut only one class, a matter of a mere two hours, for my brother's wedding; that cost me one certificate of merit.

Meanwhile, my family's financial situation deteriorated. My second uncle, as I stated previously, went to Japan and north after the 1913 uprising against Yüan Shih-k'ai failed.[3] My third uncle, who worked in a bank, had to take care of my second aunt, me, my sisters, and his own family and his children's tuition. My elder brother, Kuo-fu, however, paid for my tuition. Knowing the difficult situation we were in, I did not want to ask my third uncle for money. So, each morning I arose early to walk to school, a couple of miles away. My third uncle unfailingly gave me train fare whenever he saw me walking to school.

In marriages arranged according to Chinese customs, the most important consideration was the other family's reputation and social standing. I became engaged at the age of thirteen on the day of the Chinese August Moon festival. The daughter of Sun Jung-kiang, an old friend of my father's, was my fiancée. Her name was Lu-ch'ing. I readily gave my consent when my father showed me her photo. We then met a few times at some relatives' homes but never talked to each other. Had we conversed, we would have created a scandal because people were very conservative at the time. A few days before I was to leave for the United States for my advanced study in 1923, our parents arranged a meeting for us to say good-bye.

My Second Uncle, Ch'i-mei

When we lived in Shanghai with my second uncle, Ch'i-mei, I was too young to know him well. I learned many stories about him from my mother and brother. As I learned about him, I became deeply impressed with his integrity and accomplishments.

His most impressive feat was an ability to tell time without consulting his watch. Whenever he was asked the time of the day, he would look up at the sky and recite the time almost to the very minute and hour. Was it his natural gift? We children enjoyed asking him the time just for fun.

Uncle Ch'i-mei was courageous, smart, and cool-headed. I was told that at the age of eight he had saved the life of a neighbor's child from a fire

Second uncle, Ch'i-mei, supporter of
Sun Yat-sen, leader of the *Shao-ho*
Gunboat Uprising of December 12,
1915. A founding father of the
republic, he was assassinated by Yüan
Shih-k'ai on May 15, 1916.

in a vacant square called Sea Island [Hai tao], which lay opposite our home.
He received the least formal education in our family, not because he was
poorly gifted but because my grandfather could afford to send only one son
to school. In accordance with Chinese tradition, a family that is not well-
off would only send the brightest child to school, with the others remaining
to learn to make a living. I thought that Uncle Ch'i-mei was the smartest
among the three brothers, but my grandfather made him an apprentice in a
pawnshop. Although that arrangement was satisfactory, he was not happy
with the work, and he later went to Shanghai to become a bookkeeper in a
silk store. Still bored, he worked hard to make a living, using his spare time
to study by reading many books. From the letters he wrote to Huang K'e-
ch'iang in 1915 it is clear that he was skilled in writing. In Shanghai he
became involved in politics in the early years of the republic.[4]

Because he did not have a chance to receive a formal education, Uncle
Ch'i-mei became preoccupied with education. My third uncle, Ch'i-ts'ai,
after returning from military study in Japan and working in Nanking, put
aside three hundred U.S. dollars for Uncle Ch'i-mei's education in Japan.
Before Uncle Ch'i-mei was to leave, he learned that a local school had to
close because it could not pay the rent. Uncle Ch'i-mei immediately donated
his money to that school. He also recommended the school increase the
tuition for children of well-to-do families and eliminate personnel expenses.

Deeply impressed by this act, my third uncle tried to raise another three hundred U.S. dollars for him to go to Japan.

Uncle Ch'i mei finally entered a police academy in Japan in 1906 and quickly became known as a person easily outraged by injustices. This kind of character later influenced his dedication to the revolutionary cause. When he returned to Shanghai and engaged in revolutionary activities, he often risked his own safety to visit his comrades in jail. Such courage won him great respect from others. I still remember that when Huang Fu-shen was in jail, Uncle Ch'i-mei spared no effort trying to secure his release, spending all his savings to secure his release even though Huang was never a close friend when they were in Japan. The ideals of the revolutionary cause dictated how he interacted with other people.

In financial dealings Uncle Ch'i-mei was also very responsible. He and some friends launched the *China Gazette* [*Chung-kuo kung-pao*]. Later, when the paper fell into financial difficulty, only Uncle Ch'i-mei faced the creditors and took the responsibility for paying the debts. His partners simply disappeared. He made friends with people from all walks of life and was very popular with underworld elements of the Red Gang [Hung-pang] and the Green Gang [Ch'ing-pang].

His bravery was demonstrated by his daring attack on the Kiang-nan Arsenal [Kiang-nan chih-tsao-chü] on November 3, 1911, in Shanghai just after the October 10, 1911, Wu-ch'ang Uprising. Ch'ing troops were dispatched to the south to attack the revolutionary army, already weakened and barely able to resist. Sun Yat-sen later said that the fate of the revolution depended on the outcome of the battle for the Kiang-nan Arsenal.

After the first assault on the arsenal failed and the revolutionary forces could not overwhelm the garrison troops, Uncle Ch'i-mei single-handedly attempted to persuade the garrison's troops to surrender. His sincerity so moved the Ch'ing loyalists that they opened the gate for him, and he succeeded in having the second gate opened. Unfortunately, the soldiers at the third gate refused; instead they captured him and turned him over to the garrison commander, who decided to execute him the following morning. The news leaked out. The revolutionary troops, already outside the besieged arsenal, again attacked by scaling the wall and finally captured the arsenal. My uncle was rescued. Among those who took part in the attack were Niu Yung-chien and Chiang Kai-shek, who contributed to the victory. Both gentlemen later became my uncle's close comrades-in-arms.

This revolutionary upsurge in Shanghai in which Uncle Ch'i-mei played an important role was crucial to the success of the 1911 revolution. After the short-lived victory of the October 10, 1911, uprising, the Ch'ing troops moved southward to capture Hanyang. Without the capture of the Shanghai arsenal, other insurrections south of the Yangtze River would not have occurred, and Yüan Shih-k'ai would have remained loyal to the Ch'ing court and opposed to the revolution. Much later, had Sun Yat-sen not yielded the presidency to Yüan, the foundation for a successful 1911 revolution could not have been established. Uncle Ch'i-mei had great faith in the 1911 republican revolution led by Sun Yat-sen, and in subsequent years he also supported the national revolutions fought by the Vietnamese and the Koreans for the independence of their countries. Most Korean exiles in China knew Uncle Ch'i-mei personally. In order to coordinate revolutionary activities in his region, Ch'i-mei founded the New Asia Mutual Aid Society [Hsin-ya t'ung-chi she]. He was perhaps the very first Chinese to assist other Asian revolutions. My elder brother, Kuo-fu, later carried on his mission; I also took part in similar activities between 1929 and 1936. We often contacted the Korean revolutionaries and supported their independence movements. In 1945, when the Korean government first awarded the Medal for the Founding of the Republic of Korea, three members of my family received this medal.

Yüan Shih-k'ai, greedy and ambitious, wanted to co-opt my Uncle Ch'i-mei's talents and use his influence among other revolutionists. He first offered Uncle Ch'i-mei the sum of US$500,000 if he would go abroad and give up his revolutionary activities. That tactic failed. Yüan Shih-k'ai then openly declared he would pay 50,000 silver dollars to the assassin who would murder my uncle.

Observing that the Kuomintang was short of funds to finance revolutionary work, my uncle proposed that some comrades serve as his assassins to earn money for the Revolutionary party. His comrades declined, but this example showed his zeal for the revolution.

Yüan's determination to pay US$500,000 for Uncle Ch'i-mei's life paid off. On May 18, 1916, Uncle Chi-mei's death at the age of forty deprived Sun Yat-sen of a trusted comrade.[5] Some years before his death Uncle Ch'i-mei suggested to Chiang, who was already under his influence, that he serve as Sun's aide. The death of Ch'i-mei spurred Chiang and Huang Fu, the sworn brothers of my uncle, to support Sun. They followed the example of the *tao-yüan san-chieh-i*, in which Liu Pei, Kuan Yü, and Chang Fei swore brotherhood at the Peach Garden, vowing to protect the House of Han against the Turban rebels in the second century A.D. This is described in the celebrated novel *Romance of the Three Kingdoms* [*San-kuo yen-i*].

I only had a few personal contacts with Uncle Ch'i-mei. What I knew of him I learned from others who knew him firsthand. As for Chiang Kai-shek, I had the opportunity of being his aide for more than twenty-five years during which time I observed his actions and heard him speak. I saw in him that same spirit and bearing of Uncle Ch'i-mei.

Years at Peiyang University

In 1917, I graduated from Nanyang Railway and Mining School after four years of study. I looked everywhere for an inexpensive college. I finally learned that Peiyang University in Tientsin charged only ten silver dollars a semester; this tuition also covered textbooks and laboratory equipment to enable students to study and do research. The food consisted mainly of wheat, which was cheaper than the food in the south. To take advantage of this opportunity, I borrowed two silver dollars and paid the registration fee for the entrance examination.

In Shanghai, there were several hundred students taking that same examination for forty-five vacancies; I ranked fifth. My elder brother, Kuo-fu, was happy for me; although he had missed the opportunity to go to college, he wanted me to attend. My biggest problem was the tuition and travel expense to Tientsin. My father gave me twenty-five silver dollars. But that amount could not support even one year of college expenses. The university ruled that I must first enroll for two years in preparatory classes before I was eligible to major in mining as a full-term student.

Peiyang University was regarded as an ideal university. When I first arrived, filled with gratitude and hope, everything was novel to me. Most teachers were Americans who spoke English in class. Only a very few preparatory classes were taught in Chinese. I was surprised that even the Chinese teachers spoke English. Although I had learned some English in middle school, it was not sufficient. My English professor then was David Lattimore, the father of Professor Owen Lattimore, a famous China specialist. As a boy Owen often played soccer with us.[6]

After six months at Peiyang University, my financial difficulties worsened. My brother, Kuo-fu, came to my rescue, sending me by post six yuan each month, of which four went for meals and the remaining for other daily expenses. Life was hard. If my brother's remittance came a few days late, I went hungry. At such times, I only could buy steamed dumplings [*man-tou*] to fill my stomach.

The students came from all provinces. There were so many students that the dining hall was divided to accommodate the Southerners, whose staple food was rice, and the Northerners, who preferred noodles and bread. The latter were cheaper by two yuan, and so I joined the northern section of the dining hall. After two years, I was elected chairman of the hall's management committee to supervise kitchen sanitation and do bookkeeping.

I did my job dutifully, and I never again went hungry when my funds arrived late.

The worst problem I had to contend with was the flies. Anyone who found a fly in a dish could exchange it for a fresh dish, and I, as chairman, had to go to the kitchen to obtain a clean dish. This chore proved so irksome that I appealed to the school administration to provide us with screens for the windows and doors and covers for the dishes. We even urged the cooks and janitors to be more diligent in eradicating the flies. There always were mischievous students who, about to finish a dish, would place a dead fly in it and yell my name, demanding a fresh dish. Once I exposed this trick and reprimanded the offending student on the spot for his mischief. I warned him that if he did this again I would not allow his table to obtain clean dishes even if a fly had been cooked into the dish. The chef was grateful for my sense of fairness and, thereafter, we cooperated well. For more than two years I held this responsibility, perhaps the longest tenure in the school's history.

Peiyang's strict training had produced talented students. I performed well in my studies. The school stipulated that anyone whose average mark reached 85 and above would be rewarded with a reduced or even free tuition. For many semesters I received this favored treatment, which greatly relieved my financial burden.

I liked athletic activities at school that helped to build my body. I enjoyed tennis most of all, but I also played basketball, soccer and competed in high jumping, ice-skating, race running, and martial arts. My main regret was that, as I was short in stature, I only could compete in intramural activities but never against other institutions.

One incident I still remember clearly. In April 1922, the two-month-long first Fengtien-chihli war broke out in the Tientsin region when troops of Chang Tso-lin and Ts'ao K'un engaged in fierce combat.[7] Martial law was proclaimed at night. Transportation was suspended between Peiyang University, located in suburban Tientsin, and the city. One night, my closest friend in school, Ch'en Ju-liang, styled Fanyu, suddenly caught cholera and began vomiting and having diarrhea. His life was clearly in danger, but there was no way to send for a doctor in Tientsin because of the curfew. I recalled a booklet I had bought from a street vendor in Tientsin titled *Self-Help for Everything* [*Wan-shih pu-ch'iu-jen*]. I examined it and sure enough found a remedy for cholera. The instruction called for salt to be fried dry, along with alunite, and then dissolved in water of equal quantity and given to the patient to drink. The remedy was so effective that his vomiting and diarrhea instantly stopped. This incident greatly influenced me. After saving the life of my good friend, I strongly believed that information about medical emergencies should be made publicly available. During these past years in Taiwan, I have devoted part of my time to promoting Chinese medicine, including the founding of a Chinese medical college at Taichung in 1970 and two hospitals for Chinese medicine. That incident in my youth also revealed that the curiosity that prompted me to buy odd books could be of great service in the future.

When the May Fourth movement occurred in 1919, I was responsible for the publishing of Peiyang University's daily newsletter. During the student strike, I was busy with affairs of the newspaper, sometimes going to the city to cover important events as a reporter. I had limited opportunities to participate in other activities outside the university, such as attending meetings. But I did join a number of demonstrations and marches. Activists from two of the well-known universities in Tientsin—Peiyang and Nankai— later became very well known, among them Chou En-lai of Nankai.

The May Fourth movement attracted me to books about this new cultural movement. Because of my affiliation with a newspaper, I had access to a great variety of publications, including magazines such as *New Youth* or *La Jeunesse* [*Hsin ch'ing-nien*], *New Tide* or *The Renaissance* [*Hsin ch'ao*], and books related to the Russian revolution and communism. I devoured them with great interest. Most young people at the time had leftist tendencies, and I was no exception. Books about how the Soviet Union opposed imperialism, often vividly written, had special attraction for the young who believed they could learn from the Soviet experience.

I particularly enjoyed the writings of Ch'en Tu-hsiu. I also liked the writings of Lo Chia-lun and Hu Shih, but I cared little for Li Ta-chao's work. The most blatant slogan of the May Fourth movement was Down with Confucius [*Ta-tao k'ung-chia-tien*], which I thought was too radical and antitraditional. I had thoroughly studied *The Four Books* and *The Five Classics* and could not agree that Confucius's teaching was that bad. My way of thinking was that any rotten tradition certainly ought to be discarded or rejuvenated but that to condemn old traditions as bad and demand they be destroyed was overemotional and irrational. I was convinced that merely copying Western or Soviet ways of doing things while negating the values of Chinese cultural tradition could not make China strong. If Down with Confucius was a slogan to awaken the nation, that might be all right; if it was used to reject our traditional culture, such extremism to correct a wrong would only produce a greater loss.

I now believed that the most important task to save China was to free the country of imperialism. In the 1910s Japanese imperialism aroused the wrath of the nation, and this outburst of passion gave birth to the May Fourth movement. Why should China, as one of the allies in World War I, be treated so unfairly by being forced to give Japan control of the Shantung Peninsula as a result of the 1919 Paris Peace Conference?

The Chinese people had expected our delegates to the Paris Peace Conference to defend Chinese sovereignty and resist Japan's demands. Yet the Great Powers totally ignored truth and justice; by colluding with one another, they favored Japan. Only then did I begin to understand why the 1917 Russian revolution had opposed imperialism.

When the Paris Peace Conference convened, a great passion gripped the Chinese people. They campaigned for economic sanctions against Japan and mobilized the Boy Scouts to persuade the public to boycott Japanese goods. Stores all over the country deliberately sold only Chinese-made products and caused great financial losses for Japanese businesses in China. Bullied for years by the Great Powers, the Chinese people united to protest against foreign imperialism. The May Fourth movement served as the catalyst, causing many people to desire active participation in national affairs. Paradoxically, the Paris Peace Conference helped the Chinese people unite behind their delegates in Paris to take a determined stand on behalf of China.

During that time, I knew little of Sun Yat-sen's writings and ideas, yet I felt attracted to the idea of communism, as I was stimulated by my anger over the treatment of China by the Great Powers. Books on Marxism circulated among my schoolmates, and some endorsed communism while others supported the concept of Three People's Principles proposed by Sun Yat-sen. I still believed I was too young for politics or for joining any political organizations.

The University of Pittsburgh

After graduating from Peiyang University in 1923, I yearned to go to the United States to further my study. Tsing Hua University was selecting a group of students to go abroad and offering two scholarships to other university students, one from the South and one from the North. I registered to take the examination as a northern candidate, but I failed to pass, chiefly because a brilliant engineering classmate, Li Shu-t'ien, outscored everyone. He was one of our school's best students, having an average grade above 95. He later went to Cornell University and earned a Ph.D. in engineering, which was difficult to obtain. At Cornell, he was nicknamed "encyclopedia." His elder brother, Li Shu-hua, was a well-known physicist.

Without a scholarship, I had to look elsewhere for help. Relatives of my stepgrandmother planned to send their son, nicknamed "Pao-pao," abroad, and they offered to pay my travel expenses if I would look after him. Pao-pao, the only son, was spoiled by his father, a former diplomat, and his mother, a concubine. They were wealthy but negligent in rearing their son; consequently he had done poorly in school. I accepted the offer because I heard that in the United States one could attend college by working part-time.[8]

In the summer of 1923, we joined over one hundred Tsing Hua University graduates aboard the SS *President Jackson* to sail for the United States. On board were Li Shu-t'ien, Ku Yü-hsiu, Huo Pao-shu, and my brother-in-law Shen Pai-hsien, who was going to the University of Iowa to study hydraulic engineering at his own expense. I had originally planned to go to either the Massachusetts Institute of Technology or the Colorado Institute of Mining, but then I heard that the University of Pittsburgh excelled in mining engineering and was located in the heartland of America's coal and steel industries. I decided to take Pao-pao and enroll in the University of Pittsburgh.[9] My English was quite fluent, and I found a woman to teach Pao-pao English.

The chairman of the mining engineering department was Professor R. M. Black, who had considerable practical experience. Every week Professor Black took his students to the mines around Pittsburgh to learn firsthand what he taught us in the class. For instance, when discussing drainage systems in mines, he showed us a mine with the best drainage works and expected us to write a report soon after. After one year of graduate instruction, I had learned a great deal. I realized that American education emphasized the pragmatic approach, which was very different from education in China. I learned that the applied sciences were a major reason for the rapid industrial development of the United States.

In the summer of 1924, my classmate Tseng Yang-fu and I both received our master's degrees. My M.S. thesis title was "The Mechanization and Electrification of the Chinese Mining Industry." After graduation, I entered a training program run by the U.S. Bureau of Mines, at which time I also learned about emergencies in case of a mine explosion. After taking another examination, I became qualified to engage in mining work.

My studies now completed, I felt a sense of joy and relief. Summer vacation had arrived. My friend Hsu En-tseng and I decided to do some sight-seeing and visit factories. Our first stop was Philadelphia, where we participated in the annual meeting of the Chinese Students Association. We traveled to Chicago, Boston, Atlantic City and then to New York and Washington, D.C. While in Atlantic City we observed the annual Miss America beauty contest, which was far less elaborate than today's pageant, but it was a rare event to see girls on flower floats and in swimsuits competing for who was the most beautiful.

After Washington, D.C., we visited Niagara Falls, reached the Canadian border, then swung south to Detroit, where we visited the famous Ford automobile plant. The assembly-line speed of production and high efficiency deeply impressed me. Then we arrived in Chicago once again to visit a huge

After master's degree in coal mining was conferred by
the University of Pittsburgh, summer 1924.

slaughterhouse. Live pigs and cows entered a building, and later they were
butchered, refrigerated, or canned. That sight was truly unbelievable. We
drove all day and rested at night, mostly camping in fields and cooking our
meals, rarely staying at a hotel. What a carefree life! I learned much in those
two months of summer travel.

Joining the Kuomintang

At meetings of the Chinese Student Association, we frequently discussed
China's future. Many supported the Kuomintang [National People's party]
and many did not. There were some who criticized the Kuomintang for
allying with Russia and admitting Communists. My view was that we could
learn from the Russian revolution. While writing my master's thesis, I had

studied and begun to admire the ideas of Sun Yat-sen and his plan for
rebuilding the nation.[10] I was a member of the Pittsburgh branch of the
Chinese Students Association. Its president, Hsu En-ts'eng, and I regularly
read the *Young China Morning News* [*Shao-nien Chung-kuo ch'en-pao*], a Chinese-
language newspaper published in San Francisco. We learned about the revolution sweeping across China and Sun Yat-sen's views, especially his *San
Min Chu I* [Three People's Principles].[11] In 1925, I formally joined the
Kuomintang in San Francisco.

While I was a student at the Nanyang Railway and Mining School in
Shanghai, my elder brother, Kuo-fu, took me to hear Sun's speech. He
spoke Mandarin with a heavy Cantonese accent, but his delivery was eloquent and his views brilliant. Already impressed by Sun, I asked my brother
to buy some books for me about Sun's doctrine before I set out for America.
I had no opportunity to read them on the ship because I was seasick, and in
school I was too busy with class work. When I began to write my thesis, I
carefully studied Sun's international development plan for the first time. I
admired his original and brilliant concepts for building highways and railways, constructing three coastal ports, and establishing new industries, all
to create a new China.

Having observed the United States' achievements, I now felt I must
return to my motherland to devote myself to the revolution and national
reconstruction. I regularly met with many good friends, and we discussed
our plans for returning home after completing our studies. We were full of
enthusiasm and high hopes. I was convinced that Sun's revolution was the
first important step toward national reconstruction. We could not begin
without defeating China's warlords. We heatedly discussed Sun's Fundamentals for National Reconstruction [*Chien-kuo ta-kang*]. I subscribed to his
idea of encouraging foreigners to invest in China to launch economic development. The U.S. steel industry had been assisted by British and German
investors before America developed the world's finest steel industry. From
the outset I believed Sun's view was correct, but many people disagreed.
They argued that too much foreign investment would control our economy
in the future and that foreign investment should never exceed half the
country's total investment. These views were shortsighted because China
possessed neither the wealth nor the political independence to launch construction projects. A blueprint was necessary in which foreign aid and
technology could be tapped to promote China's development. As soon as
the Chinese people could use machinery, they would quickly acquire the
ability to manufacture those same machines. Once the unequal treaties and
extraterritoriality had been abrogated, China would be free and sovereign.
I highly valued many of Sun's brilliant ideas, especially regarding social

welfare and the improvement of the people's livelihood. Inspired by Sun's writings, I joined the Kuomintang. Many of my friends soon followed me.

A Miner in Scranton

Two months of travel with my friend Hsu En-ts'eng greatly enhanced my knowledge of the United States. When we returned to Pittsburgh, we immediately looked for jobs. I found work in a brickyard, where I learned the process of brick making from clay mixing, cutting, and heating. A month later, I was formally employed by Pittsburgh Mining Company as a miner in my regular line of work. I first worked in a mine only two and a half feet high, not high enough for me to stand up in. I had to crawl in and drag out the coal with a machine. I was soon transferred to another mine where the coal bed was seven feet thick and that had a different work routine. Later, I requested to be transferred to still another mine, with the coal bed about five to six feet thick, a most ideal mine to work. Within six months, I had worked in many different coal mines and gained a great deal of valuable work experience.

Then I moved to Scranton's white coal area to work in a larger mining company, having a work force of more than four thousand men and a pit more than three thousand feet deep. I stayed there for eight months. While in a tunnel, I once was helping an old miner repair the railway when I heard a faint sound above my head. I quickly pulled the old miner aside, just in time to avoid being hit by a huge falling rock. Another time, a colleague and I were fixing a tunnel door when I detected a coal cart sliding down the slope. I immediately pushed my co-worker aside just before the cart smashed into the tunnel door without injuring us. When working in mines one must constantly be aware of unexpected danger. My quick reactions had saved the lives of two of my co-workers, who in gratitude shared with me much of their work experience.

Being responsible for inspecting the ventilation of tunnels, I was the first to enter the mine every morning and inspect it before the work day began. If I detected gas or if the safety lamp indicated the presence of gas, I posted a Danger sign at each of the entrances to warn others not to enter. In my routine check one morning, I found the safety lamp in one tunnel indicated gas. Just as I was on the way out of the tunnel to post the Danger sign, a Hungarian miner was entering. Not only did he ignore my warning, but he was smoking a cigarette. I could not stop him. Within three minutes, an explosion in the tunnel threw me to the ground. The Hungarian miner's body was severely burned. The company's investigation proved I was not at fault, but for a long time that accident depressed me.

On another occasion I was helping an electrician named John repair wires in the mine. He asked me for a hammer. I looked everywhere and finding one that was slightly marred, I handed it to him. He said, "This hammer is just like you Chinese." Furious, I hit him with the hammer, and we started to fight. Before long other miners gathered around us to watch. The foreman asked what had caused the fight. I answered, "He insulted my country and for that I can't forgive him." After hearing my explanation, the foreman declared, "Ch'en was right." He reprimanded John and instructed the other workers that from henceforth no one would insult another's mother country. That incident taught me a lesson: one must stand up to fight whenever necessary.

While working in the mines, I often became injured and wound up in the hospital. After recovering, I returned to the mine, never missing an opportunity to learn. Of all the Chinese students studying mining in the United States, I probably worked in the mines the longest, learning about every phase of work.

One day I was the last to leave the tunnel. Before I had reached the exit I realized I had forgotten something, so I turned and went back. Suddenly, there was a big noise. The pillars had collapsed. Had I had gone ahead toward the exit I would have been buried alive under the fallen rocks. My co-workers outside thought I had been crushed to death in the tunnel. Little did they know that I knew about the emergency exits. Before long, in that pitch-black tunnel, I had found my bearings and crawled out of a small opening. That event surprised them all. Even today I retain this habit of keen alertness. Working in a coal mine was an extremely dangerous occupation, especially when safety measures were not sufficient, and casualties were high. Without pressure from the miners' unions, I do not believe that the capitalists would have been willing to spend money to improve safety measures for the well-being of their miners.

Most miners had very limited education, yet they were conceited and looked down on college graduates. One day a drainage pump motor broke down, and a miner who had been a demobilized soldier was unable to fix it after trying for half a day. The foreman then asked me to help. I was well aware that everyone in the mine was waiting for this college graduate to fall flat on his face, so I was determined not to fail. Fortunately, my efforts succeeded, and the motor was repaired.

In the eight months at Scranton, I worked in the mine all day and kept busy in the evening. The mine was some distance from downtown. I recall that I was well treated by local friends and have great nostalgia for Mr. and Mrs. Malcolm Kay. Their son, then studying at the Carnegie Institute of Technology, invited me to take lodging at their home. They treated me like a member of the family and refused to let me pay rent. After I had moved to the YMCA dormitory, I still visited them on weekends and holidays, and Mrs. Kay would teach me to play the piano and paint with watercolors. On Sundays I went to church with them—a Methodist church, I recall. I realized that the teachings of *The Four Books* and *The Five Classics* were not much different from those of the Bible. From then on, churches in Scranton began to invite me to speak. I spoke about traditional Chinese culture and the teachings of Confucius and Mencius because, as a Chinese, I felt it was my duty to introduce our culture. Each time I was invited to speak, I would borrow a projector to show slides of Peking, our old capital, and other places in China, thus introducing our people and customs to the audience.

In the Scranton area the mines employed twelve thousand miners, and I was the only Chinese. Once, I went with the Kay family to attend a New Year's Eve party sponsored by the church. One of the entertainment programs was for every one to take turns picking a question slip from a box and answer it. The question I picked was "What was the biggest news event in 1924?" Without hesitation I answered, "In 1924, the most important, significant event was the legislation passed in the United States to prohibit Chinese from immigrating. This anti-Chinese law violates the spirit of brotherhood and equality of Christianity; it also runs counter to the spirit of American democracy. The passage of this bill is a shameful stain on the United States." My impassioned, blunt words won a round of applause, and many came to shake my hand and talk with me.

In the new year the miners went on strike. Being a member of the union and having heard our union leader, John L. Lewis, speak, I also participated in the strike. But I now decided to leave mine work despite the relief allowance I received from the union. At that time, with two additional years of work experience I could have obtained a formal miner's license. However, I yearned for a change and wanted to work in a gas company. Letters and cables from my elder brother, Kuo-fu, urged me to return home immediately, reminding me that I had worked in America long enough and that it was time to return and serve China by devoting myself to the nation's reconstruction. In 1925, I sailed home by way of Vancouver.

I had been most impressed by the American management system. Its emphasis on practicality and efficiency required that every phase of work be meticulously studied. In the mines where I worked, miners offered suggestions and improvements in mining techniques. These were studied, and if deemed beneficial to the company, the company adopted them. The miners' making the suggestions received a large sum of money from the company. This excellent system encouraged and induced management to explore new possibilities while creating loyalty among employees toward the company. When I later worked for the Kuomintang and as minister of education, I also used this approach and encouraged my staff to make suggestions, which I tried to adopt if at all feasible.

Americans also practiced individual responsibility at every level. Each level reported to the one above, and each person performed his part of the work process while emphasizing practical results. This type of work efficiency was not yet possible in my country. Anything that could be done in a day would take two or three days, as though to prove that a busy person could not finish his work on time. This time-wasting, work-neglecting mentality was a common disease in all government agencies of China. It not only afflicted the functionaries in lower echelons but also plagued those on top, whose directives were often impractical and commanded no respect from their staff, who in turn sabotaged those very same directives. I found in the United States, at least in the places where I worked, that those in charge carefully measured how much each worker performed in a day, and they tried not to waste manpower or issue impossible directives that could never be realized. Emphasizing practical results also made it easy for subordinates to obey their superiors. As an engineer, I felt I must emphasize efficiency and practical results. Within my inner self, a force stirred me to become an outstanding engineer and devote myself to advancing China's industrial growth. This was the reason I worked so hard in the mines.

CHAPTER TWO

Before the Northern Expedition

WINTER 1925–SUMMER 1926

Chiang's Confidential Secretary

I RETURNED TO MY HOMELAND in September 1925. Arriving in Shanghai, I was ready to serve as an engineer at Chung-hsing Ming Company at the invitation of the company's president, Chien Hsin-chih. Soon after my arrival, my elder brother, Kuo-fu, handed me two telegrams from Chiang Kai-shek, then commandant of Whampoa Military Academy.[1] Chiang urged me to go to Canton to be his assistant. My brother also repeatedly told me this would be a good opportunity for me to work for the national revolution. Despite this opportunity I was more interested in being an engineer than a politician. But I could not resist my brother's advice. Touched by Chiang's sincerity, I sailed for Canton shortly before the lunar New Year's Day of 1926.

On January 9, 1926, Chiang received me at the Commandant's Office of Whampoa Military Academy. He immediately asked me to be his confidential secretary, before I could explain my wish to be a mining engineer. On my certificate of appointment Chiang wrote Ch'en Li-fu instead of my other name, Tsu-yen, used in school both in China and the United States. From then on, I was called Ch'en Li-fu. Chiang called my elder brother Kuo-fu, so that we always have been referred to as Kuo-fu and Li-fu, or the two Ch'en brothers. Because Chiang was Uncle Ch'i-mei's sworn younger brother, I was supposed to call him third uncle. However, to distinguish him from my own blood-related third uncle Ai-shih, I simply addressed him as Third Uncle Kai-Shek. At work, I called him commandant during the Northern Expedition and later, commander in chief [*Tsung-ssü-ling*].

Chiang had many titles. In addition to being the commandant of Whampoa Military Academy, he was a member of the Military Council, commander of Canton Garrison Command, and commander in chief of the Army of the Eastern Campaign.[1] I was his confidential secretary, but in fact I handled all his important private and confidential documents, of which many were telegrams requiring translation. I also lived at his official residence in Canton's Tung-shan district and ate three meals with him every day. Indeed we were very close.

Shao Li-tzu worked with me in a small office. Shao drafted official papers, and I translated telegrams and transcribed letters. We also dealt with documents from Whampoa Military Academy and the headquarters of the Eastern Campaign. Handling these documents required special expertise. Shao gave me much advice. Later, when he left Canton to assist Feng Yü-hsiang, I alone assumed responsibility for confidential documents.

Numerous documents passed my desk, addressing political, military, economic, private, and party affairs; they were of such a variety they could not easily be classified. The most cumbersome task was translating telegrams. In the beginning I had to spend a lot of time just checking and translating, and I usually was unable to finish my work before midnight while Chiang rose early in the morning. How could I stay in bed when he was active? I was then twenty-seven years old and full of energy. Although I often lacked sleep, I was in high spirits, worked hard, and completed whatever Chiang instructed me to do. My work required me to be at my desk all day. I hardly ever went out, and I had little social life. My work prohibited me from making contact with outside people. I met the many people who visited Chiang, but I did not participate in their conversations. As a confidential secretary in special charge of office affairs, I was quite isolated.

Chiang's life-style followed a regular pattern. He was always early to bed and early to rise. Every morning he did exercises in bed. Then he got up and sat quietly meditating for half an hour to clear his mind. Next, he listed the things he had to do for the day, and he made drafts of urgent papers that required immediate attention. Chiang wrote most important reports himself, but sometimes he instructed Shao to prepare the first draft. Chiang would revise his writings and make final corrections. Such preparatory work was always done before breakfast. Then Chiang, Shao Li-tzu, and I ate breakfast together.

I noticed that sometimes Chiang had a bad temper, especially toward military officers, but he behaved more courteously toward civilian officials. One day after dinner, I said to Chiang, "If anyone lost his temper with me, I would resign at once." Knowing that I was a man of self-respect, Chiang did not take my words lightly. For this I was grateful. At the time, I understood perfectly well why Chiang's disposition was so volatile, because a political crisis was brewing. Many old comrades imagined Chiang was

As Chiang's secretary in 1926.

left-leaning and procommunist, whereas the Communists believed him to be a right-winger. Both wanted him out of power. In these circumstances Chiang was frustrated. He held a vital military post and shouldered tremendous responsibilities, but the Military Council of the Kuomintang had ignored his Northern Expedition plan.

As an engineer I was not interested in this complex political situation. One day, I approached Chiang with two requests: first, if opportune, I wanted to resume my profession; second, if I worked for him, I would do my best to follow his instructions, but I wanted him to respect my dignity and never verbally abuse me in anger. Chiang quickly agreed, but he never fulfilled my first wish. Never using the knowledge of my profession has been my lifelong regret. As for my second wish, it was completely realized.

Chiang's Character

Looking back, I realized that during the period Chiang was commandant of Whampoa Military Academy he had a bad temper, frequently scolding his underlings. I went to see him when he was in such a mood, and I said to him, "Commandant, your temperament is most offensive. Those you have cursed can take it, but I cannot. If you should ever do that to me, I will pack up and leave tomorrow." Chiang understood I had come to help him save our country and not to beg for a government job. I had my self-esteem and dignity. In the twenty-odd years I spent with him, he never lost his temper with me. Thinking back, I consider myself most fortunate.

In those months Chiang was gloomy, even though he controlled Canton, but the Communists still plotted to get rid of him. He was always unhappy, and he often burst into uncontrolled anger. He still held military power, but his position in the government was insecure. The Kuomintang's policy was based on the slogan Party above the Government, and Government above the Military [*Tang kao-yü cheng, cheng kao-yü chün*], which meant that the party controlled the polity and the polity controlled the military, which relegated Chiang to a subordinate role. He was in an awkward position because those in control could replace him at any time. Seeing himself in this hopeless situation, he decided to resign, saying he was unwilling to carry on. Wang Ching-wei was in the Central Executive Committee, chairman of the Political Committee, and chairman of the Military Council; his adviser was the Soviet general Nikolai Vladmirovich Kuibyshev. We called him General Chi Shan-chia, or Kissan'ka.[3] Wang had the power to dismiss Chiang, but he dared not approve Chiang's resignation, fearing he himself could not control the army. Chiang faced a dilemma. If he quit he would appear irresponsible, but if he continued on the job, he would face mounting pressure. As his dilemma worsened, so did his temperament, and he often lost his temper with his staff. One day I told him a story.

> General Paul von Hindenburg had a well-known saying, "To lose [your] temper is to punish yourself." Hindenburg never lost his temper. He was a military genius, and he often was in difficult situations. As the army chief of staff under Emperor Wilhelm, he once accompanied the crown prince, Wilhelm II, in military exercises, and each commanded rival forces. He won the contest by surrounding Wilhelm II's forces. The press reported that the two teams battled even because the crown prince would have been humiliated if the news revealed his troops had lost. Hindenburg also feared that, if the truth leaked out, the crown prince would lose face and he would

have to resign. So he immediately resigned. Wilhelm I did a clever thing. He let Hindenburg resign, but sent him to East Prussia to inspect fortifications in case Russia might attack East Prussia. Hindenburg accepted this assignment and thoroughly studied the terrain. When World War I started, Kaiser Wilhelm II already was on the throne, and he appointed Hindenburg commander in chief of the eastern front. His knowledge of the area enabled him to defeat the Russian army in a bold maneuver, leading to the surrender of 240,000 Russian troops. After that disaster, Russia never dared to attack Germany. Hindenburg was later transferred to the western front to lead the fight against France. When the war ended, his troops retreated from France. Despite defeat, Hindenburg maintained strict discipline over his troops, and earned the respect of many world leaders. Germany's defeat was largely the responsibility of the commander in chief who preceded Hindenburg. World War I already was ending when he took command and his orderly withdrawal of German troops won him the respect of his countrymen. After Wilhelm II stepped down, the German people elected Hindenburg as president of the Weimar Republic.

My story about Hindenburg deeply impressed Chiang, and he forgave my remark that "if you lose your temper and curse me, I will pack up and leave tomorrow." I believe that is the reason why for the next twenty-five years he never once became angry with me.[4]

Aborted Trip to the Soviet Union

In 1926 Chiang was in a difficult situation. Wang Ching-wei was in charge, and the National government now wanted to dismiss him. The government did not dare to take such action. When Chiang tried to resign, Wang Ching-wei, the chairman of the National government [council], neither accepted nor rejected it. That decision put Chiang in an awkward position and made his life miserable. It was rumored that some leaders wanted Chiang to go to the Soviet Union to "observe and study." Such a choice, however, might result in his being detained in the Soviet Union and allow someone else to assume military power in Canton. Chiang decided to visit the Soviet Union, and he asked me to accompany him. We kept our plan secret and prepared to sail from Hong Kong to Vladivostok. We assembled out passports, steamer tickets, and luggage, and we obtained some foreign currency in Hong Kong to supplement our travel expenses.

On the day of departure, while driving to the Ch'ang-ti pier, I asked Chiang the following: "Commandant, why do we have to leave? The military power is in the hands of the commandant. Why do we not just make a stand?" Being young and unfamiliar with the complex matters at hand, I spoke with unusual bluntness. Chiang did not mind, and he immediately told the driver to return to his residence. But he changed his mind and again told the driver to drive to the pier, at which point I raised this question. "If we leave, who is going to take over the post of commandant, which Sun Yat-sen had conferred upon you?" Chiang reflected, and this time he firmly said, "Go back to Tung-shan residence." Because there was a glass partition separating us, the driver could not hear our conversation and he appeared puzzled by these conflicting orders.

Once Chiang decided to stay and make a stand—and a wise decision it was—the course of Chinese history changed. Only Chiang and I knew what took place. In 1980, at a ceremony presenting me with the Chung-shan Medal on my eightieth birthday, I felt it was my duty to tell the Central Committee that Chiang's decision was an extremely important turning point in our national revolution. Chiang already had visited the Soviet Union, and there was no need for him to go again. His refusal to go was not determined only by my advice. When a person is undecided, a few words of advice can make a great difference. As for why I had the courage to question him, only the heavenly spirit of Sun Yat-sen can explain that. History's events are so very complicated.[5]

The *Chung-shan* Gunboat Incident

After returning to his residence, Chiang kept busy and remained on his guard. Chiang's refusal to visit the Soviet Union paved the way for the *Chung-shan* Gunboat Incident on March 20, 1926, which was a scheme to kill him. The *Chung-shan* gunboat had docked in Canton. On that day, without orders, the gunboat moved to the Whampoa River, uncovered its cannons, and prepared for an attack.

On the morning of March 20, Chiang felt that something was not right when he went to the Whampoa Military Academy. He immediately set off in his motorboat and returned to Canton, where he took temporary shelter in a cement factory. From there he ordered his troops to stand ready. I usually followed Chiang everywhere he went, but this time he instructed me to remain at his Tung-shan residence.

In fact Chiang already had received some intelligence reports. I remember that on the night of March 18, around 12:30 A.M., someone came to the residence and knocked on the door saying, "My name is Hu. I have urgent matters to report only to the commandant." I replied, "He went to bed some three hours ago." The man still insisted. I had to report this to Chiang because, only a few days before, Chiang ordered me to awaken him for any urgent matters. As soon as Chiang heard that Hu had arrived, he got up at once to receive him. The two talked for more than half an hour before Hu left. I later learned that this man was Hu Kung-mien, a member of the Chinese Communist party Central Executive Committee and an old friend of Chiang's from Chekiang. By visiting at such a late hour, he obviously had important information and wanted no one to see him. That night Chiang and Hu spoke in whispers. As a rule I did not participate in such discussions. I knew that whatever was being talked about must have great importance. Later I thought their discussions must have had something to do with the *Chung-shan* Gunboat Incident on March 20.

Chiang stayed in the cement factory for half a day and one night, and nobody knew he was there. Three times Wang Ching-wei's wife, Ch'en Pi-chün, telephoned to ask the whereabouts of Chiang. I replied that he had gone to the Whampoa Military Academy. She did not believe me and insisted I tell her Chiang's whereabouts. I politely sparred with her in this way, and the third time she called she became angry, cursed me, and slammed the telephone down. At the moment I was alone at the residence. I had been politely taking all calls of inquiry, and there were many. As for Chiang's true hiding place, even had I known, I would never have revealed it.

On March 21, Chiang delivered a speech at Whampoa and then he and I departed for Humen. After arriving and taking a rest, we drafted a plan for the Northern Expedition. Chiang spoke and I took notes. The Humen Fort commander was Ch'en Shao-ying. With Ouyang Ke, deputy commandant of the Naval Academy, and Hsu Hu, Ch'en Shao-ying captured the *Chung-shan* gunboat on the night of March twentieth to suppress the rebellion. The *Chung-shan* Gunboat Incident proved instrumental for launching the Northern Expedition that brought Chiang to power. After that episode, Chiang instructed me to write Ouyang Ke and request him to visit Chiang's residence. Chiang then ordered him arrested on his arrival. Ouyang had served Chiang well and faithfully carried out his orders as I stated above. For the life of me, I could not think of any reason why Chiang had him arrested. I surmised that Chiang did not want the *Chung-shan* Gunboat Incident to become a cause celèbre and wanted someone to shoulder the responsibility for it. Chiang must have figured that the Northern Expedition still required the Communists' cooperation, and thus Ouyang Ke, who should have been rewarded for helping to seize the *Chung-shan* gunboat, was made the scapegoat. Chiang's clever tactic defused the crisis.

What happened to Ouyang Ke? Later he was released during the Northern Expedition. As for the reason, I do not remember. All I know is that he was a most ambitious man who believed that his failure to be promoted was because he came from Kiangsi Province and was despised by the Fukien clique. Chiang later appointed him to be commandant of the Central Torpedo Training School [Chung-yang yü-lei hsüeh-hsiao] in Chenkiang. His eventual fate was a complete surprise to many: he was executed by a military court for corruption. In my view, he probably was too conceited for his own good, but it was hard to believe that he could have been guilty of corruption. I tried to save him but to no avail. Ouyang Ke repented, but it was too late to save him.

Another person arrested for being involved in the *Chung-shan* Gunboat Incident was Wu T'ieh-ch'eng, the police commissioner of Canton. He was also brought to Tung-shan, then sent to Humen. Perhaps Chiang knew that Wu was a coconspirator in the plot. In this complex situation, I was not sure what relationship Wu had with Wang Ching-wei. Wu was unprincipled but smooth and tactful, traits I did not learn about until I worked with him in the Kuomintang central headquarters. Only Chiang really knew the reason for Wu's arrest, and he never confided in me.

At that time, Liu Shih and Chiang Ting-wen led the most dependable troops located in the Canton region. In the Northern Expedition these two led the first and second divisions of the First Army. While suppressing the rebellion, they disarmed the Workers Investigation Brigade [Kung-jen chiu-cha-tui], then under the command of the Communists, and took four thousand pieces of arms. They also surrounded the residence of the Soviet advisers and maintained law and order in Canton. These two men were loyal and supported the national revolution.

Chiang asked me to write to Wang Ching-wei on the night of March 23; I personally took that letter to Wang's residence. That letter contained evidence accusing him of rejecting the party faithful and siding with the Communists. The same evening Wang hastily left for Hong Kong and refused to meet with Chiang. I found it difficult to comprehend the inside story of this conspiracy against Chiang, but from all available facts, especially the letter to Wang, Wang Ching-wei must have participated in the plot. Otherwise, why had he not openly helped Chiang? And why did he hastily escape? Chiang also demanded that the Russians leave Canton, and I wrote that letter to the Soviet adviser Kissan'ka.

After the incident, Chiang held a series of meetings with important officials in Canton, such as T'an Yen-k'ai, T. V. Soong, and Li Chi-shen, asking for their opinions and to draft a policy plan for the future. They frankly stated their views about the current situation, which greatly helped Chiang.

The above facts are all that I know about the *Chung-shan* Incident of March 20, 1926. Although the Communists had tried to remove Chiang from his control of Canton, he still tolerated them. Unable to intimidate him, they incited a rebellion, hoping that Chiang would step down. They never perceived that Chiang's strong will and inside information had enabled him to take steps to put down the rebellion, thus avoiding a rupture with the Soviet Union. At that time, the Soviet advisers strongly influenced the government; Wang Ching-wei was only too willing to take orders from them. Yet Chiang had Ouyang Ke arrested. Another person involved in the conspiracy was Teng Yen-ta, then dean of Whampoa Military Academy. Chiang not only forgave him without conducting any investigation, but in July of that year he appointed him to the very important position of director of the General Political Department of the National Revolutionary Army [Kuo-min ko-ming-chün tsung-cheng-chi-pu] under the command of Chiang himself.

On March 19, 1926, the day before the *Chung-shan* Gunboat Incident, Teng Yen-ta came to see Chiang in a very nervous state of mind. Chiang was out. Teng became extremely uneasy. He did not ask Chiang's where-abouts, nor did he express any concern, as though he knew in advance what was about to happen. Actually, Chiang was not avoiding him. When Chiang later learned that Teng had been involved in the conspiracy, he pretended he knew nothing. Chiang did not have him investigated because he considered it more important to carry out the Northern Expedition with all the help he could get. I personally thought Teng was a capable, ambitious man, full of energy, an eloquent speaker, and hard-working. Chiang always cherished the talents of others, and he naturally hoped that Teng would again loyally serve him.

It is worthwhile to note that the Soviet Union at this time did not want to destroy its relationship with Chiang. An agreement for the Nationalists and the Communists to cooperate and launch the Northern Expedition was then signed. A document later found in the Soviet embassy in Peking revealed that the Soviet advisers were reprimanded by Moscow for their reckless action in Canton. Moscow realized that the success of the Northern Expedition could only benefit the Soviets, especially because our national revolution was based on *San Min Chu I*, which was compatible with ele-ments of communist ideology. Moreover, the two sides both opposed im-perialism. The Soviets also understood that if the Kuomintang failed in Kwangtung, the Communist party would not survive. The Communist party had to seek refuge under the Kuomintang in order to grow. Because of this delicate relationship, Chiang and the Soviets both tried to avoid a confrontation that might rupture the relationship.

This incident also produced an early decision to launch the Northern Expedition. By then Chiang had seized enough power to dominate the party and the government. He alone could decide when to start the expedition without seeking the approval of Wang Ching-wei and his ever-present Soviet advisers.

The *Chung-shan* Incident revealed six significant developments: (1) Many Chinese at home and abroad now realized that Chiang represented the ideals of *San Min Chu I* and was the main leader of the Kuomintang. He was not a power of the Soviet Union or the Chinese Communists. (2) Loyal comrades of the Kuomintang were encouraged and had reason to continue to work hard on behalf of the national revolution. (3) The Communists now realized that Chiang was not easily intimidated and that their pro-Wang, anti-Chiang strategy had failed. Leaders in the Soviet Union also understood that a communist takeover was still premature. (4) The cunning efforts of Wang Ching-wei and the Communists to form an alliance had been broken. (5) Chiang became the real power that would command the Northern Expedition forces. (6) Control of the Kuomintang had reverted to loyal Kuomintang members and Wang Ching-wei, and the Communists were out of power.[6] Eager to be the leader and very willing to hand over party power to the Communists, Wang Ching-Wei had fled to Hong Kong in shame. The current Kuomintang leadership began to reorganize the Kuomintang and the National government. Persons who previously had cooperated with Chiang took over influential posts: T'an Yen-k'ai became chairman of the National government [council] and Li Chi-shen, director of military affairs. All departments of Kuomintang headquarters were again in the hands of loyal comrades.

Reorganizing the Kuomintang

The *Chung-shan* Gunboat Incident greatly shook up the Kuomintang so that quarrels with the Chinese Communist party finally became public. Even in the Whampoa Military Academy, two factions secretly existed among the faculty and students: one was called the Society for the Study of Sun Wenism (Sun Yat-senism) [Sun-wen chu-i hsüeh-hui], which adhered to the Three People's Principles; the other was called League of Chinese Military Youth [Ch'ing-nien chün-jen lien-ho-hui], which favored communism. These differences also existed at the highest leadership level. Many Kuomintang members believed that a coalition with the Chinese Communist party was essential. They knew the Communists only used this coalition as a cover to work for their own purposes, but they felt that as long as the latter did not dare openly oppose them, for the interest of the party the Kuomintang had to accept them. The Communists joined the Kuomintang as individuals and then formed cells to create confusion. This short-lived coalition between the Nationalists and the Communists, however, made it possible to build the foundations for the Northern Expedition. But later on, ambitions and conspiratorial activities of the Chinese Communist party caused the two parties to split.

Chiang's speech at the Whampoa Military Academy on January 9, 1926, cited the similar goals of Sun Yat-sen's *San Min Chu I* and communist

My elder brother, Ch'en Kuo-fu,
in Canton, January 1926,
during the Kuomintang
Second National Congress.

ideology. While Chiang was still trying to resolve the disputes between the two parties, newspapers in Hong Kong and Shanghai accused him of leaning to the left and referred to Canton as "Red Canton." After the *Chung-shan* Gunboat Incident, more people became aware of Chiang's strong belief in *San Min Chu I*. Chiang now had enough power to make all major decisions. He could act on his own without being worried about the views, suggestions, and recommendations of officials in the government, party, and military. He decisively performed the daily tasks, and very soon the British and Americans recognized the National government. Moreover, the Great Powers realized that Chiang was not a communist sympathizer.

It is well known that Sun Yat-sen first allowed Communist party members to join the Kuomintang on an individual basis, hoping they would contribute to establishing the Three People's Principles in China. I am sure he was aware that they pursued their own interests and only wanted to use the Kuomintang as a shield to secretly expand their own sphere of influence. Even within the inner circle of the Kuomintang, people like Wang Ching-wei curried favor with the Communists. As Wang consolidated his power, Chiang increasingly became a thorn in the side of the Communists. According to the Kuomintang principle that the Party Was above All [*Tang-ch'üan chih-shang*], a concept borrowed from the Soviets, all military personnel took direct orders from the party's Executive Central Committee, making the army an instrument of the Kuomintang. Chiang soon found himself boxed in.

As Wang Ching-wei wielded greater and greater power in the Kuomintang, Chiang was forced to deal with more Communists. This was a major reason why many people erroneously believed he had become a "leftist." Had Chiang not decided to work with the Communists, he easily could have driven them from Canton. I view the *Chung-shan* Gunboat Incident as a major event in Chinese modern history. Some have interpreted it as an accident, and others regarded it as the product of human error. Whatever was the real cause, I believe that Chiang wisely handled the crisis.

Between 1929 and 1930, when I served as secretary-general of the Kuomintang, I presented a detailed report on the *Chung-shan* Gunboat Incident at a meeting of the Central Committee to commemorate the party's cleansing of its enemies. Senior Kuomintang members like Hsieh Tzu, Chang Chi, and Tsou Lu had opposed admitting the Communists in 1924. They had left Canton for the Western Hills in Peking, where they opened a second front by advocating the Three People's Principles in north China. The Communists accused them of breaking up the Kuomintang and weakening the party. I could not agree with this charge because those same Kuomintang members who had accepted the Communists in their midst had stayed in Canton, and only later had they changed course and attacked the Communists. Those who went to the North and advocated the Three People's Principles indirectly helped our Northern Expedition, although they were threatened by the warlords. We hoped that, after the unification of China, the two factions would come together and work for the great cause of national reconstruction.

Hu Han-min returned from the Soviet Union on April 29, 1926. A senior member of the Kuomintang, he had high status in the party. Because the important positions already had been filled, Hu could only be assigned to the Standing Committee of the Kuomintang Central Executive Committee. He was unhappy with this post, especially knowing that Chiang now had the highest positions in the party, government, and military. Indeed it was not the right time for Hu to return to China. He thought it best to leave Canton, and he departed later that year. In fact, had he stayed in this awkward situation, he would have become a target for the Communists. I thought his departure minimized friction in the Kuomintang. It was a wise act. Had Hu insisted on remaining in Canton, Borodin would have found a way to banish him, and that would have given Chiang more headaches. I do not believe Hu's departure had anything to do with Borodin, but I suspect that Chiang received some indication of this decision from Borodin.

The Communists were then under Borodin's control, and they wanted very much to remove the right-wing influence within the Kuomintang. They perceived Wang Ching-wei as being on the left, Hu Han-min to the right, and Chiang in the middle. Chiang's dilemma was that he could lean neither to the left nor to the right without destabilizing the Kuomintang. After the *Chung-shan* Gunboat Incident, the general perception was that Chiang favored the right, which made the Communists very nervous. But in fact Chiang was exceptionally evenhanded. He cooperated with the Communists in order to prepare the Northern Expedition, but that cooperation caused many right-wing members to be unhappy and forced leaders like Hu Han-min and Wu Ch'ao-shu to leave Canton. In order to heal the Kuomintang's rift, Chiang invited Chang Ching-chiang, T'an Yen-k'ai, and my elder brother, Kuo-fu, all right-wingers, to serve on his staff. Chang left Shanghai and arrived in Canton on March 22, 1926; my elder brother arrived in Canton on May 1.

While preparing the Northern Expedition, Chiang also worked, but not excessively so, to improve relations with the Soviet Union. The Soviets naturally hoped that Chiang would lean to the "left." Because of Chiang's great power, the Communists could only spread rumors to undermine Chiang's position.

I never participated in Chiang's secret meetings. I merely prepared the daily work schedule for formal meetings. But there were exceptions. In April 1926, Borodin had just returned from north China, and he had a secret conversation with Chiang. I do not know where they met, let alone what they discussed. They very likely had arranged their meeting by telephone, but someone must have taken notes. As to who that was I do not remember. The notes could have been kept in the party's office. I only know that some papers in the office, and I never examined them, were all-important for Chiang. I recall that Hu Han-min left Canton on September 22, 1925, after Liao Chung-k'ai was assassinated on August 20, 1925. Many had mistaken Liao for a leftist, but I always believed he was a loyal Kuomintang comrade. I noticed that when delivering his speeches he hardly used the words "*chu i*" [ism]. But one day he repeatedly emphasized *chu i*, specifically pointing out that what he meant was *San Min Chu I*, Three People's Principles, not to be confused with *Kung-chan chu-i*, or communism. Not only was he a loyal Kuomintang member, but he exuded enthusiasm, and he was ready at any time to sacrifice himself for the Kuomintang. When negotiating with warlords like Liu Chen-huan and Yang Hsi-min, Liao had sat on the opium-smoking couch with them to win their trust and learn their secrets. His considerable contributions to the party cannot be forgotten. During his tenure as minister of finance he solved financial difficulties incurred by the party and the Whampoa Military Academy. I think the reason so many people were suspicious of him was that his wife, Ho Hsiang-ning, and his son, Liao Cheng-chih, were both left-leaning and later enjoyed a great reputation in the Chinese Communist party.

Rumor had it then that Liao was assassinated by the right wing, involving even Hu Han-min's cousin Hu Yi-sheng. The Communists simply used this rumor to blame the crime on the right-wing faction. I do not recall the facts because when the assassination occurred I had not yet arrived in Canton. In any case, Liao Chung-kai was a true, loyal member of the Kuomintang, and there was no reason for the right-wingers to murder him. Liao's passing was an immense loss to the Kuomintang. I still remember his home, which was on the right side of Chiang's residence, and I often went there to visit his wife.

I now realize that the *Chung-shan* Gunboat Incident was indeed a conspiracy against Chiang. Owing to my youth, I did not quite understand the political situation. In retrospect I now see more clearly than at that time. For instance, Li Chih-lung, the captain of the *Chung-shan* gunboat, was a real Communist. He never should have navigated the gunboat into the Whampoa River without specific instructions from Chiang. I remember Li Chih-lung had always been a top student at the Whampoa Military Academy and was Chiang's favorite. Chiang later appointed Li as captain of the *Chung-shan* gunboat.

Before that incident Chiang had not yet consolidated his power to repulse the attacks from the anti-Chiang faction. I am not very clear about the details, but I know that Chiang's influence in the Kuomintang at that time was still not strong and that a few procommunist members who dominated Kuomintang's policy planning met no opposition. Their decisions were obeyed and carried out. Wang Ching-wei spoke very persuasively and eloquently when advocating collaboration between the Kuomintang and the Chinese Communist party. He accused anyone who opposed the Communist party of opposing Sun Yat-sen's will. If Chiang had organized his own force to challenge the Communists, they would certainly have focused their wrath on Chiang. Therefore, I believe Chiang had no choice but to contend cautiously with that treacherous group.

It was still difficult for Chiang to control the party then. Therefore, he concentrated on consolidating his strength in the military, particularly at Whampoa Military Academy. He maintained a neutral stance amid the disputes between the left and the right; yet he still hoped that the Kuomintang's right wing would win out in any confrontation with the Communists. Although he did not openly express his true feelings, if he knew the Communists had so vicious a plot in the works, he would predictably have reacted in kind. I do not know whether the military, teaching faculty, and cadets of Whampoa Military Academy fully supported him. I only know that Chiang worked hard and maintained good connections with all groups.

After the defeat of the warlords, Chiang's prestige skyrocketed, and popular respect for him greatly helped to expand his power.

The *Chung-shan* Gunboat Incident was an anti-Chiang plot that failed, and luckily it helped Chiang's later success. Chiang was able to acquire power over both the Kuomintang and the government and begin to change the political climate. Most important, Wang Ching-wei lost out, and the party had to be reorganized. At the second meeting of the Kuomintang's Central Executive Committee on May 17, 1926, many who had once supported Wang now turned to back Chiang, and those who were undecided found themselves in an awkward position. Procommunist members now noted Chiang's power, and they had little choice but to align with him.

At the May 17 meeting, there was much discussion, and finally it was agreed to reorganize the party and restrict the activities of those members who also were Communist party members. The committee also decided that in the future all department heads of the Kuomintang Central Committee must be held by full Kuomintang members. This step reduced the number of Communists in the Central Executive Committee to only one-third of the total. One resolution of this meeting was to demand that the Chinese Communist party turn over the list of those Communists who enjoyed dual membership in both parties to the Kuomintang Central Executive Committee. The first glimmer of Kuomintang reorganization was becoming clear.

The only resolution was that all Kuomintang central departments be headed by full Kuomintang members. The Communists completely rejected the demand for their name list. My elder brother, Kuo-fu, who had been elected to the Kuomintang Central Supervisory Committee, acted for Chiang as head of the Organization Department. His difficult task was to comb out the real Communists among our ranks. From the outset, however, the Organization Department had been controlled by the well-known Communist Tan P'ing-shan.

As early as January 1924, at the first meeting of the Central Executive Committee, Sun Yat-sen expressed his keen awareness of the competition between the committee members of Kuomintang and communist persuasions. He allowed the Communists to control the Organization Department, and I think there were two reasons for that. First, Sun wanted the Communists to know that the Kuomintang was sincere and that they should not be suspicious; second, Sun was dissatisfied with Kuomintang organizational security, and he wanted to use the skills of the Communists to remedy that defect. But in reality, by using Wang Ching-wei, the Communists took over the Organization Department.

Comrades like Hsiao Cheng, Cheng Yi, and Yu Chun-hsien helped my elder brother, Kuo-fu, take charge of the Organization Department.[7] He was determined to infuse the Kuomintang with new life. His first act was to recruit the American-educated Tseng Yang-fu and Lai Lien to assist him to develop a procedure to politically train cadres of every level in the party. My brother visited many local party branches under the control of the Communists and found that the Kuomintang comrades lacked enthusiasm. He realized that new cadres had to be trained to revitalize the revolutionary spirit of the party comrades in order to persevere against the Communists. Only then was there any hope to lay the foundation for developing a successful Kuomintang party.

I remember Chiang ordering my elder brother to see Ting Wei-fen and Ku Meng-yu, who had recommended that Tuan Hsi-p'eng and Wang Lu-p'ing work with my brother. Ting was a senior revolutionary from Shantung Province and had considerable party experience. He had never held any important positions, but he had worked hard to promote the party, and he enjoyed great influence among the local comrades. Ku had a close relationship with Wang Ching-wei and was influential among those belonging to Wang's faction. They had recommended Tuan Hsi-p'eng, of Kiangsi Province and a student leader in the May Fourth movement, because of his excellent organizational work. He had formed a group called the A-B faction within the party branch in Kiangsi Province. His job was to assist my brother in the training program. Wang Lu-p'ing, a Northerner, had been close to Wang Ching-wei and was also experienced in party work.

Assisted by these men, my elder brother organized programs for cadre training and reforming the party. These three experienced good relations with all factions in the party, and my brother's reorganization work smoothly advanced. During the Northern Expedition the Kuomintang built grass roots support in the Yellow River Valley and the Yangtze River Valley, and these two comrades played an important role, for they came from the Yangtze Valley and the North, respectively.

Why Chiang Was Chosen to Lead the Northern Expedition

While working in Chiang's residence, I was in the office all day, hardly ever venturing out, at least not until Chang Ching-chiang arrived in Canton. He lived nearby. After nine o'clock in the evenings, whenever I had time, I went to visit him. Chang was older, and in the Shanghai days we referred to him as our elder. He and I knew each other well. He liked me and frequently invited me for a chat when I was not working.

Each time we met, we cordially talked. Because Chang liked to discuss reconstruction and engineering projects, we usually ended up conversing about building railways and industries. He was fascinated by my experience in the United States and, especially, my observations about railway networks and industries. We seemed to talk forever.

Chang was engaged in researching how to write strokes for classifying Chinese characters. I learned his methodology, which later inspired me to invent my own system. I developed a simple system by using only five basic strokes. I even wrote a book about it titled *The Principle and Practice of Five-Stroke Indexing System for Chinese Characters* [*Wu-p'i chien-tzu fa t'i yüan-li ying-yung*], which was published in Shanghai in 1928. When I asked him to inscribe the book, he wrote, "My Way Prevails" [*Wu-tao hsing-i*], which pleased me enormously.

During the Northern Expedition, those of us who served in the confidential materials section [*Chi-yao-k'o*] at headquarters typically handled an average of 150 letters and telegrams each day. It was too much for us, and we were always busy. I decided to use my five-stroke indexing system, categorized the files, and classified the telegrams in such a way that their retrieval was made easier. Our work efficiency greatly increased and an important spin-off was to speed up our military deployments. When Chiang learned about this, he complimented us.

To tell the truth, in the few months between the *Chung-shan* Gunboat Incident of March 20, 1926, and launching the Northern Expedition on July 9, 1926, we worked day and night without any letup. My work load was seriously beginning to affect my health.

Even before the Northern Expedition, I often coughed. My doctor showed me the X-ray picture and told me that my right lung was in poor condition. He asked me to rest more often. I listened but I could not follow his orders. When our march to the North began, we were totally involved in the expedition's work with no time for anything else. I rode all day on horseback with the troops. At rest stops I had to translate telegrams on the spot. My busy, intense routine did not affect me, and indeed the fresh air seemed to help clear my right lung.

The Northern Expedition reminds me of a question I often asked myself: Why did Sun Yat-sen appoint Chiang to be commandant of the Whampoa Military Academy in May 1924?

I understand that Sun's original plan for the Northern Expedition had been aborted because of the Kwangtung Province's military opposition. They never comprehended Sun's revolutionary goals and his high hopes for the country. The military thought that as soon as Kwangtung Province was unified it could develop on its own, and they did everything possible to undermine Sun's plan for the northward advance. An example of this approach was the handling of Ch'en Chiung-ming's insurgency.

Knowing the situation only too well, Sun was determined to find some-one with talent and vision from the Yangtze or Yellow River valleys to lead the Northern Expedition. He believed that such a person would be unlikely to find a comfortable, permanent nest in Kwangtung; such a person would have the incentive to march to the North and realize national unification.

I always imagined that was the reason why Sun selected Chiang.

Hailing from the Yangtze Valley, in his early days Chiang had partici-pated in the revolution as a follower of my second uncle, Ch'i-mei. Sun surely anticipated that if Chiang was appointed commandant of the Wham-poa Military Academy, his comrades from the Yangtze Valley would follow him to Canton and that once Kwangtung Province became unified under the Kuomintang they would form a force to complete the Northern Expe-dition. These people would certainly not desire to remain in Kwangtung indefinitely. I also assume Sun must have thought that with Chiang as leader, more comrades from other provinces would support the Northern Expedition.

The person most displeased with Sun's decision was Wang Ching-wei. Wang Ching-wei was a native of Kwangtung, and the Communists tapped provincial support to elevate his power. Wang then used the Communists to expand his influence. He used all sorts of strategies to undermine the influence of people outside Kwangtung.

Wang Ching-wei clearly knew that Chiang would not stay in Canton for long, but he also was aware that Chiang could not be easily manipulated. Kwangtung Province had now been unified and Chiang was in full control, but Wang was only chairman of the Military Council. He lacked the Wham-poa connection and had little influence among the expedition troops. There-fore, Wang had no other choice but to depend on the Soviet connection to try to dislodge Chiang and have him replaced by another military leader he might be able to control.

The Soviets, as well as the Communists, also worried they might never be able to control Chiang. Meanwhile, the Communists continued to adhere to the strategy of Party above All [*Tang-ch'üan chih-shang*] to prevent any single leader consolidating power over the Kuomintang. Their scheme was to assign Teng Yen-ta, dean of the Whampoa Military Academy, to be commandant to replace Chiang and then to find another military leader for the Eastern Expedition force.

Most of the officers of the Northern Expedition force were not from Kwangtung Province. Ho Ying-ch'in, commander of the First Army group, was a native of Kweichou Province who had participated in the Kiang-nan Arsenal battle in Shanghai in 1911. T'an Yen-k'ai, commander of the Second Army group, was from Hunan Province, and Chu Pei-teh, commander of the Third Army group, from Yunnan Province. The majority of Whampoa cadets had been recruited by my elder brother, Kuo-fu, and they came from all provinces, but with a majority from Hunan Province.

I really believed that Sun Yat-sen had acted with great foresight to select Chiang as the Whampoa Military Academy commandant. Sun regarded Chiang highly because when Ch'en Chiung-ming rebelled on June 16, 1922, Chiang rushed to Canton and stayed there for some fifty-six days to help Sun. I believe that crisis enabled Chiang to win Sun's full confidence. But Chiang was not elected to the Kuomintang Central Executive Committee in 1924 when the First National Congress was held in Canton. He would assume that position only when the Kuomintang Second National Congress convened on New Year's Day of 1926.[8] Sun Yat-sen probably did not want to draw too much attention to Chiang's elevation in 1924. Chiang once told Kuomintang members the following: "A potential leader will rise some day, but he must first be unobtrusive to others for a considerable period of time."

My connection with Chiang enabled me to become acquainted with many Kuomintang members like Hu Han-min, Wang Ching-wei, Chang Ching-chiang, Tai Ch'i-tao, and T'an Yen-k'ai, just to name a few. I had little interest in politics but was fortunate to learn much from these senior party members. I observed that each had his strong and weak point. Chiang was no exception. In the 1920s, however, his weak points were overshadowed by his achievements. His views on the major issues in that period were correct. Except for his handling of the Ouyang Ke affair, it has been my observation that he never mistreated his loyal staff and had not put people to death by an unjust military court.

CHAPTER THREE

The Northern Expedition

SUMMER 1926–SUMMER 1927

The New Filing System

ON JULY 22, 1926, I left Canton with Chiang and his Northern Expedition forces.

My duty was to take charge of confidential materials such as telegrams and papers in the secretariat of Chiang's field headquarters. Eight of us worked in the confidential materials section. During the day we marched nonstop with the troops, and at night we stopped marching but kept on working. We carried on like this until we reached Heng-yang, a medium-sized city in Hunan Province.

Our mood was upbeat and our efficiency high despite being few in number. We worked fourteen to sixteen hours each day. Our enemy, the warlords, persisted in their bureaucratic ways and their troops' morale was low. Speed is most essential in military affairs. Any request from the front must be acted on immediately to enhance military efficiency. We were never bored, and we won every battlefield engagement. This experience made me realize that when one takes on important responsibilities and produces good results for others, one can succeed in any undertaking. Consider the maxim: "To share is to benefit."

We usually processed around 150 documents a day. Time was short and Chiang was always impatient. Whenever he wanted a certain paper, he required us to find it for him immediately. This challenge forced me to conceive a classification method for Chinese characters to organize our files.

With two objectives in mind, I devised the five-stroke indexing system, which, first, facilitated rapid searches for documents and, second, was a system simple both to learn and to use. There is nothing mysterious about a methodology if one will practice and learn it. Old-fashioned Chinese filing systems are complex and require a lot of time to master. I knew little about these old systems, but I knew many government agencies had used these same systems for generations.

The filing system I invented so facilitated our work that the confidential materials section made significant contributions to the success of the Northern Expedition.

The Hunan-Wuhan Battles

The battle of Ting-ssu Bridge on August 30, 1926, was decisive: our victory enabled the National Revolutionary Army to control Hunan Province and move on to Wuhan in Hupei Province. Despite high casualties on both sides, the main force of Wu P'ei-fu, which had controlled Hupei, Honan, and Hopei provinces, was defeated by the National Revolutionary Army. With Wu out of the way, he no longer could counterattack.

The battle for Wuchang was fought around seventy years ago. I still cannot forget what I saw. When the battle was most fierce, Chiang dispatched me with a letter to the Seventh Army group commander, Li Tsung-jen. I mounted a horse and rode to the front. Dead bodies were everywhere, and their stench permeated the air. From afar, I could see that the corpses had black faces, but when my horse approached and its tail moved, the flies covering the dead scattered and the black faces disappeared. It is impossible to describe my pain. I recalled the line, "One general's fame takes a toll of ten thousand skeletons," and I reined in the horse. Sitting in the saddle in a stunned state of mind, I steered my horse gingerly around the bodies so as not to let his hooves step on them.

I passed small villages along the way. When the peasants saw I wore the uniform of the National Revolutionary Army, they came out to welcome me. Some led my horse, while others brought tea and even a jug of wine and a chicken. I was deeply moved when I saw their sincere hospitality. At that moment I understood the true meaning of a line from *The Four Books*: "With baskets of food and jugs of wine, welcome the army of liberation."

Exposed to heavy artillery fire from the Wuchang City walls, Chiang left his field headquarters by train to visit the front line and direct our offensive. Chiang calmly carried out his duties without fear. For someone like me who had had no battlefield experience, that scene gave me tremendous confidence. Chiang instructed me that if urgent telegrams arrived from the front and needed an immediate reply, I should awaken him at night no matter how late the hour. I still tried my utmost to avoid disturbing his sleep. Unless something was truly pressing, I asked the chief of the general staff to handle the matter.

Having just defeated Wu P'ei-fu, we were engaged in combat with the warlord Sun Ch'üan-fang, commander in chief of the joint forces of Kiangsu, Kiangsi, Chekiang, Anhwei, and Fukien. Although our small military force's morale was high, the situation did not look good. Fighting against heavy odds, our leaders decided on a two-pronged strategy: while fighting, Sun, Chiang also telegraphed my third uncle, Ch'en Ch'i-ts'ai, to attack Sun Ch'üan-fang.

The Soviet military adviser was General Galen [Galin, Vasilii K. Blyukher]. Galen's duties were military and technical.[1] He showed little interest in party affairs and other matters. Chiang usually accepted his military recommendations.

Each night when we halted to rest, two single rooms were prepared, one for Chiang, the other for Galen. When I was invited to dine with Chiang, I found Galen at the same table. The two of them talked mostly about military strategies, and they usually agreed.

Chiang and General Pai Ch'ung-hsi, however, often differed on strategies. When that occurred, I had to step in and smooth out their disagreements. If an urgent telegram demanding help arrived, especially from Li Tsung-jen, I reproduced two copies, one for each of them. If they took different positions, I then discussed the fighting with Pai, and as a rule he complied with Chiang's wishes.

Li and Pai were from Kwangsi Province and this brought them closer. People loved to call them "Li-pai." As chief of the general staff, Pai, with Chiang's endorsement, ordered more provisions for Li's Seventh Army group. In such a situation, I always asked Pai to copy Chiang's name on the orders he issued. Pai, however, did not like the idea. To evade Chiang's detection, he preferred giving verbal instructions instead of written ones.

I should also mention T'ang Sheng-chih, commander of the Eighth Army group, a man of ambition as well as an opportunist, not worthy of trust. I believed the National Revolutionary Army took a risk when using him. But he proved helpful when the left wing used him to contain the warlords in Szechuan, Yunnan, and Kweichou provinces.

Liu Wen-tao, director of the Political Department of T'ang's Eighth Army group, served as a Kuomintang representative in charge of coordinatng the Eighth Army group and the National government. A senior member of the Kuomintang and a native of Hupei Province, he was a trusted aide of T'ang and often represented him when consulting with Chiang and serving as a go-between. Liu was known for his splendid voice. He could deliver a speech before a crowd of ten thousand without a microphone. His wife also worked in the Political Department of the Eighth Army group. She was a well-known woman who usually dressed in a military uniform and wore riding boots.

The Chinese Communist party's foundation at that time was still weak. Borodin and the Communists finally decided on a policy of splitting the Kuomintang leadership.[2] Chang Ching-chiang, T'an Yen-k'ai, T. V. Soong, Li Chi-shen, and my elder brother, Kuo-fu, were still in Canton and had been cooperative and helpful in our advance. T'an Yen-k'ai, who had become chairman of the Committee for the National government after the Chung-shan Gunboat Incident, provided support, which was deeply appreciated by Chiang.

Because I worked around the clock in the confidential materials section, I became very familiar with reports from my elder brother, Kuo-fu, then in Canton. He reported that, after the *Chung-shan* Gunboat Incident of March 20, 1926, the Communists had realized that their influence in the Kuomintang was weaker and they now plotted to divide our strength. First, they dropped hints that Wang Ching-wei would receive the chairmanship of the Standing Committee of the Central Executive Committee in order to provoke dissension between Chang Ching-chiang and T'an Yen-k'ai. Second, the Communists knew that Chang Ching-chiang and my elder brother, Kuo-fu, greatly despised their slippery tactics. When Borodin approached Chang, he learned about his principle that an "anti-Communist is not an antirevolutionist," a principle that my elder brother, Kuo-fu, also supported.

My Wedding

When I was confidential secretary at the Whampoa Military Academy, my colleague Shao Li-tzu and I managed all confidential papers. After Shao Li-tzu became liaison officer to Feng Yü-hsiang's headquarters, I found myself doing two people's work every day, toiling until after midnight. To make matters worse, Chiang rose at six o'clock every morning and often required my services, forcing me to rise before six every day. As a matter of fact, I never slept more than six hours a night. Every day I was at my desk drafting documents, writing letters, and translating telegrams. I was so busy that very soon I was overcome with spells of constant coughing. An X ray showed that my right lung was already infected with tuberculosis. The Northern Expedition was about to begin. My doctor advised me not to join the march, but I felt duty-bound to do so. I constantly coughed as I marched with the troops. Yet after we arrived at Heng-yang, a medium-sized city in Hunan Province, my condition had improved. I attributed that to walking, exercise, and fresh air.

In Wuchang, however, intense work, lack of sleep, and eating food contaminated by flies brought on dysentery, and I collapsed on a train near the frontline, too weak to move. Because of insufficient medical facilities,

The bride and groom: my wife and I after our wedding
ceremony, Shanghai, 1927.

Chiang suggested that I go to Hankow to find a doctor and rest. Our forces
had now captured Hankow, on the north bank of the Yangtze River, but
Wuchang, on the south bank, was still in enemy hands.

I set out in a sedan chair for Hankow, and on the road outside of the
Wuchang City wall, some guards on the wall started shooting at the sedan
chair. Fortunately, I was not hit. As we crossed the river, machine guns
started firing at us. I was unhurt and arrived in Hankow without a scratch.
By the time I entered a Japanese-managed hospital in the Japanese Concession, I was close to death. With rest and medicine I completely recovered.
By that time, Chiang had reached Kiangsi Province. I was ready to return
to his side and work, but he urged me to rest more. Therefore, I went to
Shanghai, and married my fiancée, Sun Lu-ching.

Poor communications at the frontlines had prevented me from informing my family and fiancée of my illness. My family had set the wedding ceremony for July 5 in Shanghai. That date approximated the launching of the Northern Expedition, and so my wedding had to be postponed despite the elaborate preparations. I had wanted to marry after the Northern Expedition, but my father and in-laws would not agree. A wedding date was set for December 9, 1926. Three days beforehand, my family, my bride, and her father and mother arrived in Shanghai, but I did not show up until the evening of the eighth, arriving by boat.

In order to be in Shanghai in time for the wedding without attracting attention, I dressed as a merchant, even wearing a pair of eyeglasses. I dared not reveal my travel plans to anyone. My whole family did not know when I would arrive, and they became extremely anxious, even discussing a postponement of the wedding. As soon as I arrived in Shanghai, I telephoned my sister-in-law and learned that my elder brother, Kuo-fu, had returned from Canton to attend my wedding. Everyone was greatly relieved.

The wedding ceremony was simple, yet modern, and took place in the Peace Hotel of Shanghai's British Concession for reasons of security. We invited only a few close relatives and friends to join us.[3] Now, with deep sadness, I wish to record that my wife, Sun Lu-ching, a person with great decency, dignity, and all traditional womanly virtues, bid farewell to me and her children on September 29, 1992. She died of heart disease at the age of ninety-two. She shared my success and failure, sorrow and happiness for nearly sixty-six years. She left me three adult sons, Tze-an, Tze-ning, and Tze-ch'uo, one grown daughter, Tze-yung. I vividly recall that eight days after the wedding, I received a telegram from Pai Ch'ung-hsi urging me to report immediately to the general headquarters of the National Revolutionary Army in Nanchang. In my absence, Ch'en Pu-lei, my substitute, had been incapable of doing my job, and Pai wanted me back at once. I left the next day for Hankow and soon reached Wuchang by way of Hunan Province, which was still partly controlled by the warlord Sun Ch'üan-fang.

The National Revolutionary Army captured Nanchang on November 7, 1926, but I did not arrive there until early January 1927. When we launched the first offensive on Nanchang, we met strong resistance. The fierce battle was the worst battle of the entire expedition. Fortunately, Chu Pei-teh's Third Army group was stationed in Nanchang, and with Chiang supervising, the enemy was broken. Our forces pursued the enemy, entered the East Gate, and captured a large quantity of arms. Among the many captives were battalion, regiment, and even division commanders of Sun Ch'üan-fang's army.

Shortly after my arrival in Nanchang, Pai Ch'ung-hsi was transferred to the front as the commander of the Eastern Route Army.

Wuhan versus Nanchang

When Borodin and his group came to Wuhan in December 1926, the Communists and their Kuomintang collaborators insisted that policy decisions must be made by the leaders in Wuhan. A struggle for power now developed between Wuhan and Nanchang.

In Wuhan, Borodin began to behave like a big boss. The Communists became friendly with Generals T'ang Sheng-chih and Chang Fa-k'uei. For that reason, from late 1927 to December 1929, T'ang Sheng-chih always opposed Chiang. Chang Fa-k'uei also became very arrogant and imperious. He ingratiated himself with the Communists in the hope of obtaining a high position in the government with a handsome salary to match. T'ang Sheng-chih wanted Wuhan to be chosen the nation's capital.

The Kuomintang party-military leaders in Nanchang and Wuhan tried to gain control over the local party branches at Canton City and in Kwangtung and Kiangsi provinces. The Communists, however, also aimed at taking over the Kuomintang's Canton municipal branch and making it their base. But when my elder brother, Kuo-fu, left Canton, he appointed Wu I-tsang to head the municipal party branch. Wu then served as head of the Kuomintang's Organization Department.

I knew Wu to be a fair-minded and upright man. At the May 1926 second meeting of the Central Executive Committee, Wu ignored all pressures and decisively ruled that the Communists be allowed only one-third of the Central Executive Committee seats. He successfully crushed the Communists' attempt to take control of the Canton municipal Kuomintang branch.

In the Kiangsi Kuomintang provincial branch many Communists operated. But they only occupied one-third of the party's membership so that our side still had a majority. The Communists began spreading rumors. For example, on February 27, 1927, Tuan Hsi-p'eng was overwhelmingly elected to the Provincial Committee of the Kuomintang branch in Kiangsi, receiving only three negative votes. But in Wuhan everyone learned from communist rumors that he had not received enough votes. This development enabled the Communists to boycott the party branch in Kiangsi and demand that another election be rescheduled for March 26, 1927. They instigated the arrests of Lo Shih-shih, Ch'eng T'ien-fang, and others on April 2, 1927. That time, I did not take part in the fight over party membership in Kiangsi because all party affairs were handled by my elder brother, Kuo-fu. The situation now had become critical, in fact bad enough to foment a conspiracy against Chiang. This new struggle centered on which city should become the new seat of the provisional central government of National China. The Communists insisted on Wuhan. Chiang preferred Nanchang. Ironically, the great majority of the Kuomintang members, including T'an Yen-k'ai, also preferred Wuhan. In order to head off a confrontation, Chiang acceded to communist demands. I believe that the Communists had wanted to minimize Chiang's military control of Nanchang. On January 11, 1927, Chiang set out for Wuhan, but I did not go along. I later learned that Chiang, after delivering a speech, was almost prevented from leaving Wuhan.[4] I also discovered that a communist agent, Chang Hsien-yun, had infiltrated my office and had relayed vital information to Borodin. Chiang quickly sent him back to Wuhan.

Meanwhile, the central leadership of the Soviet Union was reluctant to abandon its only ally in the East. In Wuhan, Borodin continued to serve as adviser to the Chinese Communist party, and both plotted for a second time to grab power. But Borodin never expected to collide with two of the most anticommunist leaders, Chang Ching-chiang and Ch'en Kuo-fu. The former openly criticized him without fear, while the latter quietly worked hard to build a solid foundation at the lowest levels of the party. Borodin soon initiated the anti–Chang Ching-chiang campaign with the slogan Down with the Muddle-headed, Old and Feeble Chang Ching-chiang. When Chang Ching-chiang was later in Shanghai, he said to me while smiling: "If I was really muddle-headed, old and feeble, would it be worthwhile to make the effort to knock me down? I may be old and feeble, but I am certainly not muddle-headed!" The Communist party now mobilized its members to smear and destroy him. But Chang and my elder brother also went after Borodin.[5]

I now raise the question of whether Ch'en Pu-lei ever proposed to Chiang Kai-shek that he use Shanghai's Green Gang to handle the communist problem in early January 1927.[6] Ch'en Pu-lei, a journalist, was very familiar with the situation in Shanghai, and so it is possible since Chiang often consulted with him. But Ch'en never told me that he had made any such suggestions to Chiang. Moreover, Chiang understood the situation in Shanghai very well, and it seems unlikely that he needed any prompting from Ch'en. As for how much importance Chiang attached to Ch'en's advice, I really have no way to judge, but I know that ever since joining Chiang's camp, he played an important role as adviser.

Early in January, Chiang decided to make Nanking and Shanghai the targets for his next offensive. There were also suggestions that Chiang should advance toward Peking along the Peking-Hankow Railway, to avoid the errors made by leaders of the T'ai-p'ing Rebellion. But those who advocated taking Shanghai and Nanking first believed that once we had taken control of the lower reaches of the Yangtze Valley, our financial difficulties would be largely solved.

Two reasons compelled Chiang to make Nanking and Shanghai the first targets of our offensive: (1) The Kuomintang Political Conference in Canton, held on November 26, 1926, decided to move the capital to Wuhan. This decision probably weakened our party's military influence in Wuhan. Disputes within the Kuomintang could have wrecked our revolutionary movement before subduing the northern warlords. Rather than Wuhan, we needed another secure site. (2) Sun Ch'üan-fang's troops were still strong. If we moved directly on Peking, our overextended battle line might tempt Sun to attack our rear. He also might attack us from Shantung Province. Chiang hoped to deal Sun a knockout blow before he even began to take on the warlords Chang Tsung-ch'ang and Chang Tso-lin.

The commander of the Sixth Army group was Chen Ch'ien, but the director of its Political Department, Lin Tsu-han, was a Communist. We were particularly worried about the loyalty of the Sixth Army group. The political departments and Kuomintang representatives in the army held great power, and they even signed orders on behalf of a military commander. Most people never understood the real function of the "the party" in the army, and the Communists often used army political departments to carry on intelligence work and to confuse the public.

Tai's Trip to Japan

After the National government was installed in Nanking in 1927, Chiang had to make clear his position on communism and imperialism. When the National Revolutionary Army reached the lower reaches of the Yangtze River in February 1927, Chiang's first step was to ask Tai Ch'i-tao to go to Japan. He left Shanghai on February 14 and returned on March 31 of the same year.

Chiang reasoned that henceforth the Northern Expedition forces would be occupying territories long dominated by foreign imperialism. Our advance into Shantung Province would inevitably worry the Japanese. And the Japanese very likely might try to oppose our plan to unify China. Therefore, Chiang sent Tai to Japan to inform the Japanese of our intentions. Tai asked Japan to support Chiang diplomatically.

In Japan, Tai met with a number of powerful political leaders. They were deeply concerned about China's future development, and they paid particular attention to what Tai had to say. It was common knowledge that Chiang and Tai had disagreements in Canton, and now Tai had surfaced as Chiang's personal representative. The Japanese now realized that the Kuomintang was a force to be reckoned with, and they perhaps envisioned the likely unification of China. Sending Tai to Japan also demonstrated that Chiang was not as radical as many foreigners had said.

During his stay in Japan, Tai did not reach any agreement with the Japanese, but he got his message across. Tai told the Japanese that Sun Yat-sen's "Pan-Asianism" meant China and Japan should work in mutual cooperation and maintain a friendly relationship. Furthermore, China's revolution would never threaten Japan, and the goal of the Three People's Principles was to promote and preserve stability and eternal peace in Asia. It was later reported that many Japanese in the audience were in tears listening to the speech.[7]

Tai was accompanied at all times by the Black Dragon Society [Amur Society, Kokuryūkai] leader Toyama Mitsuru, who was very sympathetic to the Chinese revolution. When Sun Yat-sen and Tai were in exile in Japan, Toyama had protected them. He was their closest friend. Although he had known Chiang fairly well, his friendship with Chiang was not as close as with Sun and Tai. Another person very friendly with the Japanese leadership was Huang Fu, but he played a different role from that of Tai.

Huang Fu took a neutral position. He was an official in the warlord Peking government. Cautious and prudent, Huang had keen judgment and spoke eloquently. If he had represented the National government in putting in a good word in with the Japanese, his influence would have been different from that of Tai. But he did help Chiang this time by convincing his Japanese friends that Chiang was not a Communist and that unusual circumstances had forced him to work with the Communists. I think that Huang Fu's mission was to explain the goal of our national revolution to the Japanese and discuss the future relationship between China and Japan. But I did not think that the Japanese should be informed of our intentions toward the Communists because we wanted to keep our plan of a pending purge of the Communists confidential. Huang did that.

We needed someone to assure the Japanese leaders that no matter what developments occurred in China, our side wanted friendly relations with Japan. The slogan of Anti-Imperialism reverberated everywhere in China, and we did not want to cause any misunderstanding with the Japanese or alarm them. Huang had the confidence of Chiang because, as I stated before, he had sworn a blood oath with Chiang and my second uncle, Ch'i-mei. Their political stands were not identical, but their personal relations were close. We believed that cautious measures were necessary to prevent the Japanese from interfering with our march to the North.

I clearly remember that as soon as we arrived at the lower reaches of the Yangtze River, the British changed their attitude. They now knew we were not Communists and eagerly wanted our friendship. Chiang might have sent someone to clarify his anticommunist stand as he had done with Japan. Now looking back, I think the Sino-British relationship in 1927 was similar to that of the United States and Castro's Cuba in 1960–61. The United States would not extend diplomatic recognition unless Castro openly declared he would not ally with communist countries. Before mid-April of 1927 Chiang had publicly declared he would not make deals with the Communists. Communist propaganda and communist attacks on Chiang later also convinced many that Chiang was an anticommunist.

As our forces closed in on Shanghai, foreign and Chinese banks gave considerable aid to the National Revolutionary Army, chiefly dictated by a desire to survive. My third uncle, Ai-shih, knew many Shanghai financiers when he worked in the Bank of China. He helped Chiang and later became the chairman of the National Financial Committee and the accountant general of the National government.

The National Revolutionary Army was far superior to any of the individual warlord armies. Our strategy was to divide and defeat them one by one. Chiang sent Huang Fu to negotiate with Chang Tso-lin in the North while fighting Sun Ch'üan-fang in the South. We reckoned that even if those negotiations failed, at least we had temporarily split the warlords. But as relations between the National Revolutionary Army and Wuhan rapidly deteriorated, the situation became critical. Did the warlord Peking government try to make contact with us? I am not sure it did, but I recall that Wang Ch'ung-hui went to Shanghai to conduct negotiations.

But in a matter of a few months, the National Revolutionary Army emerged victorious. The warlords wanted to talk peace with Chiang and the National Revolutionary Army and implored us to stop the offensive. The Peking government hoped for a repeat of 1911 when the northern provinces fell to Yüan Shih-k'ai because the Nationalists lacked the strength to go north after choosing Nanking as the national capital.

The Peking government, however, refused to accept the conditions put forward by Chiang, and the negotiations failed. I believe Chiang forced that outcome to avoid repeating what had occurred in the T'ai-p'ing Rebellion after the T'ai-p'ings seized Nanking. Chiang had learned from history and did not linger in Nanking, preferring to negotiate and seize the opportune moment.

The Anching Incident

On March 15, 1927, we traveled by train from Nanchang to Kiukiang where we transferred to the warship *Chih-tung*. I was one of Chiang's many aides-de-camp. The ship docked at Anching on March 19. The Communists in Anching had been bullying our comrades. Many of our comrades boarded to see Yang Hu, a senior Kuomintang member in Anhwei Province and one who had participated in the *Shao-ho* Gunboat Insurrection of December 5, 1915, with my Uncle Ch'i-mei in Shanghai.

They complained to Yang Hu and requested he allow them to impose control over the Communists. But Yang hesitated. Being young and temperamental, I urged Yang to accede to their request, and I pledged that if anything should go wrong I would share the responsibility. Only then did Yang consent to let our comrades act. Confidential telegrams still passed through my hands, and I was well aware of what the Communists were doing. With each passing day, I became more angry toward the Communists who were plotting to destroy us. In reality our national revolution was being fought on two fronts: we faced both the warlords and the Communists.

Shortly after Chiang delivered his speech at a welcoming assembly on March 23, 1927, we attacked the Communists. For the first time we confronted them head-on. I was not at the scene of the fight, but I instigated the incident and was the first to expose their true face. I ordered an all-out frontal attack on the Communists. My purpose was very simple: I did not want to see the communist influence spread in China. We had to stop it.

The Wuhan authorities later asked Chiang what had transpired. Yang Hu and I explained everything to Chiang. He said nothing and instructed me to send a telegram to Wuhan saying that everything was now normal. The situation, however, was very serious, and Chiang could have been reprimanded by the Wuhan authorities. We arrived in Nanking on March 24, the day after the National Revolutionary Army had taken the city. We discovered a great array of weapons abandoned by Sun Ch'üan-fang's troops: rifles, bayonets, swords, grenades, and so forth piled along the Yangtze River near Hsia-kuan and scattered about. One day, Chiang asked me to carry a letter to the deputy commander of the Second Army group, Lu Ti-ping. When I passed through that same area, I was reminded of the battle at the Ho-sheng Bridge when I had to cross over the countless dead bodies. Those battlefield scenes terrified me. Sun Ch'üan-fang was now unable to hold Nanking after he had lost Shanghai. Although his troops still occupied the north bank of the Yangtze River, they did not attempt to fire at Chiang's flagship. In historical perspective, what we did in Anching was the prelude to a series of anticommunist actions. Very shortly, "the Nanking Incident" of March 24–25, 1927, occurred.

The Nanking Incident

Many foreigners were massacred in Nanking right after the National Revolutionary Army had captured the city; that event became known as "the Nanking Incident." In retrospect, the incident might have been instigated by the Communists to stir up foreign resentment against Chiang. It was, indeed, a tragic affair.

The wars of those years often brought great harm to foreigners; it was unavoidable although many condemned it. Foreigners found it difficult to determine which side waging those wars was responsible for such calamities. Most foreigners in China believed that no one would dare harm them, and they often were careless in their security. No one could really tell just what exactly had caused the Nanking Incident.

Although the Wuhan government had not yet received international recognition, it was a legal government; all diplomatic matters had to be handled by the foreign minister of the Wuhan government. After the Nanking Incident, Chiang told the Great Powers to negotiate with Hangou to resolve their grievances. But Great Britain, Japan, the United States, and other nations blamed only two persons: Chiang and Ch'en Yü-jen, the foreign minister of the Wuhan government. Great Britain had been aware of the conflict between Chiang and the Communists. We could have prevented much misunderstanding if someone from the National Revolutionary Army had been sent to mediate with the British before our troops reached Shanghai. Later, the Shanghai bankers did bring Chiang and the British together.

We learned later that the people in Shanghai became more supportive of Chiang than of Sun Ch'üan-fang when they began to realize that Chiang would defeat Sun Ch'üan-fang. The friendly attitude of the Shanghai bankers toward Chiang also began to influence British thinking. The British are very realistic, and they wanted to protect their interests despite the suffering they had endured in Nanking.[8]

My Counterpart Chou En-lai

Pai Ch'ung-hsi captured Shanghai on March 21, 1927, and our flagship arrived there on March 26. Chiang immediately asked me to carry a letter to Pai, whom I had not seen in a long time. I briefed him about the Communists. Pai was strongly anticommunist, and he pointed out that we had to find another way to handle the Communists. Pai would play an important role in the Kuomintang purge of the Communists.

We set up our general headquarters in the office of Kuo T'ai-ch'i's Bureau of Foreign Negotiations. Most districts in Shanghai were controlled by the Communists. While working at headquarters, we observed them demonstrating. Chou En-lai was in charge of the communist organization in Shanghai, and he behaved as if much of Shanghai belonged to him. Because the Communists used the Huchou Association of Fellow Townsmen [Hu-chou t'ung-hsiang-hui] in Chapei as their headquarters, we naturally assumed that Chou En-lai had established special ties with the Huchou people.

I had met Chou En-lai in Peking during the May Fourth movement. While we were at the Whampoa Military Academy, we never met. One day Chou arrived to ask for the curfew password. We did not casually reveal the curfew password to outsiders because that would lead to serious security problems. Such information would have allowed Chou to use the workers to promote street violence. I flatly turned down his request. I insisted on knowing who wanted the password and reminded him that if he honestly informed me, I might consider his request. But he refused and continued to demand I reveal the password.

Chou En-lai, who then directed workers' activities in Cha-pei, used his position as representing the Shanghai workers to intimidate me. I told him that our mission was to safeguard the security of Shanghai's millions of people and that, if he only represented the workers, he must obey our orders. Unsuccessful, Chou En-lai became very angry and said, "You are really tough." The Office of the National Revolutionary Army's Chief of Staff was responsible for the curfew password. When Chou realized he could not persuade their office, he believed I would easily capitulate and confide in him. But I was not easily fooled by Chou. This was the first time I rejected a request from Chou En-lai, and it would not be the last.

After this first encounter with Chou, I found him to be a most troublesome man. I later asked him to telephone me first when urgent matters arose that I might be able to help with. But he rarely contacted me, perhaps realizing that I was difficult to deal with. In later discussions with Chou, I became impressed with his abilities. He was very capable and one of the most talented among all the Communists I knew. He once told me that he had organized 600,000 people in Shanghai.

Our forces in Shanghai were still weak. Chiang relied mainly on the First Army group, which was thinly spread over a vast area. He luckily had the support of Pai Ch'ung-hsi, and Pai's staunch anticommunist attitude won Chiang's unfailing trust. For that reason Chiang appointed him as chief of the General Staff. The commander of the first division of the First Army group was Hsüeh Yüeh, a good military man. After Ch'en Chiung-ming rebelled, he escorted Sun Yat-sen to the *Yung-feng* warship. I did not know him well until he became governor of Hunan Province in 1938. In the Shanghai period I recall him as young with radical ideas. Our intelligence information in the confidential section alerted us to keep an eye on him. But his behavior improved, and Chiang was able to strengthen his control over Shanghai.

How did the other principal commanders, after the Nanking Incident, see Chiang? The deputy commander of the Second Army group, Lu Ti-ping, was loyal and obeyed T'an Yen-k'ai; the commander of the Third Army group, Chu Pei-teh, stationed in Nanchang, was not a risk; the commander of the Fourth Army group, Li Chi-shen, was stationed in Canton, and he opposed the Communists; the commander of the Fifth Army group, Li Fu-lin, also supported us; the commander of the Sixth Army, Chen Ch'ien, might be influenced by the communist Lin Tsu-han, the director of the Political Department, and we put a question mark on him, but generally speaking he could be trusted; the commander of the Seventh Army group, Li Tsung-jen, also supported Chiang because he was close to Pai Ch'ung-hsi. As for General Ho Ying-ch'in, the commander of the First Army group, he was absolutely reliable. I think it is not far from the truth to state that nearly all military commanders but T'ang Sheng-chih of the Eighth Army group and Chang Fa-k'uei, commander of the "Iron Army," supported Chiang. The Communists badly wanted to win these two over.

Our Strategy for Eliminating the Communists

To eradicate the Communists from the Kuomintang, we began to plan for a party purge. In the middle of April 1927, my elder brother, Kuo-fu, first called a meeting of the Central Supervisory Committee [Chung-yang chien-ch'a wei-yüan-hui] to work out a solution to the communist problem within the Kuomintang. Chiang instructed that telegrams be sent to committee members in different locations to gather in Shanghai for this conference. Since most Central Supervisory Committee members were elderly people, the Communists had paid little attention to this committee. Little did they know that these elderly people played a crucial role in our party's purge. As these elders arrived in Shanghai, the Communists began to realize that they were in a perilous situation. Fearing that the Central Supervisory Committee would take action, they issued slogans such as Down with the Muddled, Mediocre, Old and Corrupt Members to sow dissension between young Kuomintang members and these elders.

On April 2, 1927, Wu Chih-hui presented a letter to the Central Supervisory Committee. It contained a proposal for a party purge and was passed unanimously by the committee. Meanwhile, Wang Ching-wei had returned from France on April 1, and he convened several high-level party meetings in which the decision was made to have the Central Executive Committee meet in Nanking to discuss the communist problem. To our surprise, on April 5, Wang Ching-wei and the Chinese Communist party leader, Ch'en Tu-hsiu publicly stated that the Kuomintang and the Communist party would continue to cooperate. Wang Ching-wei then secretly left Shanghai for Wuhan to cooperate with the Communists and prevent our party from eliminating them. The Kuomintang members were now split between Wuhan and Nanking. Wang Ching-wei's sudden change of mind proved he was unpredictable and untrustworthy. He also underestimated our determination to eradicate communist elements within the Kuomintang.

By now we had discovered that our official party seal was in Wuhan. Without it, we could not formally announce the party purge. Wu I-chang, secretary of the Organization Department, visited me about this matter. I suggested we have a new seal made to resemble the seal on old documents. When I now reflect about that decision, I view it as radical and even improper. The immediate problem for Wu I-chang, my elder brother, Kuo-fu, and me was how to identify the Communists. The Chinese Communist party had never submitted a membership list to us, and we had no way of distinguishing between a communist and a noncommunist Kuomintang member. Previously the Communist party had secretly ordered its party members to hide their true identities and continue their work within the Kuomintang.

I told Wu that the only way to solve this problem was to go to war with them because the Kuomintang and the Communist party would quickly split. We had used this technique in Anching. We immediately telegraphed trustworthy comrades everywhere to engage in hand-to-hand combat to flush out the real Communists and get rid of them by any means. Sure enough, hand-to-hand combat between the Kuomintang and the Communist party broke out in Chekiang, Kiangsi, and Anhwei provinces, and our plan was working. But the conflict differed according to area, and my elder brother, Kuo-fu, Wu, and I had to find ways to deal with this problem. Because Chiang concentrated on military affairs, he had no time for these matters.

My memory and the available records provide the following list of leaders responsible for the Kuomintang party purge in different locales: Tseng Yang-fu and Lai Lien in Kwangtung Province; Hsiao Cheng, Cheng I, Hsu Chao-ti, and Hu Chien-chung in Chekiang Province; Yang Hu, Wu K'ai-hsien, and Wang Yen-sung in Shanghai; Ch'eng T'ien fang, Lo Shih-shih, and Tuan Hsi-p'eng in Kiangsi Province; Shao Hua and Fang Chih in Anhwei Province; and Yeh Hsiu-feng in Kiangsu Province.

The Communists controlled a workers' organization called the Federation of Trade Unions [Tsung-kung-hui]. We had our own organization, called the Federation of All Workers [Kung-jen tsung-hui]. Similarly, the communist students controlled an organization called the Federation of Students [Hsüeh-sheng-hui], and we had our own, called the Federation of All Students [Hsüeh-sheng tsung-hui]; their peasants' organization was the Association of Peasants [Nung-min hsieh-hui], and ours, the Federation of All Peasants [*Nung-jen tsung-hui*]. Just as the Nationalists and Communists competed, so too did their various social organizations.

Another technique we developed was creating secret political units within social or public organizations. For example, within a trade union this unit would decide how party policy might influence union members before they held their meeting. To avoid alerting the trade union of our efforts to influence it, we carried out our political activities secretly. We tried to propagate our viewpoint to the public in the name of the trade union. Because everyone knew who our members were, we did not accomplish very much. Therefore we tried to infiltrate different organizations; we did not want them to attract the attention of local warlords.

This same tactic had long been a favorite trick of the Communists, and now we were merely copying them. But there was a difference between our goals and theirs. Our aim was to protect our political activities among the masses and be constructive. We wanted to lead the masses on the correct course, whereas the Communists really wanted to control the masses and mobilize them to rebel against the government and the Kuomintang. Some people might ask, Was not leading the masses in this way also a form of control? Of course it was. But the distinction is not an arbitrary one. One must remember that in 1927, most of China was anticommunist. Peasants knew nothing about communism. Warlords, foreign settlements, and members of the leading elite in all circles were anti-Communists. Most of them had serious doubts about communism. Thus the Communists inevitably treated all non-Communists as enemies; we wanted to mobilize all non-Kuomintang members to our cause.

When the Communists controlled the Kuomintang Central Executive Committee, our political units could accomplish little. The Organization Department had sent some loyal Kuomintang members to work among the masses, but they were mainly older people who tired quickly. They could not compete with the very young, active Communists. Only after my elder brother, Kuo-fu, took over the Organization Department did we begin to weed out the Communists' political units and replace them with our own— in a word, we used the Communists' tactics to attack the Communists. Once our political units began to influence various social groups, we could easily separate the communist and the Kuomintang members. Our targets then became evident. At the time of the purge, our political unit in the Association of Peasants was particularly effective. For one thing, the association was local in character, and the peasants were not politically conscious and typically had no interest in politics. A few Kuomintang activists did a good job organizing them, which was much easier than working in the trade unions.

For the historical record, I should mention that there was no formal plan of collaboration and no alliance in existence between the Kuomintang and the Green Gang [Ch'ing-pang].[9] The two groups were friendly, however, and Kuomintang members received considerable help from the Green Gang. The Green Gang maintained good relationships with the police and helped keep order in the foreign concessions, especially in the British Concession.[10]

The Kuomintang and the Shanghai Green Gang enjoyed close ties as early as the 1911 revolution and the second revolution against Yüan. My second uncle, Ch'i-mei, worked closely with the Green Gang although he never joined them.

The Shanghai Episode

We launched the party purge in Shanghai on April 12, 1927. A comrade who personally participated in that event later told me his account.

Before 1927, the Communist party controlled both Shanghai's Federation of Trade Unions [Tsung-kung-hui] and the Federation of Students [Hsüeh-sheng-hui], as well as having organized many other groups amid the masses. The former two associations, plus others, were under the direction of a capable communist leader named Hui Tai-ying. The Chinese Communist party used merchants' organizations to subvert the Shanghai Chamber of Commerce [Shanghai shang-hui], which was dominated by big businessmen. In order to control the entire movement, it also used the Association of Streets and Neighborhoods [Ma-lu lien-ho-hui] to influence other minor merchant organizations to prevent them from taking a neutral stand. The Chinese Communist party desperately needed their support. One must bear in mind that the Kuomintang's Shanghai municipal branch was secretly controlled by the Communists

Shortly after April 12, the Political Department of the Eastern Route Army Headquarters [Tung-lu-chün tsung-chih hui-pu] ordered Ch'en Ch'un, Pan Yi-chih, and Leng Hsin to close the Shanghai municipal branch. Kuomintang central in Nanking then appointed Ch'en Teh-chen, Pan Kung-chan, Chou Chih-yiian, and others to form an executive committee to direct party affairs in Shanghai. This committee then sent representatives to every part of Shanghai to organize groups among the masses that would be under Kuomintang control.

The Shanghai Federation of Trade Unions was actually the Chinese Communist party's headquarters. Its workers were equipped with numerous arms, supplied chiefly by Pi Shu-cheng's troops, although some came from the police in Nan-shih and Cha-pei and from the Shanghai Defense Brigade [Pao-wei-t'uan]. Loyal Kuomintang comrades had also taken arms from the Shanghai Defense Brigade in order to oppose the communist workers' pickets.

On April 12, the Eastern Route Army Headquarters moved to suppress the workers' pickets. This action set off armed conflict. Fortunately, the Eastern Route Army applied its full strength to carry out this mission; clashes were many but casualties few. The Political Department in the Eastern Route Army Headquarters then appointed Chen Chun, Pan I-chih, Chia Kung-hsia, and others to form a committee to consolidate three trade unions in Shanghai and to cooperate with the Kuomintang's Shanghai municipal branch to reorganize all trade unions. A Shanghai Party Purge Committee [Shanghai ch'ing-tang wei-yüan-hui] was established at the same time, and all Communists within the Kuomintang were finally removed. The secretary-general of the Shanghai Party Purge Committee was Lin Ch'i-han. The organization in Shanghai that contributed most to the party purge work was the Society for Joint Progress, whose leaders were Tu Yüeh-sheng, Huang Chin-jung, Chang Hsiao-lin, Yang Hu—all leading members of the Green Gang.

On the evening of April 11, the chairman of the Executive Committee of the Shanghai Federation of Trade Unions, Wang Shou-hua, a disciple of Chang Ching-hu (who was a member of the Green Gang and a Communist), was invited to the residence of Tu Yüeh-sheng on Hua-kuo Road South to meet with Huang Chin-jung, Chang Hsiao-lin, Yang Hu, and Tu. At this meeting, Wang was told that most people in Shanghai opposed the Communists and that for his own good he should quit the Communist party, dissolve the workers' picket units, and support the Kuomintang. Wang, however, rejected the suggestion and was killed in a scuffle that followed.

Huang Chin-jung, Tu Yüeh-sheng, Chang Hsiao-lin, and others then sent gang members among the workers and instructed them to mop up the workers' pickets in Nan-shih and Chapei. The Communists they could identify in the trade unions were quickly arrested and brought before the police or the National Revolutionary Army Headquarters for trial. Eliminating communist elements in trade unions was largely the task of workers in the Society for Joint Progress [Kung-chin-hui], which had connections to various trade unions. As they controlled much information, they were very successful in their work.

Because the total membership of the Shanghai Tsung-kung-hui was about 800,000, any action on their part quickly affected residents throughout the city. The Chinese Communist party called workers' strikes, which terrorized the residents. Can you imagine what would happen if all 800,000 workers had gone on strike? City life would have come to a stop, and Shanghai would never have been the same again.

In retrospect, I can say that many Kuomintang comrades in various districts and our Society for Joint Progress members in various factories acted courageously. They cared little for their safety when assisting the police and the National Revolutionary Army to root out communist elements in the trade unions. The surprise attacks on the communist command posts quickly forced communist union members into hiding. Many dared not appear in public and fled to the foreign concessions. Soon after April 12, Communists in various districts were arrested. The student unions were reorganized, and those found to be members of the Chinese Communist party went into hiding. This victory was not won without paying a price, and we incurred many casualties.

Comrade Wu K'ai-hsien was the Shanghai municipal branch secretary of our Kuomintang Organization Department. He had issued a certificate to anyone who had dual party membership but who willingly denounced his or her communist affiliation and signed an oath pledging to resign from the Chinese Communist party. A copy then was placed on file, and individuals were exempt from any punishment. Those who held dual membership and had not pledged to denounce and leave the Chinese Communist party, however, were expelled from the Kuomintang. Wu K'ai-hsien recalled that during the purge some confusion arose in our chain of command and that justice was not always dispensed. According to Wu's account, the Party Purge Committee tried but failed to save Chang Ching-i from being executed by garrison headquarters. A young student, Chang had attended Chiao-t'ung University and served as secretary of the Workers and Peasants Department of the Shanghai municipal branch. Chang was a member of both the Kuomintang and the Chinese Communist party. Therefore, he had a dual party membership but had pledged to renounce his communist membership. Yet repeated appeals for his pardon were ignored by Yang Hu, who cochaired the Party Purge Committee with Ch'en Ch'ün and also commanded the garrison headquarters. Wu's last hope was to cable my elder brother, Kuo-fu, to report the case to Chiang. Chiang's order of release came too late; the student Chang had already been executed. Wu remarked that countless people in Shanghai died during the purge. It was a bloodthirsty war to eliminate the enemy within. I must admit that many innocent people were killed. We paid a heavy price.

Our purge prevented the Chinese Communists from instigating disturbances and riots in Shanghai. After that, they dared not make a wrong move.

Thoughts on Eliminating the Communists

In retrospect, the success of the party purge was due to the combination of three factors:

1. Party seniors took action because two members of the Control Yüan of the National government, Chang Ching-chiang and my elder brother, Kuo-fu, knew about the communist conspiracy and could persuade Wu Chih-hui, Tsai Yüan-pei, Li Shih-tseng, and others to publicly denounce the Communists.

2. The Western Hills group, located outside of Kwangtung Province, had long opposed Sun Yat-sen's policy of admitting Communists to the Kuomintang and suspected Chiang of being procommunist. The *Chung-shan* Gunboat Incident of March 20, 1926, finally made them realize that Chiang was anticommunist. Yet they still wondered why Chiang continued to collaborate with the Communists during the Northern Expedition. Only when the Kuomintang began to purge itself of Communists did they return in force and help Chiang.

3. Before the *Chung-shan* Gunboat Incident, Yang Pao-an, a Communist, headed the Organization Department, and more than half of its members who worked underground in the Kuomintang provincial branches were Communists. After my elder brother, Kuo-fu, took over as acting head of the department, he sent trained personnel to staff provincial party branches. By the time of the purge, our comrades had enough force to overpower the Communists. In the National Revolutionary Army, many engaged in political training work were Communists. But most of the senior army officers hated those political commissars, who merely mouthed communist propaganda. As soon as the leading Kuomintang members decided on an anticommunist policy, those in the Political Training Department lost their influence and came over to our side.

As I recorded earlier, the decisive battle between the Kuomintang and the Communist party had begun at the end of 1926, when Chiang arrived in Anching aboard his gunboat. After the people's welcoming assembly for Chiang had disbanded, comrades on our side began fighting with the Communists. Before this fight, Yang Hu and I were both on the gunboat with Chiang. Comrades from Anhwei Province had come aboard to seek advice from Yang Hu, a senior member from Anhwei Province. They complained that, because they had been oppressed by the Communists for so long, the time was ripe to attack their tormenters. Daring not to advise them, Yang asked for my opinion. I said, "It could be done, but only after Chiang had left the meeting hall." That battle was won by our Kuomintang comrades, and from that event the struggle between the Kuomintang and the Communist party began in earnest. It set an example for how to deal with the Communists.

A comment now about the Green Gang. The Green Gang had been basically an underground, secret, anti-Manchu organization, which was patriotic and nationalistic. After the 1911 revolution, this body gradually became a mutual-aid group among the lower social class of people. Then it became involved in gambling, drugs, opium smoking, and prostitution. In Shanghai the gang really flourished in the British Concession, but it was not prominent elsewhere. The British authorities actually allowed the gang to run wild, even though they knew the Green Gang was linked to crime, primarily because they needed the gang to help them control the concession. We needed the help of the gangs to eliminate the communist influence over the lower social classes. The Kuomintang's power in the Shanghai area could not be consolidated unless communist activities among the lower social classes completely ended. The Green Gang was anticommunist and supported the Kuomintang, believing the Kuomintang was a young, dynamic power. If the national revolution succeeded, the British Concession might revert to Chinese hands with the Kuomintang in power. The future of the Green Gang could very well depend on the Kuomintang. Most important for the Kuomintang was that the Green Gang not ally with the Chinese Communist party. That prospect was worse than our cooperation with the Green Gang. Just as every coin has two sides, we cooperated because of mutual gain. They helped us eliminate communist power in Shanghai, which had greatly expanded. I have stated the facts. In this naked power struggle, how to pocket the winnings was the most important task that we faced, and theories were irrelevant. Without the assistance of the Green Gang, our national revolution would have been in peril.

Was the Kuomintang part of the Green Gang? Definitely not. Did some members of the Kuomintang belong to the Green Gang? Possibly yes. Neither group forbade its members to join the other. Were Sun Yat-sen,

Chiang Kai-shek, my second uncle, Ch'i-mei, and my elder brother, Kuo-fu, members of the Green Gang? The answer is no. Then what was my relationship with gang leaders like Tu Yüeh-sheng? Tu Yüeh-sheng was a very intelligent man with great abilities. He sensed the changing political climate. Whenever I was in Shanghai, he always treated me with great courtesy. Through him we learned much about the British Concession.

Finally, the major figure who organized and executed the purge was Yang Hu, a leader of the Green Gang and the same rank as Tu Yüeh-sheng. As I believe I recorded earlier, he played a decisive role in assisting my Uncle Ch'i-mei in the anti–Yüan Shih-k'ai *Shao-ho* Gunboat Insurrection of December 5, 1915, in Shanghai. My elder brother, Kuo-fu, greatly relied on him to recruit able-bodied young men to join the Whampoa Military Academy. We figured that, no matter what, Yang would pass whatever we suggested to Tu Yüeh-sheng, and through Tu, the Green Gang went into action.

The historical record shows that after the purge, Chinese and international Communists began attacking the Kuomintang and the Green Gang with all kinds of insulting language and terms one finds in dictionaries. How did the Soviets view the affair? They were unhappy, of course, but they had nothing to say because we won the battle. How powerful were the Chinese Communists before the purge? At the lower level of Kuomintang organizations, 70 percent of the party workers were Communists.

The Investigation Unit

Any country threatened by communist subversive activities from within and by foreign aggression from without must have sound means to investigate and gather statistics to defend itself. If you have read *Kuan Tzu*, you know that the success of the state of Ch'i during the period of Warring States (403–221 B.C.) came from its knowledge of the common people and its ability to mollify the dukes and princes and to bring them under the control of one ruler.

Our revolution started with a phase of military rule, then passed through the political tutelage stage, and later entered a stage of constitutional government. One could say it had to be born from force before it could pass through the kingly way of a benevolent government. At that time, we were in a dire predicament: from the outside we were confronted by foreign imperialists who waited for the opportune moment to move against us; from inside, we confronted certain warlords and politicians who were willing to collude with these foreign forces.

After visiting the Soviet Union, Chiang knew very well how politics was played in that country. He observed that country's well-organized agency of investigation and collection of evidence to maintain internal stability. Therefore, after our party purge of 1927, we formally established the National government in Nanking on April 18, 1927. Chiang decided to assign someone to study the communist problem. He assigned that task to me. Chiang wanted me to set up an investigation section within the Organization Department, which he headed. The section's main task was to monitor and suppress communist activities.

I had learned much about the Chinese Communist party when I worked in Chiang's general headquarters. Even so, after receiving this directive I felt at a loss for how to begin. I felt I was not suitable for this work. Moreover, I was without knowledge and experience in this line of work because I studied mining engineering and my training had been to study physical things rather than people. I went to Tai Ch'i-tao and asked his advice. After listening to my concern, Tai said: "You are an intelligent and kindly person. For this kind of investigation work, people of all types are required. But to take charge of these people, a kind and just person is required because only that kind of person can exercise control and prevent troubles." He then lectured me about Buddhism. "Go and look at the eighteen *Lohans* standing in rows within a Buddhist temple. Each is bushy-eyebrowed, with fierce eyes and three heads and six arms, to project a terrifying sight. In the middle of them we observe the gentle Buddha. Only the kind and gentle can overcome the fierce and brutal." Then he added, "Such work is exceedingly important. The Soviet Union has its organization, the KGB, and for America, the FBI. A most loyal party member must be in charge of this work, or else we will have problems. Having you manage this operation will reassure Chiang. You ought to be very careful in selecting personnel. They must be impartial, just, and unselfish or else you will have trouble." After listening to this advice, I decided to accept.

Soon after the Kuomintang headquarters were set up in Nanking, sometime in April, I assembled a unit without any formal name to begin our investigations. Eventually, the unit became known as the investigation section of the Organization Department. We were attached to the Organization Department headed by my elder brother, Kuo-fu. Chang Tao-fan, a secretary at the Organization Department, also joined our group.

I gathered some students who had recently returned from the United States. Among them were Hsu En-tseng, Wu Ta-chun, Chao Ti-hua, and Yang Teng-ying; I also recruited Chang Ch'ung, who had studied Russian at Harbin Industrial College, and Pu Meng-chiu, who had been in Germany. Their expertise varied: Yang Teng-ying studied political science; Hsu En-tseng, electrical engineering; Wu Ta-chun, statistics; and Chao Ti-hua, economics. I do not remember Pu Meng-chiu's specialty. All were party members. Aside from Hsu En-tseng, I knew none of them. They had been recommended yet none knew the workings of America's FBI or the Soviet Union's OGPU, a forerunner of the NKVD and later the KGB. But they had been well educated and were scientifically trained. They all had good family backgrounds, were cultured, polished men with fine personalities and qualities. They had been recommended, yet none were specialized in spying, espionage, or investigative works.

I first divided them into two teams: one for investigation, headed by Hsu En-tseng with Yang Teng-ying as his deputy; the other took charge of gathering data and was headed by Chao Ti-hua, with Wu Ta-chun as deputy. At the outset, each team had six or seven people, and the total number of people working on both teams came to no more than twenty. Under my leadership, this small brigade pioneered the scientific methods and organizational skills we devised to survey the activities of the Communist party. Chiang later supplied me with a list of forty names, all graduates of the Central Military Officer's Academy [Chung-yang lu-chün chün-kuan hsüeh-hsiao] who had undergone six months of special political training, and I sent them to various locations. After the purge, the Communists changed their tactics. To survive, they went underground. To make matters worse, many Kuomintang members still held dual membership and had not openly declared their party affiliation. These conditions made our work imperative. Our first priority was to induce those Communists who had gone underground to give up.

We expanded the work of our team by first dispatching several members who had been trained by Chiang to Shanghai, Hankow, and Canton, where the Communists were most active. Then, we sent people to Chekiang, Kiangsu, Anhwei, Kiangsi, and Hupei to study communist infiltration of Kuomintang local branches. We also transferred some agents to Nanking for special training. We gradually developed a working network.

Soon after, we discovered that Chiang had established a similar organization under Tai Li that performed the same work we were doing. My colleagues began to suspect that that unit must be a fake, for why would Chiang be so distrustful as to form a similar unit? The other unit never revealed itself to me. I thought to myself, if I don't ask Chiang about Tai Li's work, he will laugh at our incompetence. He will say, "You claim to be an investigation agency, but you never knew there was another intelligence unit under my command!" Then I wondered, if I do go to ask him, how will he reply?

After a long deliberation, I decided to see Chiang: "There is a man named Tai Li who claims that you asked him to do investigative work. Is this true?" Somewhat taken aback, he said: "Tai Li works in my office, and no special organization exists. I occasionally need him to investigate matters, and if he should behave improperly, you can report that to me anytime." After Chiang admitted he knew about Tai Li's activities, we were at ease. I told my colleagues: "We will do our work as though we are Chiang's eyes and ears. To rule out incorrect information, Chiang needs two sets of eyes and ears. We should not have suspicions, and we must work hard to prove ourselves. Their operation only can be beneficial and not harmful." Everyone was pleased by my reasoning and persuasion.

I was head of the investigation section of the Organization Department for less than two years when I was assigned to be secretary-general of the Kuomintang Central Executive Committee in April 1929. The investigation team members continued to consult me on many matters. That made it hard for me to remove myself completely from their activities. As for Chün-tung, the Bureau of Investigation and Statistics of the Military Committee of the National government [Kuo-min cheng-fu chün-shih wei-yuan-hui tiao-ch'a t'ung-chi-chü], at first it was an agency only "in reality but not in name." Tai Li organized that operation when he worked in Chiang's office and was assigned to investigate certain matters. After the scope of Tai Li's work greatly expanded, his unit still bore no official title. Eventually, Chiang did not want Tai Li to operate this way on a permanent basis.

On May 4, 1935, Chiang asked me to take charge of a unit called Combined Reporting on Investigation and Statistics. I asked Chen Kung-ju to assist me on military matters. I assigned Hsu En-tseng to be the director of the first branch, which specialized in community communist activities; Tai Li became director of the second branch with an emphasis on communist activities in the military; Ting Mo-tsun took over the third branch, which handled the organization's general affairs.

I was in charge of this unit until New Year's Day of 1938, at which time Chiang appointed me minister of education. I resigned as head of this unit because the jobs were so different and one person could not be in charge of both. Using this rationale I separated myself from investigation and fact-gathering work to assume my post as minister of education. My old unit collapsed, and the first branch became Chung-t'ung, the Bureau of Investigation and Statistics of the Central Executive Committee of Chung-kuo Kuomintang [Chung-kuo kuo-min-tang chung-yang chih-hsing wei-yuan-hui tiao-ch'a t'ung-chi-chü], with Chu Chia-hua as head and Hsu En-tseng as deputy. The third branch was dissolved. Later, Ting Mo-tsun joined Wang Ching-wei and performed investigation and statistical work with Wang's puppet government. From that time onward, the operations of the former first and second departments working in the Japanese-occupied areas rapidly deteriorated because of bad management.

I had initiated China's first political investigation and statistical work. For a little more than a year I had been responsible for that activity until I completely disassociated myself from that line of work. In the next ten years, the name and activities of that organization greatly changed. In 1949, Chün-tung became an agency of the Ministry of the Interior.

As I stated before, Chün-tung was the abbreviated name for the Bureau of Investigation and Statistics of the Military Committee of the National government. Its predecessor was the second branch (led by Tai Li) of the Combined Reporting on Investigation and Statistics unit, which I managed. In 1938, when I became minister of education, these two bureaus, Chung-t'ung and Chün-tung, separately continued to investigate communist activities. In the twenty years of the National government's rule on the mainland, the two bureaus coexisted, underwent many reorganizations, and performed intelligence-gathering work.[11]

I believe that our investigative activity greatly contributed to the governance of the country. The investigative units strengthened the central leadership and safeguarded political stability. This helped us resist foreign aggression and paved the way for national unification and reconstruction. I will not deny, however, that our units engaged in activities that caused considerable criticism.

Our anticommunist stand evolved from the foundations of Chinese culture. We were very lenient toward communist youths who had crossed over to start a new life. Instead of censuring them for their past mistakes, we educated them in Chinese culture and history and employed them in party headquarters at different levels. About sixteen thousand ex-Communists crossed over to our side, which proved to be an enormous problem for the Chinese Communist party in the latter part of the 1930s. The reputation of our unit quickly improved, and within a year and a half, on April 8, 1929, I was promoted to secretary-general of the Kuomintang Central Executive Committee. Secretary Chang Tao-fan then was appointed to head the investigative unit. He was replaced by Hsu En-tseng, an electrical engineer. Later, Ku Shun-chang, former head of the communist secret service, secretly defected to our side through the efforts of Comrade Ts'ai Meng-chien, our chief of investigation and statistical work in Wuhan. That defection caused communist secret service cells in many places to collapse, and we rounded up all of their people. In 1946 Chou En-lai told me at a Political Consultative Conference dinner that had he lingered five minutes longer, he too would have been captured.

Using Radio Communication and Secret Codes

Our investigation unit took great pride in operating several shortwave radio stations for communication between Shanghai and Nanking. It was a first, and the shortwave radio stations greatly helped our work. Li Fan-i, an American-trained engineer who specialized in shortwave electricity, suggested this scheme. At that time, the National government only had long-wave radio stations.

I still remember that when I first tried to sell Li Fan-i's innovative idea to other leaders, no one showed any interest. Nor did anyone understand that information could be sent by shortwave radio. But those of us with scientific training certainly knew it could be done as many countries were already using shortwave radio communication.

On August 26, 1927, Sun Ch'üan-fang pushed southward from his base north of the Yangtze River to attack Nanking. His troops crossed the river at Lung-tan and interrupted Nanking-Shanghai Railway traffic. His troops cut the electric wires between Nanking and Shanghai. Pai Ch'ung-hsi in Shanghai and Ho Ying-ch'in in Nanking had no way of contacting each other. I took this opportunity to invite Ho to use our radio station to communicate his military plans to Pai. Sure enough, the two radio stations played a decisive role in the battle of Lung-tan that defeated Sun Ch'üan-fang.

Ho later reported to Chiang that the plan to assault Sun Ch'üan-fang from Shanghai and Nanking could only have been achieved by our two radio stations. In addition to receiving a monetary reward, Chiang also appropriated funds to improve radio equipment in the military forces. We drew up plans to build a factory in Shanghai to manufacture radio equipment.

Our communication system was superior to those of the warlords and the Communists. We quickly sent confidential information and documents to the central headquarters. We also speedily sent directives on how to deal with the Communists from Kuomintang headquarters to all other party units.

Another important mission of the investigative unit was to improve the secrecy of our telegraph codes and to break the enemy's codes. At the end of 1927, when T'ang Sheng-chih of Hunan rebelled, we could intercept and interdict his telegrams. When we captured a city, we immediately secured the local telegraph bureau and had its entire file sent back to our headquarters. We had no difficulty deciphering secret codes, which allowed us to learn the movements of enemy troops. This enabled Chiang to quickly deal with the various warlords without having to deploy many troops.

I would like to record that Mao Ching-hsiang directed the team's work. Chiang later complimented our confidential section for its successful use of radio networks. He awarded us 10,000 yuan, which nearly equaled the same amount of silver dollars. I divided the 6,000 yuan among all the section members and used the remaining 4,000 yuan to establish the Cheng-chung Publishing House, which later became known as the Cheng-chung Book Company.

We invested a lot of time in inventing our code. The telegraph code used in China, originally introduced by the Commercial Press, contained about ten thousand characters. At first we merely changed the numbers to make the code secret, but later, fearing that it might be too easy for others to decipher, we decided to revise the Commercial Press's code by deleting little-used characters and rearranging others. We completely changed the order of characters and printed in boldface only the frequently used ones. The confidential section adopted this secret code. The five-stroke indexing system for Chinese characters that I invented also proved helpful in keeping our code system secret. I kept the codebook with me at all times and frequently altered the code. We sometimes divided the code into five versions (*A, B, C, D, E*) and gave these to one person who was to contact us. We agreed to use only *A* version on Monday, *B* version on Tuesday, and so on. By using a different version each day, we prevented our code from being broken or intercepted.

Our office contained a cabinet with twenty-five drawers, each labeled from *aa* to *zz* and each having twenty-five indexed file folders. The files were arranged mainly by surname, but the indexing method that I had invented had wider application, such as arranging the files by location and subject. We had roughly seven or eight hundred versions of secret codes. Each time we received a telegram we first searched for the code version that the sender used. Our indexed filing cabinet enabled us to locate the code we wanted.

The greatest advantage of our method was that any person managing the files could easily learn my indexing system. Personnel could be changed without causing any difficulties. If a particular codebook was not returned to the original place after use, however, the next user would not be able to decipher the telegram. Therefore, I ordered the twenty-five drawers of the filing cabinet locked. I even introduced a master key, which could lock all the drawers at once. Only two persons possessed this key: the person in charge of the files and me. I was satisfied with this system as it greatly increased the efficiency of our decoding.

Aside from the secretariat of the Kuomintang Central Executive Com-

mittee and the membership unit of the Organization Department, no government agencies adopted my filing system. Many personnel in charge of
government files would have lost their jobs if my efficient system had been
used. The filing department in any government agency is always the most
conservative, and those in charge could not tolerate reform.

Chiang Steps Down

A key policy of the National government in Nanking was to eradicate
communism in China, but Wang Ching-wei continued to cooperate with
the Communist party.

In May 1927, Wang Ching-wei and Ch'en Tu-hsiu issued a joint statement that caused the Kuomintang to split. The Wuhan and Nanking branches
of the National government were on the brink of war. The Wuhan group
viewed the Nanking government as antirevolutionary, an attitude that I
believed was influenced by instructions it received from the Communist
International. The Chinese Communist party had assigned Communists to
work with the left-wing Kuomintang in Wuhan to fight the right-wing
Kuomintang in Nanking. The Communist party hoped that this would
destroy the Kuomintang.

Chiang sought help from outside. He and Feng Yü-hsiang held a conference in Hsuchow between June 19 and 21 and reached three accords: (1)
the puppet Wuhan government was illegal and should be abolished; (2) the
purge should be extended to other provinces; (3) the troops in Wuhan should
return to Honan. The Northern Expedition would continue its advance with
the support of Feng Yü-hsiang's troops. Before the conference, however,
Feng Yü-hsiang had refused to have his troops return to the North because
they already controlled all of Honan Province. But after the conference,
Feng joined the Northern Expedition.

Wang Ching-wei became greatly distressed after learning that Chiang
had won the support of Feng Yü-hsiang. The Communist party, also disappointed, declared on July 13 its intention of withdrawing from the Wuhan
government. Instead of allying with Chiang, if Feng Yü-hsiang had allied
with the Wuhan government to oppose Chiang, future developments would
have been very different. Knowing communist infiltration had spread in its
ranks, on July 15 the Wuhan leadership initiated its party purge in Hunan,
Hupei, and Kiangsi provinces. Borodin, Galen, and other Soviet advisers
were expelled. The Communist party began to escalate its attack on Chiang,
publicly denouncing him as an antirevolutionary, a dictator, and a traitor to
the national revolution. They declared that Chiang had betrayed Sun Yat-
sen's teachings. The Chinese Communist party tried to infiltrate Chiang's

army and promote a massive defection. Chou En-lai and Chang Kuo-t'ao were ordered to go with Chang Fa-k'uei's troops to Nanchang and Kiukiang. They held discussions with Ho Lung and Yeh Ting, both subordinates of Chang Fa-k'uei, and talked them into rebelling on August 1. Chu Teh also participated in this armed uprising. Still waving Kuomintang banners, more than twenty thousand soldiers were involved in this episode. Their commanding headquarters was named the Revolutionary Committee of China's Kuomintang [Chung-kuo kuo-min-tang ko-ming wei-yüan hui].

On the third day of the uprising, our troops surrounded the communist insurgent troops in Nanchang. On the fifth day, the Communists broke out and fled southward to the Tung-ho River Valley of Kwangtung Province by way of Fukien. There, they hoped to establish a base near Swatow. The remnants of the communist troops, led by Yeh Ting, ran away and regrouped in Lu-feng and Peng-pai. Chu Teh and his troops first pretended to surrender but then fled to the southern part of Hunan Province.

In spring 1928, Chu Teh and Mao Tse-tung joined forces in Ching-kangshan on the border between Kiangsi and Hunan provinces. The Nanchang revolt of August 1 led to the birth of the Red Army. The revolt also brought about the Lu-feng episode, which gave the Chinese Communist party some time to recuperate.

After Wuhan joined with Nanking in a party purge, a special committee was formed on September 16 to coordinate both sides. Wang Ching-wei and Sun Fo set out for Nanking, which indicated that the Wuhan government leaders intended to move to Nanking. But before the special committee called a meeting, an important matter first had to be resolved: would this committee establish a strong central government and continue the Northern Expedition? The decision was affirmative. The Wuhan faction, however, raised a new slogan, Separating from the Communists and Opposing Chiang [fen-kung fan-Chiang]. To avoid a party split, Chiang tendered his resignation on August 12 and handed the military to Ho Ying-ch'in, but he made three requests:

1. Comrades in Nanking and Wuhan must set aside suspicion and dissension. Wuhan comrades must move to Nanking and cooperate to serve the nation and the party.

2. The armed forces stationed in Hunan, Hupei, and Kiangsi provinces must join together to advance northward and join the troops fighting along the Tientsin-Pukou Railway to complete the national revolution. Feng Yü-hsiang already had agreed.

3. Those armed comrades in Hunan, Hupei, and Kiangsi provinces must carry out a thorough purge of all remaining communist elements.

Chiang's decision was truly unselfish. Chiang knew that since the *Chung-shan* Gunboat Incident of March 20, 1926, he and Wang Ching-wei would never get along. After Chiang resigned, many senior members of the party such as Wu Chih-hui, Chang Ching-Chiang, Ts'ai Yüan-p'ei, and Li Shih-tseng also resigned. Hu Han-min later resigned.

Chiang set out for Japan on September 16, 1927. Although a collision with Japanese forces in Shantung Province seemed inevitable, Chiang wanted to discover Japan's true intentions. While in Japan, Chiang was the guest of Toyama Mitsuru. Toyama looked after Chiang and introduced him to the people he wanted to meet. Toyama Mitsuru opened many doors. Chiang had invited me to go to Japan with him, but I declined. I had neither interest in Japan nor knowledge of Japanese. I told Chiang I was exhausted, and because my health was poor, I needed rest.

It occurred to me that if Chiang did not return to Nanking, I would look for a job as an engineer because I had lost interest in politics. But looking back, I regret missing that opportunity to meet some important people in Japan. Although I had passed through Japan twice on the way to and from the United States, I never stayed in that country long enough to get to know its people very well.

After Chiang's resignation, Pai Ch'ung-hsi and Ho Ying-ch'in cochaired the Military Council. Ch'en Pu-lei, who had been my replacement in 1926, automatically took over my confidential section post.

Pai held me in high regard and wanted me to stay as his adviser at his general headquarters, but I declined. Although Chiang had not allowed me to leave, I saw no need to stay.

Aside from some very sensitive material that Chiang wanted me to protect, I indexed all the papers and turned them over to Ch'en Pu-lei including my telegraph codebooks. The section, as I recorded previously, later became part of the Military Committee of the National government.

The transfer was smooth. At the farewell dinner given to me by my colleagues, I distributed to them the few thousand yuan left in our section that had been the emergency fund if we were unemployed. Everyone was saddened by my departure. It was an emotional farewell.

I spent most of my time revising my five-stroke indexing system and produced a book titled *The Principle and Practice of Five-Stroke Indexing System for Chinese Characters* [*Wu-p'i chien-tzu fa t'i yüan-li chi ying-yung*], published by Chung Hua Book Company in 1928. In the same year I published another book, *How to Locate Clan Surnames* [*Hsing-shih su-chien-fa*], which made Chinese surnames easier to find by applying my method of classifying five hundred Chinese surnames.

CHAPTER FOUR

Working with Chiang

SPRING 1928–WINTER 1931

Chiang Returns to Power

WHEN CHIANG RETURNED TO SHANGHAI from Japan on January 10, 1928, he was alarmed by the unstable situation and the poor progress of the Northern Expedition. Various civilian organizations and high-level military leaders appealed to him to take charge. With the approval of the Kuomintang Central Executive Committee, Chiang returned to Nanking and became commander in chief of the National Revolutionary Army on January 4, 1928. I accompanied him to Nanking and was reappointed head of the confidential section in the General Headquarters.

In February 1928, I became a member of the Executive Committee of the Reconstruction Commission of the National government [Kuo-min cheng-fu chien-she wei-yuan-hui],[1] and in May of that same year I was appointed the commission's secretary-general. Chang Ching-chiang was the chairman. It was not by accident that I gained that post. As mentioned earlier, I had often visited Chang Ching-chiang in the evening while in Canton before the Northern Expedition commenced. Chang was very interested in China's reconstruction, and we held similar views.

The government's finances were in critical condition, leaving the government no resources for rebuilding the nation. I made two proposals: (1) to form an advisory corps of engineers, including foreign experts to help entrepreneurs with technology, administration, and management; (2) as soon as our financial resources improved, to start reconstruction work according to Sun Yat-sen's industrial plan in the *The International Development of China* [Shih-yeh chi-hua]. My proposal to hire foreign experts for assistance was accepted.

We first began planning the Huai River dredging-channeling project in

Kiangsi Province to control flooding that had plagued China for many centuries. We asked the best Chinese hydraulic engineering expert, Li Yi-chih, to draft the plan. Li engaged a well-known German hydraulic engineer as a consultant, and their advice, after an on-the-spot investigation, matched the Huai River project outlined in Sun Yat-sen's industrial plan. Sun's foresight was remarkable. That project was initiated by Chiang and my elder brother, Kuo-fu, who served, respectively, as chairman and vice-chairman of the Huai River Commission.

Another successful project we undertook was restoring a flooded coal mine belonging to the Ch'ang-hsin Mining Company in Ch'ang-hsin County, Chekiang Province. Liu Chang-ching, the owner of the company, had hired a British expert to restore the mine to active use, but he estimated that the total cost for repairing the entire drainage work would be at least 1,200,000 silver dollars. This high estimate frightened Liu, who came to me for help. I told him that the Reconstruction Commission would send someone to do the survey and make the estimate. I sent my friend Lu Tzu-tung, a graduate of the Colorado School of Mines who had been in a car accident with Hsu En-tseng and me when we drove around the United States. The Ch'ang-hsin Mining Company's site was harassed by bandits, making the survey difficult to carry out. Fortunately, Lu Tzu-tung was very capable. He first visited the leader of the local bandits and reached an understanding with him. He told the bandit leader about our project and promised jobs for everyone once the mine began production. The bandit leader was willing to cooperate.

Lu Tzu-tung estimated that without any unexpected crises 600,000 silver dollars could do the job, half the British engineer's estimate. Liu, the mine owner, and I agreed to help restore the mine until its production reached 200 tons a day, a self-sustaining stage, at which time the Reconstruction Commission would return the mine to its owner. He would have the option to decide whether to retain the technical personnel we had hired or fire them.

When the contract was completed, the mine owner spent a total of 640,000 silver dollars even though another flood had occurred. Seeing this project through to success was my most satisfying experience since my mining student days because I had applied my learning to this difficult problem.

The Reconstruction Commission also helped restore the Li-shan coal mine in Anhwei Province, which also had flooded. Other successful projects included revamping the Chi-shu yen [Chi-shu] dam and power plant near Shanghai and starting to reconstruct the railroads between Hangchou and Kiang-shan and between Chia-hsin and Soo-chou. We also made recommendations to finance agricultural and industrial projects. But those in charge of finance could not comprehend our proposals and would not adopt them. Unwilling to help expand the work of the Reconstruction Commission, the financial authorities established their own bureaucracy, the National Resources Commission, which absorbed the Reconstruction Commission and eliminated its original function and services.

The Tsinan Incident

On March 31, 1928, I left Nanking with Chiang to go to Hsu-chou to participate in the last stage of the Northern Expedition. On May 1 we recaptured Tsinan in Shantung Province, which straddled the southern bank of the Yellow River. Led by Chiang, our troops entered Tsinan late that night. Chiang set up his headquarters in the office abandoned by Chang Tsung-ch'ang. The confidential section ran its business in a train car at the railroad station outside the city wall. I recall that before this event, Chiang had ordered the troops to go around the city of Tsinan to avoid encountering any Japanese troops. But our commanders probably thought it best to capture part of the city on the south bank to prevent Chang Tsung-ch'ang, who might be backed by the Japanese, from attacking our troops, which were located on both banks of the Yellow River.

On May 3, we suddenly heard gunshots from Japanese troops and decided to move our radio station to headquarters. The situation became very tense. Japanese troops had surrounded Tsinan, and only one city gate remained open. Chiang, who had long anticipated this, expected trouble.[2]

After the Japanese killed the National diplomatic envoy, Ts'ai Kung-shih, Chiang ordered Huang Fu, then foreign minister, Lo Chia-lun, and Tseng Yang-fu to negotiate with the Japanese. Lo also was Chiang's speech writer.

Huang Fu lodged a protest with Tokyo. By the next morning, the situation had worsened. Huang Fu tried to persuade Chiang to leave Tsinan. Chiang flatly refused. As the situation became more and more tense, Huang Fu told me again to persuade Chiang to leave Tsinan immediately. After I assured Chiang that my staff would stay until the very last, when all telegrams had been transmitted, he consented to leave.[3] I noticed that whenever Chiang's fate hung in the balance he remained calm and unruffled. We later heard the sound of airplanes approaching. Chiang instructed me to see if they were from Nanking. Just as I looked out the window, two bombs fell into our courtyard, one landing in a garden pond to the left of the window and another on the living quarters of the aides-de-camp. The bomb that hit the living quarters exploded about fifty feet from Chiang's bedroom, killing two orderlies. These planes had been sent by Chang Tsung-ch'ang's subordinates and were piloted by White Russians. That was the first time I witnessed aerial bombing.

Later, on May 6, Chiang left Tsinan, leaving only me and my staff at headquarters. Of all the telegrams leaving Tsinan by order of Chiang, the most important was to order our troops, including those under the command of Pai Ch'ung-hsi, to cross the Yellow River. Chiang also made radio contact with Kuomintang headquarters and the National government in Nanking to advocate diplomacy rather than military force to solve the Tsinan crisis. That evening, we finished transmitting all telegrams, but because the entire city was under curfew, we had to wait until the next morning to join Chiang.

We faced the problem of transporting the heavy radio equipment. I asked Kao Lin-pai to take charge. He luckily found some street sweepers who helped move our radio equipment. With that problem solved, everyone left for Chiang's new headquarters except for myself and a colleague named Lai Shih-tu who had contracted typhoid fever. I took him to a hospital, made him comfortable, and gave him some money. Then I hurriedly joined my unit.

While retreating, we were strafed several times by airplanes. I witnessed a plane that had been hit by return fire; it exploded and disintegrated in the air. My feelings were indescribable, and that scene is still with me even today. That was the first time I saw an airplane destroyed in the air.

We safely arrived at our headquarters in Tang-chia-chuang, and Chiang was pleased to see us. I was later told that before we arrived, Chiang appeared very worried about our safety and had often asked of our whereabouts. I also heard that Chiang had high words for me, praising me as serious, responsible, assertive, and being able to calmly handle any emergency. That was the first time he mentioned my moral character and ability. My co-workers were impressed that I had not abandoned a sick colleague at a time of great personal peril.

Reunification

When the Tsinan Incident occurred, as luck would have it, the Second Army group, led by Feng Yü-hsiang, and the Third Army group, commanded by Yen Hsi-shan, were advancing toward Peking. I believe that Feng Yü-hsiang and Yen Hsi-shan had not launched attacks but had let Chang Tso-lin retreat on his own because they had an implicit understanding that Peking and Tientsin could be taken without a fight. By the time negotiations with the Japanese over the Tsinan Incident began, our forces had crossed the Yellow River and were moving along the Tientsin-Pukou and Peking-Hankow railways, thereby avoiding a clash with Japanese troops.

At the Western Hills of Peking with Chiang Kai-shek.

Yen Hsi-shan's troops occupied Peking on June 8, 1928. Chiang handled this delicate situation carefully because Japanese troops stationed in Tientsin's foreign concessions might support the Manchurian warlord Chang Tso-lin. Chiang's strategy was to avoid a conflict with Chang Tso-lin at all costs. On June 17, 1928, Chang Tso-lin ordered his troops to evacuate Peking.

Roughly three years after his death, a memorial service was held for Sun Yat-sen on July 6, 1928, at the P'i-yun Temple at the Western Hills in Peking. Chiang stood alone in the front, and Li Tsung-jen, Yen Hsi-shan, and Feng Yü-hsiang stood behind him in the same row. Civilians, including myself, were in the rows behind them. We could see Sun's face through the glass-enclosed coffin, as serene as though he merely slept.

I still remember how Chiang broke down and sobbed the moment he saw Sun's body. That was the first time I ever saw him cry. It was most moving to see him weeping like a son grieving over the death of his father. I never saw him cry again. Facing Sun's coffin, Chiang muttered an account of all the difficulties he had overcome in these past three years and he vowed to cut back the army and to rebuild the nation. The memorial service was solemn and dignified.

Chiang wanted to demonstrate his trust in Feng and Yen by stationing only a few of our own troops in the North. At that time Feng Yü-hsiang,[4] Yen Hsi-shan,[5] and Li Tsung-jen[6] were truly united with Chiang, and they were determined to work together for the good of the country. I believe that if Chiang had stationed more troops in the North, Yen Hsi-shan and Feng Yü-hsiang would have thought twice before they were foolish enough to use military force to oppose us in central China in March 1930.[7] On July 13, Chiang's generosity was treacherously rewarded by Yen Hsi-shan, Feng Yü-hsiang, and Wang Ching-wei's establishing an Expanded Conference [K'uo-ta hui-i]. This crisis became known as the Mutiny of 1930, which led to the formation of a new National government, lasting eleven days, on September 9 of the same year in Peking.[8] The espisode ended on September 20, and two days later T'an Yen-k'ai passed away at the age of fifty-two.

Members of the Central Standing Committee requested that the committee appoint Ma Chao-chun, a rival of Wang Ching-wei's, to be the Kuomintang's special agent to be sent to the North. His assignment was to mobilize Kuomintang members to sabotage Chiang's two enemies, Yen and Wang. Ma was well-known in labor union circles and very close to the working-class people.

We also learned that the Japanese had warned Chang Hsüeh-liang not to join the Kuomintang. This placed him in a predicament, for if he decided to ally with the Kuomintang he would be threatened. Chiang could have sent troops to the Northeast, but he did not want to act hastily. He hoped he could find peaceful means to induce the northeastern warlord troops to

join our ranks. After we captured Shanghai on March 21, 1927, representatives from all sides, including those sent by Chang Tso-lin, came to
negotiate peace with us. The Japanese assassinated Chang Tso-lin by blowing
up his train on June 4, 1928, at Huang Ku-tun.[9] On December 29, 1928, his
son Chang Hsüeh-liang pledged his loyalty to the National government.
Chiang sent Wu T'ieh-ch'eng to the Northeast, and he raised the Kuomintang party's blue-sky white-star banner there.[10] Chiang commended Chang
Hsüeh-liang for ignoring the Japanese threat and risking his life by joining
the Kuomintang.

In retrospect, Chang Hsüeh-liang cooperated with the National government for three reasons: first, the Northeast was threatened by the Japanese; second, reunification of the country was in sight; third, he wanted to
get revenge for the death of his father, Chang Tso-ling.[11]

On January 25, 1929, Chiang offered a proposal to cut back the army
at the Army National Military Reorganization and Disbandment Conference
[Kuo-chün pien-ch'ien hui-i], but it met very strong opposition. His proposal would have benefited the country. Chiang failed to have his proposal
effected because no military man in China wanted to slash his troops.[12]

The Nanking Leadership

The National government was proclaimed in Nanking in October 1928 with
Chiang as chairman of the National government of [Kuo-min *cheng-fu chu-
hsi*], T'an Yen-k'ai as the head of the Executive Yüan, and Hu Han-min,
head of the Legislative Yüan. China now officially entered the stage of
political tutelage under Kuomintang rule.[13]

The major diplomatic issue facing the Kuomintang was how to elevate
China's status on the international scene. The Kuomintang's first priority
was to have the unequal treaties abrogated. Although our forceful negotiations made progress, the Western nations were unwilling to give up their
privileges in China. This issue was incessantly discussed in the Kuomintang
Central Executive Committee.

On the domestic front, the most important issue facing the National
government was to reform the archaic legal system and draft new laws.
Lawmaking is vital for establishing a democratic system. We needed new
laws to implement the Three People's Principles and to establish local self-
government in accordance with Sun Yat-sen's teachings. That responsibility
fell on the shoulders of Hu Han-min, one of the founding fathers of the
republic.

The next important issue facing the National government was improving the quality of our military. Chiang initiated many reforms to raise the
standards of our military personnel. Too many officers lacked a good edu-

cation, and some had entered officers' training academies without a high school diploma. Chiang thought it important to raise the entrance standards of the officer academies. He also selected able officers from various warlord troops for further schooling and set up a war college to train more staff officers. In short, Chiang began to improve military standards and to create a modernized Chinese army. Other important programs involved road building, protecting waterways, and improving the agrarian economy.

In early 1929, Chiang assigned me to be the new chief of his political training office [*Cheng-chih hsüan-lien-chü*]. This office was under the jurisdiction of the Training Supervisory Department of Chiang's headquarters. Almost 90 percent of the staff members were graduates of Whampoa Military Academy but were without military appointments or duties. I did not feel I was qualified for the job, but Chiang insisted. He instructed me to cut back 40 to 50 percent of the personnel. He felt it wasteful to have so many people in the office. I began to interview each of them. I asked them how they felt about the recent party purge and their ideas about political training work. I also set up a special committee to review our recorded conversations.

My method caused a great stir and strong protests. Many complained that my way of questioning was too subjective. At first I disregarded these criticisms, thinking the problem was simple. Only later did I find that the issues were more complex because many of the staff members who were to become unemployed were personally close to my predecessor, Fang Chüeh-hui. Fang was also reluctant to relinquish his post.

I reported to Chiang that I was unable to carry out the reduction of staff because I did not have the talent for such political maneuvering. Chiang adamantly refused to let me resign. A week after I assumed the office, I took sick leave and left Nanking, requesting that Chiang find a new replacement. Before I took leave I had already met with all the personnel but had not yet started to make cutbacks.

I left for Shanghai, fearful of another relapse of tuberculosis. Weak and fatigued, I constantly coughed. I wanted to have a physical checkup, rest, and cure my illness. It was the first time that I had ever quit my post.

The Third Congress of the Kuomintang

The Third Congress of the Kuomintang was held from March 15 to March 28, 1929, in Nanking.[14] I was then in Shanghai, and my health was still very poor. Only later did I learn it was a very important meeting and far more significant than the two previous congresses. Because the National Revolutionary Army already controlled the Yangtze Valley, all the delegates were eager to have our party set up on a solid foundation.

Hu Han-min played a pivotal role at the conference, and he, along with

Chiang, dictated the outcome of the conference. Although Chiang headed the Organization Department, my elder brother, Kuo-fu, was really in charge.

Many congress delegates had played leading roles in combating the Communists. They despised the "leftist faction" [*tso-p'ai*]of our party, meaning Wang Ching-wei and his followers. These leftists had virtually stood aside and done nothing in our fight with the Communists.[15] Hu Han-min had never liked Wang Ching-wei. Those who followed Wang Ching-wei at the conference, like Kan Nei-kuang and Ch'en Kung-po, were known as the Reorganizationists [Kai-tsu p'ai] and received a great deal of criticism and insulting denunciations. Hu Han-min and Wang Ching-wei headed dominant forces within the party, and both posed as senior statesmen above Chiang because of age and experience. Each claimed that his faction represented the majority and that Chiang lacked support in the party. But when it became clear that Chiang's party support matched their own, they immediately accused him of manipulating the party. I learned that the persons selected for the Central Executive Committee had been decided by Chiang and Hu and that my elder brother, Kuo-fu, merely carried out their orders.

When the membership list of the Central Executive Committee was revealed, all senior comrades in the Kuomintang had been selected. But Chang Tao-fan and Yu Ching-tang, who assisted my elder brother in handling party affairs in the Organization Department, were also on the list. Our party's highest leadership body now had some new blood. It would have been unfair not to appoint to the committee junior members who were responsible and showed leadership potential. I had not expected to be chosen a member of the Central Executive Committee. I only learned that was the case from a list published in the newspapers. My elder brother later wrote me the news. I was really not qualified for the job. I was the youngest member of the Central Executive Committee.

On April 8, 1929, at the first plenary session of the Third Congress, I was elected the first secretary-general of the Central Executive Committee of the Kuomintang's Third Congress. To be elevated from the confidential section of the Organization Department to this high post in one leap came as a total surprise to me.[16] Because of poor health, I had not participated in the party congress meeting. Only later did I learn that Chiang and Hu had reached an understanding and forwarded my name.

I had not expected Hu to agree with Chiang on my nomination. I had little contact with Hu; in 1926 when he was also in Canton, we had never met. In Nanking I saw him only occasionally. I believe that he agreed principally because I was a nephew of my late uncle, Ch'i-mei. Yet he might have learned of my reputation as a good party worker. I was not thirty years of age. I really considered myself too young to shoulder these new responsibilities. I thought about asking the Central Executive Committee to allow me to step down. At the first regular meeting of the committee, on April 11, with Hu as chairman, my case was discussed, and it was resolved that the committee "telegraph Comrade Ch'en Li-fu to urge him to immediately assume office and to request Comrade Yeh Chu-tsang to be in charge until Comrade Ch'en arrives." Yeh then headed the Propaganda Department. On receiving this telegram, I again cabled Nanking to decline the offer. At the second regular meeting of the committee on April 15, my request was denied and the committee again telegraphed me to assume my office as soon as possible. The committee also asked my elder brother, Kuo-fu, to urge me to accept. I declined for a third time, honestly believing in my heart that I was not capable of taking on such a responsible position. I sincerely begged them to consider other able persons for the post so that official business would not suffer as a result of this delay.

At the sixth regular meeting of the committee my request was still not granted. As chairman of the committee, Hu then suggested that the committee await Chiang's return to Nanking for further discussion. On May 20, at the thirteenth regular meeting, Yeh Chu-tsang refused to continue in the job, and so T'an Yen-k'ai urged me to assume the office. Hu seconded the motion. My health had now improved, and I had just returned to Nanking. Sensing that I could no longer turn down the offer, I attended the fourteenth regular meeting to explain my position. Hu insisted that the matter be discussed again after holding a memorial service for the transfer of Sun Yat-sen's body to the Nanking Mausoleum. At the seventeenth regular meeting on June 20, Yeh Chu-tsang resigned as the acting secretary-general; Hu once more pressured me to assume the office immediately. On June 24, at the eighteenth regular meeting of the Central Executive Committee, I finally agreed to accept the post.

The events I have just described occurred at a time when Hu Han-min was assuming enormous responsibilities for party affairs. Each time Chiang made a tour, he instructed me to go to Hu for guidance on all party matters. Wang Ching-wei was already out of power in Nanking, and Hu was the most senior, the most knowledgeable, and the most important leader in the Kuomintang.

I had associated with very few people up until that time. For this reason, whenever there were job openings I only invited my very good friends to fill them. During this fascinating phase of my life, time passed quickly. Being both young and energetic, I felt as though I could accomplish anything. Many decades later, I behaved more cautiously and deliberated longer before making decisions.

The Secretariat was in charge of all documents of the Kuomintang Central Executive Committee. Every document that came from other departments, no matter how long or important, had to pass through the Secretariat. This agency also served as the document-transmitting center between upper and lower levels of the party. When the Kuomintang congress was not in session, the Secretariat took note of all important proposals and set agendas for the Kuomintang congress and regular party meetings. The Secretariat also carefully presented all resolutions to the Central Executive Committee and the Standing Committee.

Our agency was officially called the Secretariat of the Central Executive Committee, but when the Central Executive Committee was not in session it also served as the Secretariat of the Standing Committee. The Secretariat handled all documents and affairs between the party and the government as well. In a word, the Secretariat was the liaison both within and without the Kuomintang. For a man so young as I, without any experience in party affairs, I indeed had a heavy burden to shoulder.

The Kuomintang Senior Members

The Central Executive Committee of the Third Congress called its first meeting on March 28, 1929, in which nine Standing Committee members were elected: Chiang, Hu Han-min, T'an Yen-k'ai, Sun Fo, Tai Chi-t'ao, Yu Yü-jen, Ting Wei-fen, Yeh Chu-tsang, and my elder brother, Ch'en Kuo-fu. Whenever the Standing Committee met, each of the nine members, by an understanding rather than by design, rotated the chair.

Not every member would be present at these Standing Committee meetings; for instance, Chiang might be inspecting the troops. Furthermore, much business did not require a decision by voting. Except for very important issues, at the conclusion of each meeting the chair would ask the members if they had any questions related to the proposals under discussion. If no dissenting voice was heard, the proposal was considered passed. But issues involving policy changes had to be decided by a majority vote of the committee.

Minutes of each meeting had to be first approved by the chair, then read to committee members for their approval or amendment. To save time, reading of the minutes often was postponed until the start of the next meeting. If no corrections were needed, the minutes stood.

It was not an easy task for me to serve nine members of the Central Standing Committee. I tried to resign twice, first at the sixty-first regular meeting on December 30, 1929, then at the eighty-first regular meeting on March 24, 1930. I wrote to Chiang and Hu telling them that I believed I was too young and inexperienced for such work. Both Chiang and Hu believed I could do the job, and they assured me that if I should have any problems

I could seek their help. One of my many difficulties was that certain problems were too trivial to ask the Standing Committee for its instructions. For example, when the Standing Committee gave instructions to carry out a policy, the Secretariat would look for a precedent to draft a plan in the name of the committee. Although it was the responsibility of the secretary-general to draw up such a document, it required the signatures of the nine committee members.

It was most tedious to visit or telephone each of the nine members to get their approval for a special plan each time. Therefore, I suggested that two of the Standing Committee members take turns each day representing the committee and that they be at the central Kuomintang headquarters every morning at nine or ten o'clock to examine these official papers. In this way, these documents could be approved quickly. If there was disagreement, it would be taken up at the next meeting. With nine members on the committee, no single person was likely to take charge, and it became too big a responsibility for the secretary-general.

I arrived at the office every morning at eight. The two members assigned for that day would come in about nine. I usually spent the whole morning with them. It was a good opportunity for me to get acquainted with the Standing Committee members. As they went over the papers, I always stood at their side to see if they needed further materials but also to observe their reactions and attitudes. The committee later decided that, because they were too busy, only one member would come in each day. To inform every Standing Committee member of the week's work, I summarized the content of the papers that had been read and commented on by the rotating members. In this way I learned a great deal about these senior committee members and better understood their personalities and special qualities. I would like to record below what I thought of each.

HU HAN-MIN.   Of the nine members of the Standing Committee, Hu truly loved and was devoted to the Kuomintang. He also was the most experienced in party affairs and also the most serious and responsible. He worked with all his energy and frequently offered strong opinions.

Hu also had a thorough understanding of the Three People's Principles doctrine because of his many years devoted to party work. He was a very principled man and demanded the same of others. Perhaps his one shortcoming was to be overly critical and to speak ill of others. For this reason many people kept a respectful distance from him. Arrogant and full of his own self-importance, Hu also liked to claim a lot of credit for himself. If he did not approve of some matters, he openly faulted others at the central Kuomintang's weekly meetings and thus offended many people.

While other members often neglected their rotational responsibilities because of their tight schedules, Hu always came to the office on time. Not only did he attend every meeting, including the relatively unimportant ones called by the subcommittees, but he was never late. This attitude won him much praise from others.

Whenever there was no official business that required his attention, Hu would chat with me, telling me anecdotes of the Kuomintang and many events of the past.

T'AN YEN-K'AI. T'an's personality was just the opposite of Hu's. Dignified, poised, and intelligent, I believe T'an to have been the smartest of all the Standing Committee.

T'an could quickly reach a decision after examining official documents. I once tested to see if he really had so rapidly comprehended a document's content. I first read the document with care. After he had given the same complex document a quick glance and written down his comments, I raised a few questions. His answers proved that he thoroughly followed the content of the paper. Indeed, I saw him as living proof of a Chinese saying: "To take in ten lines at one glance."

Whenever T'an found a matter of vital importance related to current events, he wrote to Chiang and offered suggestions. He let Chiang decide whether to approve his suggestions or not. He seemed so self-assured as never to claim credit for himself.

He wrote every letter himself. His Yen-style calligraphy was so beautiful that one felt proud to receive his handwritten letter. Chiang accepted most of T'an's suggestions, but T'an never told anyone that Chiang's ideas were his. For this, I greatly respected T'an. Moreover, T'an was strongly anti-communist and he always weighed all aspects of a situation before taking action.

Some would say that if T'an was so smart, why was he willing to subordinate himself to Chiang? I believe T'an considered Chiang to be the only leader who could take the lead and solve the complex difficulties facing our party and government at that time. He regarded Chiang as the most suitable person for the country's leadership.

I later learned that, although T'an came from an aristocratic family of former officials and scholars, his childhood was quite poor, and he was such a filial son that he never wore a fur coat throughout his life because his mother had never enjoyed the same luxury. How true is the old Chinese saying: "An official loyal to his sovereign is certain to be born of a family of filial piety."

TAI CHI-T'AO. Tai too was a smart man and versed in Confucianism and Chinese Buddhism. It was as though his aspirations having been unfulfilled, he had turned to Buddhism for solace. His devotion to Buddhism had helped him to work with the minorities in the frontier region. He often told me interesting philosophical stories about the origin of the Three People's Principles doctrine. Whenever discussing official business, before he offered his opinions he usually spent about fifteen minutes to half an hour justifying his position. He was full of ideas, many so ingenious that one could not help but be persuaded. I often thought this kind of a person must be a profound thinker. His mind was like a fast-producing factory whose manufactured goods had to flow continuously because there was no storage space.

Tai was of enormous help to Chiang. He was the youngest member of the Western Hills group and a thorough anticommunist. He was the Communists' most formidable enemy because the few books he had written were of enormous influence on the public and disclosed the errors and evils of communist thinking. He was highly respected by the older generation. At critical moments, he would rely upon a principle and use impressive historical facts to win over others to his point of view. For example, right after the Sian Incident, his interpretations were most persuasive and believed by others. I frequently asked him for advice whenever I encountered difficulties.

TING WEI-FEN.   Reticent and a man of a few words, Ting was not eloquent, but the few words he spoke were always appropriate and carried considerable weight. He was a loyal member of the Kuomintang and worked well with Chiang. Few comrades on the Central Executive Committee came from the North. The northerners, especially those from Shantung Province, often visited Ting when they happened to be in Nanking. We greatly valued Ting's opinions. On matters relating to the North we were certain to get views from Ting. It was he who had secretly led a political organization called the Grand Alliance [Ta-t'ung meng] when the warlords were rampant. The Grand Alliance was quite influential in Shantung, Hopei, and other northern provinces and was a cover for the Kuomintang. Before the Northern Expedition, less-influential secret organizations in the Peking-Tientsin area like the Revive China Society [Hsing-chung-hui] and the Practice Society [Shih-chien-she] also sought out Ting for advice. At a regular meeting of the Kuomintang's Central Executive Committee, my elder brother, Kuo-fu, and I put forward a motion that these minor organizations within the party be disbanded. After the motion was passed, they were ordered to dissolve.

When war with Japan began because of the Marco Polo Bridge Incident on July 7, 1937, I received orders to become the acting dean of the Central Political Institute [Chung-yang cheng-chih hsüeh-hsiao], the post that Ting had held.

YEH CHU-TSANG.   An archetypal man of letters, Yeh was mild-mannered and even-tempered. He liked to drink and always kept wine bottles in his office desk. He was a rather passive person, although when circumstances demanded, he worked hard in a responsible and thorough way

He belonged to the Western Hills group but was not actively involved. His calligraphy was beautiful, and he was an accomplished poet. An excellent writer, he had edited newspapers run by the Kuomintang. He was like T'an Yen-k'ai in mannerisms, but he lacked T'an's fervent spirit. As a loyal party member, Yeh made special contributions to publicizing the Three People's Principles doctrine and related policy matters. In those two months of my repeated appeals to the Central Standing Committee to decline the job offer, I was lucky he acted on my behalf, for otherwise I would have had to be in office when I was ill. I was most grateful to him.

CH'EN KUO-FU.   He was a serious-minded and responsible person, a loyal party member and patriot. He had contracted tuberculosis at the age of twenty but continued to work even though ill, never giving a thought to his health. When the Whampoa Military Academy first opened, he rendered invaluable assistance to Chiang, such as recruiting cadets and soldiers and obtaining logistic support in Shanghai when the region was under warlord control.

Whenever my elder brother, Kuo-fu, formed an opinion about a difficult problem, he asked me to seek-out Hu Han-min and T'an Yen-k'ai for advice. Although a Standing Committee member himself, he wanted to avoid giving people the impression that major Kuomintang matters were decided by just two brothers. Chiang already had instructed us to defer to Hu.

Kuo-fu was never educated in natural science, but with his intelligence and innate interests, he would have made an outstanding engineer or scientist. I am not exaggerating when I say that our Kuomintang's organizational rules were largely his creation. His contributions to the party's financial management were incalculable, and without him the Central Political Institute would never had been so successful.

SUN FO.   Sun Fo loved to read. Among all the senior party members I believe he was the one who had read the most Western works. He read mainly about politics, economics, and science. He often asked others to buy newly published books from the United States and Europe for him. Whenever he became bored at meetings, he took out a book to read. His love of books was very similar to his father's (Sun Yat-sen) great interest in reading. I do not think Sun Fo held broad interests, but I admired him for his zealous spirit to search for knowledge. He did not talk much, nor did he easily express his opinions. If you did not raise a question, he could sit there for fifteen minutes without uttering a word. If he found a certain subject to be interesting, he would begin to speak, and the more he spoke the more animated he became. Yet he was impatient and easily lost his temper.

Someone made the following amusing comparison: If you went to see Hu Han-min, he spoke so eloquently that you never had a chance to open your mouth. If you went to see Chiang, he listened to you but spoke little. If you went to see Wang Ching-wei, he was very courteous and both of you conversed a great deal. If you went to see Sun Fo, neither of you had much to say. Four different styles of behavior existed in our top leadership. How lucky I was to interact with seniors who were so different in their characters!

Yu Yü-jen. A man of optimism, sincerity, and forthrightness, Yu was unruffled by the chaos around him. Personifying the strength of the North, he indulged himself in the study of important matters and was an outstanding calligrapher, which manifested his character and personality.

He was a respected revolutionary leader throughout the North, especially in the northwest regions. Hailing from Shanyuan of Shensi Province, he was particularly sensitive toward the events in the Northwest. People there viewed him as the leader, and they followed him when he backed Chiang. Yu now made his home in Shanghai, and when he was supposed to represent the Standing Committee he always showed up. His views at our meetings were highly regarded, and he was a most responsible person.

Yu had a powerful build, and when he spoke with his magnificent voice and clear diction, he was most impressive. He often read proclamations at the end of plenary sessions or the party congress. The party and country loved him.

For a long time he served as president of the Control Yüan in the National government. He was chosen to be president because he was a founding member of the Kuomintang and the republic and because he was one of the very few Central Committee members from the Northwest. As the revolution had originated in the South, it was natural that more party members were southerners. Comrades from Kwangtung Province were the majority, followed by those from the Yangtze River Valley and finally the Yellow River Valley. Although few party members came from the Yellow River Valley, our party organization leaders gave careful consideration to geographic distribution so as not to appear unfair.

Yu was not a man deterred by age. His beard extended nearly two feet, but he never acted old. He particularly liked to be around young people. I once asked him whether he slept with his long beard outside or under the bedding? He replied, "I make a knot of the beard and place it outside the bedding."

Yu wrote a book entitled *Standard Free-style Calligraphy* [*Piao-chun* ts'ao-shu] to teach readers how to write Chinese characters quickly in the free-style mode, and the work became a model for calligraphy.

Those Standing Committee members who came to the Kuomintang central office most often were Hu Han-min, Ting Wei-fen, Yeh Chu-tsang, and my elder brother, Kuo-fu. They all treated me with kindness. Perhaps because of my youth, they easily overlooked my errors. Having a simple nature, I treated people with candor and directness. Members of the Standing Committee, if not holding a job in the government, received a monthly salary of 300 yuan from the party.

The Kuomintang and the National Government

Most of the Kuomintang Central Executive Committee members held con-current posts in the National government.[17] Among the standing members of the Central Executive Committee only Ting Wei-fen and I did not hold concurrent posts.

I believe that income was a powerful reason for everyone to want multiposts. As stated earlier, the Central Executive and Standing Committee members received a monthly salary of only 300 yuan, while a cabinet member earned a monthly salary of between 600 to 800 yuan.

What about the leaders at provincial party headquarters? Did they also simultaneously hold posts in the provincial government? During the time of the Northern Expedition, local party officials wielded considerable power. Under the slogans of Party Power above All [Tang-ch'üan chih-shang] and Rule the Country through the Party [i-tang chih-kuo], local government chiefs deferred to local party leaders, and it was unlikely that party leaders wanted to become government officials just for the sake of receiving a government salary.

Between 1928 and 1931, comrades in provincial Kuomintang headquar-ters were extremely busy conducting party purge work. They helped or-ganize every basic level of local party offices and coordinate party and local government activities. As a result, the provincial and municipal government officials were induced to join the party. But the reverse also held true, as in the case of Pan Kung-chan. Pan was a Standing Committee member of the Shanghai party branch, but he was also the commissioner of the Social Affairs Bureau of the Shanghai municipal government.

Some Kuomintang comrades also insisted that party personnel should not be involved in local government; they argued that during the political tutelage period the party should function as a legislative body to check and balance local government officials. Once party members became part of a local government, the influence of party criticism would be minimized.

While representing the Central Executive Committee,[18] I once attended a party congress in Kiangsi Province in which the Kiangsi governor, Ku Chu-t'ung, was invited to make a report. Governor Ku was not only a party member but also a delegate to the congress. He was reporting both as a government official and as a party member. At that meeting the commissioner of the provincial education department also made a report. In this example, the Kiangsi provincial party had assumed the function of a provincial legislative assembly.

Still others pointed out that because qualified persons were hard to find to share the responsibilities of party and government work, why not allow provincial or municipal party members to concurrently serve in local government posts and avoid looking for talent outside the party? But that argument made it unreasonable and illogical to view the party as a legislative body.

After the purge, Chiang considered sending local party members to serve in local governments. Many party members were unwilling to accept such assignments, but others reluctantly did so. The principle of "party power above all" still prevailed, and everybody thought they should "go where the power lies."

As a matter of fact, local governments were not as corrupt as many thought. As soon as a government did something wrong, the party investigated the matter. Local governments feared the party just as they feared a legislative body. With the party leading the people, few in government dared to be corrupt or take bribes.

In fact, those who advocated separation of government and party offered good reasons. If all party members joined government bodies, they would no longer be in a position to supervise local governments. Any form of criticism was like criticizing oneself. This policy perpetuated abuses.

During the political tutelage period, the party functioned as a legislative body: the Kuomintang headquarters acted like the National Assembly, and the local party corresponded to a local council. If that were the case, then the party should pay comparable salaries to those party members serving in government. Only then could competent party members be induced to supervise the government.

It was impractical to demand that party workers conduct party work without adequate compensation. Moreover, most party members were too poor to offer the party their free time and effort. By paying capable people to work for the government, we created a system in which the party, instead of steering the government, became an opposing entity. In retrospect, this was why fewer and fewer young men and women wanted to take party work seriously.

Serving as Secretary-General
of the Kuomintang

As the secretary-general, I spent considerable time each day receiving visitors. I met nearly every party member who came to the Kuomintang headquarters from different provinces and cities, particularly those serving in the local executive and supervisory committees. They often brought their problems to my attention. Although I had not previously made their acquaintance, my post provided a unique opportunity to get to know every activist within the Kuomintang and to listen to their views. I averaged around twenty appointments each day, and many, to my surprise, were young defectors from the Chinese Communist party. I never refused to see anyone. Not only did I meet them, but I also had to appear pleased and make every effort to make them feel welcome and happy. During their stay in Nanking, I entertained and dined with them, trying to better know and understand them.

I worked hard. Each morning I arrived at the office early, way ahead of others, and stayed late in the evening, often after seven o'clock. So vigorously did I throw myself into work that I made my subordinates suffer. About forty to fifty people worked under me, either with special assignments or in the clerical section. None of them dared to arrive late or leave early. Office discipline was naturally established.

I reorganized the Secretariat, especially the clerical section, which had been responsible for copying, printing, and classifying documents. I taught the personnel a new printing method, thus increasing printed volumes from two hundred to a thousand copies. Meanwhile, I used my five-stroke indexing system in Chinese characters to file materials within the Secretariat.

I knew the entire staff in the party's Organization Department, and I now tried to improve personnel cooperation in the different departments to increase work efficiency. For example, if the Secretariat received some documents relevant to the Organization Department, I made a copy and sent it to the Organization Department; if the document also had something to do with other departments, such as the Youth or Women's departments, I sent copies to those same departments with a note that the Organization Department would contact them directly. This method enabled all concerned departments to receive the same information quickly.

The local party headquarters praised these efficiency-improving measures taking place at central Kuomintang. I took pride in these reforms. I often talked with my elder brother, Kuo-fu, of how we could peacefully bring about China's reunification and solve the many problems over the long run. We decided that the first step was to publicize the views and policies of the Kuomintang and the National government, especially to people in areas beyond our control, like Szechuan, which had submitted to the authority of the National government in name only. We took the initiative to build a broadcasting station at the Nanking Kuomintang headquarters, and then we authorized the manufacturing and selling of radio sets at a reasonable price to create a larger audience. We had films made to educate the masses and to promote their understanding of our party's policies.

Our efforts bore fruit. The Nanking broadcasting station had a great influence throughout China. Built chiefly by funds donated by overseas Chinese, the station was more powerful than those of Japan and the Soviet Union. We received more money than we anticipated, so Kuo-fu suggested that a special commission be set up to budget its allocation for useful purposes. Lin Sheng, a senior member of the Kuomintang from Fukien Province, was chosen to head the commission because of his extensive relations with overseas Chinese. Under his direction, part of the money was spent to build the broadest boulevard along Chungshan Road in Nanking, to restore the Fallen Soldiers Cemetery, and to construct the Shanghai Radio Transmitter-Receiver Factory. Our plan to build a film studio did not materialize, but we did install a quasi–Chinese Oscar award system: the Association for Film Education [Tien-yin chiao-yüeh hsieh-hui] gave annual prizes to the three most outstanding films based on their educational content. Because we lacked funds to make many films on our own, we tried to encourage the private filmmaking industry.

While secretary-general of the Central Executive Committee, I always paid attention to key issues related to the National government, and, as soon as I noticed anything, I immediately put it on the agenda for discussion by the Central Political Committee at its regular meetings. The trivial cases I simply forwarded to the government.

One last note: the Central Supervisory Committee accommodated virtually all the ideas and suggestions of the senior members. The Central Supervisory Committee supervised the policies and directives made by the Central Executive Committee. The members of the Central Supervisory Committee also enjoyed considerably more prestige because they had the right to attend the Standing Committee and Executive Committee meetings as well as the power to discipline party members.

With my wife in April 1929 when I became the secretary-general of the Central Executive Committee of the Kuomintang.

Working for the
Central Political Committee

Shortly after I assumed the post of the secretary-general of the Kuomintang Central Executive Committee in June 1929, the Central Standing Committee in early 1930 appointed me concurrently to the post of secretary-general of the Central Political Committee [Chung-yang cheng-chih hui-i]. Many years later, in April 1947, I again held these two posts simultaneously.

The Central Political Committee was the abbreviation for the Political Committee of the Central Executive Committee [Chung-yang chih-hsing wei yuan-hui cheng-chih hui-i], a unit set up within the party for the purpose of studying policy decisions. Any important issues that confronted the National government but that did not directly concern the Kuomintang were dealt with in the Central Political Committee.

The Central Political Committee was at first a simple unit, but it gradually grew and began to set up its own subcommittees on interior affairs, education, finance, economics, foreign affairs, and other subjects to study specific problems relative to these various areas. The decisions made at the Central Political Committee went through the Central Standing Committee, not directly to the government. These policy decisions were included in those made by the Standing Committee, most of which no longer needed further discussion, but a few might be listed on the agenda for final deliberations by the Standing Committee. Approval was then passed on to the National government [council] by the Standing Committee. The Standing Committee members' task was to chart broadly the scope of policy-making without attending to detail. When dealing with those units outside the party, the Standing Committee made the final decision in the name of the Central Executive Committee.

The chairman of the Central Political Committee was Chiang, who had to attend every meeting but could appoint someone to take his place if he should be absent. After every item in the agenda had been discussed and a decision reached, the chairman would ask the secretary-general to read the resolutions. When the meeting was over, the chairman carefully studied every part of the resolutions before affixing his signature.

Generally speaking, Chiang had the right to appoint anyone to act as the chairman, but sometimes he allowed those attending the conference to elect their own. If Hu Han-min was present, members often elected him to be the acting chairman, but if Hu was absent, another member would be chosen. If Chiang was in Nanking but unable to chair the meeting, he would indicate who should take his place. If he was not in Nanking, then we allowed the members to decide on their own. Later, the Political Conference members took turns chairing the meeting so as to share the privilege of being the chairman. Everyone was content with this arrangement.

During Chiang's absence from Nanking, I passed the unimportant resolutions of the Central Political Committee to Hu or the Standing Committee member who was serving as chairman. I telegraphed Chiang about the important issues, and if he disapproved, we held more discussions; but such occasions were rare.

Before assuming the post of secretary-general of the Central Political Committee, as secretary-general of the Kuomintang I handled documents and papers related to the government. The work of the secretary-general of the Central Political Committee was relatively simple. It chiefly involved preconference preparations with some routine follow-up. I had two secretaries, Ti Ying and Hu Han, to help me prepare the agenda. I directed them to search old files for precedents, which we then systematically classified. We printed them so that every attending member had a copy of the material and any precedent we had located at hand. Before discussing important issues, Chiang's approval was necessary before they were presented to the conference. Should Chiang have any instructions, certain attending members accepted and acted accordingly. After the resolutions were finalized, they had to be reviewed and signed by the committee chairman, who was Chiang.

The post of secretary-general of the Central Executive Committee was more important than that of the secretary-general of the Central Political Committee because the former wielded greater power in decision making, which affected the entire party. All Kuomintang agencies were under the former's indirect supervision, whereas the latter did not control any subordinate units.

But the Central Political Committee was significant for two reasons: (1) the issues debated in conference meetings were relevant to legislative principles and policies; (2) those attending these conferences were senior party members. The Central Political Committee's resolutions were not made public but passed on to the Standing Committee. Often, they were leaked before they were finally sent to the National government to be implemented. Secrecy was essential because newspaper reporters swarmed around the headquarters' offices rather than the government agencies to gather their news. The Kuomintang headquarters had little need for lavish display. The Kuomintang was the backstage manager, and the executive branches of the government were supposed to make the important announcements.

The Central Political Committee held its regular meetings on Wednesdays, while the Standing Committee held its on Thursdays. The Executive Yüan met on Mondays. In principle, any policy decisions by the government were to appear in Tuesday's newspapers. But leaks often occurred right after the Central Political Committee had met. As a result, government announcements were eclipsed by news leaked from the conference. If the government's words were to have any significance, the party should remain invisible behind the scenes. But the public seemed to ignore the government's announcements, and so we decided to make our party decisions more confidential.

Chiang's Power Expands

The National government held great power and influence when Chiang was its president and Hu Han-min was president of the Legislative Yüan. In the early stage of the Nanking National government, governance was not always clearly defined. Having a National government was essential because we were just beginning to establish the new Five-Power System as suggested by Sun Yat-sen.

The nominated council members of the National government were usually put forward by the president to the Central Political Committee, which in turn passed them on to the Central Standing Committee. I was among those elected to the National government council.

Whenever disputes occurred between two ministries, the Executive Yüan was to resolve them. If disputes occurred between two yüans, the National government council, which met once a week, would adjudicate. Whether or not the dispute was resolved by the council, the case would go to the Central Executive Committee to be transmitted to the Central Political Committee.

The National government council also had a voice concerning important legislation. The council discussed the laws and regulations to be implemented and sent its views to the Central Political Committee for further study. The committee then forwarded its views to the Central Standing Committee for final approval before being transmitted to the National government and the Legislative Yüan.[19]

The president of the Executive Yüan, T'an Yen-k'ai, passed away on September 22, 1930. Chiang took over that post on November 24 of the same year. I began to worry about this action.[20] Once Chiang had assumed the presidency of the Executive Yüan, who was going to arbitrate disputes between the presidents of the two yüans? Hu Han-min, the president of the Legislative Yüan, had always been very outspoken and critical of others. If he should now find fault with the Executive Yüan, that would be tantamount to criticizing Chiang.

The status of the Executive Yüan was certainly enhanced during Chiang's tenure as president, the significance of which did not escape news reporters. That was a natural development because whenever a strong, dynamic man leads, power goes with him. All power accrues in the hands of the person who makes final decisions.

Military matters also came to the attention of the highest levels of the Kuomintang. Chiang, however, only reported the most important military matters to the Central Political Committee, which he chaired. He was also the commander in chief of all three armed forces: army, navy, and air force. Those positions augmented his power. Needless to say, the power he enjoyed was immense, and no man could compete. Reports of other military matters were brought to the Central Executive Committee meetings by the minister of war, mainly past and future developments in general rather than specific terms because our military strategies were confidential at this time.

The Central Political Committee also had the right to make a military decision. For example, when the Nineteenth Route Army rebelled in Fukien Province in November 1933, the committee ordered its commander dismissed. The committee also decided on whom to appoint as minister of war and also had the authority to adopt military regulations. However, for security reasons, military policies were rarely discussed beforehand. The

Political Conference always expressed its support for any of Chiang's military actions. A voice of dissent could create a grave situation because to oppose a military action or to have discord over military matters might bring civil war.

Our rule that the "party above the military," as I noted above, was only a formality. Strictly speaking, it was difficult to have the party control the military. The Central Political Committee had no means to handle military affairs. Although a Military Council existed, it had no muscle because the person in charge wielded no real power.

The real issue, of course, was who was in charge. If the leader of the party, the government, and the military was one and the same person, he naturally had no need to report to the party about military matters. Meanwhile, Central Political Committee members also had no need to learn about military strategies. The situation might be different if a person of little consequence was put in charge of military affairs.

To finance the government, every agency of the National government sent its budget to the General Accounting Office [Chu-chi-ch'u], which had been under the supervision of my third uncle, Ch'en Ai-shih, ever since 1931. The military budget was part of the total government budget. It was very difficult to reduce the military budget at this time, and the government even set aside a special reserve fund for military uses such as secret military operations.

The General Accounting Office was a special agency whose decisions had to be approved by the National government council. Budget drafts first were sent to the Central Political Committee, then to the Finance Committee for detailed discussions, and back again to the Central Political Committee for approval, then to the Central Standing Committee, and finally back to the National government. It usually took months to go through this cumbersome, complicated, but necessary process.

On the Cultural Front

In April 1928 I founded the *Capital News* [*Ching-pao*] in Nanking. This daily newspaper's name symbolized the nation's capital, Nanking.

The purpose of founding this newspaper was to publicize Sun Yat-sen's Three People's Principles so as to give ordinary people some guidance and moral inspiration and make the Northern Expedition succeed in its mission. The paper vigorously opposed any alignment with the Soviet Union and steadfastly opposed any collaboration with the Chinese Communists, but it promoted cooperation with all friendly nations on an equal basis.

I was chairman of the board of directors. The paper was launched with some of the cash award I had received from Chiang, along with contributions from many friends. My duties at the confidential section often delayed my arrival at the paper's office until nine or ten o'clock in the evening. I wrote editorials and articles on special topics and read the final proof. I often stayed up very late.

In the second year, when its circulation reached 13,500, it surpassed the *Central Daily News* [*Chung-yang jih-pao*]; the *Capital News* was soon Nanking's top newspaper. I should stress that because of my work at the confidential section where firsthand news was abundant, the *Capital News* often scored the most rapid, interesting, exclusive stories. I naturally could not print any reports that were state secrets or confidential in the military sense. Our paper often scored first because my work at the paper did not start until near midnight when other papers already had gone to print; our late stories, therefore, made the news.

On May 1, 1928, the *Capital News* published an exclusive story reporting the recapture of Tsinan. We made a scoop because I happened to be on the frontlines at the time and telephoned the paper's office as soon as victory was assured. Other papers could not compete with us. The *Capital News* also printed many well-written articles that interested readers. There were daily commentaries on women, education, and other topics, supplemented with good illustrations. We were also the nation's first newspaper to use cartoons to caricature the dark side of society. Each day the artist Liang Ting-ming used his satirical brush to attack hoodlums.

Every Sunday we printed a pictorial supplement similar to the *Shanghai Times* [*Shanghai shih-pao*]. The pictorial supplement of the *Shanghai Times* only printed pictures of beautiful women and movie stars, whereas our pictorial supplement poked fun at society and politics through photos and cartoons.

Our paper's influence increased dramatically. When Peking was recaptured, we suggested that the city's name be changed from Peking to Peiping. In an editorial I pointed out how improper it was to continue using Peiching, the "northern capital," for Peking, and Nan-ching, the "southern capital," for Nanking because Nanking was designated the nation's capital on April 18, 1927. I argued that Peking would only confuse the people into thinking that our nation held two capitals. We also suggested that the province of Chih-li be renamed Hopei because Chih-li Province literally meant the province in which the nation's capital was sited; if this logic ruled, then Kiangsu Province, where the capital Nanking was located, ought to be called Chih-li. Then we suggested that Kiangsu University be renamed Central University [*Chung-yang ta-hsüeh*] because it was located in the capital of Nanking where the National government was installed. All these suggestions were adopted by the government.

Our commentaries supported the government's policies. We wrote editorials on foreign policy to help readers better understand the issues; we supported social reforms and attacked corruption and dishonesty.

Although our paper's position appeared neutral, we supported the government. On small matters we criticized the government; anytime we detected that the government had mishandled matters, we exposed them immediately. For this reason the *Capital Times* was popular among the readers. The people also liked the serialized novels we published in the paper's supplement. All these features made the *Capital Times* not only the leading newspaper in Nanking but increased its circulation in cities along the Nanking-Shanghai Railway and elsewhere, where newspaper readership traditionally had been monopolized by the *Shanghai Times*. Our editorial department was gradually strengthened by new talents, many of whom became well-known scholars.

We also had had an unpleasant encounter with Ch'en Shao-kuan, deputy commander in chief of the navy. Columnist T'ang Po-kung, in his daily column on historical topics, one day wrote about the navy of 1912. The deputy commander in chief, then in Hankow, heard that the *Capital Times* had attacked the navy and immediately ordered sailors from his fleet to come to Nanking to take over our newspaper office. One of our editors was arrested. After this incident, we found it very difficult to run a newspaper with an editorial policy such as the *Capital Times*'s. Whenever we criticized someone, that person went to complain to Chiang.

One additional matter at the *Capital Times* made us happy: the British news agency Reuters translated our commentaries on international topics into English and sent them abroad. When the U.S. secretary of state, Henry Stimson, passed through Shanghai, he made a point of meeting with our chief editorial writer, Chen Min-keng.

Approximately one and a half years after the *Capital Times* was founded, I passed its management to Shih Hsin-chia and the paper's name changed to the *New Capital Times* [*Hsin-ching jih-pao*]. The paper lasted until Japan initiated its attack on China in 1937. The tens of thousands of silver dollars it earned enabled my elder brother, Kuo-fu, and I to print *Current Affairs Monthly* [*Shih-shih yüeh-pao*], a monthly magazine exclusively devoted to current affairs. We interpreted international and domestic news of great importance and reported on topics such as public health and scientific progress. Our model was *Time*, of the United States, and *Le Monde*, of France. I was publisher of the magazine, and Chen Min-keng, the editor in chief. Staff members in the editorial department were renowned scholars, specialists, and well-known public figures. This magazine turned out to be quite popular, and when its circulation reached 11,000, it became the third-ranked periodical of the nation, after *Eastern Miscellany* [*Tung-fang tsa-chih*] of the Commercial Press and *New China* [*Hsin Chung-hua*] of the Chung-hua Publishing Company.

During my tenure as secretary-general of the Central Executive Committee, I also founded *Political Review Monthly* [*Cheng-chi p'ing-lun yüeh-kan*] with my elder brother, Kuo-fu. The two of us and the managing editor, Cheng Yi-tung, funded the magazine. Our purpose was to promote a new concept, "one ideology (Three People's Principles), one organization (Kuomintang), and one leader (Chiang Kai-shek)." We hoped to support Chiang as the top leader of the Kuomintang both in name and in fact. Our party lacked a real center of gravity, thus creating a situation where "nothing could be accomplished without clear directives and no directives could be justifiable without proper jurisdiction." This condition had to be changed so that our nation could deal with its internal and external problems.

Having been involved in radio stations, newspapers, journals, and magazines, my attention now turned to the publishing business. Wu Ta-chün and I founded Cheng-chung Publishing Company in 1930.

At the start, the company's initial investment was only 4,000 yuan, part of the monetary reward from Chiang for deciphering telegram codes. I was the publisher. One overriding thought governed our ventures in newspapers, magazines, and publishing: We viewed cultural work as vital and important for the success of the Kuomintang. In the beginning, the company published only books and materials related to the party. By 1931, I felt that one person's energy was too limited and that I could not possibly wear so many hats at once. I now decided to transfer company management to the Secretariat of the Central Executive Committee. Not only did the party increase the company's capital but it returned the money we had invested, and we retained copyright of our publications.

By 1935, the company began to publish middle school textbooks. It opened a retail outlet in Shanghai and invited well-known educators in different locales to be our representatives. In the following year, two additional retail outlets were opened in Wuchang and Changsha and a printing plant was built in Shanghai. Some years later, we contracted to publish Chiang's diary, his remembrance of that half-month in Sian, and Madame Chiang's reminiscence of the Sian Incident. Each of these three books sold half a million copies, earning a great deal of money for the company.

The Kuomintang headquarters later combined its San Min Chu I Publishing Company with Cheng-chung to become the San-min Publishing House. Famed for its high printing quality in Nanking, San-min became "No. 1 in printing," and Cheng-chung, also well known for its printing quality in Shanghai, became "No. 2 in printing."

Chiang versus Hu:
The Provisional Constitution Dispute

After the 1930 mutiny ended, Chiang accepted the suggestion of Wang Ching-wei, Yen Hsi-shan, and Fcng Yü-hsiang that a provisional constitution for the political tutelage period [*Hsüan-cheng shih-ch'i yao-fa*] be drafted. Hu Han-Min believed it was still too early to talk about a provisional constitution I sensed a dispute emerging between Chiang and Hu. As president of the Legislative Yüan since October 1928, Hu believed he held the highest authority in any legislative matters, and he thought that although much had been accomplished, the time was not yet ripe to proclaim a provisional constitution.[21]

Hu had great influence. A Kuomintang leader who enjoyed seniority, he could keep his power as long as the party controlled the situation. If the Kuomintang's importance were reduced, however, Hu's power would be reduced and the members of the Political Study Group [Cheng-hsüeh-hsi] would enhance their position. This group used all means to boost its own standing. I once heard Chang Ch'ün say that "the Whampoa clique has weapons as its backing; the CC clique (see Glossary) has the masses as its base; the Political Study Group looks impressive but actually has nothing behind it." The point was that if we created a provisional constitution, it would elevate the people's power and reduce the Kuomintang's power. The Political Study Group would be only too happy to use the people's power to reduce the power of the Kuomintang and confront Hu Han-min. But elevating people's power was also the Kuomintang's policy, except that the party's strategy called for a tutelage period to precede the constitution period. In my view, the time was not yet ripe to switch to the constitution period.

My understanding about this simmering dispute was the following. It was too early to proclaim a provisional constitution. Why? Because Sun Yat-sen clearly had stated in his *Fundamentals of National Reconstruction* [*Chien-kuo ta-kang*] that before entering the constitutional stage, the first step was to establish self-governance for the county [*hsien*]. Only after all counties had achieved self-governance could all the provinces achieve self-governance, and only after more than half the provinces had achieved self-governance could the nation enter the constitutional period. Sun's idea of political tutelage was very clear: to work from the lowest level upward until self-government had engulfed the nation.

I always had doubts about this issue because we had never followed Sun's instructions as set forth in *Chien-kuo ta-kang*. We would never have failed in 1949 if we had truly followed Sun's teachings in the first place. The first step should have been to train people to practice governance at the county level so the people could elect their governing officials and establish their legislative bodies. This basic step was truly ignored by our party. No one knew how long it would take for a county to successfully achieve local self-governance as Sun Yat-sen had described.

But what was my view of the National People's Convention [Kuo-min hui-i], which the Kuomintang called for in 1931?[22] The Kuomintang had unified the entire nation in name but not in reality, and the purpose of the 1931 convention was to secure the people's formal recognition of the three stages of national reconstruction as formulated by Sun Yat-sen: military operations, political tutelage, and the constitutional period. That is to say, the people must accept the concept that "political tutelage was designed to educate and enable them to govern themselves."

In talking with Hu Han-min, he suggested that I be appointed the acting secretary-general of the National People's Convention. He had always been considerate toward me, but that day I was not in a good mood so I said, "I don't want to be the acting secretary-general." As soon I said that, I left. Someone later told me that he was quite bewildered by my behavior. The fact was I believed it was too much responsibility for me to take on. My behavior was not political. I hardly ever lost my temper, and I regret having created this misunderstanding between Hu and me. Chiang believed that the decision to draft a provisional constitution was a political decision and that the purpose of drafting a provisional constitution was to discourage those who wished to inspire support outside of the party. I realized that many ambitious men within the party were unwilling to act on Sun's teachings. The moment they were denied high positions in the party, they looked for power elsewhere in order to act against the party. Actually, it was not the party but Chiang they resented. This meant Chiang had to win popular support from within in order to resist threats from without.

Hu took a very tough stand on the issue of a provisional constitution. From his many years of dealing with Wang Ching-wei as an adversary, Hu always opposed whatever suggestions Wang made. Hu insisted that it was a mistake for Chiang to announce the drafting of a provisional constitution without the party's approval. From Hu's point of view, Chiang was only one member of the Central Executive Committee. Hu was not wrong as far as party discipline was concerned. If I were the judge, I would say that Hu was legally right but that Chiang was politically correct. It was very unfortunate that Hu's opposition to the provisional constitution caused Chiang to take him into custody on March 2, 1931, and that his resignation was approved by the Central Executive Committee on the following day.

I think Chiang's move was a well-planned act.[23] Chiang had not informed me beforehand; perhaps he thought I was too close to Hu. In truth I greatly respected Hu. At that time Yang Yung-t'ai, a leader of the Political Study Group, was very close to Chiang. It is important for me to record that the Political Study Group had opposed Hu when the Kuomintang in Kwangtung adopted the seven-director system on May 20, 1918.[24] Whenever the opportunity arose, as a member of the group, Yang wanted to get even with Hu. He considered Hu the personification of the Kuomintang; to counter Hu was to counter the Kuomintang. Yang was a complete politician. When he came to see Chiang he always brought two plans, pro and con, for any important issues to be discussed. He first sounded out Chiang's opinion. If Chiang leaned toward the pro side, he presented his pro plan and vice versa. In fact, the Political Study Group had no formal organization, and its members maintained close contact with one another for selfish reasons. They never worked among the lower-class people but concentrated their effort on high-level personalities by closely observing Chiang and Wang Ching-wei; in every possible way, they catered to that leadership and those around them. Their aim was to win over the trust and goodwill of those leaders and then use that in their schemes to be appointed to high places.

Yang Yung-t'ai and his group constantly made Chiang aware that he was unable to have his way because of party elders like Hu Han-min. Pouring oil on the fire, they falsely accused Hu of being the one who had incited the troops to mutiny. Although the Kwangtung troops and Liu Shih might have maintained friendly relationships with Hu, I never believed Hu would act directly against Chiang the way Wang did.

Between 1930 and 1935 Liu Shih was the governor of Honan Province. Chang Ting-hsiü, the secretary-general of the Honan provincial government, was a follower of Hu. Yang Yung-t'ai then accused Chang as the contact man sent by Hu Han-min to Honan to do liaison work for him. In fact, as a fellow native of Kiangsi Province, Liu Shih had known Chang Ting-hsiü for quite some time. It was not Hu who had recommended Chang Ting-hsiü for the secretary-general post.

As for the story about the collusion between Hu and Hsu Chung-chih, my understanding was that when Chiang dissolved Hsu's army on September 10, 1920, Hsu naturally was very displeased, especially since Chiang had once been his subordinate. Kwangtung provincials are more or less partisan, but I did not believe either Hu or Hsu had the strength to go against Chiang and his National government.

One evening when going to the bathroom from his bedroom, Chiang saw a guard nearby looking very secretive as though he had something to hide. Chiang immediately suspected the man had come to assassinate him, and he ordered him arrested and handed over to Tai Li for interrogation. It was later learned that the guard was connected with Wen Chien-kang, who was a coarse man with no training in law and then the director of the Bureau of Public Security in Nanking. He was also very close to Hu.

When Chiang accused Hu of sabotaging the government, I believed, as stated before, that Hu was one of the most trustworthy members of the Central Executive Committee but that his candid and critical attitude had offended many. As the president of the Legislative Yüan, he believed his position resembled the speaker of a parliament. He freely spoke at weekly memorial meetings and cited shortcomings of the government administration, thus causing embarrassment for many high-level officials. Had T'an Yen-k'ai still been alive, Hu would not have been taken into custody because T'an was good at arbitrating disputes between different parties.

The following are the probable reasons for Hu's confinement: (1) Hu openly denounced and criticized the government. His attacks on those whom he considered inadequate inflicted harm on them. For this reason, no one stood up to defend him. (2) The falling-out between Yang Yung-t'ai and Hu started long before, when Sun Yat-sen experimented with the seven-director system in Canton. Yang accused Hu of acting in conspiracy with the military people. The idea of a conspiracy infuriated Chiang, and Yang had a good opportunity to sow discord, which was the main cause for Hu losing power. (3) Chiang believed Hu's addresses to the public and his conduct impeded his governing. At this juncture, any criticism of the government from Hu greatly displeased Chiang because Chiang felt he was responsible. Moreover, anyone who agreed with Hu was made to appear to have deserted Chiang. It was in essence a power struggle, and Chiang, with power already in hand, naturally did not want anyone to oppose him. Furthermore, because the nation had not yet been unified, some of Hu's actions were certain to cause trouble.

On a night in March 1931 when Hu had been taken into custody, I was the only one who dared to speak out for him. I vividly recall that evening; all members of the Central Executive and Supervisory committees were invited to Chiang's residence at the [central] military academy for dinner and a meeting.

Hu, already under house arrest, was not present. When other committee members learned of the news, no one dared to utter a word of dissent. They played it cozily. As soon as the meeting was over, I grabbed Yeh Chu-tsang and asked him to accompany me to see Chiang. Yeh did not say a word while I tried to persuade Chiang to rescind his order, counseling him not to go to extremes. I said that in view of Hu's resignation it was no longer expedient to confine him. Chiang answered: "It's already done. There is no way to pretend any further." To this day I still wonder why there was not a single person who would defend Hu. Apparently, these senior members were afraid and dared not speak up. Hu's fondness for denouncing and criticizing others had set him apart from the other seniors. His relations with many Kuomintang members were very poor.

It is astonishing that I was so naive as to challenge Chiang's decision!

But I only worried about the next day's news reporting Hu's arrest. I realized that if this incident gave the foreign press an unfavorable impression, it would not help Chiang's career at all. Who was to take Hu's place and handle his responsibilities? Undoubtedly, there was only one person and that was Chiang.

Did Hu's imprisonment have an impact on the Kuomintang? Although Hu played a key role in party affairs, he had not attempted to place his own trusted aides in local party headquarters. He occasionally recommended someone, but he was not insistent. Nor was he enraged if someone he had recommended did not turn out well. In this respect, his way of doing things was different from that of Wang Ching-wei. Hu's was a gentleman's style, while Wang nurtured his own organization: the Reorganizationists [Kai-tsu-p'ai]. Hu had followers among the Kuomintang, but they were not organized. His imprisonment therefore did not influence the low-level cadres of the party. Although many comrades felt he was wronged, their feelings never produced significant conflicts or troubles.

Did Hu's imprisonment cause Sun Fo, Lin Shen, and others to leave the National government in Nanking? Those Kuomintang seniors who chose to remain in the national capital now became very careful in expressing their opinions. They believed that Hu's fall had been caused by his sharp tongue. The real truth was that the conflict between Chiang and Hu was more than a clash of differences over personalities; differences over substantive matters were key factors as well.

The National People's Convention

The National People's Convention [Kuo-min hui-i] was "to be convoked with the least possible delay," according to Sun Yat-sen's will. It was convened between May 5 and May 17, 1931, in Nanking. To the best of my memory, the following is a summary account of the convention and some important matters and resolutions that were discussed.

More than 450 delegates, including the Panchen Lama of Tibet, attended the National People's Convention. Three proposals were presented: (1) to draft a provisional constitution of the Republic of China for the period of political tutelage; (2) to define the direction of educational policy; (3) to prepare measures for industrial development. Chiang, chairman of the National government [council], spoke at the opening ceremony, held on May 5. The next day, the delegates, including Central Committee members and members of the National government, were led by Chairman Chiang to visit Sun's mausoleum. In spite of bad weather, the swearing-in ceremony was held at the mausoleum.

A presidium of nine was elected at the preparation meeting, held on May 7. Yu Yü-jen represented the party, and the National government presented the name of Chang Hsüeh-liang as a member of the presidium. The temporary president of the presidium, Yu Yü-jen, announced the election results at the second preparation meeting on May 7: Chang Chi, Tai Chi-t'ao, Wu T'ieh-ch'eng, Chou Tso-min, Lin Chih-fu, Liu Ch'un-i, and myself with three alternates, P'eng Chi-ch'ün, Ting Wei-fen, and Hu Shu-hua. Yeh Chu-tsang was nominated as secretary-general, and he asked my help. I became the assistant to the secretary-general.

The provisional constitution was discussed on May 8, and on the following day, a resolution to "abrogate the unequal treaties" was approved. Ch'en Pu-lei, Shao Li-tzu, and Liu Lu-ying were designated to draft a statement of declaration.

On May 12, a "Provisional Constitution of the Republic of China for the Period of Political Tutelage" was adopted after three readings. On May 13, two resolutions titled "Embrace Sun Yat-sen's Legacy in Its Entirety" and "Define the Direction of Educational Policy" were adopted. On May 14, a resolution to "Prepare Measures for Industrial Development" was passed. At that same meeting, Chen Chi-t'ang was warned that he should repent and allow for the peaceful unification of the nation.

On May 15, seven resolutions and two telegram texts were approved, and June 1, 1931, was set as the date to promulgate and begin to enforce the provisional constitution for the political tutelage period. The delegates also drafted a resolution to appeal to the entire nation to support peace. On May 16, the National People's Convention passed a motion to commend Chiang for his services, and before a national anthem was approved, the party anthem would be used as the national anthem. The convention issued a proclamation emphasizing three themes: (1) embrace Dr. Sun Yat-sen's legacy in its entirety; (2) abrogate the unequal treaties; (3) uphold peaceful unification of the country.

In his speech at the closing ceremony on May 17, Chiang stressed these goals: (1) strengthening national unification and abiding by the rule of law; (2) acknowledging democracy as essential for national reconstruction; (3) cultivating the untiring effort of the nation; (4) promoting education; (5) maintaining local law and order; (6) accomplishing local self-governance. The people's convention also declared its determination to wipe out the Chinese Communists.

This national convention demonstrated that the Kuomintang was not a party representing only a minority of the people and that nonparty people could fully participate in national politics. The political atmosphere was new and dynamic. The warm words of delegates made me feel the convention was proceeding smoothly and was agreeable to the wishes of Sun Yat-sen.

Members of the presidium of the National People's Convention (Kuo-min hui-i) of 1931. From right to left: Lin Chih-fu, Ch'en Li-fu, Tai Chi-t'ao, Wu T'ieh-ch'eng, Ms. Liu Hsüan-i, Chang Hsüeh-liang, Chang Chi, Yu Yü-jen, Chou Tso-min, Yeh Chu-tsang.

Yet the convention only looked good on the surface. The fact of the matter was that it did little for the common people.

For the China of May 1931, a provisional constitution made sense if people needed their civil rights protected, and it might be an effective instrument to deal with those who violated its rules. But strictly speaking, had the provisional constitution been adopted earlier, Hu could have used the law to challenge Chiang's right to restrict his freedom. In fact Chiang never publicly stated the charge against Hu. He merely wrote a letter to Hu on February 28 refuting Hu's opposition to his proposal of convening the National People's Convention and drafting the provisional constitution of the political tutelage period. On March 1, Chiang put Hu under house arrest.[25] Such was Chiang's use of power.

The convention adopted the provisional constitution for the period of political tutelage, an issue causing the dispute between Chiang and Hu as I noted above. That action received the unanimous support of the convention's participants. While the convention was in session, Hu remained under house arrest in Nanking. Many delegates wanted to visit him, but they were dissuaded from doing so. They were mainly party seniors who merely wanted to show Hu some sympathy and say a few words of comfort. But Chiang feared that those who wanted to see Hu might be persuaded by him to cause trouble at the meetings. The final question was whether Chiang could minimize discontent among the senior Kuomintang members because of his arrest of Hu. The answer is clear from future internal developments within the Kuomintang: obviously not.

Three days after the convention ended, the Communists stirred up trouble in Honan, Hupei, Anhwei, Hunan, Kiangsi, and Fukien. On May 25, T'ang Shao-i of Kwangtung circulated a telegram demanding Chiang step down from the political scene. On May 27, sixteen notables including T'ang and Wang Ching-wei held the Extraordinary Conference of the Central Executive and Supervisory Committees [Chung-yang chih-ch'en wei-yuan-hui fei-ch'ang hui-i] in Canton. On the next day, with the support of Li Tsung-jen from Kwangsi, they installed a military government [*Chün cheng-fu*] in Canton to show their defiance of the Nanking government. These acts were related in various ways to Chiang's arrest of Hu. Provincial sovereignty was another issue because these oppositionists were mostly Kwangtung people.[26] The alienation of Kwangtung meant the breakup and setback of the party and our inability to make our national goals a reality.

On December 15, 1931, at the Central Committee's provisional meeting, Chiang reluctantly resigned from the chairmanship of the National government [council], presidency of the Executive Yüan, and as commander in chief of the army, navy, and air force. As I mentioned above, Chiang simply had made too many enemies and thus for the second time was forced to step down at the peak of his powers. He promised to leave for Ningpo and then go on to Hangchou for rest. He appealed to those in Kwangtung Province to unite with the nation and assist our mother country.[27]

As head of the Organization Department of the Kuomintang, I was still busy working with other comrades at the central level to find solutions to save the nation, and so I remained in Nanking and did not go with Chiang.

On December 27, the provisional central government of the Chinese Soviet republic openly proclaimed its aim to overthrow our National government, and the following day Lin Shen was elected as the chairman of the National government council and Sun Fo was our new premier. Meanwhile, the Japanese Kwantung Army had fomented the September Eighteenth Incident in Mukden and invaded many of northeastern China's major cities and towns. Beset with internal troubles and foreign invasion, China now faced great peril.

CHAPTER FIVE

Between Two Japanese Attacks

SPRING 1932–SUMMER 1937

My Calamities

BY THE TIME I BEGAN TO SERVE in the National government, the Chinese aviation industry was off and running. I had the chance to fly on business. Air travel presented more dangers than today, but each time I landed safely. Could this be divine providence, and was I being "unexpectedly saved from a perilous situation"?

In early January 1932 I first encountered personal danger in the sky. Chinese Communists were stirring up trouble in Honan, Hupei, Anhwei, Kiangsi, and Fukien provinces, while the Japanese Kwantung Army, having occupied Mukden, pushed onward to take Changchün and was closing in on Jehol Province. Our national trouble deepened from domestic subversion and foreign aggression. After a peace conference had been called in Shanghai, delegates from both Nanking and Kwangtung went to Hangchou to meet with Chiang for advice about the nation's new difficulties. Chiang had now retired from active political life. The Central Executive Committee then reconvened and decided to invite Chiang to return to the government. I was ordered to fly to Hangchou to see Chiang, present him the committee's request, and urge him to return immediately to deal with the national crisis.

The airplane I took was a two-seat trainer, with the pilot in front and me in the backseat. The cockpit had no cover. As my mission was urgent, the last available training airplane was assigned to fly me to Hangchou. The pilot's name was Shih Man-liu.

Before the plane approached Chien-chiao Airfield in Hangchou, the sky suddenly clouded over, followed by lightning and thunder. Soon a torrential rain fell. The raindrops striking my face brought pain. The sky was dark with flashes of lightning. Looking down, we could not see the ground. Both the pilot and I were terrified because the fuel gauge now registered empty. We luckily found an opening in the clouds and made an emergency landing. After we touched ground, I asked the pilot, "What if we had not succeeded in landing?" He replied with fear still clouding his face, "We only had fuel for five minutes of circling. After that, the plane would have dropped and we would both be dead!"

Shortly after my terrifying experience in the sky, my cousin Ch'en Hsien-fu, the eldest son of my second uncle, Ch'i-mei, left Shanghai for Hangchou to sign up for the Air Force Academy entrance examination. Hsien-fu was an impulsive person and full of patriotism. Incensed by the September Eighteenth Incident, he made up his mind to enroll in the Air Force Academy. No one in the family could dissuade him.

It so happened that Shih Man-liu, the instructor who piloted the trainer, was on the same train sitting across the table. They struck up a conversation, and Shih learned that he was my cousin and told him about his piloting me to Hangchou. The two naturally became friendly.

Shih told my cousin that he was a senior instructor in the air force and would be willing to accompany him to the academy. After they had arrived at Chien-chiao, Shih took my cousin Hsien-fu on one of his training rounds despite regulations that untrained cadets could not fly.

Two trainers took off at the same time, with Shih Man-liu's plane flying in front and another plane following. The propeller of the plane in the rear collided with the tail of the plane in front, causing it to lose balance and crash. Both my cousin and Shih lost their lives.

After the tragedy, I felt as though Shih Man-liu had cursed my family, as if he had demanded payment of a debt, and that tragedy was simply fate! While I was lucky to have escaped my doom, my cousin could not escape meeting him on the train. It was like the saying "the road of a wrongdoer is narrow—he is sure to be found out." When I think about my cousin and me both flying with Shih Man-liu, a chill still passes over me and I marvel at how fate determines a man's destiny.

During my life I have rarely been superstitious. One time, however, on a return trip from the United States, I took the maiden flight of China National Airlines to China.

Before the trip, friends advised me not to take the maiden flight because it might be dangerous. I was not moved and was determined to take my wife along as we had planned. When we stopped at Hawaii for refueling, many overseas friends and relatives came to the airport to welcome us. While descending the plane, my wife lost her balance, fell, and injured her ankle. We were forced to change planes for a later flight to Shanghai.

When one leaves home, unexpected things can happen. Luck or misfortune are determined in a single instant. Such an episode makes one wonder whether our fate is indeed prearranged by certain unknown forces.

The Land Commission

The fourth plenary session of the Fourth National Congress of the Central Executive Committee was held in January 1934,[1] and Kuo-fu and I, along with others, reported on our party's land reform policy.[2] The many proposals on the land problem and the National Economic Commission's proposal submitted to the Central Political Committee in February of the same year were then debated in the Central Political Committee. The committee resolved that: (1) the Land Commission be formed by the National Economic Commission, the Ministry of Interior Affairs, and the Ministry of Finance. That commission would make a systematic survey of land in different provinces and municipalities within six months and then present recommendations for the Central Political Committee to appraise and decide. (2) All proposals regarding the land question submitted by the Fourth Congress of the Central Executive Committee and the National Economic Commission were to be assembled and studied by the commission. In August of the same year, the Central Political Committee at its 419th meeting recommended that I become director of the Land Commission. I was then thirty-four years old.

The commission's task was gigantic, being responsible for a nation consisting of twenty-two provinces and more than eight hundred counties. The commission worked a year and three months on a natural land survey. More than a thousand Kuomintang members were mobilized to go to the countryside to survey the land. The commission was short of funds and unable to purchase mechanical calculators, so we borrowed some twenty calculators from different government agencies at night when not in use and returned them the next morning. If done today, we would use computers and we would not have depended on such primitive means of calculation. But in our case, spirit won over matter [*Chin-shen chung-yü wu-chih*] as shown by our achievements.

The majority of the commission's staff, whether working inside the office or out in the field, were government employees. They received no additional pay but a small allowance for expenses. They worked hard round the clock because they knew the task had to be completed to produce a satisfactory land policy. To serve the people, "the equalization of landownership" had been proposed by Sun Yat-sen during the earlier days of his revolutionary career. After thirty-three years, the Kuomintang had only begun to initiate the basic statistical survey work to begin revamping the land laws. It was long overdue. Furthermore, a Japanese invasion appeared imminent, and the party was giving maximum effort, day and night, to preparing military resistance, so that less attention was provided to improve the people's economic livelihood. When the war of resistance against Japan began, we had to ignore the land problem, and because half the country's land had fallen into enemy hands, we could do little anyway. The meddling of white imperialism actually gave red imperialism an opportunity to rob the people of all land under the guise of "land reformers." Sun Yat-sen's goals of "land to the tiller" and "equalizing landownership" simply could not be achieved. In retrospect, I wish to record that all reports and government documents show that the land survey efforts of National government in Chekiang in 1928–1930 did not meet rural family resistance. Peasants were cooperative. I believe it is unfair to state that the Kuomintang did not pay attention to the needs of rural areas or that we betrayed Sun Yat-sen's Principle of Livelihood [*Min-sheng chu-i*]. Circumstances prevented us from implementing our land program. Once the victory over Japan was in sight, the Sixth Kuomintang Congress, which was convened on May 14, 1945, introduced outlines of land policy [*Tu-ti cheng-t'se kang-ling*]. We hoped we could accomplish Sun Yat-sen's law of land reform after the war was won.

The failure to enact Sun's land policy truly embarrassed the Kuomintang. We sincerely believed that if the tiller cannot have land, he will not increase his output even under threat of force. Who is to say that people who live every day on the brink of starvation will not risk their lives to overthrow such a regime? Today, we still call for China's national unity under the doctrine of the Three People's Principles and that can only mean "land to the tiller," which is an incentive for peasants to rise up, take back their land, and launch a revolution to overthrow the communist regime.

Wang Ching-wei's Narrow Escape

In 1935, Wang Ching-wei had two posts: president of the Executive Yüan and foreign minister of the National government. Wang assigned his deputy T'ang Yu-jen and a department head, Kao Chung-wu, to deal with an expected Japanese invasion. One day, I visited our Japanese specialist, Tai Ch'i-tao, to ask advice for coping with Japan's aggression. Tai had conceived of an overall strategy designed to change Japan's attitudes toward China.

I asked Tai if he would go to Japan to convince senior officials that the Soviet Union was working behind the scenes to provoke a Sino-Japanese war. If such a war started, both sides would lose while the Soviet Union would benefit. Tai smiled and said: "This is a very difficult task. If those in charge of our foreign affairs have no intention of sending an envoy to Japan, who will volunteer for this important assignment?"

Upon hearing this remark, I realized that Tai was willing to go but that the Foreign Ministry had no plan to send him. So I visited Wang and presented my proposal: The Soviet Union wanted to provoke a war between Japan and China because its objectives were to break the Axis powers' alliance and to remove the risk of being attacked on both the eastern and western fronts. To counter that strategy, we should give Japan an incentive to advance to the North rather than to the West. When the two powers began fighting they would weaken each other, and that would minimize the threat of a possible Sino-Japanese war.

But Wang believed Japan could not be persuaded to alter its plans to advance westward, and he was unwilling to consider my suggestions. I was so disappointed that I made no mention of Tai. I now realized that Wang was not a great statesman after all. To bring about drastic change, one needed great ideals and a daring resolve to succeed. If Wang only relied upon people like T'ang Yu-jen, who merely secured advantages by exchanging small favors, then a war between China and Japan was inevitable.

As the war rapidly approached, China suffered unending internal troubles and foreign aggression. Matters of vital importance needed discussion, and a plenary session of the party congress was convened.[3] Before the opening ceremony we first went to Sun Yat-sen's mausoleum to pay homage and then back to the Kuomintang headquarters to prepare for the meetings, after which time group pictures were to be taken. On November 1, 1935, when photos were being taken to commemorate the start of the sixth plenary session of the Central Executive Committee of the Fourth National Congress, an assassin suddenly started shooting at Wang Ching-wei. A bullet entered Wang's back. Although severely wounded, fortunately he was not killed. Guards killed the assassin, a news agency reporter, on the spot. A body search revealed an entrance permit belonging to a man named Sun Feng-ming, which had been issued to the Morning Light News Agency [Shen-kuang t'ung-hsin-she]. With the suspect dead, investigations proved difficult.

Oddly, Chiang was not at the picture taking. Many suspected a political assassination, arguing it had been instigated by war advocates angry with Wang Ching-wei's weak diplomacy. Then Wang's wife, Ch'en Pi-chün by maiden name, publicly asked at Kuomintang headquarters why Chiang Kai-shek was not at the picture taking. This accusation set off rumors, which caused political instability. Chiang was absent at the picture taking because he felt ill and had returned to Kuomintang headquarters directly from Sun's mausoleum, but the unexpected event was just too coincidental to allow for that rational explanation.

That evening, Chiang called me in and told me that this case must be immediately investigated and solved to dispel rumors and prevent the political situation from worsening. He asked me how many days I would need to break the case. I already had ordered Hsu En-tseng and Tai Li to launch an investigation. We had no clues because the assassin was dead and the news agency no longer existed, but I daringly promised Chiang the case would be resolved in a week's time.

As soon as I left his office, I launched an inquiry of those persons who had sponsored Sun Feng-ming's Kuomintang membership. Anyone connected with that action was questioned. We finally arrested Sun's coconspirators Ho Pu-Kuang, Chang Ming-yin, and others in the vicinity of Chenkiang, and they confessed to plotting to kill Wang. This was the first time I had linked a party member to his sponsors to break a case. Kuomintang headquarters set up a special subcommittee of inquiry, and Ch'en Pi-chün was a member. We handed the prisoners over to the subcommittee for interrogation. The conspirators were members of Wang's clique who were enraged by Wang's abandoning them after his rise in the political arena. Now that the truth had come out, the storm subsided. Just when the entire nation should unite to counter foreign invasion, we were threatened by an incident that might have precipitated civil war. Luckily, I was able to clear up this case in only five days so that Chiang's name was cleared. For this Chiang expressed his appreciation to me.

Letter from Chou En-lai

While preparing to resist Japanese aggression, the faculty and student body of the Central Political Institute [Chung-yang cheng-chih hsüeh-hsiao] unanimously decided to move the institute from Nanking to Lushan in Kiangsi Province, then to Chih-kiang in Hunan Province, and finally to a hot spring named Nan-wen-ch'üan on the outskirts of Chungking. When the institute was being transferred to Lushan, Dean Ting Wei-fen resigned. Chiang appointed me acting dean. While the institute was in Lushan, I lectured six hours to students on the Three People's Principles. A few days later the generalissimo ordered me to Sinkiang, ending my acting deanship of the institute. Chiang had reasons to send me to Sinkiang. Long before the war of resistance, he had wanted me to accomplish two things: First, he wanted me to talk with the Chinese Communists to obtain a joint declaration that our common goal was to resist Japan if war with Japan should occur. Second, he wanted me to negotiate with the Soviet Union to ensure that, should the Sino-Japanese war occur, the Soviets would support National China.

Negotiations with the Chinese Communists were undertaken secretly because we did not want the Japanese to know lest they start the war earlier. During the anticommunist campaign in September 1935, when our troops were encircling the remnants of communist troops, Chou En-lai began inciting students to demand that the National government resist Japan's aggression. Even Chang Hsüeh-liang admonished the National government for not fighting Japan, and he tried to make Chiang appear as the nonresistant general [*Pu-ti-k'ang chiang-chün*], a title he had earned when he had unceremoniously relinquished his authority over the Northeast. Chiang, however, had long been actively preparing for war. His tactic was to gain time and to speak lightly of national sacrifices until war actually came. When it did come, he did not intend to be idle. Chou En-lai feared that Yenan and its areas might risk being overrun by the Japanese. He wrote a letter to Kuo-fu and me expressing his hope that if we called off our campaign of suppressing the Communists, they would be willing to obey and follow the leadership of the National government and join in the fight against Japan. This letter was forwarded through Hong Kong by Huang Hua-piao and Tseng Yang-fu; a translation of the original text follows:

Messrs. Kuo-fu and Li-fu:
Since we parted company ten years ago, our nation's crisis has worsened. Newspapers report that you are planning to ally with Russia. Although such reports may be only rumors, your recent way of thinking is quite obvious. Mr. Huang [Hua-piao] just came from Chin-ling [Nanking], and I have learned that Mr. [Tseng] Yang-fu's plans are actually in the minds of men of wisdom [my elder brother, Kuo-fu, and I],[4] calling out for echoes from afar. I can see that the atmosphere in Nanking today is far different now than in the past. For many years my party [Chinese Communist party] made similar appeals. Now, with the encouragement of both of you, cooperation between our two parties will again be possible. With this single action, our national crisis definitely will take a turn for the better.
It is already well known that the invaders [Japanese] are penetrating deeper, and their puppet troops [of Manchukuo] have recently overrun Sui-yuan [Province]. Japan has even set up its air force headquarters in Camp Ting-yuan. The Northwest is in danger of falling at any moment, but the Kuomintang troops and the communist troops are still fighting each other. This state of affairs not only is pleasing to the enemy of our nation, but saps our national strength and will destroy both of us. Ever since our First Army reached the Northwest, our side has repeatedly asked for a cease-fire. Our Second and Fourth Army have now entered Shensi and Kansu from the north. Their goal is only to join forces in fighting against Japan, because to defend the Northwest is to defend China. Our side now takes this opportunity to send an official letter to your party Central [Executive Committee], stating our general policy and expressing our sincerity in wishing to establish collaboration between our two parties. We hope a new path will thus be open to facilitate the preservation of our nation and resisting foreign aggression. Because both of you are highly placed in the center of your party [Kuomintang] and are close to Mr. Chiang, I implore

朱天山先生：

岂本十年，国难日亟。据我山先生有鉴诚之举，谁肯道路传闻，甚之乃窥见山先生最近趋向。董君远金陵来，知朱甫先生的军刮分，正为贤者所注目，特为应逸，想见军中今以之空气之非若此。故连年不顾，何以山先生为之振导，使山先生亦应合作。国难好机，实非此一举。近来介入盖深，修军侵略，已成事实……年航空经济互实误於军连营，西北……桓叠一新，窃谓救速杆雅为计。

……尤其继在旦夕，乃西与此军既好放对，此不惜为者於说之机之顺且互消国力，自遂其志。故方且一方面军刮西北源之敌作战，安成今之西山方西军此之北人陕甘。其目的合於会会处。盖任之中央公西，表示此意。故方以杆路连卖意，合作之希望为诚厚，以冀救已藥难，得阙新经。山先生为者定十框，为屏生，又记切无间，尚请更进一言，立停军事行动，实行联诚援共，一致扶已列氏，从璧一新，窃谓雄扶，溪杆雅为计。

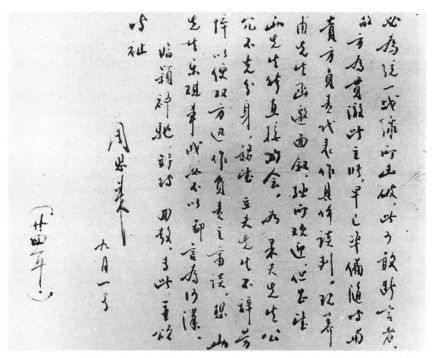

(*on facing page and above*) Chou En-lai's three-page letter to my elder brother, Kuo-fu, and me, September 1, 1935.

you to advise him to cease military action at once and to unite with the Soviet Union and with the Chinese Communist party to fight against Japan on a common front. Such efforts will revitalize anew our nation. In spite of the cunningness of the Japanese bandits and those venomous traitors, I can speak with certainty that they will be destroyed by our united front. Now that Mr. Yang-fu has written to invite me to meet with you, I welcome this occasion and hope that the two of you will attend in person. If Mr. Kuo-fu cannot spare his time from his busy schedule, I hope at least Mr. Li-fu will be present so that both sides can enter into responsible negotiations. I believe you both want this to be a success and will not dismiss my suggestions as nonsense.

Wishing for a speedy reply, I am,

Sincerely yours,
Chou En-lai
September 1st

(Received in September, the 24th year [1935] of the republic)

Negotiations with the Chinese Communists began in the earlier part of

1936. Our side was represented by Chang Ch'ung and me, and the communist representative was Chou En-lai. Because these negotiations required the presence of the Third Communist International, Pan Han-nien participated.[5] Before they would agree to come to Shanghai, these two representatives first requested our guarantee of their safety. Chang Ch'ung contended that if we accepted the Communists' surrender in principle and halted our attacks, the Communists would agree to any conditions we demanded. If a Japanese invasion of China occurred, that would give them an opportunity to survive. But they could go back on their word any time, and by then we would be so engaged in war with Japan that we might find it difficult to suppress the Communists should they not fight the Japanese.

We knew how their minds worked, and they knew how we would react. They had never kept their promises, and deception was their strong point. But in order to show the world that the entire nation was united in its effort to resist Japan in case the war became a matter of necessity, we proposed they issue a joint declaration in which four points were to be included:[6]

1. The Chinese Communist party will strive to fulfill completely Dr. Sun's San Min Chu I [Three People's Principles], which is most suited for China's needs today.

2. The Chinese Communist party will abolish its policy of sabotage and sovietization, which aims at overthrowing the National government, and will stop the forcible confiscation of landlord property.

3. The Chinese Communist party will abolish all existing soviets and allow democratic government, so as to achieve unified political administration throughout the country.

4. The Chinese Communist party will abolish the name and insignia of the Red Army, which will be reorganized as the National Revolutionary Army and subject to control by the government's Military Commission to make ready to fight the Japanese.

The Chinese Communists naturally agreed to these four principles. At our invitation, Chou and Pan came to Nanking. I went to talk with them in person, which put them at ease. After a number of talks, we reached a general agreement on the language and terms of the joint proclamation. Chou En-lai then wanted to report back to Yenan. I directed Chang Ch'ung to accompany him to Sian and to see Chang Hsüeh-liang on the way. I calculated that Chou would tell Chang Hsüeh liang about the agreement, which would restrain Chang from making brash statements about resisting Japan and restrain his military forces. Pan remained in Nanking and Shanghai to continue the negotiations.

Only a few days later, on December 12, 1936, the Sian Incident began. Chang Ch'ung and Chou En-lai were then in Sian, but we who were not in Sian were in the dark as to what was actually taking place. For the testimony of history, here I would like to record that on September 22, 1937, the Chinese Communist party did make known to the public a communiqué entitled Together We Confront the National Crisis [*Kung-fu kuo-nan hsüan-yen*]. The above-mentioned four points were clearly stated. From then on, the Communists, who had no true desire to fight the Japanese, were only interested in expanding their military strength.

Negotiations with the Soviet Union

From Chou En-lai's letter, Kuo-fu, Chiang, and I immediately knew that the Chinese Communists were acting under Soviet direction. We believed that Soviet policy was the following: (1) destroy the alliance of the Axis powers (Germany, Japan, Italy); (2) encourage a Sino-Japanese war in the East and a German-Franco war in the West so as to enable the Soviet Union to remain neutral without adversaries on either side; (3) cooperate with Chiang in order to get him to stand up to Japan without worrying about his internal troubles. Therefore, I was instructed to conduct negotiations with both the Chinese Communists and the Soviet Union.

On Christmas Eve 1935, Chiang sent me to the Soviet Union for secret talks. I had never engaged in diplomacy before and I felt quite apprehensive. Chiang gave me guidelines and insisted that I travel in absolute secrecy. Bearing a passport with the false name of Li Fu-cheng, Chang Ch'ung, alias Kiang Yung-ch'ing, and I boarded the German ship SS *Potsdam*. On the same ship were Ambassador Ch'eng T'ien-fang and his entourage, traveling to their post in Germany. In the second-class cabins there were some twenty-odd students from the School of Submarine Warfare [Tien-lei hsüeh-hsiao] who had attended my lectures and were going to Germany for advanced study. In the ten-odd days of voyage between Shanghai and Marseilles, it was almost impossible to keep my mission secret, but I managed to do so after some detailed planning. The only person aware of our presence on board was Ambassador Ch'eng T'ien-fang, but he made no contact with us. As the ship passed through Hong Kong, Bangkok, Benin, Singapore, Ceylon, the Suez Canal, and Egypt, finally reaching Marseilles in France, there were eight checkpoints along the way. At each checkpoint, the passengers were required to appear on deck to answer roll call. Although I wore dark glasses as a disguise, my gray hair was difficult to conceal, so I feigned sickness, stayed in the cabin, and had meals sent by room service.

At each port, all passengers were required to go on deck to be inspected, which usually took more than a half an hour. In order not to reveal myself during these inspections, I asked Chang Ch'ung to stand at the head of the first row; then, after being called, he took my passport and stood at the last row to be the last one called. In this way I avoided revealing my identity because the inspectors were usually too tired to inspect all personnel by the end of taking roll.

Whenever we docked at a new port, we waited until all the other passengers had gone ashore, and then we left the ship; we usually returned to the ship after only a quick sight-seeing tour. In Singapore, Benin, and Ceylon, we went ashore to see the sights and never encountered any fellow passengers. In this way, we managed to keep our identities secret and finally arrived in Egypt. During this period, Ambassador Ch'eng kept in touch with me only by ship telephone. When we arrived at Marseilles, the inspection was more elaborate. We were all gathered in a big hall where our passports were examined. Again I asked Chang Ch'ung to go first and I waited until the last, at which time everyone had become exhausted, and so I passed inspection easily. We returned to our cabin, tipped the room attendant, and asked him to direct us to a travel agent. Then we quietly boarded the night train for Berlin. From beginning to end we had never revealed our true identities.

Arriving in Berlin, Ambassador Ch'eng went to the embassy to assume his post. Under Hitler's rule, Germany was full of secret agents and we were concerned about our safety. Chiang cabled us to lie low in Berlin and wait for instructions for an appropriate time to travel to the Soviet Union. All cables were forwarded by Ambassador Ch'eng, and one read: "Too early yet. Go first to France, Switzerland, Italy." In each country we stayed in the best hotels in order to avoid attention because no Chinese would check into a deluxe hotel. We usually stayed in the hotel during the day and went out only in the evenings to night clubs or movies. Therefore, we never encountered anyone we knew.

We later traveled to Hungary and Czechoslovakia, where we also checked into the most expensive hotels. Our ambassador was Liang Lung, who must have wondered about these two Chinese, Li and Kiang, and why they did not register at the embassy. After some checking he found out that the two Chinese were only passing through and about to leave soon. At that time, an international fair was being held, and China had sent a delegation to participate. He invited us to dinner. Not wishing to reveal our identities but not wanting to be discourteous by refusing his invitation, I sent Chang Ch'ung to dinner and asked Ambassador Liang to convey my thanks with an excuse that I was ill. Since the ambassador did not recognize Chang Ch'ung, our secret was intact. We then moved to another hotel to conceal our whereabouts. We again received cabled instructions asking us to delay our plans. So we went back to Marseilles where we ran into a Chinese, Feng Ti, who had graduated from Whampoa Military Academy's first class. I told him to keep quiet: "We have a secret mission. You must not tell anyone. If this news is leaked, you will be fully responsible!" We then traveled to Hungary, Yugoslavia, Austria, and other minor countries in Europe before we returned to Hungary to await instructions.

One day Ho Yao-tsu, Chinese ambassador to Turkey, came to Hungary and told us that the "situation was not favorable. We hear Japan learned of Generalissimo Chiang sending Ch'en Li-fu to the Soviet Union, and the Soviets are very uneasy for fear this information would provoke the Axis powers to attack them. So Generalissimo Chiang has instructed me to tell you there is no need to go to the Soviet Union." Our mission to Moscow had been canceled.

While I was abroad, newspaper accounts of all Central Executive Committee meetings never mentioned my presence, and that aroused some suspicion. I had fortunately prepared more than ten letters, all written with my own hand, to be posted by my wife in Hangchou to tell Nanking friends and relatives that I was recuperating in Hangchou from illness. A letter would be mailed every few days as a ruse to keep my mission secret. But Japan spread rumors that I had been sent to the Soviet Union, which caused the Soviets to worry about the Axis powers. Chiang was forced to change his plans and ordered me to return and conduct negotiations with Soviet ambassador Bogomoloff in Nanking. To avoid attention, Chang Ch'ung and I returned home separately, I by way of Vienna, Yugoslavia, and Greece to cross the sea to Haifa. I then took the Dutch KLM flight from Gaza to Singapore, where I boarded a freighter for Shanghai, not realizing that the freighter, after docking at Hong Kong, was ordered to sail first to Japan to load coal. At the port in Japan, I was lucky not to be detected by the Japanese customs officers. If discovered, I would have found it difficult to explain myself to the Japanese.[7]

In 1936, I conducted talks with Soviet ambassador Dimitri Bogomoloff in Nanking in the hope that the Soviet Union would sign a military alliance with us to deter Japan.[8] Bogomoloff feared that, should Japan attack China, the Soviet Union, bound by this agreement, was required to assist us in fighting Japan; if that was the case, Japan could ally with Germany to invade the Soviet Union. The Soviet Union wanted to avoid being attacked on both sides, so Bogomoloff considered a military alliance with China too risky. Our talks did not proceed as we had expected. We then discussed the signing of a mutual nonaggression pact. While talking, I once asked Bogomoloff, "Which China would be more advantageous to the Soviet Union, a China of Three People's Principles or a China of communism?" The ambassador appeared surprised at my question and stated that the latter would be more to the Soviet liking. I said: "You are wrong. Only Three People's Principles can be communism's best friend. Just imagine a nation of 500 million people, once communized, would it still take orders from a nation of 200 million people?" Bogomoloff seemed disturbed and passed on my words to his government.

Later, our talks returned to the substance of military aid. The reason we really wanted to sign a nonaggression pact with the Soviet Union was to discourage that government from aiding the Chinese Communists during a Sino-Japanese war. Although I conducted negotiations between China and the Soviet Union, the Sino-Soviet Treaty of Nonaggression was signed by Foreign Minister Wang Chung-hui on August 21, 1937, in Nanking and remained in force for a period of five years with a two-year extension.[9] The attack on Pearl Harbor on December 7, 1941, changed the entire situation, but the Soviet Union kept its commitment to us. The most important section of the treaty was Article Two: "In the event that the Contracting Parties should be subject to aggression by one or more third Powers, the other Contracting Party is obligated not to render assistance of any kind, either directly or indirectly, to such third Power or Powers at any time during the entire conflict, and to refrain from taking any action or entering into any agreement which may be used by the aggressor or aggressors to the disadvantage of the party subjected to aggression."

While negotiations were going on, we realized the Soviets hoped the war would be fought only between Japan and us or between Germany and France, so the Soviet Union could avoid involvement. The Soviets' objective was so obvious that we knew that if we asked for military aid, they would not refuse. We hoped that during the advent of war, the Soviets would continue to support us with all kinds of weapons, such as airplanes, tanks, antiaircraft artillery, and cannons. We gave them a detailed list of the weapons and their amounts and when we expected delivery. We knew that, once war had broken out, the coastal ports would no longer be available and that the only passageway to the Soviet Union was through Sinkiang Province. I was later sent to Sinkiang to discuss with Governor Sheng Shih-tsai how to transport gasoline and store it at intervals to supply our troops without delay. During our negotiations, we also asked the Soviets to stop supplying the Chinese Communist party with arms because we did not want to "be attacked from the front and rear." My insistence upon this demand perhaps prevented them from helping the Chinese Communists during the war. Then the Soviets, on April 13, 1941, suddenly signed a mutual nonaggression pact with Japan as well.[10] That action, along with our policy mistakes in dealing with the guerrillas, helped strengthen the Chinese Communists. Moreover, the Soviets went back on their word to us and assisted the Chinese Communists near the end of the war. Here I can say that owing to the Treaty of Nonaggression in 1937, the Soviet Union granted us three loans totaling $250 million in 1937, 1938, and 1939, at a low interest rate of 3 percent. By the end of 1939, they had given us approximately one thousand planes, two thousand pilots,[11] and five hundred military advisers. The United States, in contrast, from 1942 to the end of the war in 1945, provided China with only $500 million in credits. Of the $50 billion in lend-lease the United States dispensed, China only received $26 million in 1941 and $210 million in 1946, eventually coming to a total of U.S.$1.54 billion, or less than 3 percent of the total amount. The U.S. policy was "Europe First, Asia Second."[12]

The Sian Incident

About six or seven days before the Sian Incident,[13] I had received instructions to allow Chou En-lai to pass through Sian on his way back to Yenan. As I stated in the previous paragraphs, Chang Ch'ung was to accompany him to Sian and meet with Chang Hsüeh-liang to discuss our negotiations and reassure him that the National government was determined to fight Japan. We did not want Chang to use the concept of resisting Japan as an excuse to maintain his military strength. For that reason, Chou and Chang Ch'ung were in Sian when the incident occurred.

The National government convened an urgent meeting the night of the incident [December 12, 1936] and made these recommendations: (1) Severely condemn Chang Hsüeh-liang and Yang Hu-cheng; China's long history had taught us that whenever a head of state was abducted, he was invariably executed if the government appeared weak to respond. The National government decided to send armed forces. (2) Designate Ho Ying-ch'in to take command of the forces and make a speedy attack. (3) To take other measures to rescue Chiang.

I discussed the third point with Tseng Yang-fu and asked Tu Tung-sun to rush to Shanghai at once to fetch Pan Han-nien back to Nanking. The next day I told Pan to cable the Third International the following: "The behavior of the rebellious Chang [Hsüeh-liang] and Yang [Hu-cheng] in abducting Generalissimo Chiang has been condemned by the military and the people of the entire nation. If anything should happen to the generalissimo, China will be without a leader to fight Japan and the Japanese army could easily occupy China. This will not benefit the Soviet Union. The National government is taking a stern attitude in coping with this situation."

Another cable was sent the next day: "Hope you have received yesterday's cable. If Comrade Chou En-lai is still in Sian, please cable him immediately and order Comrades Mao Tse-tung and Chou En-lai to persuade Chang and Yang to spare Generalissimo Chiang. Such a step will be helpful to both China and the Soviet Union."

Since I had Pan's secret code in my possession, I used the secret code for both cables and they were directly transmitted from Nanking to Moscow.

The following day the Third International replied: "Two cables from Comrade Pan Han-nien received. Suggestions agreeable. Orders to do same already cabled to Comrades Mao Tse-tung and Chou En-lai."

I felt more at ease after receiving this cable. When Chiang finally returned to Nanking, I accompanied him from the airport to his official residence at the central military academy. Chiang called me in while he was in bed. I could not wait to ask, "How was Chou En-lai's attitude in Sian?" The reply: "Very good." Then I suggested, "The government forces are already there, perhaps we can take this advantage to attack Yenan." Chiang, his head bent over, did not answer. Seeing he was tired, I hurried off. I was pleased that the two cables of Pan Han-nien's had borne fruitful results.

The Japanese Parliamentary Delegation

In the spring of 1937 a fifteen-member delegation of Japanese parliamentarians came to Nanking and insisted that they see me. I received them with a tea party in my residence on Ch'ang-fu Street, Nanking. After exchanging a few words of greetings I asked: "Why are you gentlemen so anxious to see me? Is it because the newspapers have reported I am the one most strongly advocating resisting Japan?"

This caused them to smile. I then continued: "My strong anticommunist stand is well known to all. Now that I am also strong in my anti-Japan stand, doesn't that make me a man of overwhelming arrogance? I want to take this opportunity to tell you gentlemen that my anticommunist stand is based on a rational point of view in which I believe communism is absolutely unsuitable for China. As for my anti-Japan stand, your country does not treat us as brotherly neighbors. Your bullying leaves us with no choice but to defend ourselves. So my anti-Japan stand is emotional but not rational. If China and Japan do not realize that the Soviet Union is driving a wedge between us, then we are really bringing troubles upon ourselves. I predict the outcome of a Sino-Japanese war, so please take note." Some of the visitors actually took out their notebooks and recorded what I said.

"Your country will be controlled by capitalists while China will be ruled by Communists. Both sides will lose, and neither side will gain. So I hope you gentlemen will exert your influence to stop your young military men from being exploited by another country. Do not deceive yourselves and others. I also ask you to read Sun Yat-sen's speech on 'Pan Asianism,' which he delivered at Kobe November 28, 1924. If after reading that, you see clearly the paths China and Japan should take, I shall consider myself very lucky."

I knew very well that a few legislators like this delegation could do little about the brashness and recklessness of Japan's young military leaders. But I thought they should at least be aware of the future consequences. After the war, Japan broke an espionage case and discovered that the young military men were actually being encouraged by the Soviet Union to invade China. By then it was too late, and a great wrong had been perpetrated.

In 1961 when I passed through Japan in my travels, the Speaker of the House entertained me and my wife at a dinner at his residence, to which was also invited Ts'ai Meng-chien. I told of my speech to the Japanese delegation before the war. He heaved a sigh, saying: "That was fate. No such errors should ever be committed again."

CHAPTER SIX

The War of Resistance against Japan

AUTUMN 1937—SUMMER 1945

July 7, 1937

THE NATIONAL GOVERNMENT DECIDED to engage in the war of resistance the day after the July Seventh Incident, 1937.[1] That day I arrived at the Organization Department of the Kuomintang headquarters to find a dozen Chinese and foreign reporters waiting in my office. As soon as an American newsman saw me, he quickly asked me in a surprised manner, "There is such a disparity in strength between China and Japan, how can you repel Japan?" I said: "You Americans ought to know your history. According to your way of thinking, America would still be a British colony. When Washington touched off the French and Indian War in the Ohio Valley in 1754 he only had a few pistols and rifles, which were no match for the weapons of British soldiers. Washington relied on the will of the people, and this is a powerful but invisible force, superior even to guns. With the people behind him, he won the final victory. Today, as we face Japanese aggression, the entire Chinese nation is fighting back. Generalissimo Chiang's decision only follows the will of the people. The question today, therefore, is not 'whether we can fight' but 'whether we ought to fight.' If we ought to fight, then we must fight to the last man. America's War of Independence finally succeeded with the assistance of France. Who knows if our war with Japan might bring help from other countries? There is a saying that 'A just cause garners abundant support.' You gentlemen are wrong to assess us only by our material strength. You must realize that spiritual and moral strength are far more important than material strength. The Northern Expedition of a decade ago was the most recent example showing that we can win against heavy odds."

In the war of resistance, the military asked me to organize a military engineering corps [*Chün-shih kung-tso t'uan*] whose mission was to build a pillbox line between Liu-ho and Chia-ting to prevent the Japanese forces from advancing westward. The Japanese quickly occupied Shanghai and were ready to move westward to attack Nanking. To block their forces, we needed a strong defense line supported by machine guns.[2] Some time earlier, I had gathered a group of engineers from Nanking and Shanghai to form the Learning Society for the Study of Sun Yat-sen's International Development of China [Kuo-fu shih-yeh chi-hua yen-chiü hsüeh-hui], with the objective of estimating the number of engineers for each industrial project of Sun's development plan. We formed a military engineering corps with myself as its head. We speedily completed the national defense line project, but it was regrettable that the military did not use the pillboxes. We had worked hard to build them and at the risk of our lives, but they were soon overrun by the Japanese.

In his book *China's Destiny* [*Chung-kuo chih ming-yün*], Chiang mentioned Sun's industrial development plan, and he too suggested that the engineering projects be studied, such as the length of railroads and highways, the quantity of electric wires required, and how many engineers and workers were required to complete the projects. The charts listed in his book were produced by members of the Chinese Engineers Society, which already had made that appraisal. This society is still active and deserves praise. At its annual meetings, I am honored to be invited to participate and give lectures on special topics.

Mission to Sinkiang

Why did Chiang send me to Sinkiang in 1937? I had known Sheng Shih-tsai ever since the Northern Expedition. His appointment as governor of Sinkiang Province did not occur until April 2, 1940.[3] While he was still a young military officer on the general staff and I was a section chief of the Northern Expedition headquarters on the Northern Expedition, Sheng had observed me marching during the day and then working as soon as we stopped. He knew that no one worked as hard as I did, and he admired my energy. Not long afterward, he went to Sinkiang and defeated Chin Shu-jen, then leader of Sinkiang. He took over Chin's place, and became Sinkiang's top leader. Sheng Shih-tsai telegraphed Chiang to request the National government to send me and Chi Shih-ying, a senior member of the Legislative Yüan. I was working in the Organization Department, and Chi, who had once served with Sheng in Kuo Sung-ling's insurgency group against Chang Tso-lin, was also too busy to leave. Chiang instead sent Huang Mu-sung, who possessed little knowledge about politics but happened to be Sheng Shih-tsai's former teacher. Huang spoke to newspaper reporters of "plans for Sinkiang" before leaving. A distrustful man, Sheng hoped the National government would send someone to help him after he had seized Sinkiang by force. He wanted the National government's recognition. I went to see Sheng's teacher and told him that Sheng only wanted the National government's recognition and that his conversation with reporters might mislead Sheng into believing that "the National government wanted to send you to control him." Huang replied that he had no intention of ruling Sinkiang and that he had been misquoted by reporters. Soon after he arrived, Sheng put him under house arrest. Much time elapsed before he was released.

Later, Huang Shao-hsiung and Pai Ch'ung-hsi of Kwangsi colluded with Wang Ching-wei to seize Sinkiang. Huang Shao-hsiung sent a telegram to Sheng's subordinates warning them about Chang Li-yuan, an army commander of ours who might overthrow Sheng Shih-tsai. But that telegram fell into Sheng's hands, exposing the conspiracy of Wang Ching-wei and the Kwangsi faction. Chang Li-yuan became very displeased and considered breaking with the National government. Chiang was in Kiangsi for the anticommunist campaign, so I went there to brief him on the deteriorating situation in Sinkiang. Chiang then sent a high-ranking person to carry his handwritten message to Sinkiang to appease Sheng. Only then was the Sinkiang situation stabilized.[4]

Chiang knew of my relationship with Sheng. When Sheng first wanted me, Chiang did not send me. When I reported the Sinkiang situation to Chiang, he sent another with his letter to appease Sheng. Finally, at the outbreak of the war of resistance, Chiang turned to me.

Euro-Asia Airlines flew over Sinkiang. One day, a flight carrying many German military advisers made an emergency landing in Sinkiang and was seized. The president of the Executive Yüan, Wang Ching-wei, twice telegraphed Sheng Shih-tsai to ask him to release the airliner. The requests were ignored by Sheng Shih-tsai as revenge for the treachery concocted by Wang and Huang Shao-hsiung against Sheng. In the meantime, Germany sent an ultimatum to Wang, demanding that this issue be resolved within forty-eight hours. Embarrassed and helpless, Wang politely expressed his wish to see me. He asked me to help, showed me a message already drafted in my name, and pleaded with me to sign. The day after the telegram was sent, Sheng Shih-tsai released the airliner. Sheng's kindness toward me did not escape Chiang's attention.

I had just finished negotiations with Soviet ambassador Bogomoloff. The Soviet Union wanted our war with Japan to be protracted; by remaining neutral, it could avoid attack from both the East and the West. I took this opportunity to ask the Soviets for planes, tanks, and antiaircraft artillery.

Fearing that Ambassador Bogomoloff might retract his word, I insisted that he write the numbers down in his handwriting. He finally relented. I placed his written promise in a safe place. When Chang Ch'ung was later sent to Moscow to seek weapons, their Foreign Ministry refused to oblige until Chang Ch'ung showed them the promise written in Ambassador Bogomoloff's own hand. They shipped weapons to China in batches, which had to pass through Sinkiang. Chiang, therefore, sent me to Sinkiang to talk Sheng into supplying us with fuel. I accompanied Soviet ambassador Bogomoloff, who was on his way back to Moscow on a China National Air Corporation charter plane, to Sinkiang. When the plane landed in Tihua, Sheng was at the airport to meet us along with a battalion of cavalrymen who kicked up a large cloud of dust. How impressive it was!

That day, Sheng hosted a big welcoming party for me. The Soviet ambassador and I sat on one side as honored guests. The Soviet consulate in Sinkiang then had a staff of hundreds, being many times larger than the Soviet embassy in Nanking. The Soviets wanted a foothold in Sinkiang. Sheng treated me very well and put me up in the Western Garden within the compound of the governor-general's [*tupan*] official residence, which was lavishly furnished. I learned that many executions took place in that compound. When Chin Shu-jen ruled Sinkiang from 1928 to 1933, he often invited guests to banquets to watch the executions as after-dinner entertainment; such barbarism still prevailed in the frontier regions in our time. After I settled in the Western Garden, I heard stories that the place was haunted, but I was not afraid.

Sheng treated me royally. Visitor movements in Sinkiang were restricted, but I was free to visit and give speeches anywhere. A teachers' college run by Mrs. Sheng even invited me to lecture—an unprecedented event. One day, Sheng sent me four suitcases of paper currency to use as spending money. The currency system in Sinkiang differed from China proper, where one yuan issued by the National government was worth a few thousand Sinkiang yuan. But four suitcases of paper money meant a great deal to me. If I declined to accept the money, I would have offended Sheng's feelings; if I accepted I would be accepting a bribe. So I thought of a way that proved satisfactory to both sides: I suggested that Sheng build a Sun Yat-sen Memorial Hall, and when I departed, I contributed the money for the hall's construction. Sheng was very pleased.

Our discussions on supplying us with fuel went well. He readily gave his consent. We planned to use the most ancient form of transportation to transport the fuel for the most modern form of transportation: a camel would bear eight barrels. The plan worked well, and the fuel arrived at its destinations without any difficulties. Our fuel in Sinkiang was sufficient for the military equipment sent by the Soviet Union, and the planes flew over

Kansu Province to Sian and onward to Hankow. As soon as we completed our negotiations, I was ready to leave.

On the day of my send-off ceremony, something unpleasant happened. Sheng invited all the government officials to attend, including the provincial governor and the heads of provincial agencies and military commanders. A vice-governor and a few heads of departments of the Uighur nationality attended. After Sheng had spoken, I also spoke a few words. Then Sheng asked me to retire, but he ordered some of the attending officials to remain. Being highly suspicious, he immediately ordered the vice-governor and several heads of agencies to be arrested and accused them of plotting to overthrow him. His use of my departure to arrest those government officials made me extremely uncomfortable. Perhaps he was just paranoid.

Sheng was the kind of man who trusted no one but his own wife. He later not only alienated the Soviets, but he also rebelled against the National government. I tried to persuade him to be loyal to Chiang. I told him that inasmuch as Chiang had confidence in him, he should remain loyal and devoted to the National government, if only to protect Sinkiang from being overrun by the Russians. He positioned machine guns in front of his official residence at night, a terrifying scene. He had all his filing cabinets locked, which meant he had to unlock these himself whenever he needed documents. He trusted no one. He was a very capable man, but his flaw was his distrust of people. In the end there was no one in whom he could confide, except his wife, not envoys from the Kuomintang headquarters, not his subordinates of many years.

Sinkiang is very fertile, and its water comes from the snows on T'ien-shan Mountain, which melt and flow to villages so that the people need not dig wells. They plant wheat in the rich, black soil, which extends two or three feet in depth. The people say that "one year's harvest satisfies three years of need." After sowing the wheat seeds, nature takes its course. There are few birds to destroy the crops, and "water comes from heaven" (heaven here means T'ien-shan). Seventeen Chekiang provinces can fit within Sinkiang, and in theory the province should support a population seventeen times that of Chekiang's 27,000,000, which would be over 400,000,000. But in the latter part of the 1930s, Sinkiang was scarcely populated, with little more than 3,000,000 people. Its resources include large amounts of oil and coal, and its coal is the best in the world. I know that because I studied its coal; some coal lumps are three feet long and one and a half square feet wide, and so heavy that a donkey can carry only two. After burning, the coal leaves only a little white ash and little residue, proving that it is of the best quality. T'ien-shan Mountain also has jade and gold. The gold mines yield "dog head gold," lumps as large as dog heads. The Soviet Union always had an eye on Sinkiang because of its great wealth.

When Sheng held his welcome party for me, I had noticed a tall Russian, a third secretary from the Soviet General Consulate, who closely observed me. When Ambassador Bogomoloff failed to return to his post, Chiang sent me to the airport to meet the new ambassador, and I suddenly realized that he was the same tall man I had seen in Sinkiang. Why, I wondered, had a low-ranking diplomat in Sinkiang suddenly become the new ambassador. I asked Chang Ch'ung to inquire when he was in the Soviet Union. He learned that the new ambassador had once been the Soviet deputy defense minister but had been demoted to third secretary of a consulate. (In communist countries promotions and demotions are unpredictable because the Communists "treat people as objects," without any feelings.) The tall man had been sent to Sinkiang to make a geographic survey, which shows that the Russians have never given up their aggressive designs on Sinkiang's rich resources. When I was in Sinkiang, the Soviet consul general was very friendly toward me. He went hunting with me and one day even gave me an excellent hunting rifle as a gift when we failed to shoot anything. At that time China and the Soviet Union had good relations.

On our trip to Sinkiang, Bogomoloff and I had to board a plane in Wuhu, Anhwei Province, because the Japanese were bombing Nanking airport. The Japanese probably had intelligence reports of our movements, for as soon as our plane took off, they also bombed the Wuhu airport; but we escaped the attack. While returning from Sinkiang, I also flew on a special charter plane without passengers. Sheng had given me many Hami melons, and once again a cavalry of several hundred horsemen arrived for my departure, making for a spectacular send-off. We were forced to land at Hami and spend the night because of a huge sandstorm. In Hami I had the chance to taste real Hami melons, which were sweet but small. The Hami melons that Sheng had given me were larger.

In Hami I stayed at the home of Doctor Yaolo, the Sinkiang representative of the National Assembly, who took me to the local theater. Sinkiang theater can present some very cruel drama, and that night the play *Wusung Slays His Sister-in-Law* was performed, in which a pig's heart and intestines were used on the set. After the killing, Wusung took those bloody organs out of his sister-in-law's body. I found the performance cruel and barbaric.

Men and women in Sinkiang use no saddles when riding horses. When in love, the boys court the girls on horseback, and once a boy has caught up with the girl, he kisses her and she must marry him. Sinkiang held other surprises for me. Why is the Gobi Desert called Gobi? The Gobi Desert contains a mixture of sand, cement, and pebbles, which makes the surface hard and flat like an airfield, and such material is called *gobi*. When the sandstorm forced us to stop at Hami, our plane landed on that very gobi. The next morning our plane had vanished. It took a long time to locate it because the plane had been blown miles away by the storm. A car towed it back, and we were soon airborne.

We first flew to Lanchou and then to Sian. Twenty minutes before we arrived in Sian, we learned from radio reports that Japanese airplanes were flying toward us. The pilot asked me what course to take. I thought that if we headed straight for Sian we certainly would be attacked, but there was not enough fuel to fly to Lanchou. After some deliberation I told the pilot to remain on course. After we had landed in Sian we learned that twelve Japanese planes were flying over Sian and southward to bomb Han-chung. When we touched ground, not a single person was at the airfield because the air alert had sent them into hiding. Once again, we had survived.

Chiang Ting-wen, governor of Shensi Province, came to meet me, and we had a luncheon at his mansion. We then flew to Hankow, and again an air alert siren resounded as we landed. We quickly unloaded my luggage and Hami melons, and the plane took off for Ichang. The Hankow airport was soon bombed by the Japanese. In Wuhu, the airport had been bombed as soon as I boarded the plane; in Sian, we nearly ran into enemy planes; in Hankow, the airport was bombed as soon as I left the plane. It was a miracle that I escaped three times in a row! If I had decided to fly to Lanchou when we approached Sian, we would have been forced to crash-land. I realized that, at a critical moment, the first thought is invariably correct because of its purity and clarity. I relied on intuition: fly ahead! In that way, I escaped a disaster.

We were lucky that Sinkiang could supply us with fuel. After the Japanese seized Nanking and moved to attack Hankow, our airplanes supplied by the United States were nearly destroyed, but the planes, tanks, and antiaircraft artillery promised by the Soviet Union arrived just in time. The Japanese had no knowledge of this, so when they tried to bomb Hankow, twelve of their planes were shot down by our air force. That was an unprecedented victory. The Japanese were shocked because they thought we had no planes left. For this glorious victory in the air, I was awarded an air force medal after the war. I felt very honored being the first civilian to have received such an award.

A Proposal to the German Ambassador, Oskar P. Trautmann

Unable to repulse the Japanese attacks in April 1938, the National government retreated from Nanking and moved to Hankow. The Japanese had just damaged a foreign warship in the middle of the Whampoa River in Shanghai, which made the foreign powers lodge a protest (I do not remember this vessel's nationality). But Germany took this opportunity to assign Ambassador Oskar P. Trautmann to mediate between China and Japan in an effort to prevent the war from spreading.[5] I was then in Hankow. Ambassador Trautmann came to see me. Although I previously had discussed with the Chinese Communists our interest in fighting Japan and had negotiated a nonaggression pact with Soviet ambassador Bogomoloff, I still believed that the Chinese Communists and Soviet Union could not be trusted. I now thought that if the opportunity arose, they should be eliminated for the good of our country and the world. I advanced this proposal to Trautmann: "The Japanese warlords have long intended to invade China. If you want them to stop the war, you had best conceive a scheme to select another target rather than to attack us. I think the Axis powers should work together, with Japan advancing northward into Russia and Germany advancing eastward. That should be your common goal."

I urged Trautmann to advise Hitler that he should not simply invade weak countries but should inspire the respect of all people for Germany. He should call for the liberation of all colonies in the world and for Japan, Germany, and China to unite to defeat the Soviet Union. Chiang did not know about my proposal to Trautmann to persuade the Germans to select a different target of attack. Just imagine, if they had accepted my suggestion, the course of Chinese communism would have been very different.

I then suggested that we three nations should conclude a secret pact, with our first objective being the defeat of communism and our second objective, liberation of the world's colonies. Once these were accomplished, the British Empire would be finished. Sun Yat-sen's Principle of Nationalism [*Min-tsu chu-i*] would materialize, and we could pronounce equality for all nations in the world. We Chinese wanted no territory and wanted to see the liberation of India, Korea, and Annam [Vietnam]. China already was self-sufficient in land, people, and resources. Japan could promote trade with the liberated colonies of Asia and the South Seas.

We would permit Japan to pass through our territory to attack the Soviet Union, but once the war was over, we expected Germany to guarantee Japan's withdrawal from China. The liberated colonies in Africa could be Germany's sphere, so that the original goals of the Axis could be realized. The United States would not disapprove of our suggestion; Germany need not attack France; Japan need not invade China. If Germany agreed to this proposal, we could support an anticommunist regime in Russia once the Soviet communist government had been overthrown and communism abolished. As for the Baltic states of Lithuania, Latvia, and Estonia, we would be happy to see their independence.

I put forward these thoughts to Trautmann and asked him to convey them to Hitler.[6] It is possible that the German Foreign Ministry may still have my proposal on file, but any Englishman or Russian who might find it would perhaps not forgive me. Before Trautmann received any reply from

Berlin, the Japanese troops already were advancing westward. Trautmann failed in his mediation and returned to Germany. If my plan had been considered, the world would be entirely different today.[7]

Chiang versus Wang

The Kuomintang Extraordinary National Congress convened in Wuchang on March 29, 1938, with 355 registered delegates for the sole purpose of electing Chiang as the party leader [*Tsung-ts'ai*] of the Kuomintang. Our slogan was One Doctrine, One Leader, One Organization. We hoped that during the war, total power—party, political, and military—would be concentrated in Chiang's hands. The main reason my elder brother, Kuo-fu, and I published the magazine *Political Review Monthly* [*Cheng-chih p'ing-lun yüeh-kan*] was to promote this concept. At the Extraordinary National Congress of 1938, Wang Ching-wei became the main obstacle preventing Chiang from achieving total power. Wang was senior to Chiang, and he was unwilling to yield. Although an intelligent man, Wang possessed one huge shortcoming: he always wanted to be the top man. The person who pushed him was none other than his wife. His wife, Ch'en Pi-chün, had greater ambition than her husband. She thought if Wang became "number one," she would be "the first lady." On election day, with 355 delegates present, we faced no difficulty in obtaining a majority. As the motion was made, I saw Wang looking very unhappy. I immediately suggested to Chiang that a new post, deputy party leader, be created for Wang. That was done, but even after Chiang and Wang were elected, Wang was never satisfied. He then proposed the party form a National State Council [Kuo-min ts'an-cheng-hui].

The National State Council was to include all other political parties in China such as the Chinese Communist party, the Chinese Youth party, the Democratic Socialist party, and leaders of all leading circles without party affiliation. By heading the People's Political Council, Wang would be the leader of all political parties in China, including the Kuomintang. Before the council was formed, I contacted the leaders of these parties. In name, the council was to be the highest organ within the power structure of the Kuomintang, and it also accommodated the non-Kuomintang members. I believed that having this council would greatly legitimize the Kuomintang's standing in the country. Such elites as Tseng Chi and Carsun Chang expressed an interest in joining us, if only to unite the nation in resisting foreign aggression.

Using the Kuomintang's name, Wang Ching-wei wrote a letter recognizing the legitimate role of the China Youth party and the Democratic Socialist party in national politics. Strictly speaking, Wang had no authority to deal with them on behalf of the Kuomintang. By now, his obvious desire to become the leader of all other parties, political organizations, and factions far exceeded my expectations. I had hoped that an alliance with the minor political parties could lead to a united front for coping with the Chinese Communists. Yet I worried about the possible conflict between the Central Executive Committee and the National State Council. What should we do if these two organs within the Kuomintang produced different interpretations or decisions about the same issue? Wang explained to Chiang that the Central Executive Committee could act like the Senate of the United States and that the National State Council was merely the equivalent of the House of Representatives. The Senate held more power than the House. The Kuomintang should adopt the European and American political forms. On this point, Chiang did not oppose Wang. Consequently, the motion to establish the National State Council was approved in the Central Political Committee and the Central Standing Committee. Fortunately, an article in the charter of the National State Council stipulated that the selection of the council's organizing members must be nominated by the leader of the party [*Tsung-ts'ai*], giving Chiang the final say. Chiang later instructed me to submit a list of names for him to recommend to become members of the National State Council. I used a single guideline to decide the final list: loyal comrades of the Kuomintang must make up the majority, with the rest—including members of the China Youth party, the Democratic Socialist party, and Wang Ching-wei's faction—having no more than 40 percent. This decision was absolutely necessary. If a motion required a vote, democracy would rule and we being the majority would win. If other parties made trouble about important resolutions, we would use democratic balloting to deal with them. After the National State Council was established, Wang Ching-wei became its chairman and he considered himself the leader of leaders, just like Chiang's position as party leader of the Kuomintang's National Congress. Those thoughts gave him some peace.

While Wang Ching-wei believed he was the leader of the leaders, he lacked resolution in the war against Japan. He was a defeatist and always pessimistic. He predicted disaster from the war. Wang often said to us, "Ah, how can we fight this war?" After we had retreated to Chungking, Wang Ching-wei was already prepared to flee.[8] In any war a leader's determination is vital. If the leader's convictions falter, his followers lose confidence. We were able to fight the war to the finish because we relied entirely on one person's resoluteness—Generalissimo Chiang's. It was never easy. Battle after battle, we lost ground. We retreated from Nanking, then from Hankow, and finally we reached Hunan Province. If the Japanese had then mobilized a million troops to encircle us, instead of choosing to fight us in piecemeal fashion, we would have been finished. They used only small elements of their army to attack us, adding some troops here and there. Chiang judged the Japanese to be "small-timers" and thought they lacked the vision to win big. The Japanese did not make the necessary investments to defeat us. Chiang's strategy at that time was to "use space to gain time." China was so large that it was not easy for the Japanese to fight everywhere. Once the enemy troops were in our terrain, they could not suppress and control every patriotic citizen.

Our policy and our strategy were certainly correct. After Nanking fell, I worried about the Japanese strategy. What would we do if the Japanese armies used the Kwangtung-Hankow Railroad on the south and the Peiping-Hankow Railroad on the north to encircle us in Hankow? I expressed my concern to Chiang, who replied: "No, the Japanese certainly do not have such a bold vision. We will entrench ourselves, and slowly turn defeat into victory." Chiang's judgment proved to be correct.

I figured Wang Ching-wei was going to flee. He was very unhappy at not having been elected as the Kuomintang's party leader. He was still not satisfied even after becoming the head of the National State Council. Fearing that if the war was lost he would be in trouble, he tried to collaborate with the Japanese, who were always looking for a Chinese to serve as their puppet. Besides, Japan wanted to divide China into a number of small states. Wang Ching-wei's background made him their ideal choice, so he and the Japanese were soon colluding with each other.

Wang Ching-wei's aide-de-camp, who happened to be a good friend of my aide-de-camp, leaked to him the news that Wang Ching-wei considered our situation too risky and was ready to defect. I instantly telegraphed Chiang, who was then in Hanchung, Shensi Province, saying that from reliable sources (which I did not reveal), I had learned that Wang might defect. When Chiang returned, Wang Ching-wei was already gone, having fled to Hanoi on December 20, 1938. He no longer believed our side could win the war. Chiang wanted me to fly to Hanoi to persuade him to return. When I was ready to leave, on the morning of March 22, 1939, I read in the newspaper that Wang Ching-wei's secretary, Tseng Chung-ming, had been attacked by an assassin in Hanoi. The report stated that had the assassin not entered the wrong room (that of Wang's secretary), Wang Ching-wei would have been killed.[9] The rumor was that Tai Li had sent the assassin. I had no idea exactly what had happened, so I went to Chiang for instructions. He immediately told me to cancel the trip. Fearing another assassination attempt, Wang Ching-wei took a roundabout way to reach Hong Kong, arriving there on December 25, and finally Japan. He began working with the Japanese and later set up a puppet government in Nanking in March 1940.

Often I asked myself, despite the agreements he reached with the Japanese on November 1, 1939, and again on October 30, 1943, was Wang

Ching-wei truly pro-Japanese? My answer was, and still is, no. Despite his great dissatisfaction with Chiang and maybe other elements within the Kuomintang, Wang was a great patriot, a Nationalist, and a faithful follower of Sun Yat-sen. After his puppet regime was first set up in Nanking on March 29, 1940, he did not entirely disassociate himself from Chiang.[10] Compared to Hu, Wang was much more individualistic. Hu, in my opinion, only considered himself a senior member of the Kuomintang. He shared power with Chiang. Hu believed that Chiang should follow the Confucian tradition; Chiang should listen to him and ask his advice. Chiang's critical view of Hu was evidenced in the letter he wrote to Sun Yat-sen as early as March 2, 1924.[11] Ever since the Northern Expedition days, Chiang never thought Hu could be the heir of Sun Yat-sen, nor did he take into account the possibility of Wang's succeeding Sun. He believed their shoulders were not broad enough to bear the responsibility Sun left to them. It was he, Chiang, who should be the leader of the future Kuomintang. I clearly remember that shortly after Hu's arrest in March 1931, Chiang instructed me to reveal to the public a confidential letter Sun wrote to him on October 9, 1924.[12] In that letter Sun made known that he had serious doubts about Hu and Wang. The letter justified Chiang's belief in Sun's expectation of him. The point I would like to stress is that, burning with his personal ambition, Wang always wanted to be the top man, in the commanding position after Sun's passing. For that, he could even use resisting Japanese aggression to behave as a turncoat, a "traitorous Chinaman" [*Han-chien*]. The wounds created by the *Chung-shan* Gunboat Incident and the Wuhan-Nanking split, as I recorded before, never healed. Differences between Wang and Hu were evident, and the conflicting interests of the two with Chiang were even more evident, making cooperation either between any of the two or among the three impossible. In the short run, Chiang won the quarrel. In the long run, however, the departure of Wang at this critical juncture of our history fragmented the Kuomintang. Indeed, in retrospect, it was a great misfortune for all of us.

As I mentioned above, when I took the post of minister of education, I had resigned from the Investigation and Statistical Department, which was then reorganized into three divisions. The third division, led by Ting Mo-tsun, was eliminated. Ting had no job and went to Hong Kong. Ting was a good friend of Chou Fo-hai's, and so he joined Wang Ching-wei's puppet regime.[13] Ting, who served as head of their secret service, was acquainted with many people who had worked for the first and second divisions in Shanghai. As soon as he arrived in Shanghai, he located those former employees of the Shanghai Investigation and Statistical Bureau and used my name to tell them he was acting on my behalf. Those people did not know Ting was a defector. Some, believing I was still in charge over Ting, joined his ranks. By the time I telegraphed them that Ting had joined Wang Ching-wei, it was too late. Ting was clever and shrewd. He had obtained the addresses of our secret communication centers in Shanghai. We suffered great losses because of him.

Before Japan surrendered, Ting was the puppet governor of Chekiang Province, Chou Fu-hai was the president of the puppet Executive Yüan, and Li Chün-lung was the puppet mayor of Shanghai; thus Ting was in Chekiang, Chou in Nanking, and Li in Shanghai, three very important localities. When Ting learned the Japanese were about to surrender, he started communicating with us by telegram and pleaded for leniency.[14] I sent a man named Chao to see Ting Mo-tsun. My message to him was the following:

> Now that the war will soon end since the atom bomb was dropped in Hiroshima, I want all of you who have served in the Nanking puppet government to do three things for us. Although you are traitors, if you carry out these requests, I can guarantee that you will not be put to death. First, you must remain in Nanking, Shanghai, and Hangchou, and you must not allow the Chinese communist New Fourth Army [Hsin-ssu-chün] from north of the Yangtze River to take over before we arrive. Second, you must control the puppet troops along the Nanking-Shanghai Railroad and along the Shanghai-Hangchou Railroad. This is very important because we want to use these two railroads to transport our troops speedily without any delays; and third, as soon as the war ends, you must find the quickest way to contact General Ku Chu-tung, commander in chief of the Third War Zone (the area around Kiangsu and Chekiang) and allow the National government's troops to move immediately into the three above-mentioned localities. You must accomplish these three assignments. Your lives depend on your accomplishments.

I wanted Ting to reply immediately. But Tai Li held a grudge against Ting because Ting had had many of Tai Li's underground operatives killed. I especially instructed Ting to make contact with Tai Li by sending the telegram through Tai Li's station. By handling the matter this way, Tai Li should understand the significance of my communication with Ting. Ting's telegram later informed me that he undertook to see that the three tasks were responsibly carried out. As soon as the Japanese surrendered, he and his cohorts immediately assisted National government troops in moving into Shanghai, Nanking, Hangchou, and the areas along the Shanghai-Nanking and the Shanghai-Hangchou railroads, so that these areas could not be occupied by the New Fourth Army. I now had to fulfill my promise of sparing his life.

But circumstances are difficult to control. Chou Fu-hai, a good friend of Ch'en Pu-lei's, tried to save himself. He asked Ch'en Pu-lei to speak with Chiang on his behalf and begged for forgiveness. Although he was spared execution, he later died in prison. Ting Mo-tsun could have survived. One day, he became ill in jail and was allowed to leave the Nanking detention center to visit a doctor. He took the opportunity to go sight-seeing at Hsüan Wu Lake and happened to meet a reporter from the *Central Daily News* [*Chung-yang jih-pao*]. The reporter wrote a story titled "Ting Mo-tsun Goes Sight-Seeing at Hsüan Wu Lake Free as a Bird," and it was published. Chiang saw it and asked me, "Why was Ting Mo-tsun out of jail?" After investigating and learning that he had been allowed to leave the jail to see a doctor, I reported that to Chiang and added that we did not know why he was at Hsüan Wu Lake. Chiang became angry: "If he was sick, how could he go sight-seeing at Hsüan Wu Lake? He ought to be shot."

If Ting had behaved well in jail he would have been spared. But Chiang had retained a bad impression of him. Because I had given Ting my word he would not be executed, I pleaded with Chiang to give him life imprisonment instead of execution. The generalissimo refused my request. I had no choice but to send someone to inform Ting Mo-tsun that "there is nothing I can do to save you now. Although I had given you my guarantee, you did not behave well. Why did you go sight-seeing at Hsüan Wu Lake?" Before his execution, Ting Mo-tsun wrote me a letter: "I am grateful to you. I know you have done much to help me. I was too careless. I only blame myself for this big blunder." Actually, the reporter's story had killed him.

Li Chün-lung's whereabouts were not known; possibly he was executed by the Communists. Wang Ching-wei later died in a hospital in Japan during surgery to remove the assassin's bullet that had been lodged in his body since December 1939.[15] In retrospect, Wang was a brilliant man. He was very close to Sun Yat-sen and one of the founding fathers of the republic. He could deliver speeches that truly moved people. His translations from the classical writing style to the vernacular were quick and accurate and required no editing. Although his speeches aroused people, their contents proved to be without substance. They were stereotyped as though written from a fixed formula. After listening to him, you realized there was nothing special that interested you further. But upon delivery, his speeches cast a spell on the audience. Wang was so spellbinding that the elderly Wu Chih-hui once called him a seductive "fox spirit." Let me repeat: His greatest failing was that he wanted to be the boss. He was willing to receive anyone who could support him. He was happy when the Communists flattered him. When Yen Hsi-shan and Feng Yü-hsiang carried out their "mutiny" in 1930, he joined them because they highly praised him. When Japan made him head of the puppet government in Nanking, he was only too happy to accept.[16] He lusted to become the top leader even if he had to betray his country. It has been said that Wang Ching-wei's career was ruined by his wife, Ch'en Pi-chün, and there is some truth in such an assessment. In my opinion, his life was a failure.

Chiang's Strategy of Divide and Rule

Before the war with Japan began in 1937, the Communists had incited the young people with rumors that the National government was so weak that it dared not fight Japan. Meanwhile, the Soviet Union hoped for an open break between China and Japan. The Chinese Communists followed the Soviet line. Young people then were often critical of the government for its failure to take a strong stand against Japan. We could not tell our young people we were involved in preparing for a war with Japan. We found it impossible to speak openly because we did not want Japan to learn how militarily weak we were. Should our plans become known, Japan would certainly advance the date of its attack and catch us unprepared.

In 1935, the students and youths already were publicly demonstrating on the war issue, and Chang Hsüeh-liang followed their lead by uttering lofty demands. At this time, Chiang had sent me on the mission to the Soviet Union.[17] Before leaving, I presented a report to Chiang that suggested that these demonstrations should not be allowed to continue and that he should secretly assemble the university presidents and their student leaders for a closed-door meeting in Nanking. I urged Chiang to tell them in person that we would definitely go to war but that our national plans could not be revealed. The more advanced our preparations, the better chance we had to win; we must not let the enemy know these details. Chiang accepted my proposal and successfully handled this matter. I definitely knew that both the Chinese Communists and the Soviet Union wanted us to fight Japan. They did not care if China was sacrificed.

Chiang knew that these youths were being deceived and used by the Communists. We wanted to prevent this from happening. Chiang approved the organization of two secret groups within the Kuomintang: one named the Blue Shirts Society [Fu-hsing-she][18] and sponsored by the military, mainly graduates of Whampoa Military Academy [Chün-fang],[19] the other the Blue and White Corps [Ch'ing-pai-she], backed by the party [Tang-fang]. Neither of these groups recruited youths in the name of Kuomintang. Organizing small rings within the party was risky and illegal. These groups became active in 1935, and by 1937, when the war of resistance began, most of our youth had returned to the fold. With that success, on July 9, 1938, Chiang then ordered the two groups disbanded and incorporated into a united organization under the guidance of the Three People's Principles. It was named San-min chu-i Youth Corps [San-min chu-i ch'ing-nien-t'uan], which was strictly a political move.

People always accused us of setting up small factions within the party; actually we were under orders to do so, but we also were accused of forming the much-talked-about CC Clique.[20] In Hankow, I had written a report to Chiang to inform him that, with the war already six months old, our units of the Blue and White Corps were no longer needed. He agreed that the two should be disbanded. At the meeting to announce their termination, Chiang asked me, as an instructor [*chih-tao-yüan*] in the Blue Shirts Society,[21] to speak after he had spoken. This is what I said: "In war, we need regular armies to face the enemy's regular armies, but we also need special forces to conduct guerrilla warfare. The Blue Shirts Society and the Blue and White Corps are like the special forces. While the regular armies do battle, our special forces recruit patriotic youths to assist them. Our regular armies have now started to fight, and the special forces are no longer needed and must be disbanded. No matter our actions, we will only follow the orders of Chiang. We have no special mission for ourselves.

Chiang was extremely pleased with my speech. After the San-min chu-i Youth Corps had formed, Chiang assumed its directorship and made Chen Cheng his deputy. Why was the San-min chu-i Youth Corps created on July 9, 1938? Because the Kuomintang wanted to abolish the probationary membership system. Probationary members participated in small group meetings to learn about the party, but the party never held a formal basic training program for new members. An important objective of the Youth Corps was to train young members. The Kuomintang elected me to draft the organization rules for the Youth Corps. All probationary party members first had to join the Youth Corps; on reaching twenty-five years of age, they automatically became regular party members.

I did not think the Youth Corps should become a separate entity but only provide training for the party's youth. This arrangement was supposed to prevent disputes. Chiang appointed Chen Cheng as secretary-general of the Youth Corps and Kang Tse as the head of its organization division. A man of ambition, Kang wanted the Youth Corps to become a separate unit. His idea was entirely different from mine. He was unwilling to let Youth Corps members become party members when they reached twenty-five. As director of the Youth Corps, Chiang ignored the organic rules and allowed Kang to sign a directive that corps members could remain in the Youth Corps after twenty-five years of age and were not required to join the Kuomintang.

This new ruling caused trouble. We had become two parties with considerable friction between party and Youth Corps. This was exactly what the Communists had always wanted, quarrels between the party and the

corps. On this score, Chiang was wrong. When I first drafted the organization rules, I clearly explained to him that an independent unit must not be
created outside the party and that the Youth Corps and party should be like
a middle school and a university, with students of the former entering the
latter on graduation. But now we had a middle school with a university, as
well as a university without a middle school. The former possessed new
blood, but the latter only became old and weak. Without considering the
natural metabolic process, the two units had become adversaries.

This had happened because of the ambitions of Chen Cheng and Kang
Tse, who coveted the leadership of the Youth Corps and hoped to take over
the party some day. Every provincial Kuomintang and Youth Corps headquarters were in conflict with each other, creating great trouble for ourselves.
Finally, on June 30, 1947, Chiang ordered the corps to be integrated into the
party.

These disputes had created the impression that in the Kuomintang I was
in control while in the corps Chen Cheng and Kang Tse led. When I drafted
the organization rules of the Youth Corps, I anticipated the danger of creating
two separate units and thus specified that the corps should serve only as a
training unit for the party. But our leader, Chiang, had other thoughts. In
his leadership position, he did not share my concern because he believed that
the party and the corps would obey his orders. But when these disputes got
out of control, a motion was carried at the fourth plenary session of the
Sixth Congress of the Central Executive Committee, on September 12,
1947, that the corps be merged into the party. So much time and energy had
been wasted on this matter.

I must mention yet another incident during the early phase of the war.
Each time our government retreated, either from Nanking or from Hankow,
Chiang was always the last one to leave. Before his withdrawal he always
telephoned his closest aides. He would say to me over the telephone, "Li-
fu, you can go now." I would say, "The generalissimo himself has not left,
how can we leave before you?" Again he would say, "You first must go, and
I'll leave soon after!" It is not easy to be a leader. Chiang had to concern
himself with the safety of others, and that indeed is a sign of a great leader!

One further incident was most interesting. To leave Hankow we could
either fly to Chungking or take a boat from T'ung-ting Lake by way of
Changsha and Kwei-yang to Chungking. Chu Chia-hua wanted me to fly
with him, and Ch'en Pu-lei wanted me to take a boat with him. They both
gave me tickets. I could not decide with whom to go. That night I had a
dream, although I hardly ever have dreams. I dreamt that a tiger dropped
from the sky to attack me. I woke up wondering what the dream meant.
Would a tiger dropping from the sky signify a curse upon me? Perhaps it
was all right if I went up to the sky. So I decided to fly and wrote to Ch'en

Pu-lei to inform him of my decision and to return the boat ticket. The day we safely landed in Chungking, reports confirmed that Japanese planes had strafed a boat on T'ung-ting Lake. My first thoughts were "How terrible for Ch'en Pu-lei" and "Is he in danger?" When Ch'en later reached Chungking he said: "In my cabin there were two beds, one for me, the other for you, but it remained empty. That day when the Japanese plane attacked, three bullets hit your bed, and you would have been killed. Now I just thank God that you did not travel with me!" I then told him of the dream I had about the tiger coming from the sky. Such a dream would have prompted some people to avoid flying. However, I believe that the first thought is always the correct one. I intuitively knew I must take the plane. Had I taken the boat, the Japanese air attack would have been my misfortune and confirmed the curse from the sky. This experience was like my flight between Sinkiang and Sian; when we encountered a formation of Japanese planes, I decided not to return to Lanchou. Thus, I escaped one disaster after another. Thinking back, I realize how very lucky I have been.

The Chinese Engineering Society

During wartime in 1940, I was the president of the Chinese Engineering Society. I knew of the importance of Sun's International Development of China [*Shih-yeh chi-hua*] for postwar reconstruction, and so I proposed at our annual meeting in Chengtu that a society be formed to study Sun's industrial plan. The proposal was approved, and I was elected the new organization's president. Our preparatory committee consisted of about a dozen members, all of them presidents or vice-presidents of specialized engineering societies. We invited a group of experts to create more than ten special task forces. The society started its operation in March 1941. Nearly all special engineering societies, engineers, agricultural specialists, and staff members under the jurisdiction of the National government worked together on a variety of research programs. We had estimated in 1943 that, to meet the postwar challenges, China must build 20,000 kilometers of railroad, smelt 9,000,000 tons of iron, manufacture 150,000 machine tools, assemble 12,000 airplanes, and train 250,000 engineers. The society met four times in 1943 and held eighteen special meetings for its task forces. We made field trips and completed preliminary but detailed plans for carrying out a variety of projects while collecting statistics on population, resources, and the geography of different locales.

On April 20, 1943, a Conference on Industrial Reconstruction Plans [*Kung-yeh chien-she chi-hua hui-i*] was held at Chungking, at the the Central Library [Chung-yang t'u-shu-kuan] in which more than a hundred experts from various fields attended. After much deliberation and discussion, we finally drew up a sixteen-point Program for Industrial Reconstruction [*Kung-yeh chien-she kang-ling*]. By 1945 the society felt that this program depended too much on theory and needed to be revised, so a fifth meeting was convened. The participants included some twenty top scientists and engineers of the country. Many constructive ideas were introduced, and a ninety-one-point booklet called the Fundamentals for Implementation of the Industrial Reconstruction Program [*Kung-yeh chien-she kang-ling shih-shih yüan-che*] was printed.[22] That report presented the country's goals and how resources could be coordinated and organized to achieve them. In his book *China's Destiny*, Chiang listed estimates of our group for each of the engineering projects we had researched and studied in depth.

CHAPTER SEVEN

Wartime Education Minister

JANUARY 1938–DECEMBER 1944

Making Education Policy

SHORTLY AFTER THE SEPTEMBER EIGHTEENTH INCIDENT in 1932, I refused Wang Ching-wei's offer to be minister of education. He was then president of the Executive Yüan. Then on New Year's Day 1938, Chiang called me in and offered me the post of minister of education. I was taken by surprise and could not immediately decide. Many young students of the Japanese-occupied area had retreated inland, and the task of educating them had become increasingly difficult to manage. Education Minister Wang Shih-chieh could not handle the problem and wanted to resign. I believed that education, investigation, and statistical work were very different in nature and that I could only handle one assignment at a time. Chiang agreed, but he wanted me to concentrate on education. I held the position until November 20, 1944.

As I was no longer in charge of investigation and statistical work and had reorganized that activity into the Central Bureau of Investigation and Statistics and the Military Council Bureau of Investigation and Statistics, other work had been transferred to Tai Li.[1] In the past I never had argued with Chiang about my assignment, but this time matters were different. To be minister of education one had to be of high moral character to persuade others. But investigation work was easier because one could simply resort to pressure or force to achieve one's ends. These two missions were not compatible and could not be undertaken by a person of similar character. I apply the philosophy of the doctrine of the mean whenever I perform any job, and to have done both jobs would have been excessively imbalanced.

Chiang was insistent that I become minister of education, and so I accepted the responsibility of managing National China's education under wartime conditions until December 1944. In those seven long years, I tried to care for the destitute students, to revive education behind our military lines, to expand schools of all levels, to reform the entire educational system, and to train and recruit students for the war effort. I am proud of what I did, and much was accomplished. My work efforts were recorded in the ministry's reports and other publications such as newspapers, journals, magazines, and the second edition of *National Education Yearbook*.

My background as a mining engineer may appear to have no direct relevance to administrative work in education. But that was not the case. In my heart I believed myself qualified for the job. Whereas a mining engineer's job is to discover and develop underground resources, an education administrator must discover and develop human resources. In America, education work is often referred to as "human engineering." This comparison might be a forced analogy, but I believe it is correct. As a matter of fact, I had been involved in educational and cultural circles long before World War II.

After the Northern Expedition, I fully recognized the need to make known the beliefs and ideals of our party to the people. I made more than ten thousand speeches to students and teachers above the middle school level, and I gave lectures to students at the Central Political Institute [Chungyang cheng-chih hsüeh-hsiao] and at colleges and universities. My lectures entitled "On Vitalism" [*Wei-sheng lun*] were published to discredit Marxist materialism [*Wei-wu lun*] and were reprinted several times. After the September Eighteenth Incident of 1932, I frequently visited Peking and Tientsin to lecture and interact with young people in educational circles of the North. In March 1931 I served as a member of the board of directors of National Chi-nan University. In May 1937, I served as acting dean of the Central Political Institute. I had cosponsored educational reform with other senior members at the congress of the Kuomintang.

When I first took office at the ministry, two big problems required immediate resolution. Students and faculty in the war zone could no longer pursue an education and had fled to the interior. These exiles needed help. The problem we had to decide was whether schools that had moved to the interior should be allowed to continue or be combined with others. On the eve of the war, some people had wanted to radically change our educational system and had advocated paramilitary education. I had to choose between traditional education or a paramilitary education curriculum.

In trying to wage war and reconstruct our country at the same time, I concluded that education should not be interrupted because our national reconstruction needed qualified people. Moreover, even our war efforts required trained experts, which only our school system could produce.[2] On this matter, Director Wu Chun-sheng of the Department of Higher Education had brilliant ideas. Before he came to the ministry he had published an article called "Education at a Time of National Calamity," which argued

As minister of education of
National China in 1944.

that during a time of national calamity the education system must have
special programs added to the regular curricula. In brief, the education
system had to be tailored to achieve the grand ideal of national salvation.
That meant education should focus on the unique conditions of our day so
as to prepare society for future hardships. I agreed with Wu's ideas, and I
resolved that we should not reduce the number of schools but increase them
according to need. In this way, we resolved the problem of "quantity" of
education.

As for the problem of "quality" in education, I believed that regular
education must be maintained in order to train qualified personnel for national reconstruction and that special training should be supplemented to
meet the demands of military recruitment. On the basis of this principle, I
issued a formal letter to the nation's students in March 1938 that set forth
our educational policy and direction for youth. Our National government
still adhered to the period of political tutelage in which every important
policy decision for the nation had to be approved and supported by the
Kuomintang. Therefore, I presented my education plan at the Extraordinary
National Congress of the Kuomintang, which convened on April 1, 1938,
to debate policy related to war and national reconstruction. With the consent
of the National State Council it became the centerpiece for our wartime
education. There were four elements: (1) revise educational systems and

teaching materials and pursue the wartime curricula; (2) train personnel with different skills and assign them to suit the war needs; (3) emphasize the cultivation of national ethics, intensify scientific research, and expand scientific facilities; (4) train the youth to serve society and further strengthen our capacity to fight the war of resistance.

In addition, I presented a program outline for all levels of wartime education that specified nine educational principles and seventeen ways of implementation. The nine educational principles were (1) advance education by mental, physical, and disciplinary means; (2) combine the civil with the military; (3) place similar emphasis on agrarian and industrial demands; (4) have consistency in educational and political objectives; (5) link education of family to school; (6) use scientific methods to reorganize and teach literature, history, philosophy, and art to build national character based on Chinese tradition; (7) increase natural sciences training to meet the pressing needs of national defense and production; (8) revamp the social sciences to learn, suit our own national conditions, and encourage innovation; (9) make clear our educational goals; work to equalize education and training in different localities; make compulsory education universal for all; implement our social and family education program. These principles were applied to our school system at all levels for curricula, teachers' training, and a variety of other related fields.

Our most impressive achievement during the war of resistance was, under great adversity, increasing the number of schools at all levels. That development alone made it possible to increase learning and promote our culture, while increasing the supply of qualified people for the nation's reconstruction and for waging war.

The number of colleges, faculty, students, and graduates during the war rose greatly over those of prewar days because we attracted refugees and built new colleges. At the secondary school level, the number of normal schools and professional schools decreased in number, but faculty, students, and graduates increased in number compared with prewar days. Secondary school education grew in the government-controlled areas, and the National government also ran thirty-one middle schools, three middle schools for overseas Chinese, thirteen normal schools, two normal schools for overseas Chinese, and thirteen professional schools. At the primary school level, local governments operated the schools.

New Type Of Schools

Education at all levels was greatly influenced by the war. Many new schools were created simply to satisfy wartime requirements. In those terrible years, everyone connected with education worked hard and made great personal sacrifices to carry out the policies of the Education Ministry and to educate the citizens of the next generation.

North China and areas along the coast were the first to fall into Japanese hands, and our greatest concentration of colleges and universities appeared to be lost. The Ministry of Education somehow had to transfer those institutions and their resources to the interior. In 1939, of the 108 prewar institutions at college level and above, 17 were closed, 52 had to move behind the lines, and 14 were outside the enemy-occupied area. Twenty-five of them moved to foreign concessions in Shanghai or to Hong Kong, but these closed down after World War II broke out in the Pacific. Some faculty and students moved to Chungking and attended other schools or started classes on their own. In fact, all national college-level institutions at the time, except the Sinkiang College of Arts and Science, continued to stay open despite the war.

The ministry also helped some private and provincial colleges and universities, repairing bombed campuses and resupplying lost library equipment. Many colleges had to move several times before reaching safe haven and reopening. In addition, the ministry built new teachers' colleges and industrial, agricultural, and medical schools to handle wartime needs. It was a difficult time. Consider how many times the Kwangtung Provincial College of Arts and Science had to move. First, it moved from Canton to Wuchow in Kwangsi Province, then to Tun-hsien, the third time to Yonghsien, the fourth time to Ju-yuan in Kwangtung Province, a fifth move to Lien-hsien, a sixth to Chüeh-kiang, a seventh move back to Lien-hsien, and the eighth move to Loting.

The institutions that moved farthest away were Peking University and Tsinghua University in Peking and Nankai University in Tientsin. They first moved to Changsha and combined as Changsha Provisional University. Then they moved to Meng-chih and Kunming and became known as the Southwest Associated University. Many faculty and students moved from Changsha to Yunnan by foot, experiencing great dangers and privations but managing to reach their destination safe and sound. The quickest move was undertaken by National Central University [Chung-yang ta-hsüeh]. When its faculty and students, along with books and equipment, were shipped from Nanking along the Yangtze River to Shapingpa in Chungking, the livestock belonging to the college of agriculture were driven over land and safely reached Chungking. These are some examples of the unique national migration of universities during the war of resistance.

Faculty and students demonstrated great courage and an iron will. Educational administrators of the central and local government expended great energy at enormous risk to select campus locales, find money, and provide instruction. Everyone worked and sacrificed on behalf of the nation.

I decided that reform must first start with pedagogical education. I established teachers' colleges in certain universities, as well as two new independent teachers' colleges, one for men, one for women. I later added a few more, such as the teachers' colleges in Kweiyang, Nanning, and Hupei. I also changed the teachers' college of the Southwest Associated University [Hsi-nan lien-ta, abbreviated as lien-ta, or lienta] into a separate entity, renaming it the Northwest Teachers' College to train more secondary school teachers.

During my tenure as minister of education, the then Southwest Associated University was very cooperative despite the liberal tradition it inherited from its predecessor, Peking University. A three-man committee including Chiang Mon-liu of Pei-ta, Mei I-ch'i of Tsinghua, and Chang P'o-lin of Nankai was helpful in the time of need. The well-known and widespread radicalism, the strong antigovernment and, to some extent, procommunist student activities of the university did not take place until autumn 1945, after Mao Tse-tung's visit to Chungking. By then I was no longer in charge of education. As I recorded earlier, I left the post on November 20, 1944. It is fair to say that I was not involved in the post–World War II student movement in China. Chiang did not assign me such a job.

Practical education had been the main theme before the war. But during the war, even more attention was turned to promoting medical schools, engineering colleges, and technical schools. These schools required much equipment, which meant more money. Our ministry persuaded the government to appropriate huge amounts of funds to open these new schools.

We also nurtured young talent in music by founding the National College for Social Education and the National Academy of Music. National Chung Cheng University was established in Kiangsi because that province had never had any institutions of higher learning. After Chekiang University had moved inland to Tsunyi, Kweichou Province, it helped start National Ying-shih University. Finding employment for graduates was easy. In pre-war days, a common aphorism was "unemployment awaits graduation," but during the war, college graduates quickly found good jobs created by military, industry, and commercial demands. The Committee of Cooperation between Reconstruction and Education [Chien-chiao ho-tso wei-yüan-hui] also distributed jobs to graduates. Students of engineering and accounting schools were especially in demand.

Wartime College Education

Before the war, an investigation team sent by the League of Nations had evaluated our university system. Its report condemned the illogical geographic distribution of our colleges and universities and complained that the curriculum was unsuitable to China's needs. The report went on to describe the poor quality of many of our professors and their poor teaching methods, which were based primarily on learning by rote. But these criticisms did not receive much attention because of the outbreak of war. After my appointment to the Ministry of Education, I determined that I would not only expand college education but improve it. On the issue of irrational geographic distribution, it was true that institutions of higher learning had been concentrated in a few places, but this problem was partially solved by wartime migration. I used logic to apportion migrating institutions to various localities.

The restrictions imposed by war and changing war zones, however, did not enable us to achieve an ideal distribution. When the government seat was in Wuhan, I planned to incorporate colleges of arts, sciences, and law into one university and place that institution in a specific area behind the lines. I also tried to separate certain technical institutions teaching agriculture, engineering, medicine, commerce, and education from their universities and locate them in different locales according to government and societal need.

The investigation team from the League of Nations had pointed out that in Chinese education "the influence of foreign education is so great that foreign languages are used as tools to do research on important subjects. Material used and illustrations quoted are drawn from foreign sources." The investigation team also stated that "visitors to China, having inspected curriculum of history, political science, or economics in some of the Chinese universities, should well be forgiven for not being able to determine whether such an approach has been designed for Western students studying China or for Chinese students studying the West. It is particularly apparent that in the teaching of natural sciences, stress is placed on foreign circumstances."[3] After assuming the office of minister of education, I had similar feelings about the inadequacy of China's college curriculum. I learned that most universities and colleges were even managed by the foreign powers. Their curriculum usually did not demand high standards, and this was particulary true for Chinese history, language, and literature. I resolved to invite experts to establish new standards for college curriculum and to classify classes as either "required" or "elective." I soon discovered China had no institutions researching fertilizers. We lacked schools to develop applications for hog bristles, tung oil, tea, porcelain, and silk fabric. A disparity existed between national reconstruction and the education system. No wonder China's economy had not improved. I organized a committee in the ministry to study these problems, and I urged that our colleges and universities create new curricula to meet the need of the nation.

The next step was to examine the contents of teaching materials for curriculum subjects. We collected syllabi for different subjects from all the colleges and universities we could contact. We invited hundreds of professors to meet and exchange ideas. After two years and hundreds of meetings, we compiled forty-two syllabi to be used in select schools on a trial basis. I then decided we must edit and publish specific books for college use. In 1941, we formed a special committee to handle this problem. By 1943, under difficult war circumstances, we had published 163 books, of which 58 were by contracted authors, 88 were solicited from the public, and 17 were reprints of old books. But the books we published for college use differed from textbooks in that they were edited only for university students and faculty members to use as reference books. They were not required as textbooks. Yet some scholars at the time believed that the books we published infringed on academic freedom. They were mistaken.

Next, the ministry examined and approved teachers' qualifications. In the past, there had been no standards for teaching faculty in universities, especially at the rank of full professor. Most faculty were overstaffed. This was criticized by the educational investigation team sent by the League of Nations and by the Chinese literati. In 1940, I proposed tentative standards for regulating the qualifications of university and college teachers and setting their salary schedule and imposed certain rules for examining and verifying the qualifications of university and college teachers. Teaching faculty were to be divided into four ranks: professor, associate professor, lecturer, and teaching assistant. Methods to examine and verify their qualifications and set salary ranges as well as the requirements for promotion and tenure were also established. A small number of professors were very unhappy with these rules because they believed that academic qualifications to teach and do research should not be decided by the government. But later they dropped their protests when they learned that examination and verification would be done by a committee created by the Ministry of Education. Of these committee members, twelve were directly appointed by the ministry and thirteen were elected by the presidents of national universities and approved by the ministry. Although a vice-minister of the ministry and the director of the ministry's Department of Higher Education were automatic committee members, scholarly specialists made up the majority. Their opinions were respected, and examination and verification were conducted fairly.

Meanwhile, the ministry also stipulated that qualified teachers should take sabbaticals and receive research subsidies and fellowships. Those with seniority and prestige, if elected by their peers, could become ministry-appointed professors. These incentives convinced critics that our reforms aimed to achieve academic excellence by encouraging academic faculty to realize their full potential. Between 1940 and 1944, some seven thousand members of the teaching faculty of the nation's colleges and universities were evaluated and more than fifty-eight hundred passed those exams. Teaching assistants and lecturers who had accrued years of experience with outstanding records as well as publications were promoted. In the past, only those with advanced degrees from abroad could become a professor or associate professor, while those with Chinese degrees were denied promotion even though they had experience, outstanding records, and published works. This new measure was an incentive to teaching assistants and lecturers with Chinese degrees to improve their teaching and research.

Unified College Entrance Examination

To unify exam standards for students, I put into practice a unified college entrance examination system for designated districts in nineteen provinces and their cities. The League of Nations education investigation team had recommended this unified entrance examination system, but it was never implemented. Wartime conditions made it acutely necessary to have this unified examination system, and in 1938, it began to operate. A Committee of Unified Student Enrollment was formed with a subcommittee located in each of the entrance examination districts to manage recruitment, examination, and correcting examination papers. Dates and subjects of exams were uniformly determined, and test questions were uniformly issued by the Ministry of Education. The final decisions to admit and distribute students were made by the ministry's Committee of Unified Student Enrollment.

This system worked for three consecutive years, during which entrance exams were standardized, students' travel reduced, admissions made more fair, and, above all, fees to take entrance exams eliminated. We also worried about enemy air raids. Should an air attack on an examination location take place on exam day, or should students disperse because of an air alert, the concept of unified exams would be destroyed. It was also difficult to keep test questions confidential because they were reprinted in each district. But meticulous preparation and diligence paid off, and we succeeded beyond our expectations. As the war continued and transport became more difficult, the ministry tried to combine student enrollments in various districts. This step brought complaints from many institutions.

To elevate student learning skills, I also changed exam methods and instituted a final graduation examination in addition to term-end and year-end exams. This method combined the European and American methods for student graduation that is used today. The European method institutes no exams during the school year and has only one final graduation exam. The American method emphasizes regular and term-end exams, and a student accrues credits for graduation. Before the war Chinese universities had adopted the American system, but the League of Nations education investigation team judged this method "highly unsuitable" and suggested that students graduate only after passing a final examination.

I adopted a compromise method: students would earn credits for term-end and year-end exams, but they also had to pass a graduation examination. The graduation examination would cover not only the courses of the last term but also main courses from the previous years. By still having regular term-end and year-end exams, students were constantly supervised and encouraged to learn. A student, however, could not graduate by merely accumulating credits but also had to review and reexamine the main courses of previous years. This method induced students to remember what they learned and relate it to subject matter they were studying. This method also improved students' attitudes because they understood that studying was not merely preparing for exams. This method was superior to the method then prevailing in Germany, Great Britain, and France.

The Ministry of Education also conducted "school work examination contests" to encourage students to be diligent in their day-to-day studies. These contests served as an incentive for students and to spot talent. For example, the Nobel Prize winner Yang Chen-ning, while a student at Southwest Associated University, won first prize in the nationwide exam contest in physics. The Hong Kong English-language newspaper reporter Chang Kuo-hsing won the first prize in a nationwide English examination contest. Many still remember his expression of joy when he held up a pair of new tennis shoes he had just bought with his prize money.

We also tried to improve university administration efficiency, no easy task. In 1939, I issued a twelve-point directive for university administrative organizations, specifying that each institution must have three administrative offices: one for academic affairs, one for student affairs, and one for general administrative affairs and that the dean of each office was to be appointed from the teaching faculty.

We also proposed an office for moral teaching with these ideas in mind: (1) to plan and oversee the mentor system; (2) to handle student affairs concerning loans, relief, medical care, and military conscription; (3) to help our young people not to be led astray by wrong thinking and end up hindering the war effort.

I believed that our war for survival required that every teacher in charge of student activities must set himself as a model and hold lofty ideas for students to follow. With Chiang's approval, I wrote an *Outline of General Ethical Teaching* [*Hsün-yü kang-yao*] for all school levels. I reassessed the four Confucian virtues, *li*, *i*, *lien*, *ch'ih*, and combined them to argue for self-discipline and service to the nation and to apply them to earn one's livelihood. DeBary interprets *li* as regulated attitude; *i*, right conduct; *lien*, clear discrimination; and *ch'ih*, true self-consciousness. My outline encouraged all young men and women to "believe in oneself while believing in the *tao*; govern oneself while governing things, educate oneself while educating others, and defend oneself while defending the country." I am happy to say that more than a hundred thousand well-qualified young persons were educated and trained by this argument. Although many had to remain on the mainland after 1949, those who came to Taiwan succeeded in all aspects of life. In Taiwan today, the majority of those above sixty years of age who have served in government, military, society, and academic circles probably received a wartime college or high school education. Their contributions to country and society have made Taiwan modern and prosperous today. Many hundreds of Chinese scholars in mainland China, in the United States, and in overseas Chinese communities have been praised for their accomplishments, and many were trained in the wartime universities.

Wartime Secondary Education

As a rule, the Ministry of Education did not directly administer secondary and primary schools. The ministry only made policies and programs to devise rules and regulations for local education administration. To develop wartime secondary education, the ministry issued a directive in 1938 suggesting that every province designate three kinds of middle-level schools (middle, normal, and vocational), according to population size, transportation, the economy, and the level of cultural activities. Our idea was to found different schools in each district while avoiding duplication, concentration, and lopsidedness. The middle school district would consider the proportion of primary school children entering schools of a higher grade. The vocational school district would coordinate its schools with the local economy. The normal school district would pay attention to the need for qualified primary school teachers within the district.

In 1942, the ministry again issued a new directive advising local middle schools to build more new buildings and construct classrooms within its

financial capacity. I would say that secondary education in wartime China
was reasonably well distributed by area and size of population. Our efforts
would become the blueprint for developing a postwar secondary education
system just before the fall of the mainland in 1949.

The ministry also worked to revise curriculum, class schedules, and
course criteria. By the latter part of the war, textbooks used in middle and
primary schools were all edited under the auspices of the ministry and then
published by commercial presses. It is fair to say that, before World War II,
the government examined and approved textbooks for middle and primary
schools before being sent to the publishers. By the latter part of the war,
however, the government prepared the textbooks. This undertaking was
severely criticized, and even after the war, many accused the government of
practicing "thought control" or "competing with civilians."

During the war, when middle and primary schools behind the lines
increased in number, textbooks were urgently needed. The ministry requi-
sitioned the Cheng Chung textbooks, but Cheng Chung's coverage was
incomplete and there were not enough books to go around. Other publishers
then reprinted old and sometimes outdated textbooks used in the early years
of the republic. But even these could not meet the demands. To cope with
this unusual situation, we instructed primary schools to substitute students'
calligraphy classes for book copying so that students without texts could
use the copies. Meanwhile, the scarcity of printed materials created serious
problems. Old books were printed only on coarse paper, and their type
shrunk in size. Printing quality was poor and not up to standard. To maintain
middle and primary school education levels and to protect the eyesight of
schoolchildren, the ministry had to find some solution. The responsibility
for editing middle and primary school textbooks was assigned to the National Bureau of Editing and Translation [Kuo-li pien-i kuan], in accordance
with the new curriculum criteria. We handed these materials to publishers
who volunteered to undertake printing, issuing, and distribution. I thought
we had solved a problem created by war, and we certainly were not imposing
"thought control," let alone "competing with civilians."

Public Education

Public education in National China was financed and administered by local
governments. According to my recollection, public education suffered greatly
as a result. Why? The main reason was that elementary education was not
universal and mandatory and that few pupils could afford to attend these
schools. To promote universal education as required in the Kuomintang
constitution, the National government promulgated measures to enforce

compulsory education. No real results were achieved. In 1936, however, we had observed some progress. The percentage of school-age children attending schools had increased from 29.82 percent in 1934 to 53.0 percent in 1936. The percentage of school-age children going to school eventually reached 70 percent. But the war had greatly set back our public education, especially in the enemy-occupied areas. I requested that all provinces and municipalities behind enemy lines continue enforcing compulsory education in accordance with the 1935 program. I also made some basic changes by establishing a public education system to increase the number of public schools, thus increasing the ratio of school-age children attending schools and lowering the illiteracy rate each year.

In 1939, the National government also promulgated a new local administrative system called the new county [*hsien*] system.[4] The chief political and commercial activities of a new county were always centered in a small town [*chen*] or market town, usually an unwalled city. There were two levels of local administration under the jurisdiction of a new county or town, namely, the village [*hsiang*] and a group of households called *pao*. The village was also a suburban district of around 12,500 households, whereas the pao contained 6–10 *chia* in which each chia comprised 6–15 households. More specifically, a pao could have from 36 to 150 households. Thus, under the new wartime county system, each county had a nuclear school and each pao had to have a public school. Furthermore the nuclear school and the pao public school had three divisions for children, women, and adult men, the idea being to teach adults who never before received any schooling.

The village or town administrator was also the nuclear school principal and the leader of the village militia; the pao chief, pao public school principal, and pao militia leader were the same person. Where education and economy were well developed, principals of the village or town nuclear school and the pao public school were required to be full-time professionals.

The village or town nuclear schoolteacher also served as chief cultural officer of the village or town administration; the pao public schoolteacher also served as cultural secretary of the pao office. This public education system evolved with the new county system. In that same year, nineteen provinces and municipalities, comprising a total of 26,414 villages or towns and 303,792 pao, implemented this public education plan, and the total number of public schools (including nuclear public schools) reached 254,377. In 1946 these same nineteen provinces and municipalities outside enemy-occupied areas totaled some 34,110,000 school-age children. The number of those children attending school reached some 17,220,000. Those children not at school but who had already received some compulsory education numbered as high as 25,000,000, or more than 70 percent of school-age children attending school, a great improvement from the 53 percent of the prewar days.

Social Education

For the purpose of winning the war, the government greatly emphasized social education. The ministry originally managed institutions relevant to the nation's culture and learning, such as libraries and museums. When Japan invaded China, we had to relocate various libraries and museums to prevent rare books and treasures from falling into the hands of the enemy. We removed as much as possible to Chungking and later to Taiwan before the mainland fell to the Communists.

Between 1942 and 1944, we established many new libraries, museums, and art galleries in Lanchou, Chengtu, and Chungking. We created a National Institute of Tung-huang concentrating on Buddhist studies in Kansu. These institutions were built from scratch, but they were not quite as elaborate as the institutions they replaced. They were simple and crude at first, but gradually they expanded and improved. We had to improvise and make use of any labor, materials, and skilled people we could find. We even employed more than 1,800 destitute, homeless, unemployed men and women to serve as social education workers. After a relatively short period of training, we sent them to the Southwest, Northwest, and Szechuan-Sinkiang areas to work.

They trekked through high mountains, into the cities and townships, along highways and waterways, as well as into remote villages, to carry out war and social educational work. We used our traditional drama and music to create orchestras, choruses, radio broadcasts, and motion pictures. In each area, we recruited devoted young men and young women who were junior middle school graduates to work in remote areas. We developed national academies of music and drama. Despite their amateur character, they truly boosted the morale of the public to support the war effort.

I also pushed a new program called "education with electrical audiovisual aids," and I encouraged the provinces to organize an education office with audiovisual aids. Touring teams were sent to nineteen provinces and municipalities to demonstrate their use. By the end of 1944, we had fifty-two such teams performing wartime cultural work. I would like to say that, for the vast majority of the population in China, motion pictures and radio broadcasting were two of the most effective tools to carry out successful social education, especially during the festival celebrations and holidays. I later designated more days of the year for special occasions like February 15 as Drama Festival Day; March 25, Art Festival Day; March 26, Broadcasting

Festival Day; April 5, Music Festival Day; and September 9, Sports Festival Day.

I recall that before the war, May 4 was informally recognized as the day to commemorate the youth. But I thought the uprising of March 29, 1911, was more representative of the spirit of young people's patriotism and struggle than the fourth day of May, so I made March 29 Youth Day. I was equally happy to designate September 28, traditionally recognized as the birthday of Confucius, as Teachers' Day.[5] (To show respect to teachers, the California Teachers' Association has for some time designated May 10 as the Day of the Teacher, and President Bush declared, in 1990, that October 3 would become National Teacher Appreciation Day.)[6]

Art education also flourished during the war. Besides organizing the Central Gallery of Art and the Institute of Tun-huang Studies, we sent an investigation team to observe and study art relics in Shensi, Honan, Kansu, and Ningsia. We arranged for an exhibit of Tun-huang art in the wartime capital.

Shansi and Fukien provinces each had a science institute before the war. During the war, the Ministry of Education not only established a National Science Institute but also urged and supervised the provinces and municipalities to establish science institutes. We tried to popularize science education for students in middle schools that had little equipment by encouraging observation and experimentation. Szechuan, Hunan, Hupei, Kiangsi, Kweichou, Kwangsi, Sinkiang, Yunnan, and the municipality of Chungking complied with the ministry's order to establish science institutes.

The shortage of audiovisual equipment and materials was a big problem. The ministry each year had difficulty obtaining foreign exchange to purchase shortwave radio receivers to distribute to the provinces and municipalities. We created a workshop in the ministry to make experimental slide projectors using vegetable oil or calcium carbide. Domestically produced glass, ground by hand or with water power, was used to make lenses. Thirty slide projectors were produced in this fashion that were good enough to show glass slides. We experimented with transparent slides to print stories of historical figures. This kind of slide projector was distributed to schools and social organizations in remote areas without electric power.

To increase the supply of audiovisual equipment and to expand social education for the people, I decided to ask the United States for help, hoping our American friends would lend a helping hand with three hundred movie projectors and overhead projectors and, if possible, some two hundred slide projectors and any recordings that were educational. I presented this plan to John K. Fairbank,[7] who was then the director of the United States Information Service in Chungking, as he was preparing to leave China for the United States. I appealed to him, saying that we urgently needed the above items to use in our mobile units that traveled to remote areas in the interior provinces. I wanted our people to understand our country and the world. I told him I knew there might be some surplus educational materials in the United States and requested that he obtain some for us.

Fairbank responded that I would use them to publicize Sun Yat-sen's Three People's Principles among less-educated people. Fairbank, however, did not say if he thought it was wrong to use the movie and slide projectors to make Sun Yat-sen's ideals well known to our people, even if it was my true plan. The unfortunate fact was that Fairbank, to my surprise, on the basis of his own speculations, flatly declined my request and showed neither sympathy nor understanding. I could think of no reason except that he might fear my project would hinder the expansion of the Chinese Communist party.

My program to educate peasants in the impoverished villages might greatly alarm the Communists, but it was definitely not contrary to the friendly spirit of the U.S. policy. For example, on July 7, 1942, the occasion of China's resistance to Japan's five years of aggression, the United States issued a five-cent stamp in memory of Sun Yat-sen's arrival at Denver, when the Double Tenth Uprising of 1911 occurred in Wuchang. Indeed the year 1942 was significant in the development of Sino-U. S. relations, such as the presence of Stilwell's mission in China on March 4. On October 10, old colonial powers openly relinquished their unequal treaties. Madame Chiang Kai-shek visited the United States, arriving on November 18. The point is that my conversation with Fairbank took place in the early part of November 1943, about a year after all these events had taken place.

Moreover, in the area under the jurisdiction of the National government, I tried to restrict the spread of communist propaganda. As a Harvard University professor, Fairbank's liberal-left stand and his involvement in Chinese internal affairs to undermine the National government and weaken the Kuomintang during wartime in Chungking were well known to the diplomatic and civilian circles.[8] I regret that he accused me of using "thought control" while he orchestrated a "down with Ch'en" campaign on the Harvard campus. Some American newspapers even printed stories with the headline "Ch'en Li-fu's Thought Control." I also publicly stated: "How can thought be controlled? Have you ever seen any attempt in history to control man's thought that succeeded? Even God cannot control the thought of mankind. How can I, Ch'en Li-fu, control the thoughts of others? My main mission is education, and to educate our young generation is at the core of our national interests and educational plans." This unfortunate episode left people no doubt that Fairbank and I were at odds. As a matter of fact, in the first place, the way Fairbank spoke about me made his intention of interfering in our wartime educational policy well known in Chinese intellectual circles, and, second, he made me famous and, to a certain extent, highly controversial. It might be a historical coincidence that at the time Fairbank was attacking me the Chinese Communists were teaching Marxism and Leninism to the general public in the Yenan area. They widely publicized the argument that my educational policy had only one purpose, to Kuomintangize education [*Tang-hua chiao-yü*].

Educating the Minorities

China's border regions in 1939 were inhabited by culturally deprived minority nationalities. A national conference on education adopted a plan to promote education in border areas and a program to implement frontier youth education. Education was to be limited to "the inhabitants of Mongolia, Tibet, and other places whose languages and cultures are of a special nature." Education was to foster national consciousness in accordance with the educational aim of the Republic of China, which was to unify our nation's culture.[9] The border education program also tried to increase ordinary knowledge; improve work skills; upgrade life, physical culture, and health; and rigorously train people to defend against any invaders.

In 1943 we started seventeen national elementary schools for school-age children in the border regions. Taking into account the special circumstances of wartime, we built national secondary schools, national border normal schools with laboratory schools, coastal frontier schools, border middle schools, and border vocational schools to reach some 5,858 students, excluding students in laboratory schools. In 1939 and 1940 we sent individual groups to Chahar, Kansu, and Sinkiang and obtained recommendations for the Miao and Yi minorities in the Southwest. We also formed a Summer Border Service Corps, similar to today's U.S. Peace Corps, for university students by selecting teachers and students from universities to supply educational and medical services. On a higher learning level, we promoted specialized courses, studies, programs, and departments in border regional universities and colleges. In 1945 a national institute of border culture and education was instituted. Shortages of teaching materials, textbooks, and dictionaries were severe. There was a lack of teachers who possessed special knowledge of Mongolian, Tibetan, and Islamic languages, and there were few schoolhouses, recreational, athletic, or sanitary facilities. Yet I believe that one of the great influences of World War II on China was the new focus on the border regions, the minorities, and their welfare.

Overseas Chinese

As Sun Yat-sen said, the overseas Chinese were the mother of our revolution. During the war, the overseas Chinese made great contributions in funding and supporting our war effort against Japan. The war dealt overseas Chinese education a severe blow, as many language schools folded, leaving some overseas Chinese youths destitute.

When war broke out, some twenty-odd overseas Chinese schools in Hong Kong, Vietnam, and Burma moved to the interior. First, we helped them with funds to settle in Fukien, Kwangtung, Kwangsi, and Yunnan. Next, we took care of those students who returned to their motherland for schooling, granting relief to 14,286 overseas Chinese students. The record showed that not a single person of this category was left destitute or homeless.

We also began and financed five additional elementary schools for Chinese in foreign lands. Within China, we built new schools to accommodate the returned Chinese from abroad. In 1940, we launched three national middle schools for overseas Chinese in Paoshan of Yünnan Province, Chiang-chin of Szechuan, and Yo-ch'ang of Kwangsi and two normal schools for training overseas Chinese teachers in Fukien and Kwangtung provinces. Fifty classes were added to receive overseas students from Hong Kong and Macao immediately after Pearl Harbor. Special quotas and preferences for admission were granted to overseas Chinese students at national universities and colleges. This same policy extended into the post–World War II years and in Taiwan. Chinese schools abroad that registered with the ministry during the war received assistance in the form of guidance, textbooks, teacher training, and money. The Chinese schools that remained open in Hong Kong, Macao, the Philippines, Burma, India, Malaysia, and Indonesia worked for one purpose: to defeat the Japanese and win World War II for China and its allies.

Research Activities

In 1936 China had twenty-two research institutes covering thirty-five disciplines with a total of seventy-five postgraduate students. The war brought about the relocation of these universities, and research work suffered. From 1938 to 1944, Chinese university research institutes had increased to forty-nine, to cover eighty-seven disciplines with a total of 422 postgraduate students. Their goal was to train students and encourage professors to engage in research through programs of scholarships, fellowships, research grants, and research awards.

Even a scholar of the stature of Professor Joseph Needham praised our efforts. He was then in charge of the Sino-British Scientific Liaison Office at the British embassy in Chungking. He wrote an article in the British science journal *Nature* reporting on how scholars in Chinese universities did research under difficult conditions.[10] The work at National Chekiang University expecially impressed him. In 1941 I asked the Institute of Physics of the National Research Academy of Peking to produce two hundred microscope sets for other colleges. That same year that academy also established an institute to produce biologic specimens. In 1943 the academy had opened a scientific instrument manufacturing plant. At that time, the National government had negotiated a loan with the United States using our tung oil as collateral. I made a special request for one million U.S. dollars to allow our universities to buy books and instruments from the United States, and these were shipped to China by the end of 1942. I purchased these items with foreign exchange funds, and I asked friendly nations such as the United States and Great Britain for donations. Oxford University in England was the first to respond, and other countries followed simultaneously. Between 1940 and 1941, England sent us sixty-two boxes containing a total of 3,769 books and 146 pieces of fifteen types of journals. From America, China received more than three hundred boxes of publications for distribution to different universities. Through these gifts our research work could continue, and talented people were trained, especially scientists who later achieved great successes.

I installed a fourth division in the ministry's Department of Higher Education to manage only cultural exchanges and students going abroad to study. When the war first started, we limited students going abroad, mainly to conserve China's foreign exchange reserve. In 1939, the ministry established special rules for selecting students to study abroad on the basis of relevance to national defense. We still held examinations to compete for scholarships allotted by the British government (paid for from its Boxer Indemnity Fund) and by the endowment fund of the National Tsinghua University (paid for from the United States' portion of the Boxer Indemnity Fund). We also had a competitive examination for scholarships to commemorate the 70th birthday of Chairman Lin Sheng of the National government. In 1944, the British Society of Culture provided ten scholarships and the British Society of Industry donated ten industrial internships to study in London. India agreed to an exchange program of ten students. Candidates had to pass examinations, and the outstanding students were selected to go abroad. In 1943 the first examination for self-supporting students going to America was held. Out of 751 students taking the examination, 327 passed it. In December 1944, a second examination was held to compete for British and American scholarships and 193 students passed. Successful candidates were supported abroad by foreign exchange obtained at a cheaper official rate. Some of those same students later attained important positions in the fields of government, education, research, commerce, and industry in the United States and elsewhere. Some became world renowned, such as Nobel Prize winners Yang Chen-ning and Li Cheng-tao and former Hong Kong University president Huang Li-song.

The enemy sometimes blocked travel abroad; flying became the only sure means of leaving or returning to China. Student travel was particularly dangerous. Even so, scholarly exchanges continued among China and the United States, Great Britain, and India to include such notables as Joseph Needham of England and Sarvetalli Radhakrishnan of India, who later became India's president. Between 1941 and 1943, fourteen such scholars came to China. In the same period twenty-five Chinese scholars, including Professors Chang Chi-yun, Chou Hong-ching, and Sa Pen-tung, went to England, America, and India to lecture or do research. Another professor going abroad to teach independently was Professor Chen Shen-sheng, later an internationally known professor of mathematics at Berkeley. The Ministry of Education arranged for him to fly in a military transport plane to the United States. He wrote to thank the Ministry of Education personnel who made that trip possible. Financially it was difficult to send students abroad during wartime.

The United States and Great Britain sent their people to China to engage in cultural cooperation, such as Professor Joseph Needham, already mentioned above, and, from the United States, Professor John K. Fairbank. Their work affected China in different ways.

Professor Needham was sympathetic to the Chinese culture, and when in Chungking, he came to see me and discuss his plans. What interested him most were China's scientific achievements and scientific ideas in ancient times and their significance in the cultural history of mankind. He wanted to study, make comparisons, and then publish the results. I fully agreed and encouraged him to do this, introducing him to the people and agencies concerned. Professor Needham later assembled a group of Chinese and British scientists at the Sino-British Science Liaison Office in the British embassy in Chungking to study ancient Chinese science and wartime Chinese scientific research. He also visited all the major academic and cultural centers behind the front lines.

After the war, Professor Needham returned to visit universities in Peking and interviewed Chinese craftsmen from whom he learned how ancient Chinese instruments were made. Many years later he produced the magnificent multivolume *Science and Civilisation in China*, which is still highly regarded by leading scholars. We have completed a translation of the work, and I was the chief translator.

Professor Fairbank, who was then stationed in Chungking and in charge of the U.S. embassy's press and cultural work, did not help to increase the understanding of Chinese culture abroad but, in my opinion, played a negative role. He and his wife, Wilma, actually undermined our government's credibility abroad. They spread rumors, attacked Chinese government officials, and provided false information to the United States government, which helped to produce incorrect policies that eventually benefited the communist forces.[11] Almost fifty years after World War II, and after seeing the publication of many scholarly and popular books in different languages interpreting wartime China-U.S. relations,[12] I personally regard Fairbank's arrogant behavior to be at the same time amusing and regretful. Although he headed an important U.S. office in Chungking, he failed to promote the U.S.-China cultural and educational relationship. I still strongly believe that, to some extent, his activities in wartime China helped bring about the collapse of the National government on the mainland. I never doubted that he was a hero to the Chinese Communists, and for that reason Fairbank and his wife, Wilma, were among the very first to be invited by the Communists to visit China's mainland. He encouraged the so-called Chinese liberals and progressives to vilify the government, and his rumors and falsehoods greatly discredited our government. Fairbank's behavior did not promote cultural cooperation but was instead a form of cultural sabotage. His actions were the exact opposite of Professor Needham's contribution. Needham also leaned toward socialism, but he did not subvert Chinese culture. The two of them should not be compared. In retrospect, I would like to state that I still hold the opinion that the daily activities of the Fairbanks then made me and many of my contemporaries, foreign and Chinese alike, believe that they [the Fairbanks] were at least proleft or leftists, if not communist sympathizers. Many may agree that they were leaning toward the ultimate goals of the Chinese Communists. To some extent, I have wondered if Wilma Fairbank was then actually a Communist. Of course, many would definitely say that she was not.

In 1944, I set up fifty scholarships in ten universities:[13] Oxford University and London University in England, Harvard, Yale, Michigan, Chicago, Columbia, and California universities in the United States, Calcutta University and the International University in India. Each scholarship carried a stipend of U.S. $1,500 per year. Eligible to apply were non-Chinese students who had good records in these universities and who chose to study Chinese language, history, literature, art, politics, economics, or geography for more than one year. Their applications were judged by each university. I later added four more universities to the list: Southern California, Washington,

and Stanford in the United States and Cambridge in England, giving each
five scholarships. These scholarships, which continued until 1948, nurtured
many China scholars in Great Britain and the United States. Among those
students who received Chinese scholarships, two became famous: Professor
Richard L. Walker, an anticommunist scholar, taught at Yale University and
the University of South Carolina, lectured in National Taiwan University,
and served as U.S. ambassador to South Korea. Professor Wm. Theodore
de Bary, a noted sinologist of Columbia University, is a leading scholar who
enjoys a great reputation for academic excellence in the United States.

The Youth

The National government was challenged by the Japanese, their puppets,
and the Chinese Communists. We had to win the support of the young
people because bringing more young people to our side strengthened the
conscription system and increased support for the government.

The young men and women who could afford to attend middle schools
or universities were usually from middle-class families. Their parents and
relatives could never be enticed to collaborate with the Japanese, the Communists, or the puppets if we supported their educational training. The
young men and women who headed for the free zones usually had high
hopes and trusted the National government. If they came to the free zones
and received no assistance, they were easily enticed into becoming students
at the communist-sponsored Resisting Japanese University [K'ang-jih ta-
hsüeh] in Yenan. Therefore, if we wanted to stop them from going to the
area controlled by the Communists, we had to help them. The first thing
we did was to bring into being a student loan system for basic needs: clothing,
food, shelter, and transportation. Second, we set up underground schools
in the enemy-controlled areas, and, third, if that was impossible, we created
secret posts or stations for them to collect educational information. In the
ministry, we had a commission for recruiting and training unemployed
youths. In 1943, we divided the territory behind the enemy lines into 102
districts, appointed a supervisor for each district, and recruited, overall,
154,896 young men and women. We then put them into schools. All war
zone students, including those from Hong Kong and Macao, were sent to
colleges with corresponding departments or courses. A great majority of
these students finished their study this way, which was a major reason for
the dramatic increase in the college student population during the war. Such
wartime youth relief work was a heavy burden for the National government.
As for how many students benefited from the loan system, the records show

the total number to be 128,000. Have they ever repaid their loans? Of course not.

The military conscription of young men deserves a few words. When war first broke out, some people advocated changing education completely to wartime education; others suggested that all college students reaching the required age should be inducted by drawing lots. I thought that while youths should be encouraged to volunteer for the army, inducting all college students required more careful study. The European nations, the United States, and Japan differed from China in that (1) their manpower was limited and so they had to induct all able bodies irrespective of education level, and (2) their education systems were fully developed and a great many more people had received higher education. China's manpower was abundant, but in 1937, college-educated people numbered only forty thousand in the entire nation. Not even one of every ten thousand persons had attended college. Our nation's future depended on these young educated people, so they should not be inducted like others. College students also could serve as reserves and contribute to the war effort in other ways. My idea was they should continue their education while participating in military training and be ready if needed in the future. The supreme authorities of the military agreed with me, although many opposed this view. But even in the United States, were not medical students deferred during the Second World War? And in the Vietnam War, were not college students and graduate students also exempt from military service? A sensible conscription policy conserves talented people for effective use during war and after the peace.

Once my policy was approved in 1938, all youth in the entire nation were informed that Japan had invaded China because we were weak and backward in science and industry and that we must develop that education area despite the war. Our policy had four elements: (1) those who wished to engage in military service would be released by the Ministry of Education; (2) those unfit for military service would continue their education; (3) those already in school, at any level, must respond to the government's call when needed; (4) the government would insist that any youth not serving in the army must attend school.

As the military situation worsened, educated youth were badly needed by the military. Our ministry helped mobilize college students for the armed forces. First on the list were medical students. Graduates of medical and pharmaceutical schools were inducted and sent to serve at military hospitals or government-run medical and health units. Beginning in 1941, 15 to 20 percent of that year's medical graduates were allowed to remain at school, but the rest were assigned to military medical hospitals and other related services.

The next to be drafted were engineering students. In January 1941,

Szechuan and Kiangsi provinces were building military airports, so we allowed engineering students in their senior year to work at those sites. In early 1943, around 10 percent of the graduates of engineering schools were drafted. The great majority of students drafted were interpreters. In the fall of 1941, juniors and seniors of every university's foreign-language department were called up, first to be trained in the Corps of Combat Zone Service [Chan-t'i fu-wu t'uan], then to serve as interpreters for American pilots who had volunteered to help the Chinese Air Force. In 1944, the total of students serving as interpreters reached 3,267 and the total of students called up to serve in medicine and engineering was 3,104. These numbers do not include those students who volunteered to serve in the military or to work as interpreters. All draftees gladly answered the government's call, and they risked their lives to complete their missions. So many students came forward to volunteer that by the end of 1943 some fifteen thousand youths had volunteered to serve. In the winter of 1944 we tried to encourage 100,000 young people to enlist, and tens of thousands volunteered at this critical time to serve their country, especially in the Youth Army [Ch'ing-nien-chün] in the China-Burma-India area.[14]

Many institutions in the North such as the American-sponsored Yenching University and the Catholic Fu Jen University had remained in Peking. We asked Leighton Stuart, then president of Yenching University, to keep an eye on these institutions. As an American missionary and educator, he could fly from Peking to Chungking via Hong Kong. We asked him to contact these institutions in the North, including many schools run by the Catholic church.

We also opened a merchant marine school in Chungking with departments for shipbuilding, ship piloting, and ship engineering. I introduced a five-year vocational training school system for specialized professional education, founded a national central library system, and rescued or purchased more than 120,000 volumes of rare books now located in Taiwan in the Central Library, Palace Museum, and Academia Sinica. These collections contained 344 books of the Ch'ing dynasty, 6,219 books printed in Ming, 230 books from Yüan, 210 books of Sung, and 5 books of Chin, along with 153 Buddhist scriptures found in the Tun-huang caves.

During the war in China, no one ate well or dressed well and everyone was exhausted. The population suffered incredible undernourishment. Stress and tension were part of our daily life. Disputes erupted between faculty and students and among students as well. We tried to introduce a new spirit to counter the desire for material comforts, as in Chiao-tung University and Chung-yang University where Generalissimo Chiang Kai-shek launched a General Spirit Mobilization Campaign [*Chin-sheng tsung-tung-yüan yun-tung*]. It was a difficult time; sacrifices had to be made, but in the end our nation was victorious.

Chiang Becomes a University President

Tensions in the student population soon came to Chiang's attention. One evening in February 1943, Chiang summoned me to dinner; his son, Ching-kuo, was also present. After dinner, Chiang suggested the following: "I am concurrently the commandant of all military schools. What do you think if I take over the presidencies of all universities as well?" I said: "Military schools are different from universities. Military schools stress absolute obedience, and they are easy to control. But universities are not so simple. I am afraid there may be difficulties if the generalissimo wants to take over the presidencies of all the universities. I think a better way is to concurrently become the minister of education. If that became the case, I could be your deputy minister." I responded in this way because I did not want him to assume additional worries. He thought this over for a minute, then said, "Then, let me try one university, how about that?" Too embarrassed to disagree with him, I acceded to his request and suggested Chung-yang University. So he became the president of the Chung-yang University. By law the minister of education could give orders to university presidents. But with Chiang as president, I could not order him around. It was for that reason that I had suggested he become education minister and I his deputy, for as his subordinate, how could I issue him orders? But I later thought of installing a new post called education director at the Chung-yang University that would receive orders from me. I assigned Vice-Minister Chu Ching-nung to that post, and we solved the problem. Always in motion, Chiang was never at the Chung-yang University. Cadets in military schools might not see their commandants very often, but universities were different. A university president had to be on the job. Although Chiang did come to the university when an urgent matter arose, many students neglected to salute him because they did not recognize him. After a few months, he realized the difficulties and stepped down as president. That position then went to Ku Yu-hsiu.

A Suggestion to Hu Tsung-nan

As minister of education, I twice missed the party's Central Committee meetings: the seventh plenary session of the Fifth Party Congress in July 1940 and the eleventh plenary session in September 1943. I missed those important meetings because I had been instructed to go on inspection tours of schools and colleges in Shensi, Kansu, Chinghai, Ningsia, and Sinkiang in the Northwest and in Szechuan, Yunnan, Kweichow, Kwangsi, Kwang-tung, Kiangsi, Fukien, Chekiang, and Anhwei. I went everywhere not occupied by the enemy. I lectured at universities and at middle schools. The elementary school students stood at attention along highways when our entourage passed.

When our inspection delegation arrived at Sian, Hu Tsung-nan invited us to take a look at his troops. On a big drill ground, he and I rode on the same horse to inspect the troops. Afterward, we returned to his home. He asked me for an appraisal of his troops. I said: "Your troops look very good. But are they prepared for a show?" He asked me why I spoke in such a joking manner. I replied: "If I were you, I would assemble all troops and airplanes. On a certain night, I would bomb Yenan flat and occupy it." He said, "The old man [Chiang Kai-shek] has not given the order." I replied: "Ah! For a matter like this who would need an order? If you had done it, Chiang would have been very pleased. You should expect punishment only after you have performed the deed. But would he punish you? He would be so very happy! If only you would do this! You know your troops are directly subordinate to Chiang's command. They were his crack force during the Northern Expedition. Chiang has given you his best units to command. If you should perform this great deed, you might even become his successor in the future. It is regrettable that you lack the resolve to act."

Yet he never seriously considered my advice. If he had listened to me then, we would never have come to Taiwan. Later, when Hu died in Taiwan, I was asked to write an eulogy for him. I said I was unwilling to do so because if I should write anything, I would have to include this episode, which would be uncomplimentary to him. This episode is important in the history of the anticommunist war. If he had accepted my suggestion, history would have been otherwise. At that time, Chiang was so fond of Hu that he even tried to introduce him to the second daughter of H. H. Kung, but Hu declined the offer. Chiang regarded him highly, but Hu lacked that bold vision. I remember even saying to him: "If you do this, I shall share the blame with you. If Chiang wants to investigate, I am willing to go to prison with you." Looking back now, how regretful I feel about this missed opportunity!

We then arrived at Ningsia to meet the governor, Ma Hung-k'uei. He also welcomed me with great hospitality. I was invited to speak at the party given by local leaders. I thought I should touch upon the Koran, but I had no knowledge of it. So the night before, I made a quick study of the Koran. When I spoke, I related the essentials of the Koran to Sun's Three People's Principles. The audience was impressed and believed I understood the Koran quite well. Actually, I had studied the Koran until two o'clock in the morning.

Ningsia impressed me in certain ways. Ningsia was different from other provinces in the Northwest because it had many man-made canals supplying water for irrigation. The Ningsia and Kansu terrain contained fine sand, like powder, and sand-formed rocks and cliffs. Some sand cliffs were five hundred to a thousand feet high but very solid. On both sides of the channels, green trees grew abundantly, blocking out the sandy terrain and giving the region the name of Green Ningsia. Ningsia's water channels had created good farmland. Governor Ma encouraged the people to plant trees, and the air was fresh and clean. He carried out many compulsory policies that benefited the people. I approved of his management, and I urged him to buy a large dragline excavator to expand the canal system because that would enhance Ningsia's prosperity. Ma was a dictator: whatever he decreed, everyone assiduously obeyed.

When I arrived in Chinghai, I found the land composed of sand covered with a layer of pebbles. This was a new phenomenon, and I learned something new. At nightfall, after the sun had set, the pebbles became wet with dew, which then penetrated the soil and made it moist below the surface. The farmers sowed wheat in the cracks of the pebbles, and even birds could not destroy the young shoots. As the soil underneath was moist, wheat grew. Even under such arid conditions, the people used their knowledge of the land to grow food. They were intelligent and knew how to use natural resources. They even gathered pebbles from the hundred-foot-high sand cliff to use to irrigate the soil.

In Chinghai, the people ate mostly beef and lamb; the high animal-fat content provided them with energy and heat when the nights became cold. The Chinghai people also liked to eat *shuan*, or instant boiled mutton. Their religion was Lamaism. I visited Lama temples in which the roofs were made of pure gold. Religion exercised a great influence on the people's belief, and a man was allowed to have four wives. What was the reason for the polygamy? Take a family with four sons for example. Three became Lama monks. Because a Lama monk could not marry, the remaining son was obliged to have four wives. This custom was a natural way to maintain the population, for otherwise the birth rate would have drastically declined.

After consuming beef, we drank tea to help digest the meat. Tea drinking was most important in people's lives. The Ch'ing court had started an agency called the Department of Tea and Horses [Ch'a-ma ssu], which shipped tea from the Yangtze Valley to Chinghai in exchange for horses. This enabled the Ch'ing to have field-mounted soldiers and the people in Chinghai to have their tea, fulfilling that principle "Each supplying what the other lacks, and each taking what he needs."

But in Chinghai I fell ill with dysentery, and a physician could not be found in the rural villages around us. My illness became acute, and a veterinarian was finally called who gave me an injection with a medicinal value only slightly less than he would have given to a cow. I failed to improve, and I was forced to return to Chungking, my strength greatly drained. I later checked a medical book and found that the injection I had received was twice the volume necessary. According to that book, such an excessive amount of medicine could cause a patient to tire and suffer aches in all body joints, followed by death.

The Salt Supply

Salt production, distribution, and consumption had been a long-standing problem in Chinese history ever since Emperor Wu of Han reintroduced the Ch'in dynasty–type monopolies for salt and iron. Debate over the efficiency of such monopolies intensified with the publication of *Discourses in Salt and Iron* [*Yen-t'ieh lun*] in 81 B.C. In Szechuan, people produced salt from an artesian well. After I arrived in Szechuan, I visited such an artesian well, and I learned how China's rulers had tried to manage an economy. Salt production in Republican China has been divided among several regions, and National government regulations dictated that provinces should use only the salt produced in their designated regions. For Szechuan and Kweichow, their salt came from the artesian well, a system of salt supply called *yin-an*. Half a year before the war, some legislators of the Legislative Yüan had tried to abolish this yin-an system of regulating production by salt regions. Anyone violating the predesignated boundaries by producing salt was punished as a private salt supplier.

Why was regional designation so necessary? If the salt produced in Region A was priced at eight cents per catty [1 pint], in Region B at twenty cents per catty, and in Region C at twenty-five cents per catty, their costs and prices were different. To maintain the balance between salt production and sales volume in each area, the regions agreed each would consume its own salt. If regional division did not exist, the salt produced in Region A might be sold in Region B, the salt produced in Region B might be sold in Region C, and so on. The salt industry in the region of the highest price was sure to collapse. The yin-an system was designed to protect the salt workers' livelihood and their industry. We might refer to this arrangement as an embryonic planned economy, or Chinese style of economic protectionism.

Although salt is basic for mankind, individual daily consumption is not great, so every region's inhabitants were willing to spend more to buy salt in their own region even if the price was higher. This form of pricing guaranteed the livelihood of salt workers and their industry. Such a system had its merits, first, to guarantee a supply of salt for all consumers, and, second, to maintain employment for an important industry. But some in the

Legislative Yüan did not approve of this system and wanted a free market system instead. They drafted a New Salt Law [*Hsin-yen fa*] and wanted to abolish the yin-an system in order to install a free market system.

I protested as soon as the draft bill was put forward. At that time, salt produced at Ch'ang-lu in the Tientsin area was the cheapest, being only eight cents a catty. Kiangsu salt was twenty-five cents, Chekiang salt was twenty-eight cents, Fukien salt twenty-seven cents, and Szechuan salt about thirty-four cents a catty, the highest price in the country. In a free market, every salt industry except the one in Tientsin would crumble because they could not compete. In other words, if Ch'ang-lu could expand the supply of salt to meet the demand, the salt industry elsewhere would close down, especially in Szechuan. The Japanese had invaded the North, and if Tientsin had increased salt production and displaced the salt industries elsewhere in China, or if the Japanese had prohibited the production of Tientsin salt, China would be without salt, which might make us lose the war. For that reason, I opposed the free marketing idea for the salt industry. I suggested that we should keep the decentralized salt-pricing system. But free markets were irresistible and a trend of our time. Then I proposed an acceptable formula for all parties involved called the scheme for civilian producing, government purchasing [*Min-chan kuan-shou*] and government shipping, civilian selling [*Kuan-yün min-hsiao*], which saved salt production everywhere. The government set a salt price to purchase the salt from the merchants, who purchased salt from the salt farmers and then set their price for sale to the consumers. Consequently, salt production everywhere was preserved and continued without fear of any uninterrupted supply of salt. Fortunately, the New Salt Law the Legislative Yüan had drafted (as I recorded above) did not have time to be carried out, as the war broke out. During the war we used salt shipped from Fukien, Chekiang, Hunan, Anhwei, and Kiangsi. After Pearl Harbor, artesian wells were extended until they reached rocks that contained salt. Boiling water was then introduced to melt the salt rock, turning it into a salt solution.

In the Kweichou area, salt was especially precious. Inhabitants hung chunks of salt with a string above the cooking pan. When dishes were being prepared, the salt chunk was pulled downward to meet the pan. In northwestern China, we intensified stone salt production, and through eight long years of war we produced enough salt to satisfy the people.[15]

CHAPTER EIGHT

From Victory to Defeat

SPRING 1945—WINTER 1949

Mao Tse-tung in Chungking

ON BEHALF OF GENERALISSIMO CHIANG, Wu T'ieh-ch'eng, secretary-general of the National government, sent a telegram inviting Mao Tse-tung to come to Chungking. Mao arrived on August 28, 1945. I recall that the telegram was sent without prior discussion within the National government. The invitation was probably sent on Chiang's orders. After Mao arrived, he met with Chiang and called on several important Kuomintang and National government officials. He came to my home, which I had named *Kao-lu*, a thatched hut in the mountains. A corner of our reception room had not yet been repaired after the Japanese bombing, and chairs in the room were either broken or old. After exchanging greetings in which I apologized for the shabbiness of my house, I told him frankly why I was opposed to communism and Communists. Mao seemed surprised because everyone had been very courteous to him since his arrival. I was the only exception.

I said: "Dr. Sun Yat-sen's Three People's Principles is a doctrine that combines the best of all the major doctrines in the world. Sun's ideas also are compatible with the spirit of the Chinese cultural tradition. By fusing the latter with the former, Sun produced a unique doctrine that can deal with our many problems and restore our confidence, allowing us to stand on our own two feet without depending on any imperialist power. Three People's Principles is an independent ideology most suitably designed to enhance the self-confidence of the people in a semicolony like China. But communism originated from Soviet imperialism, which has encroached on our country. You must realize that cultural and ideological encroachment is more serious than any other form of invasion. Communism actually existed in China during the period of the Warring States some 2,400 years ago.

People such as Hsu Hsing and Chen Hsing believed in it. But Mencius attacked its absurdity by explaining that manual and mental labor should be treated equally in importance as merely a division of labor. If you, Mr. Mao, had read *The Four Books*, you should remember this. With the Three People's Principles the Chinese people are enjoying freedom and equality."

I continued: "Now China is one of the five powers. The unequal treaties were abrogated with the exception of those with the Soviet Union. We will never willingly be subjects of the Soviet Union. I can say unequivocally that the Chinese people will never tolerate the alien communist ideology, which will be buried in the end. Historically, the invaders of China came mainly from the North. The white bear of the North Pole is known for its viciousness and cruelty. Don't underestimate it. Don't take it lightly. We should not underestimate the Soviet Union, nor should we overestimate it. If China is to avoid becoming a battlefield for the Great Powers, we Chinese must adhere to the Three People's Principles. That is why I am fundamentally opposed to communism."

Mao said: "It is too early yet to put communism into practice. What I want to talk about today is the new democracy."

I replied: "I have already read your *New Democracy*. It is not any better than Sun's Principle of Democracy [*Min-ch'üan chu-i*]." The conversation was disagreeable, and we parted company.

Little did we know that the National government would be forced, not long after, to go to Taiwan. When Mao came to power, he immediately began to practice communism and clung obstinately to his course. Fearing that the Chinese Communists would grow too strong, the Soviet Union lured them into Korea to fight the United States, thereby weakening them. The two sides later agreed that China would supply manpower and Russia would undertake the expenses. But after the Korean War was over, the Soviet Union reneged on its promise and refused to pay the cost. Only then did Mao wake up. Realizing he had been duped, he turned against the Soviets. Both sides fielded huge armies on a border thousands of miles long, facing each other like enemies. After Mao allied with the Soviet Union, not an inch of the vast Chinese territory occupied by Russia was returned. The unequal treaty has not yet been abrogated. When these conditions are compared with the joint declaration drafted on January 26, 1923, by Sun Yat-sen and the Soviet representative Adolf Joffe, they are as far apart as heaven and earth. After all, Sun Yat-sen was a great statesman who, while allied with the Soviet Union, yielded no ground.

As for the Soviet Union, from 1931 to 1939, our National government signed nine agreements and treaties with it (on commerce, normalization of relationship, postal service, nonaggression, loans, and aviation) in good spirit and on an equal footing. On the basis of this record, I believe Chiang

sincerely wanted peace with that country. Our anticommunist policy and
strategy were principally aimed at the Chinese Communists, not the USSR.
We hoped a treaty like the Treaty of Nonaggression of 1937 could be reached
with the USSR after the war was over. It has been said that Stalin intended
to resolve difficulties between China and the Soviet Union by direct contacts
with Chiang. From the spring of 1942 to the summer of 1945, to the best
of my knowledge, Stalin made at least two requests to see Chiang in the
Soviet region in a designated place near the long Sino-Soviet border.[1] Chiang
flatly declined all invitations. Why? My personal observation is that Chiang
learned a bitter lesson from the Sian Incident. He feared that Stalin might
detain him as a hostage. He did not want that to happen again. He had little
trust in Stalin.

As for how Outer Mongolia got its independence, I recall that U.S.
ambassador Patrick Hurley informed Chiang of the decision President Roosevelt had made at the Yalta Conference on June 15, 1945. The direct consequence was that, in a hasty manner, a thirty-year treaty with the Soviet
Union was signed on August 14, 1945, the same day Japan declared its
unconditional surrender. I do not know whether Chiang was under pressure
from the Yalta Conference, but at the Central Political Committee meeting
he moved that Outer Mongolia be allowed its independence.[2] On August 9,
1945, Chiang invited the entire Legislative Yüan to the meeting so that the
motion could be carried. At the time, Tai Ch'i-tao's ideas and mine were
similar: we should not formally recognize the independence of Outer Mongolia but allow some flexibility so that in the future we might be able to
reclaim that territory. We presented our suggestion to Chiang in person, but
he rejected it without giving any reasons. He behaved as though there were
difficulties he could not talk about. The motion was finally approved, but
the future seemed more uncertain. At this point, I cannot speak on behalf
of Tai, but I myself took the position that the thirty-year treaty with the
USSR was basically sound and workable. The treaty could give us more
time to work out our differences with the USSR and, we hoped, end with
permanent peace. The borders between the two countries were long, and
there were complicated problems to resolve in the areas of Manchuria,
Mongolia, and Sinkiang as well as Soviet interests in our harbors, the Yellow
Sea, and the Pacific. A good relationship with the USSR was desirable and
definitely could have helped us reach accord with the Chinese Communists.
Chiang's thoughts and directives can be seen from the six conversations
between T. V. Soong and Stalin in Moscow from June 30 to July 12, 1945.
It is my opinion that negotiations would have been more favorable to us
had we known that the United States was to use the atomic bomb to end
the war with Japan.

Signs of Defeat

When the Japanese surrendered, Chiang appointed Ho Ying-ch'in as his representative to accept their surrender. I paid General Ho a special visit and suggested that he request that the Japanese troops help us safeguard the two roads from Nanking and Pukou to Tientsin. If we could induce the Japanese armies to help us defend the areas along these two railroads, our troops concentrated in the Southwest and the Northwest could directly go to the North. But Ho ignored my suggestion and forced our troops to go to Shanghai and then to board sea transports for Tientsin and Peking.

Our first failure after Japan's surrender was not co-opting the wartime guerrilla forces in the North and in the Northeast who had fought behind Japanese lines. I must say that these guerrilla forces who were so active in China's northern and the northwestern provinces during World War II were truly comrades of the Kuomintang. As we worked closely to win the war over Japan, they helped us tremendously. As soon as Japan surrendered, they needed to be integrated into our National army. Unfortunately, that never materialized. Some military authorities like Chen Cheng refused to recognize their importance and snubbed them. That strong feeling of rejection made them join the Communists, which was a disaster for us. It was like driving fish into deep water, and we unwittingly strengthened the Communists with tens of thousands of new recruits. In retrospect, Chen Cheng unquestionably made many contributions to our military efforts, but we suffered a great loss because of his unwillingness to reorganize and integrate those guerrillas into our armed forces to defeat communist expansion after 1945. I think that Liu Fei, a communist agent high in our military apparatus, might have influenced Chen Cheng's erroneous decisions.

Our second failure was mishandling financial matters. Whenever the Japanese occupied an area, they exchanged their military currency with paper currency issued by the National government on a one-to-one basis. In this way, they gradually absorbed our currency and forced the people in that occupied area to use Japanese military currency. The currency issued by our Central Bank then no longer circulated. At that time, when a banquet table including such delicacies as sharks' fins and birds' nests cost but three or four yuan, a person having ten thousand yuan in paper currency was considered very rich. In the occupied areas, when ten thousand yuan was exchanged for ten thousand yen of Japanese military currency, the people did not feel the hardship. After Wang Ching-wei set up his puppet government, however, he issued his own currency, whereby ten thousand yen in Japanese military currency could be exchanged for only five thousand yuan in puppet currency, which meant a drop in value of 50 percent. After Japan surrendered, people in the former occupied areas naturally welcomed the government currency, but the minister of finance, Chiang's brother-in-law T. V. Soong, who was in charge of currency exchange, stipulated that the exchange rate be two hundred yuan in puppet currency to one yuan of government currency. He believed that only a small amount of government currency was required to exchange for all the puppet money. Our people suffered greatly. Those who had five thousand yuan in puppet money could exchange it for only twenty-five yuan in government money. Moreover, government currency had already been devalued, which meant that a person with ten thousand yuan would end up with only twenty-five yuan in hand.

At the start of the war, I had spent ten thousand yuan to help two universities relocate: one was Fuhdan University and the other Ta-hsia University. Both were in Shanghai and did not have funds to relocate. That example shows how a rich man's wealth of ten thousand yuan could be quickly reduced to twenty-five yuan because of the war. This monetary policy paved the way for a communist victory.

Our government's financial policy now turned a man with money into a man without money, and for those without any money to start, it was disastrous. I had not quite understood the phrase "People impoverished, wealth drained" [*Min-ch'iung ts'ai-chin*], but I now understood its meaning. A mistaken economic policy could drive an entire population to poverty. The rich became poor, and the poor were utterly destitute. In other words, we greatly helped the Communists by turning the people into proletarians.

Shortly after VJ-day, we returned to Shanghai to find everything extremely inexpensive. One yuan of our currency allowed us to purchase items worth two hundred yuan in puppet money. Everyone went on a buying spree, and that made the common people hate us. A failed military policy meant losing valuable guerrilla forces who were forced into the communist camp; a failed financial policy helped the Communists by reducing rich people to the status of proletarians. These two failures, in my opinion, eventually forced us to flee to Taiwan.

If I were to write the history of those years, I would conclude that Chen Cheng and T. V. Soong were mainly responsible for turning the mainland over to the Chinese Communists. The common people quickly began to hate the Kuomintang, but at the outset they only wanted a government to bring them hope. A great psychological turnabout had helped the Communists achieve their victory.

T. V. Soong's Financial Policy

During the war, we knew about the close relationship Chi Chao-ting had with the Communists. H. H. Kung had given him work because they came from the same province. When T. V. Soong later took over the post of finance minister from H. H. Kung, he continued to employ Chi. Those at the investigation bureau had already warned Kung and Soong of Chi's background. Kung trusted him and ignored our advice. T. V. Soong had come from abroad, possessed little knowledge of the Chinese language, and used English in his daily dealings and also in written communication. Chi Chao-ting also had a good command of English, and the two of them got along fine. Both Kung and Soong thought highly of Chi's ability, but Chi actually was a spy working for the Communists. He specialized in feeding ideas to Kung and Soong that would damage the country and discredit the National government.

One very bad idea was repaying the principal of gold deposit certificates at 60 percent of their value. Twice I spoke against it at the Supreme National Defense Council meetings. I argued: "Issuing of gold deposit certificates was initiated by the Executive Yüan and approved by the Legislative Yüan. How can we now allow only 60 percent of their value to be repaid when held by the people?" Chiang replied: "This is Minister Soong's suggestion after long deliberation. He says that is the only way. Do not doubt him."

I said: "There were maids and chauffeurs who borrowed money to buy gold deposit certificates, if only to express their patriotism. But now they are asked to cash in an ounce or two of gold at only 60 percent of its value. This is unconscionable." Hearing this, Chiang said, "Then how about repayment at 100 percent for those who cash in no more than two ounces."

Chiang trusted Soong too much. He thought Soong was the expert in financial affairs. But many matters require only common sense. At that time, quotations of gold deposit certificates rose and on the black market were valued even more than the official rate, which reflected their demand. In the first period the government issued 2,000,000 yuan and certificates. The government could have issued another 5,000,000 yuan in the second period to meet market demands and redeem the first issue at face value without imposing a discount. Our government's financial credit rating would be maintained. Why did Soong not do this? Why did he let our government's financial credit rating fall to rock bottom?

Moreover, the government also had issued U.S. dollar deposit certificates, bought chiefly by patriotic overseas Chinese. These certificates were supposed to be paid back in U.S. dollars when they matured. But Soong refused to let the certificate holders cash them in at maturity. This behavior was like repudiating a debt. Again, the government lost its credit standing. Such financial policies were irrational. Overseas Chinese begin to lose their trust in the government. After the mainland fell, Chi Chao-ting was appointed by Mao to be the chief of his Foreign Trade Board, proof that Chi had long worked for the Communists.

Because of these errors in our financial policy, along with the great gap in the exchange rate between government currency and puppet currency, the rich became poor and the poor became utterly destitute. Chi Chao-ting's bad ideas had a hand in this, and our postwar policies were wrong in every respect.

When asked on whom shall we put the blame, my response is as follows: Every big decision had to be cleared by Chiang. When I recall those painful years, it is difficult to assign full responsibility. We cannot put the blame entirely on Chiang alone. Certainly, T. V. Soong's monetary policies made many people shudder at that time. When H. H. Kung was relieved of his office, he turned over a great deal of gold to Soong, along with much silver. The decision to sell gold in large quantities seems to me to be inconceivable. The entire nation was at the brink of financial and economic chaos, and people had panicked. Those who opposed T. V. Soong in Shanghai spoke out loud and clear. Labor unions and commercial associations went on strike. Chiang even sent me to Shanghai to see if I could calm the unrest.

As soon as I arrived in Shanghai, I invited leaders of labor, commerce, and society to talk. They complained that T. V. Soong's management was bizarre and unreasonable. The economy would be doomed if he continued to manage in this way. I asked everyone to be calm; with reason we could resolve this predicament. I gave a speech to the leading elite in Shanghai titled "What Should Be Our Economic Policy of *San Min Chu I*?" [*San-min chu-i ti ching-ch'i cheng-ts'e yen-kai ts'-mo-yung*]. I criticized the foreign banks in Shanghai that were engaged in commerce; the foreign banks bought agricultural products cheaply and shipped them to their own country, processed them, and then resold them to us at a higher price. The management policy of foreign banks in Shanghai was threefold: to ignore agriculture, give short shrift to industry, and emphasize commerce. Our economic policy should foster agriculture, promote industry, but not exaggerate commerce.

The day after, newspapers like the *Central Daily News* [*Chung-yang jih-pao*] published my speech. T. V. Soong, then president of the Executive Yüan and holding the post of finance minister, heard about it and ordered Chiang Meng-ling, secretary-general of the Executive Yüan, to bring a newspaper to Lushan to complain to Chiang about my attacking his economic policy. Chiang immediately sent me a courteous telegram: "Dear Li-fu, if you have any opinions about finance, please tell me. Don't express them publicly."

I took the newspaper article and went to see Soong. I said: "Dear T. V., take a look at this. Does my speech condemn you or help you? Please take ten minutes to read it carefully." After he finished reading it, he said: "No, you did not condemn me. Your message is well written!"

I said: "In my speech, I only explained that in recent years our financial policy had copied that of the foreigners and emphasized commerce. It was not suitable to the needs of China today. I suggested a thorough examination of our financial policy and then launching a reform. This would exonerate you. I did not expect to cause any misunderstanding with you. I am leaving Shanghai for Nanking tomorrow."

He said: "Don't leave. Tomorrow I will invite the responsible persons in finance, industry, and commerce in Shanghai to a meeting at the Central Bank. I especially want you to speak." I knew of his arrogant personality, but this act of his was unprecedented. I said: "I have already bought my train ticket to return to Nanking. I cannot delay." But his repeatedly sincere pleas for me to stay finally persuaded me to return the train ticket. That night Soong also invited some twenty leaders of Shanghai's financial, in-dustrial, and commercial circles to the meeting the next day at the Central Bank.

My speech again emphasized the economic policy of the Three People's Principles. I pointed out that the financial system used by the National government had been adopted from the imperialists who had occupied China for many years and exploited our resources. That system was unsuitable for China's needs and should not be blamed on Soong. I hoped that he and others would cleanse that system of its age-old malpractices and adopt the economic policy as set forth in the Three People's Principles.

My speech lasted about forty-five minutes, and Soong sat quietly in his chair listening to me. I was told later that it was rare for T. V. Soong to hear others speak and behave so patiently. After I finished my speech, he asked if there were any questions in the audience. His extemporaneous comment was that my speech made good sense. He hoped that everyone would reflect on it. In my speech I had stated: "I am not a student of political science, economics, or banking. I only speak as a true believer in the Three People's Principles who wants to see the present financial system reformed to meet the needs of the country and society. I certainly believe Soong has the daring and resoluteness to carry out such a reform."

After the unrest in Shanghai caused by the anti-Soong strikes had quieted down, I went back to Nanking. Upon Chiang's return from Lushan, I wrote him a report, describing what I had observed and heard in Shanghai and how I placated the unrest. I pointed out that, for the moment, the problem had been solved but that our financial policy was on the verge of bankruptcy and required an immediate change. After reading my report, Chiang ordered the formation of a Committee for Economic Reform [Ching-chi kai-ko wei-yuan-hui] and appointed me as its chairman and Liu Chien-chiung as my deputy.[3] Besides T. V. Soong, many of its members were scholars and experts. Soong regularly attended the meetings, which must have been difficult for a financial expert long known for his arrogance. We then drafted a plan for economic reform, had it approved as law, and, before I was to leave for the United States to observe democracy in action, presented it to Chiang for the Ministry of Finance to implement.

I believed it required military power to found a state but economic power to strengthen a state. Although Sun Yat-sen understood economics, he was not skilled in military affairs and had failed to unify China. Chiang was a genius in military affairs but lacked experience in economics; therefore he failed to keep order in the world he had fought to control. If, despite all the problems we encountered after the war, we had kept H. H. Kung in charge of financial and economic affairs instead of allowing T. V. Soong to take over, we would not have been forced to come to Taiwan. Looking back, I can only heave a sigh of immense regret. Still, I want history to judge him fairly: He should be well regarded for his great contribution to the financing of the National revolution during the years of the Northern Expedition and after Chang Hsüeh-liang pledged allegiance to our National government and endorsed the Three People's Principles in December 1928.

Marshall's Mission

After I had served as minister of education from January 1, 1938, to November 20, 1944, Chiang summoned me to be director of the Kuomintang's Central Executive Committee's Organization Department and to take charge of the National Assembly's election of representatives as well. He had decided to recall the National Assembly to draft the consitution.[4] So I resigned from the Ministry of Education. On August 14, 1945, Japan surrendered unconditionally. In the latter part of November, Chiang invited me to lunch at his Wangshan official residence in Chungking along with his elder son, Ching-kuo. After the meal, Foreign Minister Wang Shih-chieh came by to report to Chiang that the United States would send General George C. Marshall to China to mediate the dispute between the Nationalists and the Communists.

After I heard Wang's report, I candidly and resolutely told Chiang: "This is no good. Anyone else coming here would be better than General Marshall!"

Chiang asked, "Why is that so?"

I said: "First, the problems between the Nationalists and the Communists could be better solved by going to the Soviet Union for talks. If we let the United States be the mediator, it will be too embarrassing for the Soviets, who will only raise obstacles. Second, in my opinion, the Communists are experts in delaying tactics so they will gain time to build up their armies to confront us. The United States has little understanding of the communist problem in China and is easily duped. Third, my guess is that opportunities for mediation between the Kuomintang and the Communists are few and far between. General Marshall is a heroic figure and lauded by the entire world. To come here as a mediator, he must succeed, not fail. But if he should fail, how would he take it? Most likely the blame will be on us, but then how are we to handle it? For these three reasons, I believe General Marshall is not the person for the job."

Chiang seemed moved by what I had to say. He asked Minister Wang, "Have you already sent the cable of consent?" Wang answered that the cable had already been sent. (Actually that day was a Saturday, and there was still time to retract the cable.) Wang then added: "The United States is not very well versed in the problems of the Chinese Communists. It will be a learning experience for them if they participate in the mediation."

Chiang kept silent. But I continued, "In the future, when we learn that the loss outweighs the gain, it will be too late to lament."

On December 23, 1945, as a special envoy of President Truman, General Marshall flew to Chungking. The next day was his birthday. Chiang prepared an elaborate banquet to welcome him and to celebrate his birthday. Little did we know that he would have the impertinence to speak with the tone of a colonial governor and severely lecture us. All the civil and military officials attending the banquet were offended and felt unhappy.

After the dinner, Chiang asked Marshall to meet with Wang Chung-hui, then secretary-general of the Supreme National Defense Council, Wu T'ieh-ch'eng, secretary-general of the Kuomintang Central Executive Committee, and myself, director of the Kuomintang Central Organization Department, so the four of us could discuss the issues. After he had introduced us he said to Marshall, "If you wish to know more about our political and Kuomintang affairs, you may contact these three gentlemen." Marshall then spoke a few words with us and left.

The next day, Wang, Wu, and I paid a courtesy call on Marshall, repeatedly assuring him that if he needed any help, he should feel free to call on the three of us. After that we did not receive so much as a phone call from Marshall, let alone see him.[5] After a few weeks, I spoke with Wu T'ieh-ch'eng, wondering whether the three of us should go pay him another visit. Wu consulted Foreign Minister Wang, but Wang did not agree, so we gave up that idea.

A few months later, I went to Shanghai to deal with student unrest. It so happened that Leighton Stuart was passing through Shanghai on his way to Nanking to answer Marshall's summons. Stuart's assistant, Fu Ching-po [Philip C. Fugh], learned that I was in Shanghai. Pan Kung-chan arranged for me to have a talk with Stuart that lasted seven hours. During the war, as I previously stated, Stuart had often come to Chungking from Peking and frequently met with me. I had trusted him as a courier to relay information to schools in Peking. I met him in Shanghai, suspecting that Marshall must have an important assignment for him. Many leftist students from Yenching University had already infiltrated the U.S. embassy. If Stuart should be appointed the ambassador, they could take advantage of him and do a lot of damage. So I took this opportunity to brief him in detail on the history of the off-and-on cooperation between the Chinese Communists and the Kuomintang. I wanted him to be cautious and well aware of the Communists' plot to seize power. Being pure-minded and a lifelong educator, Stuart became livid with anger when he heard about the Communists' conspiracy. This seven-hour talk enabled me to inform Stuart on how to handle situations in the future. Finally, I asked that Stuart, if he had the opportunity, suggest that Marshall be well briefed in advance. Although our side would do its best to help achieve Marshall's mission, the Chinese Communists would only use these negotiations to gain more time. I cautioned that the chance for Marshall's success was very small. For that reason, he should be prepared for the worst.[6]

On July 11, 1946, Stuart was appointed the United States ambassador to China and presented his credentials on July 19. Sure enough, he told Marshall all that I had told him, and Marshall suspected that I had been prompted by Chiang. Actually, Chiang had never discussed Marshall with me. Long before Marshall came to China, I had expressed my views to Chiang. Events only proved my predictions were correct.

One day, when Chiang was meeting with Marshall, he asked Chiang: "Mr. Leighton Stuart met Mr. Ch'en Li-fu in Shanghai and was told that my mission probably would not succeed and that I should be prepared for that. Is that true?" Chiang smiled: "Ch'en Li-fu went to Shanghai on business. I have not seen him for several weeks. He is full of philosophical ideas, why do you not invite him for a talk?" Thereupon Marshall searched everywhere for me, hoping to talk with me. I received a long-distance call at home, left Shanghai for Nanking, and made an appointment to see Marshall at his residence.

At first, Marshall did not seem very friendly when he asked me about my attitude toward the peace talks between the Kuomintang and the Communists. I said: "I am a member of the Kuomintang, moreover the director of its Organization Department. At these meetings we are free to speak out, whether pro or con, about the peace talks. But once the Kuomintang has made its decision, every party member must obey. As the director of the Organization Department I particularly should set an example."

Marshall said: "Chou En-lai says you are sabotaging the peace talks, you are against me, and you personally directed your people to attack their *New China Daily* [*Hsin-hua jih-pao*] office at Chiao-Ch'ang-Kou in Chung-king. Is that true?"[7]

I asked, "Do you have any concrete evidence?" I told him that as a student of mining engineering I respected science and was ashamed of such absurd nonsense. I assured him that Chou's words were sheer smear, and I added: "I remember that day you first arrived in China when, after the banquet, the generalissimo had specifically introduced Wang Ch'ung-hui, Wu T'ieh-ch'eng, and myself to consult with you. We even called on you the next day, repeating our offer of service. But months passed and you never contacted us. I first thought that you must already be very knowl-edgeable about Kuomintang affairs. After listening to you, I realize that what you know are the statements of only one of the parties, which contrast sharply with facts. No wonder the peace negotiation is having difficulties. If you have the time, I am willing to tell how it happened."

Marshall said, "Please go on."

Thereupon I stated that, after eight years of war, we welcomed peace negotiations so that the National government would have a chance to catch its breath, to rebuild its army, and to reconstruct the country. Who would not have embraced such an opportunity? Moreover, the Kuomintang had already made its commitment to do this, and it was impossible for any one person to oppose and sabotage the peace negotiations. Being a high-level cadre of the Kuomintang, I had all the more reason to obey. Otherwise, should not the leader of the party penalize me for violating party discipline?"

Marshall was surprised to hear this, but he did not seem to doubt my sincerity. I went on to tell him that before he came to China, I had indeed raised my objections to the generalissimo about his mission. I then listed the three reasons I had given Chiang. I told Marshall that my main reason for thinking this way was that, in the past, I had frequent contacts with the Chinese Communists, especially Chou En-lai. I had come to the conclusion that the Communists were merely exploiting the Chinese people's mentality of being "tired of war after so many years of warfare" to instigate peace talks to gain time. They were not sincere, and there would not be any good results.

I added: "Because I respect your position, I did not want you, a heroic figure in the world's eyes, to take on this mission that is bound to fail. At the very beginning, I had told the generalissimo that anyone but Marshall could undertake this task. It is regrettable that those responsible for these

diplomatic negotiations with our government have had hardly any contact
with the Communists. They have no foresight, and yet they urge you to
come and engage in this thankless task. What I worry about day in and day
out is that, if the negotiations should fail, how can you step down with
honor? For these reasons, when I met Mr. Leighton Stuart in Shanghai I
suggested to him that you must be prepared ahead of time. Today, I am
delighted to be able to tell you in person what I have wanted to say. You
should know that my objection to your assuming this mission was raised
long before you came. In raising my objection I had only goodwill for you
in mind. After you came I only hoped to be of help to you but was given
no opportunity. Now that I can see you in person, I cannot help but tell you
all I know."

Marshall was very moved by what I told him. Realizing that he had
been duped, he wanted me to go on talking. I repeated: "Chou En-lai's
words were all fiction.[8] The *New China Daily* has been stirring up trouble
by planting rumors and hurling abuse at the government. The people are
extremely disgusted with it. That day when the masses marched passed the
New China Daily, someone upstairs threw down a teacup and hurt one of
the marchers. The masses became so enraged they demolished the newspaper
office. At that time I was chairing a meeting at the Ministry of Social Affairs.
Who attended the meeting and when and where the meeting took place and
all are on the record. How could I have the time to go to Chiao-ch'ang-kou
to direct the masses? If you do not believe me, you can ask those who
attended the meeting and you will find out that what I say is the truth."

Having heard all this, Marshall wanted to know the history of the
breakups and makeups between the Kuomintang and the Chinese Communist party. I told him as much as I could remember. I also mentioned
how I and Soviet ambassador Bogomoloff deliberated over the Sino-Soviet
Nonaggression Pact and how I, Chou En-lai, and Pan Han-nien discussed
and decided on the statement of "Together We Confront the National Crisis"
[*Kung-fu kuo-nan*] on September 22, 1937. Marshall showed great interest
and was never bored with my narration. It was close to eight o'clock in the
evening, time for his dinner engagement with Chiang. I wanted to stop, but
Marshall urged me to go on, saying that it would be all right if he got to
Chiang's residence a few minutes late.

Not wishing to disappoint him, I told him how, after the purge of 1927,
I set up an investigation and statistical team modeled on the American FBI.
High-level officials on the team had been in the United States studying
engineering or science. Between 1927 and 1937, that activity was directly or
indirectly under my supervision until I was appointed minister of education.
That was the period when American technology defeated Soviet technology.

We uncovered more than a hundred communist underground units, and about sixteen thousand Communists either defected to us or were captured, many of whom later were employed by the Kuomintang at all levels and proved to be a good investment for us. (Chou En-lai himself told me that he was in Shanghai's International Concessions then, and five minutes later he would have been captured by us.) Ku Shun-chang, head of the Communists' secret service, surrendered to us, which caused great fear among the Communists. During the war, when I served as minister of education, all measures I adopted were designed to block the Communists from influencing our youth. Chou looked on me as his number one enemy. I was not surprised that he used all possible means to slander and smear me. I sincerely believed communism was unsuitable for China as well as America.[9] And Chinese culture was much superior to that of the Soviet Union. It is a culture that loves peace, and it will make great contributions to the future world. I then quickly came to the conclusion: "Should you have any questions, please feel free to give me a ring." I said good-bye and left. This meeting lasted more than four hours, and I must have made an exceedingly deep impression on Marshall, as later events revealed.

I went to see Chiang and briefed him about my meeting with Marshall. Chiang asked, "Has General Marshall ever invited you three to talk?" I said: "Never. This was the first time, and I was the only one he invited." Only then did Chiang tell me that Marshall had misunderstood what I had told Stuart and that Chiang had suggested that Marshall should see me. Chiang thought that the reason Marshall had not interviewed the three of us on matters concerning the Kuomintang was that Marshall held preconceived ideas before he came to China. I recalled the first speech Marshall delivered in Chungking, and that fact was evident. The three of us were prevented from approaching Marshall. A distance had been created, which was a gross error. Furthermore, Communists were at Marshall's side, and their mission was to isolate Marshall from us. It was inevitable that Marshall's judgment was tainted, and he trusted the wrong side. (I should record here that on August 15, 1964, at the request of the State Department, I met with U.S. officials at the Sheraton Hotel in New York City to discuss the question of "the loss of China." I stated that the failure of Marshall's mission weakened and isolated Chiang; at the same time the position of Mao Tse-tung in the Chinese Communist party was immensely strengthened.)

The San-min chu-i Youth Corps held its Second National Congress in Lushan September 1–12, 1946.[10] At the closing ceremony, Chiang gave a detailed speech analyzing the international situation to the entire membership. Afterward, he invited me to return with him to his official residence. He was visibly angry about Marshall's attitude. I took this opportunity to tell him that I had objected to Marshall's coming all along for precisely the same reason. Marshall wanted his mission to succeed and so had to accept the Communists' unreasonable demands and force us to accede to them. We had to endure and not quarrel with Marshall because the responsibility of any failed peace negotiations would fall on us. Should he leave empty-handed, Sino-American relations would be damaged, much to our disadvantage. Chiang listened to me in silence.

Not surprisingly, Marshall's mission did fail. The communist tactic of using the negotiations to gain time succeeded. In order to save Marshall's "face," President Truman had to think of some other reason for calling him back, so the White House announced he would be secretary of state.

On January 8, 1947, when leaving China, Marshall issued a personal statement, the entire text of which was cabled from Washington, D.C., by the Central News Agency.[11] It stated: "The greatest obstacle to peace in China has been the complete, almost overwhelming suspicion with which the Chinese Communist party and the Kuomintang regard each other. On the one hand, the leaders of the government are strongly opposed to a communistic form of government. On the other, the Communists frankly stated they are Marxists and intend to work toward establishing a communistic form of government in China, though first advancing through the medium of a democratic form of government of the American or British type. The government leaders are convinced in their minds that the communist-expressed desire to participate in a government of the type endorsed by the Political Consultative Conference last January had for its purpose only a destructive intention. The Communists felt, I believe, that the government was insincere in its apparent acceptance of the Political Consultative Conference resolutions for the formation of the new government and intended to use coercion by military force and the action of secret police to obliterate the Communist party. Combined with this mutual deep mistrust was the conspicuous error by both parties of ignoring the effect of the fears and suspicions of the other party in estimating the reason for proposals of opposition regarding the settlement of various matters under negotiation."

Marshall had seen through the Communists, their insincerity as peace negotiators, their malice in creating difficulties, and their ultimate goal. Moreover, Marshall also stated that the "dominant group of reactionaries" in the Kuomintang had opposed every effort he made to influence the formation of a coalition government. Tillman Durdin, a newspaperman with the *New York Times* in China from 1930 to 1937, was closely in touch with Marshall, and for some time he assisted Marshall in an official capacity during Marshall's thirteen-month service as special envoy to China.[12] Durdin came to see me and asked me what I thought of Marshall's statement. He believed that Marshall had me in mind when he made his statement. He also believed, and the *New York Times* reported, that I was regarded as "the civilian leader of the most uncompromising anticommunist wing of the

Kuomintang." He asked for an interview. Informed about Durdin's intention, and wanting verbal precision, I asked my friend Li Wei-kuo to translate my comments on Marshall's statement of January 7, 1947, into English. The text was sent out by the Central News Agency in New York, and during the interview, I handed him a copy in person. The whole text appeared in the *New York Times*, January 14, 1947:

> First of all, I wish to congratulate General Marshall for his achievements in fulfilling his mission since his arrival in China. He contributed much toward bringing together the various political parties, though it is regrettable that the Chinese Communist Party finally decided to abstain from participating in the National Assembly. He contributed toward expediting the successful convocation of the National Assembly, and above all, the adoption of what he described as a "democratic constitution which in all major respects is in accordance with the principles laid down by the all-party Political Consultative Conference of last January."
>
> Secondly, I admire him for the insight he has shown in his study of the Chinese problem. I fully share his point of view on the Chinese Communist Party. If, however, he could have devoted a little more time in contacting members who take a leading part in the Kuomintang, his appraisal of the Chinese situation, in its proper breadth and depth, might have been more enlightening.
>
> Thirdly, General Marshall is correct in pointing out that China's communist problem is different in character from that of the U.S. He is also right in warning the American public against the danger of evaluating the armed and powerful Chinese Communist Party by the standards used in evaluating small communist groups in America.
>
> Fourthly, General Marshall shows remarkable knowledge in pointing out that the Chinese Communist Party is determined in conducting "a very harmful and immensely provocative" propaganda without regard for the facts, without any regard for the suffering of the people, and that they are equally determined in engineering the overthrow of the Government and the collapse of the national economy.
>
> Fifthly, General Marshall is particularly sound in calling our attention to the fact that the Chinese communists are Marxists of the pure breed and "intend to work toward establishing a communistic form of government in China," and that in this sense they are a different species from agrarian reformers, as some Americans have unwittingly considered them to be.
>
> Sixthly, I entirely agree with him on this thesis that China henceforth should bring about constitutional democracy by enforcing the new constitution and welcoming the minor political parties into the Government.
>
> What is regrettable—and indeed a shame to us—is that General Marshall, a great friend from a great ally, in spite of his advanced age and in spite of hardships and pains, has labored and struggled in China's cause during the last 13 months and in the end has earned the distrust of a handful of the Chinese, that is the Chinese Communist Party. In the deliberate misrepresentation and abuse of the action, policies, and purposes of the American Government the communist propaganda has been without regard for the truth, without any regard whatsoever for the facts, and has given plain

evidence of a determined purpose of misleading the Chinese people and the world and to arouse a bitter hatred of Americans—it has been difficult to remain silent in the midst of such public abuse and wholesale disregard of facts, but a denial would merely lead to the necessity of daily denials, an intolerable course of action for an American official. When I read these sentences I could well imagine putting myself in his place, how painful and disillusioned at heart he must have been.

But to those who are familiar with communist tactics, it is not surprising at all. Is it not true that during the past 20 years the Chinese communists have every day been using the same method, and even more vehemently, against the Government of their own country and their own people? Have they not been purposely distorting the truth, misrepresenting the facts, and indulging in vicious and abusive propaganda with the plain intention of misleading the Chinese people and the world and arousing a bitter hatred of the Chinese Government and the Kuomintang? Take myself as an example. I was the first pioneer in blazing a trail for cooperation between the Kuomintang and the communists. In fact, I was the man who actually brought to consummation the plan of cooperation for the initial period. Yet today the one who has suffered most from their misrepresentation, insults, and abusive tactics is none other than myself. In view of my own experience, anyone, accustomed to communist tactics, should not take their attacks on the U.S. as something unusual or surprising.

Most Kuomintang delegates in the National Assembly are persons who have either been schooled in Anglo-American liberalism or influenced by it. Unfortunately, they are the same persons who have been painted by communist propaganda as "reactionaries" or "die-hards." In point of fact, however, they are also the "liberals" who have adopted a democratic constitution which in all major respects "is in accordance with the principles laid down by the all–party Political Consultative Conference of last January." The communists are always masters in devising catchwords and slogans and in using them as deadly ideological weapons. They do so without the slightest moral scruples and with such persistence that people are unconsciously influenced and in the end take the thing at its face value. During the last 20 years, those who have uncovered or frustrated the communist plot of "establishing a communist form of government in China" have come under the label of "reactionaries and die-hards."

The study of political problems is the same as that of scientific problems. When a scientist approaches a problem of science, he must keep himself in close contact with the phenomena under study, and, by thoroughly investigating and analyzing all the relevant facts involved, discover the truth. The same method should be used in the study of the problems of politics. Staying [in] China for thirteen long months, possessed of immense wisdom and enthusiasm, and armed with a scientific method and mind, General Marshall, after a careful study of the situation, has come to discover [that] "a very harmful and immensely provocative phase of the Chinese Communist Party procedure has been in the character of its propaganda" and that "the dyed-in-the-wool communists do not hesitate at the most drastic measures to gain their end." Also it is no wonder that the General should have realized that the Chinese communists are Marxists of the pure breed and that their action and words are merely the means and policy with which

to attain their ultimate aim of "establishing a communist form of govern-
ment in China." So, while the "democratic form of government of the
American or British type" is the very ideal that the Kuomintang has been
for years advocating and striving to achieve, this form of government, as
General Marshall has rightly put it, is only a medium through which the
Chinese Communist Party intends to reach its final goal.

I heard that the U.S. embassy cabled the complete text of my afore-
mentioned statement to Marshall. By then Marshall's understanding of me
had become quite different from previous times. After he read my six-point
reflections, he hopefully would no longer regard me as a "die-hard element"
and a "reactionary."

In retrospect, the Communists' strategy was to divide the enemy. In
Kwangtung they branded Hu Han-min as the rightist, Wang Ching-wei as
the leftist; their tactic was to back the left and to condemn the right. After
the Northern Expedition forces had taken control over the provinces south
of the Yangtze River, they created terms like CC, Central Club, CC Clique,
attacking my brother Kuo-fu and me in order to divide the Kuomintang's
Central Executive Committee. Later they fabricated Chiang, Soong, Kung,
and Ch'en as the Four Big Families [*Ssu-ta chia-tsu*] and made all kinds of
false charges to malign those in the government. After the war of resistance
against Japan broke out, they again tried to break up the Kuomintang by
dividing it into "liberals" and "die-hard elements." Those who took a strong
anticommunist stand were branded as "die-hard elements" and/or "reactionaries" because these people persisted in opposing communism and refused to be threatened or lured by the promise of gain. Those who were
most virulently attacked by the Communists were actually the people whom
the Communists feared the most. Since I had taken command of investigation and statistical work, I had been responsible for more than sixteen
thousand Communists defecting. My policy during my tenure as minister
of education had impeded communist expansion. Therefore, I naturally
became the number one target of their attacks. But I had disciplined myself,
and I was unassailable. All kinds of accusations only enhanced my reputation.

That reputation prompted Frederick Grain, China correspondent for
the American magazine *Time*, to interview me in May 1947. I explained to
him the main sources of Chinese culture were the *I-Ching* [*Book of Changes*]
and Confucian philosophy, and I described in detail the history of nationalist-
communist cooperations and split ups. Little did I know that on the cover
of *Time*, May 25, 1947, my portrait would appear, painted by Artzybasheff,
a famous White Russian artist. The caption of the cover says "China's Ch'en
Li-fu, the essence of life is the performance of benevolence." A three-and-a-
half-page article described my thoughts, beliefs, personality, personal integrity, and achievements. Grain reported that I "want the West to try to see

Cover of *Time*, May 25, 1947.

China's problems through Chinese eyes." He continued that "when George Marshall, like many another American, last year suggested coalition with the communists, men like them were shocked (although Ch'en has been too correct to say so)." Grain suggested that "to Marshall and other Americans, communism still seems a distant threat. Ch'en and his friends have had the Reds breathing down their necks for twenty years. It has been war, bitter, open, accepted." I thought the tone was fair. Grain had not told me about the honor before the publication. Indeed, it was a surprise. As was customary, the original of the cover portrait was given to me as a gift. Such public display boosted my international reputation. The next year, when I visited the United States and Great Britain, those who received me often used my portrait on *Time*'s cover as a topic to begin a conversation. But within China, a number of people were quite unhappy and jealous of me.

Student Unrest in the Kuomintang Party School

I have already mentioned above that it was my elder brother, Kuo-fu, who initiated the training program for the Kuomintang. He realized that in our struggle with the Communists, the party could not exist and grow without a corps of strong and able cadres. So he had proposed to the Central Executive Committee that a party school be established in 1927–1928. When the School of Kuomintang Affairs [Chung-yang tang-wu hsüeh-hsiao, abbreviated as t'ang-hsiao, party institute] was founded, Chiang became its head, but my elder brother was actually in charge. It later was renamed the Central Political Institute [Chung-yang cheng-chih hsüeh-hsiao] and was supported by the Kuomintang. Unlike other schools, it was not under the jurisdiction of the Ministry of Education but was administered by the Kuomintang's Central Executive Committee. Its president was Chiang, and the school's Administration Committee was composed of party seniors such as Hu Han-min, Ting Wei-fen, Ch'en Kuo-fu, and Tai Chi-t'ao. I later was invited to be a committee member. Acting out of their respect for my brother, these elder party members did their best to help Chiang, and the school ran smoothly.

The committee held immense power and responsibility and determined all policies and decisions affecting the school. Chiang's instructions were obeyed only after the committee's deliberations. Chiang was often with his troops and spent little time at the school, so the Kuomintang seniors performed most of the administrative work.

At that time, my elder brother, Kuo-fu, was considered too young among the seniors, yet he spent the most time at the school. As director of the General Affairs Department and later the acting dean, he worked hard to improve the school's training and reputation. He worked closely with the students and often spoke individually with each one. He understood the students' problems and helped to solve them. Thus the students had a very good impression of my brother. The school affairs planned by him first had to be approved by Chiang and then by the Administration Committee. Whenever Chiang had ideas, he wrote them as suggestions for my brother to pass on to the relevant departments to carry out. The institute was unlike any other four-year college or university in China. The institute relied on military discipline, and its entrance examination was exceptionally difficult.

It discouraged personal relationships. If a member of a Kuomintang veteran's family wanted to attend the school but failed the entrance examination, recommendation letters intervening on the applicant's behalf were useless. On the average, one out of twenty who took the entrance examination was accepted as compared with one out of five passing the joint college entrance examination. This low rate of acceptance also had something to do with the fact that all institute students studied completely free and at public expense. Many young men from low-income families applied. Students in the school received strict discipline and acquired a strong belief in the Three People's Principles. After graduation and more training, they moved to important posts. Students took required courses in political science and economics, but the institute also had departments offering cooperative services, public administration, training for dealing with Mongolian-Tibetan problems, and journalism, none of which could be found in other universities. Many personnel in cooperative banks and local government were graduates of the institute. Many journalism graduates worked in important newspapers. The institute attracted the best talent in the country.

Institute students also achieved good scholastic performance. When I was in charge of the Ministry of Education my research revealed that graduates of the institute usually came from the upper and upper-middle levels of the civil service. All public servants who passed high-level civil service exams were required to go through a training period at this school. This school trained the best personnel to rebuild the country. My brother devoted the best part of his life to this institute. His love for the students was so extraordinary that they looked on him as their father or elder brother. Because of the institute's success, the Communists attacked the teachers and students of the institute, labeling them members of the CC Clique. I must make clear that my elder brother, Kuo-fu, never had an adequate education, and perhaps this was why he was so fond of education. His fulfillment of his duties at the institute clearly confirms my belief.

My brother greatly expanded the Kuomintang's influence and strengthened its organization; he also was involved in the party's financial affairs and made good use of overseas Chinese contributions by constructing the Chunghan Road, which extended from south to north in Nanking City, the Cemetery of Soldiers Killed in Action, the Central Broadcasting Station, and the Guest House for overseas Chinese.

During the war, Chiang also founded the Central Cadre Training School [Chung-yang kan-pu hsüeh-hsiao] and appointed his son, Ching-kuo, as its dean. This school also produced many talented personnel. But many people also wondered why it was necessary to have two schools for the same purpose. Chiang headed both schools. As the dean of the Central Political Institute, my elder brother, Kuo-fu, felt there was no need for the two schools to exist. He realized that he was getting old and that it was only logical to let younger men take over. He petitioned Chiang to merge the two schools into one and suggested that Ching-kuo should assume the deanship. The petition was sent, but months passed without any word from above.

This was in spring 1947. At this time Chu Chia-hua and I exchanged jobs. He took over the Ministry of Education, and I returned as the director of the Organization Department in the central Kuomintang. Within the Central Political Institute there was a Kuomintang branch, of which I was also a member. But Chu had not informed me that Ching-kuo was to be the dean of the institute. When the sudden order came, Chu Chia-hua was in Hangchou, and my brother was also caught unawares. Students were upset by the sudden news, and many became angry. They put up posters everywhere to object to Chiang Ching-kuo's being appointed their dean.

When Chiang heard what was happening, he called me in, asking, "Do you know that there is student unrest in the party institute?" I said, "No, I don't know." He asked again, "How come you don't know?" I replied by asking, "Just exactly what has happened?" He said, "When it was announced that Ching-kuo would be their dean, many students objected." I said, "Minister Chu made this announcement without notifying me, that's why I had no idea." He said, "Quickly go and take care of that matter, and do not allow any misunderstanding to develop!"

Many people thought the Central Political Institute was controlled by my brother and me. I had been teaching a course on the Three People's Principles for many years,[13] and the students and I got along well. One might say that the students held a certain respect toward us, the two brothers. When the student unrest erupted, Chiang naturally wanted me to handle it. He ordered me to go quickly and solve the problem and not cause any further misunderstanding. I immediately rushed back to the school. Our postwar demobilization had been completed; the school had moved from the South Warm Hot Spring [Nan-wen-ch'üan] in Chungking to its original campus in the Red Paper Corridor [Hung-tze-lang] of Nanking. Arriving at the school, I asked the administration to assemble the entire student body. I spoke to the students: "You should not object to Ching-kuo. You ought to welcome him." I mentioned many reasons, and the students finally accepted my advice. Immediately they took down the posters attacking him, and they even sent delegates to welcome Ching-kuo as their new dean.

But having handled the affair as Chiang had ordered, I was maligned by many people. "Ah, how powerful you are! With one speech you could turn the situation around!" Then, Ching-kuo decided to refuse the deanship, which finally went to Ku Yu-hsiu, a vice-minister of education. Evidence surfaced later that Chu Chia-hua's negligence had caused the student demonstration and incited other students of the Youth Army [Ch'ing-nien-chün], who had fought in the China-India-Burma theater at the war's end and were under communist influence. The truth was this well-planned plot was designed to stir up student discontent against Ching-kuo. Thinking back, if Minister Chu had notified the institute's Kuomintang branch in advance, we would have had time to prepare the students for the news and they could not have been so easily duped by the Communists.

Some time later, as the president of two Kuomintang party schools, Chiang ordered the Cadre School and the Central Political Institute to merge. After we moved to Taiwan, the school was reopened and became the National Chengchi University. Its president was appointed by the Ministry of Education, a practice that continues today.

The National Assembly of 1948

As I stated earlier, I was transferred to the Kuomintang Organization Department in February 1947 to help elect the National Assembly. The National Assembly was convened on March 29, 1948, and closed on May 1, 1948, in Nanking with 2,908 delegates. The most serious problem at the convention involved the participation of other political parties. For many years, minor but friendly parties had not actively engaged in political activities because of the war. Their politicians were scattered around the country, were not vigorous, and lacked experience. They were unable to compete with the Kuomintang candidates. To remedy this situation, the Central Executive Committee offered a few seats each to the Youth party [Ch'ing-nien-tang] and the National Socialist party [Min-chu-she-hui tang]. But getting our elected candidates to give up their seats proved to be exceedingly difficult. Kuomintang candidates, elected after many years of hard work, were asked to sacrifice their seats to members of the Youth party and/or the National Socialist party who had never served in office. In my opinion, this was too much to ask. But the decision had been made, and the Organization Department had no alternative but to enforce it. This was a very undemocratic act because the person receiving the majority vote should be elected, not the person who got fewer votes. For example, if a Kuomintang member received more than thirteen thousand votes and a Youth party member received some three thousand votes and we insisted that the one receiving thirteen thousand votes yield to the one receiving three thousand votes, we had obviously violated the spirit of democracy, not to say the law. But many of our party comrades, after much persuasion and agreeing to take the interest of the country into account, gave up their seats, but in their hearts they probably were unwilling. Many commented that while the Youth party and the

National Socialist party received the nominal benefits of democracy, the Kuomintang still appeared to be dictatorially opposed to the will of the people. This sort of criticism was very painful to endure. I consulted with Wu T'ieh-ch'eng, the secretary-general of the Kuomintang Central Executive Committee. I said: "Instead of yielding seats in this manner, why not just change the election law and give more seats to the Youth party and the National Socialist party? It would be much simpler, and it would not violate the principles of democracy. Let's say the Central Executive Committee selects a number of representatives who can bypass the election; then those political parties who are unable to get their members elected can be selected instead. This way will be much simpler." Wu did not like my idea, so I was unable to present this solution at the regular meeting of the Central Executive Committee.

But the Organization Department had been given an odious task, which became my responsibility after I had been sent back to the department. The Youth party and the National Socialist party were still not satisfied with the 120 seats promised them, and they demanded 200 seats. That made our job all the more difficult. After much negotiation, we gave them a few more seats. But those who had been persuaded to give up their seats had friends in the National Assembly who were indignant at this injustice. The meetings of the National Assembly did not go smoothly either because some Kuomintang members, unhappy with the handling of this matter, defied the party's authority by taking opposite stands on issues they had been instructed to support. I was overcome with remorse. By not insisting on the proper method of election, I had committeed the gravest mistake in my entire life. I violated the basic principles of democracy, which under no circumstances should I have done. I had been unreasonable and without human feelings to ask elected Kuomintang candidates to give up their seats. The consequences were tremendous, and I must take full responsibility. At that time, Li Tsung-jen ran for the vice-presidency.[14] Many people who originally would not have supported Li Tsung-jen now came out for him because they were disgusted with the Central Executive Committee. In fact, many were disgusted to the point of hatred. Although the Kuomintang did not want Li to be elected, he was elected by a majority. When politics are mixed with strong personal feelings, there can be disaster.

I reported to Chiang in advance about Li's candidacy, urging him as follows: "Li Tsung-jen wants to run for the vice-presidency. A policy decision on this matter should be made early. Are we willing to allow him to run? If not, we must stop him early. Otherwise, after he has spent a lot of money, energy, and effort campaigning everywhere, it will be difficult to stop him." On hearing this Chiang was very hesitant. He was too embarrassed to curb Li. In principle, anyone should have the right to run for office.

To stop him would be undemocratic. For this reason, Chiang did not attempt to stop him.

Within the Kuomintang, Li had a considerable record of achievement. Born in Kweilin in 1890, he supported Sun Yat-sen in the South and participated in the two Eastern Expeditions in 1925. He was commander of the Seventh Army group during the Northern Expedition. He was with Chiang for the five anticommunist campaigns. He split with Chiang in 1936, but his superb performance in defeating the Japanese at Tai-erh-chuang in April 1938 won him a nationwide reputation. With this background, he ran for the vice-presidency. Actually, I felt that, as leader of the Kuomintang, Chiang could tell Li in advance: "Do not run this time. This is my show. Wait for the next turn and I will support you." That would have been proper.

When the National Assembly first considered electing the president, Chiang recommended Hu Shih to run and sent someone to ask Hu if he would run. Hu Shih replied that it would be an honor for him to be the president, so he agreed to run. Chiang, however, was only being courteous when he invited Hu to run. Perhaps Chiang had thought that with a man of letters as president and him serving as vice-president, a fight over that seat could be avoided. At the time, I believed Chiang should not have acted so presumptuously in yielding the presidency to others. In retrospect, Chiang's modesty was perhaps a good counterbalance for his ego, but he did not realize that many Kuomintang seniors did not agree with his action. Their way of thinking was like this: "We have no objection to you, Chiang, becoming the president. But today you are yielding this honor to a non-Kuomintang member. He is not even the leader of a minor party. Are you saying that those of us who have gone through fire and water to follow Sun Yat-sen and his revolution are not qualified for the office of president?" Their consensus was that Chiang's modesty revealed that he was thinking only of his own interest and not of others. Many leading members of the Kuomintang believed that Chiang's decision was wrong. They did not object to Hu Shih but felt there was no person other than Chiang who was suitable to be president. So, finally, they nominated Chiang as the candidate of the Kuomintang for the presidency.

After Chiang's nomination was firm, others naturally began to campaign for vice-president. The Northwest nominated Yu Yü-jen, but he was advanced in years. Kwangtung nominated Sun Fo, who was the son of Sun Yat-sen and was credible. In Hunan, the military personnel and elite nominated Chen Ch'ien, a native of Hunan who had seniority because he had been the commander of the Sixth Army group in the Northern Expedition. Including Li Tsung-jen, there were four people running for vice-president.

In the election meeting of the Kuomintang, Chiang was unanimously chosen as the candidate for president. Afterward, I wrote a note to Chiang:

"According to the American tradition, the vice-presidential candidate is chosen by the president. Would this not be a good opportunity for you to name the person you have in mind? This is entirely proper. Besides the United States, many other countries also allow the president to name his vice-president. Nobody would object if the name is put forward by the president."

But he did not take my advice. He announced that the vice-president should be "freely elected." Of course, as all four nominees informed me, the Organization Department could not assist one particular person because the Kuomintang had decided to freely elect the vice-president. As the director of the Organization Department, my power to help a candidate had evaporated in an instant. In truth, Chiang had not thought this through. Although he had Sun Fo in mind to be his vice-president, he still proposed a free election. He had not forseen that if the Organization Department helped Sun Fo, the other three nominees would have been unhappy and I would be blamed for going against Chiang's decision. Once Chiang decided on a free election for vice-president, my department's credibility was in jeopardy.

In making his decision, Chiang wanted to avoid offending any one candidate, but, at the same time, he hoped the Organization Department would help elect Sun Fo. Sun Fo had the air of a spoiled son of a prominent family. He never went out to campaign. Without campaigning, a candidate cannot expect to win. Furthermore, Sun Fo did not have much money and was not willing to spend the money that he had. Li Tsung-jen, on the other hand, was very active, and many people wanted to help. He tried to keep in touch with every member of the National Assembly. In addition, Li's wife was an able and attractive campaign worker who worked hard on his behalf. In comparison, Sun Fo's campaign was weak. Despite our help behind the scenes, Sun Fo received 1,295 votes to Li's 1,438 votes. Li was elected vice-president.

Before the vice-presidential election, Li was having difficulties and had written a letter to Chiang saying that he wished to withdraw. But, surprisingly, Chiang did not accept Li's request and encouraged him to stay in the race. I thought Chiang had made three wrong moves. First, he had not stopped Li from running; second, he was unwilling to name his vice-president, thereby losing his second chance; third, when Li requested to withdraw, Chiang did not accept it. As a result, Li Tsung-jen was elected and his victory displeased Chiang, which meant that it was difficult for Chiang and Li to cooperate at this critical juncture of history. Li's election in 1949 contributed much to the fall of Kuomintang in 1949 on the mainland.

Once the election was an established fact, there would not have been problems if Chiang had accepted the outcome. Chiang, however, was the kind of person who could not conceal his displeasure. Li was aware that

Chiang was displeased with his election as vice-president. It was a great misfortune that they began to have an aversion for each other. At that time the Communists were advancing from Tsinan, while Li's Kwangsi troops were stationed in Honan Province. Had his troops moved eastward toward Shantung, they could have attacked the Communists' rear. Li's Kwangsi troops, however, took no action. Not only that, Li's commanders defied Chiang's orders. Li and Pai hoped that the troops directly under Chiang's command would be defeated, while their troops remained intact. Their intentions were truly reprehensible. Many feared that we would defeat ourselves before the enemy defeated us.

This episode explains why we were defeated in the most vital battle of the war, the Battle of Hsuchou-Pangfu from November 8 to December 16. Because of our defeat, all land north of the Yangtze River fell into Chinese communist hands.[15] The Kwangsi troops retreated southward along the Peiping-Hankow Railroad, allowing the Communists to take control north of the Yangtze River while we controlled the provinces south of the Yangtze River. The impact of this military disaster was great. The best troops of Chiang were gone. Nationwide martial law was imposed. We had to retreat to the South, and Sun Fo was named the new prime minister. Peace negotiations then resumed, and the Communists wanted Chiang to retire from the political arena, saying that any issue could be discussed so long as Chiang retired. Chiang's thinking then was that, if he was an obstacle to peace between the Kuomintang and the Chinese Communists, he should step down, and he did. This act, according to the 1947 constitution, made Li the acting president. This was the third time that Chiang stepped down from power. Sadly, Li was incapable of commanding any troops but his own from Kwangsi; those troops not from Kwangsi were unwilling to obey Li's command. Military coordination broke down, and our fate was sealed. The new political reality was the following: Out of office, Chiang was no longer the commander in chief of the three armed forces. Constitutionally he could no longer issue instructions. Our military leaders at that moment could not decide between Chiang and Li. The most important question was whom should they follow? Here matters of loyalty and discipline were at stake. The record shows some switched to Li, some abandoned their troops, and some defected and surrendered. Military morale had virtually collapsed and was lower than I had ever seen since I returned to China from the United States in 1925. Chiang's troops, now south of the Yangtze River without a commander and having no cohesive strategy, were like a pile of sand. They were repeatedly defeated, and our situation became hopeless.

As for why the mainland fell to the Communists, certainly one factor was that the Kuomintang made a wrong move in the election. That mistake caused the National Assembly to fail in its task. We should never have given the seats of our elected Kuomintang members to other minor political parties. That was not democracy. A solid, united party such as ours only became splintered; we had no detailed plan that had been thoroughly thought out before the election took place. To make matters worse, Chiang came up with his idea of yielding the presidency to Hu Shih. Although Chiang detested Li Tsung-jen, he did not stop him from running. One mistake after another finally generated political consequences that greatly influenced our military defeat. The victory we had anticipated in August 1945 was now totally lost.

The World Moral Rearmament Movement

After the presidential election in China in April 1948, the legislators gathered to elect the president of the Legislative Yüan on May 17. To console Sun Fo for not becoming vice-president, Chiang nominated him for the post and me as vice-president. In running for this office, I had the support of the Kuomintang. The other candidate was Fu Ssu-nien, who had the support of the San-min chu-i Youth Corps. In this election, we witnessed the Youth Corps' defiance of the Kuomintang whereby Kuomintang members who worked for the Youth Corps disregarded the party's decision and voted for a non-Kuomintang member. In any case, I received 343 votes and Fu received 236. I was elected vice-president. Sun Fo became the president of the Legislative Yüan. As soon as the election of the Legislative Yüan was over and even before I assumed office, Chiang decided to send me abroad.[16] To allow me to go abroad, Chiang had to find a pretext and so assigned me to the United States and Great Britain on a mission to observe democracy in action. I believe that Chiang had my advancement in mind, and I was grateful. I resigned my post at the Central Political Council effective June 2, 1948.

Chiang's instruction to me coincided with an invitation by Frank Buchman, leader of the world Moral Rearmament [MRA] in 1948. In the name of forty-five U.S. senators and representatives, Buchman had sent invitations to government officials and well-known public figures in twenty-four countries to take part in a mammoth rally. Buchman heard that I was advocating Confucianism and promoting ethical values in China. He asked Leonard G. Allen, of the U.S. Economic Cooperation Administration, to go to China and invite me to take part in the rally. Marshall had just failed in his mission and was about to become the secretary of state. With Chiang's approval, I combined his assignment of observing democracy with the invitation from Buchman into one trip. The MRA convention was to be

With Frank Buchman, leader of the world Moral Rearmament
movement.

held in Los Angeles and Switzerland. (Because Switzerland later recognized
the Chinese communist regime, I had some difficulty in getting a visa to the
second convention in 1950. The Chinese Communists were then actively
engaged in political activities within Switzerland, and they did everything
to prevent me from entering that country.) Buchman guaranteed that the
Moral Rearmament movement would not engage in any political activities,
and so the Swiss State Council approved my visa and permitted me to enter.

The world Moral Rearmament movement was founded by Frank Buch-man. Alarmed by the communist influence all over the world and the general degeneration of social morality in every country, he hoped to save the world by reaffirming a sense of morality among people. A former missionary in Kiangsi Province in China, he profoundly respected Chinese culture. As a noted public figure, he started the world Moral Rearmament movement with four articles of faith: absolute honesty, absolute purity and love, ab-solute benevolence, absolute unselflessness. MRA members were required to abide by these four rules. To realize the first article, absolute honesty, members were to sit in silence every morning for self-examination with "turning an enemy into a friend" as one of the objectives. Participants were invited to speak of events that actually occurred in their lifetime. The second article, absolute purity and love, was applicable to our modern society. The Moral Rearmament movement owned a huge structure in Caux, Switzer-land, that could accommodate a thousand people and large buildings in London and Los Angeles, all made possible by fund-raising appeals by Frank Buchman. He had the warm support of many.

When our plane landed in Los Angeles on May 31, 1948, my delegation was made up of Lo Shih-shih, Hu Chien-chung, Ch'en Shih-fu, Leonard G. Allen, and my wife, Sun Lu-ching. Buchman welcomed us at the airport. Led by police cars, our motorcade noisily arrived at the movement center. Some seventy to eighty people, mostly young, greeted us with songs. They asked me to speak. I expressed my thanks for Buchman's invitation and praised the importance of his work, which I said would greatly influence the rearmament of social morality. The day's meeting scheduled me as the main speaker. My topic was "Chinese Culture and the World Moral Rear-mament Movement," which received much applause from the audience. Actually, the four "absolutes" that the movement advocated were quite similar to our Chinese traditional Confucian moral concepts.

I was invited to an auditorium in Hollywood to make a three-minute speech. In addition, the local municipal government asked me to speak at its welcome party. The ideas for these speeches were mine, but to avoid problems of language, they were written in English by Ch'en Shih-fu and Allen. Lo Shih-shih and Hu Chien-chung added valuable information to the speeches. All the speeches were well received and praised by the audiences. The *New World News*, a widely circulated magazine then published by the movement, put a picture of my wife and me on its cover for its July 1948 issue.

After the rally, all the participants were invited to Washington, D.C., to attend a luncheon given by Secretary of State Marshall and Paul G. Hoffman of the Economic Cooperation Administration. Before my trip, Chiang had given me letters of introduction to many influential people in

American political life but missing was one single letter—to Secretary of State George C. Marshall. I had said to Chiang before my departure, "It seems like I will have to call on Secretary of State Marshall!" He said, "You do what's best!" On hearing that remark, I found it difficult to ask him to give me a letter of introduction.

After I arrived in Washington, D.C., I called on every one on my list; it would have been discourteous if I had not paid a visit to Marshall. We had once had a four-hour-long talk during his mission to China. Unexpectedly, Marshall and I met again at the luncheon and sat next to each other. Marshall and I were happy to see each other. Marshall gave the welcoming speech in which he emphasized the importance of moral rearmament. I gave a thank-you speech.

Sometime later, when Marshall was in the hospital for a physical examination, I asked the Chinese embassy to contact the State Department to express my wish to pay Marshall a courtesy call. Diplomats in our embassy told me: "Don't try to see him. He has misgivings about you. He won't receive you!"

I replied, "He definitely will see me!" They did not know that I had once conversed at a long meeting with Marshall and that he was very pleased with my talk. So I said: "You just go ahead and make the arrangements for me. I am only making a courtesy call." The result was that, when Marshall came out of the hospital after his physical examination, I was the first visitor he received.

The notice of the State Department read fifteen minutes for Ambassador Ku, fifteen minutes for me, altogether thirty minutes. Ku accompanied me. Marshall was very happy to see me, and the three of us spent an hour and fifteen minutes talking. There were many visitors waiting; they all wondered why Marshall spent so much time with me. When Ku and I came out of his office, reporters surged toward me asking, "What have you been talking about with Marshall today?" I said, "This was a courtesy call." Reporters asked, "How could a courtesy call last an hour and fifteen minutes?" I replied, "Why don't you ask Ambassador Ku?"

Ku also had not seen Marshall for a long time. Accompanying me, he did not expect Marshall would receive me first and be happy to see me. Marshall began by asking about the health of President and Madame Chiang. Then he expressed his regret for having failed during the nationalist-communist peace negotiations. He said that the slowness of political undertaking and the rapidity of military operations were as far apart as heaven and earth. He said that democratic politics worked very slowly, unlike military operations in which one command was all that was required; democratic politics required many steps in complex undertakings before a single task could be accomplished. Marshall expounded on many important ideas in regard to democratic politics for me, and he spelled out the reasons why the U.S. government was not able to give aid to China quickly. As soon as he found out that my trip to America was for the purpose of observing democracy in action, he was very helpful, immediately calling his secretaries over and telling them: "Mr. Ch'en wants to see our democratic politics in practice. Whatever material he needs you must do your best to provide!"

Ku had not known of Marshall's long talk with me in China, so he was very surprised at Marshall's kindness toward me. Only after I told the ambassador did he understand the special relationship between Marshall and me. In the past, Marshall had not understood us very well, and that had led to his failure in the mediation. He and I had a long heart-to-heart talk only once, but his memory of it was still fresh. This time, when I came to see him, he was very kind to me and very willing to help me. On bidding me good-bye, he even asked me to convey his regards to President and Madame Chiang. Regarding this meeting, the Chinese embassy personnel felt surprised that we talked at such length.

Twenty years later, I had an opportunity to read the U.S. State Department annual publication, *Foreign Relations of the United States*, 1946, 1947, and 1948. I discovered detailed conversations that took place between principal officials of our government and the U.S. diplomats during those stormy years. The documents also included many recorded conversations attacking our National government. I blushed with shame when I read them. I found out that, in the conversations with Marshall, some of my countrymen had labeled me as "leader of reactionary CC Clique" and "former head of all secret police or plainclothesmen operations in China." Fortunately, I had never said any word detrimental to our government. This only demonstrates that, when conducting talks with foreigners and their diplomats, one should be extraordinarily careful because one's remarks might be recorded without one's knowledge.

While I was in the United States, I visited President Truman and many important figures in the executive branch and in Congress. With Buchman's help, these visits were arranged by Moral Rearmament, and everything went smoothly. Each time I visited a dignitary, I presented a letter of introduction from Chiang. On meeting President Truman, I told him that our country faced a very perilous situation, and I expressed my hope that the United States would give us help as early as possible. We talked about loans and military aid. President Truman asked me about the problems with the Communists. I said: "You've raised a good question. I am one who has long dealt with the Communists. Please feel free to ask any question." I said that the biggest weakness of the Communists was their lack of trustworthiness: they often did not keep their word. I told Truman that "one has to be on guard in dealing with them, and one must not use our moral standards to

judge them, yours or mine, or otherwise one will be taken in by them." I
told him that I hoped the U.S. government would come to our aid early so
that no time would be wasted. President Truman was sympathetic and gave
me promises. In the United States, I met and talked with Henry Luce, the
founder of *Time* magazine, as well as the executives from the Hearst newspapers. Then I was invited to give a speech at the China Institute of America.
In each speech, I always stressed that communism was incompatible with
Chinese culture to help the American public understand my reasons for
opposing communism. I wanted to demonstrate that I was not the "die-
hard element" as portrayed by communist propaganda.

Chiang had instructed me to go to America to observe democracy in
action and nothing else. But once I was there, I took the opportunity to call
on the secretary of defense, the secretary of the Treasury, and other principal
government leaders, with some effective results. Secretary of State Marshall
asked them to speak to me, and some loans were approved by Congress.
When I went to see the secretary of defense, James Forrestal, he immediately
summoned officials in charge of arms and ammunition in the Pacific, asking
them how much surplus arms and ammunition were still available in the
Pacific region. He ordered them to ship that surplus to China as soon as
possible. Forrestal invited me to lunch, and in the middle of the meal he
repeatedly reminded his subordinates to rush arms and ammunition to China.
I still remember his warmth and enthusiasm. The year 1948 being an election
year, I also made a courtesy call on Thomas Dewey, which lasted for a few
minutes.[17]

Afterward, I visited England, a country advanced in democratic politics.
I talked with the Speaker of the House of Commons, the chancellor of the
Exchequer, and other important ministers and officials. I learned much about
democratic politics in England. At a luncheon hosted by the Speaker of the
House of Commons, he told me:

> You should not regard democratic politics as controlled by the people.
> Democratic politics means that representatives should do their best to
> inform the common people of the two sides of politics—namely, about the
> party in office and the party out of office; at this moment the Conservative
> party is in power, and the Labour party is out of power. Parliament sets up
> a small group composed of members from both the Conservative and the
> Labour parties. Whenever there is an important proposal to be debated in
> Parliament, this group discusses it and reaches an agreement. That is re-
> turned to Parliament, and the party in office will defend this proposal to
> the utmost, while the opposition party will find all kinds of reasons to
> oppose it. Such debate educates the people because we want the people to
> know both sides of this proposal. But when the issue is finally put to a
> vote, the voting will be done in accordance with the agreement previously
> decided on by the former group. On the surface it looks as though the

party in office and the party out of office are fighting tooth and nail with each other, while in fact important government decisions have often been decided well in advance. This is the inside story of democratic politics. All important proposals have their pros and cons. The fact is the welfare of the country and the people must come first. After the debate, the motion will be amended and approved. The pro side wins, but actually this is all prearranged. Therefore, on the surface, we are two opposing parties, but for the important issues concerning the country, we still consult with each other in advance so as to come to terms with each other!

The speaker's words were a revelation to me. Based on the major premise of maximizing a country's welfare, different parties should neither fight nor insist on sticking to their own arguments. After I returned home, I reported in detail to Chiang what I had observed.

The Competition for the Premiership

I recall that shortly after Chang Ch'ün assumed the office of premier on April 23, 1947, he recommended to Chiang that I should take over his post during the cabinet reshuffling. Chiang asked my opinion. I said: "There are many qualified elders who have more experience than I. Please consider them first. If you really cannot find any suitable person, then come to me. Persons like Wang Ch'ung-hui and Sun Fo should be quite suitable."

Chiang asked Sun Fo, who then was the president of the Legislative Yüan, to be the premier. On December 22, 1948, Sun Fo consented. Our political situation was worsening by the day. The Battle of Hsuchou–Pangfu had been a disaster for us. The government now considered moving to Kwangtung.[18] If Sun Fo should become the president of the Executive Yüan, he would greatly benefit by the support from his province as he was a Kwangtung native. Before he would agree to become the president, he required that Wu T'ieh-ch'eng, Chen Cheng, and I should join the cabinet. If Sun Fo moved to the presidency of the Executive Yüan, I, as vice-president of the Legislative Yüan, would be promoted to acting president of the Legislative Yüan. Wu T'ieh-ch'eng, however, appeared to want the presidency of the Legislative Yüan. Because Sun Fo insisted that Wu and I both join the cabinet, I felt compelled to tell Chiang that if I left the Legislative Yüan for the Executive Yüan, the Legislative Yüan would fall into chaos. If Chiang insisted I move to the Executive Yüan, however, I would do so.

The reshuffling of the cabinet controversy, which lasted more than ten days, was a hopeless tangle. Everyone was anxious. What would happen if it was put off indefinitely? At that time, we received news that our troops were again retreating in defeat. Chiang gave orders that the new cabinet be swiftly formed. Sun Fo then suggested that Shao Li-tzu join him, which put Chiang in an awkward predicament. Perhaps I should note here that by the end of 1948, Shao Li-tzu was publicly recognized as a pro-Communist. The unexpected military setback made Chiang accept the unfortunate political reality. Besides, Sun Fo wanted all factions to be represented in his cabinet. Shao, in the eyes of Sun Fo, might serve as a bridge between the Kuomintang and the Chinese Communists in case peace negotiations became a necessity. Noting this, I at once stated that "in order to speed up the reorganization of the Executive Yüan, let me step down!" Only then was a new cabinet, headed by Sun Fo, completed, with Wu T'ieh-ch'eng as vice-premier as well as the minister of foreign affairs. I became a minister without portfolio.

After Sun Fo's swearing-in as the new premier, the political situation took a turn for the worse. On January 21, 1949, Chiang retired in seclusion.[19] Vice-President Li Tsung-jen took over as the acting president. Before Chiang's retirement, those conspiring to overthrow him had spread the rumor that if Chiang should retire and Li Tsung-jen act as president, the United States would immediately give aid to the National government. This rumor encouraged Chiang to decide firmly to retire and go into seclusion. Chiang left Nanking for Hangchou at 4:00 P.M., January 21, 1949, and I resigned the following day.

Very shortly, communist troops were advancing southward across the Yangtze River. The government sent Chang Chih-chung and Shao Li-tze to negotiate with them. Instead of returning, they defected to the Communists.

The communist conspiracy was now public knowledge. They had pretended to negotiate peace terms with the government, but in fact were stalling in order to cross the Yangtze and attack, thus forcing the government to move to Kwangtung. Li Tsung-jen also harbored evil intentions. By pressuring Chiang to retire, Li had thought he could save the situation. Little did he know about communist deception.[20] They totally ignored him and moved their troops south of the Yangtze River. Meanwhile, his Kwangsi troops under the command of Pai Ch'ung-hsi had retreated back to Kwangsi. They naively believed that once they had retreated to Kwangsi, they could recoup by using American aid and then fight back, but, in fact, they were already impotent and American aid never came.

The nation's situation worsened every day, so much so that Sun Fo also wanted to resign from his premiership. On March 23, 1949, Ho Ying-ch'in replaced him. To weaken Li's growing power, the Kuomintang tried to find ways to support Ho Ying-ch'in. After becoming acting president, Li's ambition grew. To control the Executive Yüan and force Ho Ying-ch'in to resign, he colluded with Chu Cheng by nominating him as the new premier. If the Legislative Yüan approved that appointment, the government was in deep trouble with Li and Chu in charge. The newly elected president of the

Legislative Yüan was Tung Kwan-hsien, with Liu Chien-ch'ün as vice-president. We made every effort to convene the legislators in Canton, but those supporting and those challenging this appointment could not agree. Tung tilted toward Li Tsung-jen, so I warned Liu that he must vote no. On May 31, 1949, with only a one-vote margin, the motion for the appointment of Chu Cheng as the new premier was defeated. When Chiang heard the news, he was very pleased.[21] He then suggested Yen Hsi-shan's name to Li, and the Legislative Yüan soon passed this motion. Yen became the next premier. After a long conversation with Chiang in Kaoshiung, he took over the office on June 11, 1949.[22]

By now, the military situation was so bad that our troops were retreating in defeat once again, and the government had moved from Kwangtung to Chungking. Many legislators did not think conditions in Chungking would be any better. They came to me, asking me to plead with Chiang to return to office and take up the government leadership.[23] They said that if Chiang remained in seclusion, the country was lost. Legislator Kiang I-p'ing, a lawyer, volunteered to draft a telegram, which he sent in my name to Chiang, asking him to come out of retirement. In the meantime, acting President Li Tsung-jen had deserted the government, leaving the affairs of the state in a mess at this critical time. Li flew to Kunming alone, without any thought of others. I telegraphed Chiang, already in Taiwan, and reported to him the dangerous situation in Chungking. I also passed on to him Li's words: "If Chiang does not come to Chungking, neither will I." Chiang replied that he would immediately go to Chungking.

It was very risky for Chiang to fly to Chungking. As soon as he arrived, on November 14, 1949, troop morale was restored for the time being. Li, the acting president, never fulfilled his promise to go to Chungking. Instead, on December 5, he left Kunming for Hong Kong, and from there he flew to the United States. Shortly afterward, Chungking's military situation became critical, with communist troops advancing and the currency depreciating day by day. Moreover, the underground secret service of the Communists was far superior to ours. They observed every act of our government. Our situation was best summed up by the proverb "Defeated troops in retreat are much like a mountain collapsing." Shortly after Chiang arrived in Chungking, the government again, on November 21, moved from Chungking to Chengtu. I went along. The situation was so chaotic that the automobile assigned to me had been seized by others. People everywhere were shouting and crying. I shall always remember the sad scene. On leaving Chungking, Chiang's limousine had difficulty reaching the airport. That was November 30; on the same day, Chungking was in the hands of the Communists.

Most of the military leaders in Szechuan Province, like Teng Hsi-hou and Wang Tsuan-hsü, and Liu Wen-hui of Sinkiang Province could not be trusted. Yang Sheng was somewhat more reliable. Just at this time, Premier Yen Hsi-shan unexpectedly made a proposal at a cabinet meeting to have a policy for settling accounts with the landlords. That sounded just like the Communists. I was so angry that I burst out at the meeting, "The Communists have not even arrived yet and we want to persecute the landlords ahead of them?" President Yen withdrew his motion as soon as he saw my indignation.

It was now December 1949, and two of our airlines already had defected to the Communists. The communist underground was extremely active. Every day our people were becoming more anxious. The only military planes at the Chengtu airport were the planes that had transported us from Chungking. Although having Chiang in Chengtu made people a little more calm, conditions were exceedingly tense. Hu Tsung-nan's northwestern troops were of no use. As I stated before, Hu's troops had been Chiang's main troops under his control, and they had the best possible U.S. equipment. Without fighting a battle they had been defeated, and this puzzled people a great deal and continues to confound historians even today.

I later learned that some of Hu's troops had received orders to deploy to Sinkiang to suggest that the government might consider moving there. But everything was in confusion. Lung Yun of Yunnan had just defected. Lu Han, Yunnan's governor, released captured Communists and obviously had changed his stand. But the government considered retreating further. One evening after dinner I went to see Chiang. He was in a very bad mood. As soon as he saw me he exclaimed: "How strange! Today, when I summoned all the generals to a meeting, no one came!" He looked grave, and he was angry.

I said: "The situation is very critical. All these military leaders are probably no longer reliable. What do you think we should do?"

Chiang replied, "You, Premier Yen, and the others should fly to Taiwan." Right away I asked, "Where would you go?" He said, "I am going to fly to Sinkiang." I said, "You cannot go there." He said, "Why?"

I said: "There are only two regiments of Hu Tsung-nan's troops deployed there. Should you go to Sinkiang, you will be unfamiliar with the place and the people, while Liu Wen-hui has already been in control for over ten years. If he should come to the airport to ask you to make a speech, a repeat of the Sian Incident might happen. Then what would you do?"

Hearing this, Chiang changed his mind: "Then I shall go to Yunnan." I said: "Lu Han is also untrustworthy. You must absolutely not go to Yunnan."

Chiang then accepted my advice. He wanted to send his son Ching-kuo instead. But Ching-kuo was unwilling to go because he did not know Lu Han well. Chang Ch'ün was sent on December 9 and was immediately detained by Lu Han for three days. These men, all opportunists, now realized the desperate situation, and they quickly defected to the Communists. Indeed, it was frightening to see how quickly people changed their minds. It seemed that during that critical moment of history, the military force Chiang had tirelessly built up since 1925 totally collapsed. It was, indeed, the worst disaster in his entire career. Once the military defeat was apparent, all other things were lost. Like the floods of the Yellow River, everything swiftly washed away, so fast, so quickly, and so suddenly.

Flying to Taiwan

I was under orders to accompany Premier Yen Hsi-shan, who was nominated premier on June 2, 1949, to fly to Taiwan. Among our group was Chu Chia-hua. The plane took off at night and flew over the mainland. By the time it reached the border of Szechwan and Hupei, a cold current caused the wings of the plane to freeze with heavy ice, and the plane dropped seven hundred feet. We had to find a place to land. When I saw a brightly lit city on the ground, I though it was Hankow and took out a pistol from my briefcase, ready to commit suicide. Only after the pilot's announcement did I realize that we had returned to Chengtu. So I was a victim of a false alarm.

I later learned that the reason the plane was so heavy was that it carried tons of gold bars, all part of Yen's luggage. The next day, before we took off, the pilot told me that in order to avoid the same incident, the plane must be lightened. I spoke with Yen. He insisted that all the gold bars be placed on board, but he was willing to leave behind a few of his bodyguards. We arrived in Taiwan safe and sound. I later learned that when Yen left Shansi Province, he had left behind many followers who depended on Yen for their livelihood. For Yen those gold bars were a matter of necessity. But our lives were almost lost because of his gold. What irony!

I Am Named a War Criminal

One note is worth adding about the total defeat we suffered on the Chinese mainland in 1949. On December 25, 1948, the Chinese communist radio station in Yenan broadcast the names of forty-five leaders of the Kuomintang and the National government as "war criminals well known for their heinous crimes and who, all Chinese agree, should receive just penalty." My elder brother, Kuo-fu, and I, not surprisingly, were included in the list.[24] At the end of this near half-century drama, with only three of the forty-five surviving,[25] the question to ask is why did the Chinese Communists hate the "two Ch'en brothers" so much? In their publications, propaganda materials, and mass media, we were labeled as leaders of the reactionary CC Clique or the right-wing CC Clique. The Communists identified our family as one of the Four Big Families along with the families of three others: Chiang Kai-shek, T. V. Soong, and H. H. Kung. They claimed that the wealth and power of China were totally centered in the hands of our four families. The Communists also had another favorite slogan: The Country (China) Belongs to the Chiangs, and the Party (Kuomintang) Belongs to the Ch'ens [*Chiang-chia t'ien-hsia Ch'en-chia-tang*], to convey the impression that we two brothers managed, controlled, and monopolized the entire Kuomintang. Their slogan attempted to divide Chiang and me and, at the same time, alienate me from the party. The Chinese Communists also branded the CC Clique as made up of die-hard elements and selfish irreconcilables in the Kuomintang, to set them apart from other liberals of the country. The fact is that those who had a strong, unshaken faith in the Three People's Principles, the most revolutionary doctrine of twentieth-century China, were those whom the Communists feared most. To call them die-hard elements and selfish irreconcilables was cunning and suited the Communists' purposes. But people were unaware of this tactic and merely repeated the views of others, so that my brother and I were always referred to as CC, members of the Four Big Families, and die-hards. But the Chinese Communists never mentioned that the two of us were corrupt, selfish, or betrayed our cause. What did we believe in and fight for?

First, we believed that the communist ideology would never succeed in the Soviet Union, in China, or anywhere else in the world. If we could not beat them, somebody else would. We also believed that the Communist party, as a political, social, economic, and military institution, would never be accepted by the common people in China. Fundamentally, the tactics it used were brutal, cruel, ruthless, and beyond the tolerance of human nature. For us, Chinese culture and the traditional Confucian family values, ethics, and moral beliefs were deeply rooted in the hearts and spirits of Chinese people. Communism would eventually be rejected by the people. The 1991 collapse of communism in the Soviet Union proved that I was correct.

Second, we believed that Sun Yat-sen's Three People's Principles better served the needs of China than any other ideologies or isms of the twentieth century, including communism and Mao Tse-tung's thought. If we had worked harder, we might have had a chance to save China from the unnecessary sufferings caused by communism that occurred in the past half-century.

Third, we believed that the Republic of China must be maintained and nurtured. Created by Sun Yat-sen and many others, they unselfishly gave their lives and property to the cause of revolutionary change. My family was deeply involved in founding the republic. Why should we let the Soviet-supported Chinese Communist party destroy that republic? We wanted to make China an independent, free, wealthy, and democratic nation. We contributed our energy, property, and lives to the goals set forth by Sun Yat-sen. To some extent, the Chinese Communists also agreed with our efforts at nation building.

But the Chinese Communist party has never been an ordinary political party. It behaves like an unarmed army, having a strong organization and strict discipline and being skilled in the techniques of propaganda. Once that party has decided on an assault plan, it mobilizes its members to attack by waging a propaganda war, mixing right and wrong, and calling something white when it is black. The average person unfamiliar with its activities is easily fooled. The Communist party places a high priority on deceiving and winning over the people to obey its will. If you evaluate that party's propaganda by ordinary ethical standards, you will have already lost the battle. The object of that party's attack is to destroy its formidable adversary.

In political life, my brother and I supported Chiang Kai-shek to defend Kuomintang authority against the assault of the Chinese Communists. Our national revolution was waged by the Kuomintang, an anticommunist, anti-Soviet party. Events like the *Chung-shan* Gunboat Incident of 1926, the Northern Expedition, the purge of 1927, and later incidents in China made the Chinese Communists well aware of who we were. From 1925 to 1950 my brother and I managed the investigations, organizations, training programs, and activities of our party and government. To defeat communism was our ultimate goal. Unfortunately we failed.

Let me now comment briefly on the origins of the CC Clique. In one of his articles my elder brother, Kuo-fu, wrote that prior to the Northern Expedition, the Kuomintang comrades could not openly engage in party work in areas controlled by the warlords. In order to survive and develop, Kuomintang activities had to assume different forms with different organizational names. Many small groups evolved within the Kuomintang, but our Organization Department managed their activities. After 1928, these small groups had to be dissolved to unify the power. But among them, the Revive China Society [Hsing-chung-hui] and the Practice Association [Shih-chien-she] in north China insisted on maintaining the status quo. The Central Executive Committee sent me to investigate why these organizations continued to exist. Only then did I learn that they had been duped by the Communists' argument that our party's Central Executive Committee was dominated by a small faction called the Central Club with the initials CC. Their message was: "Why should you be disbanded? You are being duped."

Their mendacity produced a certain effect. Only after I had explained the fallaciousness of the communist charge did leaders of these two groups, Chang Ching-yüan and Tung Kuan-hsien, realize they had been fooled.

They printed an advertisement in a newspaper explaining that the rumor of a CC, a clique headed by Ch'en Kuo fu and Ch'en Li fu, was merely a lie to foment discord within the Kuomintang. But since the release of that information, the term *CC Clique* has been interpreted to mean a reactionary, antiliberal, anticommunist political force that dominated the Kuomintang. More specifically, those individuals of the Kuomintang associated with Kuo-fu or myself were naturally branded as members of the CC Clique. After some years, the term *CC* became common usage in society, with even the press and U.S. diplomatic papers using it to refer to those individuals who were politically affiliated with my brother and me. The truth of the matter is that the so-called CC Clique term was fabricated by the Communists without any substance, but as time passed, the term seemed real and took on a life of its own. One can only admire the skillfulness of communist propaganda. I assume the term *CC* or *CC Clique* will permanently remain in modern Chinese history. Sometimes I thought that if I had been as powerful as the Communists portrayed me, we might never have failed as we did.

While we were in Kiangsi during the five anticommunist campaigns to eliminate communist activities,[26] Chiang observed with his own eyes that the rural areas were without financial institutions. Only then did he understand that a nation must have a banking system to help the peasants. So in 1935 he appointed my elder brother, Kuo-fu, to be chairman of the board of the Farmers Bank of China [Chung-kuo nung-min yin-hang]. My elder brother changed the bank's policy of supplying loans only to commercial firms to one of also lending to the farmers; he also tried to create a rural cooperative banking system and served as chairman of the board managing the Cooperative Fund. He later was appointed director of the board of the Communications Bank. The Communists cited these promotions in their attacks on my brother to discredit him and list him as one of the Four Big Families and "a supportive instrument of American imperialistic policies." *The Four Families of Chiang, Soong, Kung, [and] Ch'en [Chung-kuo Ssu-ta chian-tsu]*, authored by the Chinese communist theoretician Ch'en P'o-ta in 1946, is such an example. On April 5, 1949, the communist official organ the *People's Daily [Jen-min jih-pao]* urged that the properties of the "Four Big Families" be confiscated. Again, in its overseas edition of January 27, 1992, the paper renewed the issue of the "Four Big Families." As a matter of fact, they found no property owned by my brother Kuo-fu and me either at home or abroad, but they accused us of being a "Fascist CC Clique" and "the center of the Chiang family's imperial reactionary political life." Communist viciousness is unparalleled.

My brother and I did our very best to defeat the Communists. We treated our comrades with sincerity and kindheartedness. We encouraged them to be loyal to the national revolution and to its leader, Chiang, and to work together in a common cause to make the Three People's Principles a reality. Those who do not know the truth might say, "Without a small clique how could you two brothers have pushed the other comrades around so easily?" They do not understand that with total sincerity, one can persuade another to do incredible things. Our hope was to develop the Kuomintang and to save our country. The slanders or praises of others are really beyond our control. We leave them to the judgment of future historians.

In retrospect, let me put personal emotion, sentiment, and feeling aside to make a brief statement that can testify to the history of modern China after 1925. The true target the Chinese Communist party desperately wanted to attack was the Kuomintang. And within the Kuomintang, it definitely saw my brother and me as a danger to its survival and existence and a force to totally destroy. It sounds flattering, but it is a fact few can challenge. Nevertheless, their wish partially came true in 1949 when Chiang decided to withdraw to Taiwan.

CHAPTER NINE

The Hopeful Years

1950–1993

The Kuomintang Reform in Taiwan

AFTER THE KUOMINTANG REESTABLISHED its headquarters in Taipei in August 1949, its leaders agonized, pondering what kind of lessons to learn from past mistakes.[1] I proposed to Chiang that we needed quick but effective reforms; among my suggestions were that all members of the Kuomintang must be reregistered and that the party census needed to be retaken. When presenting this proposition, I further stated that it was best to lay the blame for all party inadequacies, deficiencies, and mistakes on the two Ch'en brothers. After completing this, reform would be started and my brother and I should take no part in the affairs, allowing Chiang to restore the Kuomintang's prestige and rally his followers. Chiang listened without responding.

But Chiang, two days after the conversation, gave me an order on the spot to gather a small group of Kuomintang faithfuls and draft a plan. He also appointed me to head a committee of nine to review the plan. After numerous meetings and discussions, I presented a plan proposing a possible date to convene the Kuomintang Reform Conference [Kai-tsao hui-i]. At one Central Executive Committee meeting during this time, some senior members like Ch'en Shao-ying and Li Tsung-huang suggested that party reform was absolutely necessary. They said the best way was to allow Kuomintang cadres to make recommendations to Chiang and let him carry out any decisions. They believed this approach was more democratic and would spare Chiang any embarrassment.

On hearing this, Chiang went into a rage. He feared that too much discussion about reform would only create more problems. So he admonished the two members: "You may not want me to handle the reform, but there are only two ways to go: the first is for the Kuomintang to drift into obscurity; the second is you must empower me with authority and trust me. It is wrong to reform the Kuomintang in a democratic way. If you do not trust me to handle the reform, then I do not give a damn. You can go ahead on your own!" Chiang's outburst was so unexpected that everyone at the meeting was dumbstruck. Chiang went on to say, "If you do not trust me to do the reform, you go ahead and follow Ch'en Li-fu!"

It so happened that I was not at that meeting because of illness. When someone later told me of Chiang's outburst I was very puzzled. He might be in a rage, but how could he speak like this? Did it mean that he thought I advocated democracy to oppose him? I had suggested a Kuomintang reform, and I was under his order to draft a plan. My original idea was that my brother and I should not participate in the reform to demonstrate that this Kuomintang reform had produced a new spirit and a new way of doing things. Only then could the reform succeed. In addition, my elder brother, Kuo-fu, was constantly ill and I was tired. I now considered taking the blame and resigning from active political life.

When I learned of Chiang's outburst, I knew there must be a hidden reason. That awareness merely strengthened my wish to retire, and I now wanted to quit my government jobs and the Kuomintang and leave for the United States. I had, in fact, already made it quite clear to Chiang that my brother and I were responsible for party errors and that we had absolutely no desire to stay on. Our intentions were made so clear that, really, there should not have been any misunderstanding. Chiang's outburst indicated to me that he thought I was opposing him. I was so distressed by this idea that my pent-up anxiety remained within me for a long, long time. On reflection, I became convinced that this outburst by Chiang might have conveyed political undertones traceable to an incorrect statement uttered on a public occasion by Chen Cheng.

When Chiang nominated Chen Cheng to be the new premier and president of the Executive Yüan on March 8, 1950, the constitution required that the nominee must first have the advice and consent of the Legislative Yüan before being appointed. Chen Cheng sent Yuan Shou-ch'ien to ask me for my help in garnering support among the legislators. He was approved by 82 percent of the total votes. Chang Tao-fan reported the balloting result to Chiang. Chiang said, "How could there be so many votes?"—as though blaming us for helping too much. Later, Chen Cheng hosted a dinner, at which both Chiang Ching-kuo and I were present, thanking the legislators for their support. So pleased was Chen that he joked: "In the past, the so-called CC term meant Mr. Ch'en Kuo-fu and Mr. Ch'en Li-fu. Now CC means Ch'en Li-fu and Chen Cheng!"

What he jokingly said was a political blunder. Chen Cheng's support came from the San-min chu-i Youth Corps, while everyone considered me to have Kuomintang backing. From a leader like Chiang's point of view, the merging of the Kuomintang and the Youth Corps in September 1947 constituted a political threat because the balance of forces had been upset. To thank me for my help, Chen Cheng had inadvertently made a bad joke. Anyone hearing it would have formed the impression that the two Ch'ens had ulterior motives and wanted to join forces. That move could only hurt Chiang Ching-kuo, who was being cultivated to succeed his father. Because of this terrible misunderstanding, I decided to retire to a remote land.

By then, as premier, Chen Cheng was trying to expand his authority into the Legislative Yüan. When the government retreated to Kwangtung in February 1949, the premier was Ho Ying-ch'in. To avoid giving too much authority to acting President Li Tsung-jen, and because of difficulties in convening the Legislative Yüan, the Central Executive Committee had decided to grant more power to the premier. But now that we were in Taiwan, the political reality was very different. At a meeting chaired by Chiang, I explained that when we were in Kwangtung, it was difficult to convene the Legislative Yüan meetings. The Central Executive Committee had increased the power and responsibility of the premier in order to take necessary actions. But on March 1, 1950, Chiang returned to power and resumed the presidency. Constitutionally, the premier must confine himself to his own sphere of authority and could not seize the power of the Legislative Yüan. Chen Cheng, of course, was unhappy to learn this.

Days later, Chen Cheng was still unwilling to relinquish his power-grabbing ambition. He prodded the Youth Corps' supporters in the Legislative Yüan to propose reducing the legislative power of the Legislative Yüan. When this proposal was voted down and the news leaked out, Chen Cheng, who happened to be at a meeting at the Executive Yüan, lost his temper. Those legislators who opposed this proposal were the senior members of the Kuomintang, outside politics and without any particular connection to me. Without finding out who these people were, Chen called them members of the CC Clique. He angrily exclaimed: "They must be of the CC Clique! Nowadays, who can hold the job of the president of the Executive Yüan but Ch'en Li-fu. I quit!" He then ordered his vice-premier, Chang Li-sheng, to draft a letter of resignation for him and to give it to Chiang. The rumor later circulated that Chiang would send me into exile on Green Island [Lü-tao] and treat me as he did Hu Han-Min.

When the news of this incident came out, quite a few uninvolved legislators told Chen Cheng: "You wrongly blamed Ch'en Li-fu. He never expressed any opinion to other legislators about that proposal. You were wrong to accuse him!" Only then did Chen Cheng realize that he had wrongly blamed me. I felt he had been very unfair, and I was very indignant about the matter. Before I went to Taichung to see Chiang, I made my feelings clear to a lot of people: "From now on, if Chen Cheng wants to have anything to do with the Legislative Yüan, please do not come to me!" While I was in Taichung, Chen Cheng, realizing he was in the wrong, asked Hsu Shao-ti, a legislator, to represent him and apologize to me for his insensitivity.

This incident, plus the fact that Chiang had misinterpreted my suggestion for party reform, spurred me to think of retiring and going abroad. The world Moral Rearmament [MRA] movement had again invited me to a rally in Switzerland, so I took the opportunity to speak to Chiang. In my farewell letter to him dated August 18, 1950, I mentioned again that, "having been under the president's tutelage for twenty-five years, I am ashamed that I have not accomplished more, and I feel very guilty. Now that I am going abroad, should any political problems arise, please do not come to me any more. I have never been interested in these." Before I left, I wrote two other letters, one to my close friends urging them to continue to be loyal to Chiang, and another letter to senior Kuomintang members explaining that because I had not performed well, I was taking the blame, resigning, and going abroad.

The Kuomintang underwent reform in those years, and all members were required to register again. I did not do so, and Chiang had not listed me as a member of the Reform Committee [K'ai-tsao wei-yüan-hui], which was formed on August 5, 1950. But he designated my brother Kuo-fu as an advisory member. Little did I know that when I arrived in the United States from Switzerland, a new party membership registration card stamped Che-kiang No. 1 was awaiting me in the hands of Yu Kuo-hua, who had been asked by Chiang to give me the card. This seemed to indicate that Chiang wanted me to continue as a member and not leave the Kuomintang. I thought it would be impolite to decline, so I accepted. From then on I stayed out of political life and started my new carefree life in America by founding a newspaper in New York City's Chinese community and managing a chicken farm in New Jersey to make a living. It seems the very essential question left here is what would have happened to me if I had not taken advantage of participation in the MRA convention in August 1950 to leave Chiang for my own good? The answer would be if Chiang had not sent me into exile on Green Island, Chen Cheng would have had me arrested if he had become the president.

My family in 1950: (from right to left) second son, Tze-ning, eldest son, Tze-an, youngest son, Tze-ch'ou, my wife, Sun Lu-ching, and daughter, Tze-jung.

Founding the *China Tribune*

After the MRA convention, I decided to live in the United States for good. But I had to find the means of earning a living and do something useful in my remaining years. I wanted to leave something behind.

The first thing I did was to raise money to purchase a newspaper that was already very influential among the overseas Chinese. It was called the *China Tribune* [*Hua-mei* or *Hua-mei jih-pao*]. Chinese Communists then in the United States were also looking to purchase a Chinese-language newspaper, and they were also interested in the *China Tribune*. When my friends in New York heard of this, they attempted to persuade me to buy it. They did not want to see the paper become a tool of Chinese communist propaganda. The newspaper asked for US$20,000. I went to Hsu Kan, former minister of food and the minister of finance of the National government, who happened to be in the United States. I asked him, "Does Chiang know you are in America?" He said, "No." I said: "If Chiang does not know, you had better be careful. How could you come to America if Chiang has not permitted you to?"

Then I told him that if he wanted Chiang's forgiveness, he could do something meaningful for the cause of the National government: purchase the *China Tribune*. He said he could contribute only $10,000. I had to raise the rest. I finally collected the $10,000 from old friends such as Pan Kung-chan, Hsiang Ting-jung, Lai Lien, Hsüeh Kwang-ch'ien, Tung Ling, and Chen Ching-yün. I contributed as well, which made seven of us. Now that we owned a newspaper, we began expressing our views in the New York Chinatown area, counterattacking the Communists to recover the mainland.

I enlisted the services of first-rate professionals to write editorials. Among them were Pan Kung-chan, former editor of the noted non-English daily Shanghai *Shen Pao*, and Lai Lien, editor of the *Central Daily News* [*Chung-yang jih-pao*]. We gathered the best Chinese men of letters in the United States. Our paper became influential in American public opinion, and virtually every overseas Chinese subscribed to our paper, making it a powerful voice speaking out for the recovery of the mainland and reconstructing our country. Our paper became a spiritual fortress of anticommunism in the eyes of the overseas Chinese. It was not until 1969 that I broke away from the paper financially and yielded my share to Chu P'o-shun, but I retained the title of honorary chairman of the board of directors.

Running a Chicken Farm

Most of my other friends accepted teaching jobs after they had settled down in the United States. Having studied mining engineering, I could have taught mining engineering or even the philosophy of Chinese culture. My daughter had just graduated from high school, and she planned to go to Lakewood in New Jersey to attend college. That area enjoyed a good reputation for chicken farming, and many people spent their summer vacations there. Ninety percent of the first-rate hotels were run by Jewish immigrants; they closed in winter but opened for business in the summer.

A friend of mine, Hu Ting-an, had served as the head of Kiangsu Medical School. He suggested that we go to New Jersey to run a chicken farm. We surveyed more than sixty chicken farms before we decided on a relatively cheap one. The purchase price was US$47,000, with a down payment of $20,000, the rest to be paid up in ten years. That was a big sum of money, and I had only $4,000 in my possession. I had no alternative but to borrow

from friends. H. H. Kung was generous enough to let me borrow $8,000.
But my partner, Hu, could afford only $4,000. We had to ask our friends to
chip in to cover the remaining $4,000.

Why did I choose to run a chicken farm? I thought I had worked for the
Kuomintang and the National government long enough. I had tried to please
Chiang and many other people in and out of the political world, but in the
end I believed few appreciated my services. From now on, I was not going
to serve another person. It was a wonderful feeling to realize I was finally
free. By taking care of chickens, I would no longer have to please anyone.

That year, egg prices were high in America and chicken farming was a
good business. Within half a year, we had earned $5,000. Feeding the chick-
ens was performed by machines. Whenever we needed to buy more feed,
one telephone call sufficed. Our chicken farm, however, was not modernized
or managed scientifically, and we were frequently short of drinking water.
We used our first profit of $5,000 to purchase three chicken-feeding machines
and to dig a deep well. We were now raising a total of five thousand chickens,
and feeding them kept us busy. After working on this chicken farm, my
chronic backache disappeared. I was in good health and could bend and pick
up a bag of feed weighing a hundred pounds without any strain. Fortunately,
my three sons, including my youngest son, who was only eight years old,
helped out whenever they had time.

I learned a great deal while managing that chicken farm. I was lucky
that chicken cholera and other diseases dangerous for chickens never struck
our farm. If only 70 percent laid eggs, our five thousand chickens could
produce 3,500 eggs a day. It was a profitable business.

To perform a job well, one must have a thorough understanding of it.
Take chicken raising, for example: when one buys small chicks one must
learn to distinguish a female chick from a male one. Only a female chick
would produce eggs, and you would lose money if you bought a lot of male
chicks. It was not easy to distinguish a male chick from a female one. Experts,
who used microscopes to distinguish between the two, could tell whether a
chick was male or female only twenty-four hours after it emerged from the
eggshell. Determining the sex of chickens was not 100 percent accurate, and
some chicks escaped correct identification. The Japanese were quite good at
this art. The law of nature indicated that, on average, of five thousand
newborn chicks, half were male and the other half female. Raising chickens
was not easy, especially in winter because heating equipment was necessary.
As the chicks grew, a veterinarian had to give them injections. Then the
chicks were allowed outdoors, but we also had to guard against raiding
skunks. Windows had to be closed day and night.

The sale of eggs also required certain procedures. We normally used
machines to select and classify eggs according to weight and eliminate the

small ones. We then washed them clean. To keep the eggs fresh, we packaged them the same day and sent them to buyers who shipped them from Lakewood to markets in New York City.

But our good times did not last very long. Soon after the completion of an East-West superhighway, egg prices dropped drastically because eggs raised in the West, where production costs in open fields were low, were now transported in refrigerated trucks overnight to New York. These eggs were sold at a lower price. The market formerly enjoyed by New Jersey chicken farms declined. The chicken-raising business in New Jersey suffered a slump, and many farms closed. My next-door neighbor had the foresight to tell me that "once the superhighway is open to traffic, the eggs will flow steadily from the West. Competition will be tough; we will no longer compete in chicken farming." He decided to sell his chicken farm.

But I dared not take that step. If I sold my chicken farm, what could I do? My chicken farm income declined by more than $3,000 per month, and it became more and more difficult to earn my livelihood. Mechanized farms still barely broke even, and survival was impossible for any farm using manpower to feed the chickens. My first partner, Hu, had left the farm after three years, and my eldest son had gone to college, leaving only me, my wife, and my youngest son to manage the farm. No matter how we tried to cut costs, we could not make ends meet without asking friends to loan us money. However, each time I borrowed money, I made certain that I returned the loan within two or three months, and I never once lost my credit with my friends. Chiang heard of my predicament and, without my asking, sent me as a gift two or three thousand dollars each year. This money became the source from which I drew funds to repay my debts. Receiving that fund was like "receiving charcoal in a freezing winter," and I was grateful for Chiang's concern.

I had begun my chicken-raising business in 1953, and by 1961 I could no longer afford to go on. I was forced to close my chicken farm, thus ending eight years of painstaking work. There is a proverb that goes "Fortune never arrives doubly; misfortunes never come singly." How true! Right after I went out of business, I encountered more bad luck. When I started my chicken-raising career, I had insured the farm buildings for $16,000. Now that I was no longer in business, the insurance agent I had dealt with for eight years offered me this sound advice: "Now that you're no longer raising chickens, why take out so much insurance? Reduce it a little!" So I reduced the insurance to only $4,000. Little did I know that just after I had reduced my insurance, a forest fire would engulf my chicken farm. On that day, my whole family had been invited to spend the day with friends in New York City.

We used three acres of our thirty-acre farm for living quarters. The leaves had fallen, and the dry season increased the danger of fire. Luckily, I had raked the leaves from around my house the night before we went to visit friends. When the fire devoured the leaves, it did not reach my house. Of three rows of chicken barns, only half a row remained untouched by fire. My new automobile, to be used for transporting eggs, was parked in the garage right next to the chicken feed storage building, and it was destroyed. We hitched a ride with friends to New York City. This fire was a total shock, and it happened right after I had reduced my insurance valuation for the property. Such bad luck was totally unexpected, but that was life.

When I bid farewell to my elder brother, Kuo-fu, in 1950, he was already very ill. We somehow had a premonition this would be our last time together. Sure enough, on August 25 the next year, at age sixty, my brother passed away. Chiang's telegram conveyed that news to me, and the message implied that I need not go home because everything would be taken care of. I fully understood. The Kuomintang was undergoing reform, and it would be inappropriate for me to return. But ten years later, in 1961, my father became very ill. Chiang telegraphed me to return right away. My wife and I made the trip overnight and arrived in Taipei to see more than a thousand people who had come to the airport to welcome us. They had done this on their own. I was deeply moved by their kindness. Chen Cheng, sincere or not, was at the airport to take us to my father's home. My father had already lost consciousness after a stroke. He held my hand tight as though he was aware I had returned home. When Chiang received me, he expressed concern about my father's health. Shortly afterward, my father passed away. After the funeral, we returned to America by steamship via Japan. I left Taipei hastily because I thought someone might think that Chiang would ask me to take up some government job. I had asked my friend Shen Shih-hua to take care of my chicken farm before I had left New Jersey, and I had to get back to the farm.

The Princeton Medical Books Project

I became idle after my chicken-farming enterprise. About that time, a Chinese-funded foundation wanted to reclassify several thousand Chinese medical books stored in the Princeton University Gest Oriental Library's East Asian collections. They asked me to take charge. I thought that rearranging these Chinese medical books would be meaningful work. So I agreed to take the job. The collection was particularly strong in pre-twentieth-century works on traditional Chinese medicine and publications of the Ming period. I.V. Gillis and Pai P'ing-ch'i had coauthored a book, *Title Index to the Catalogue of the Gest Oriental Library*, published in Peking in 1941, and in 1974, Ch'u Wan-li of National Taiwan University would write *A Catalogue of the Chinese Rare Books in the Gest Collection of the Princeton University Library* introducing the collection. In 1954, Hu Shih also had written an article about the library.[2]

The impressive collection of Chinese medical books had been assembled by Guion Moore Gest, a Jew. Why did he collect so many Chinese medical books? First, he was a very rich man who had been afflicted with a serious eye disease in his early years. Specialists all over the world had not been able to cure him until he learned of a well-known eye medicine of Tingchou of Hopei Province in China. Gest used that medicine and was soon cured. He thus considered Chinese medicine to be a miracle. Thereafter, he annually appropriated a certain amount of money to friends in the U.S. embassy in Peking to collect Chinese medical books for him. The collection rapidly expanded.

Gest first took the collection to Canada and housed it temporarily in the basement of a government agency. He later met Albert Einstein and asked him whether he wanted these books. Einstein said: "My research center is very small, and there is no place for the collection. The newly built Princeton University library should be spacious enough to have these books deposited there." This was how the Gest Library came into being.

This book collection was so large that Hu Shih had spent two years cataloging it. In accordance with the foundation's wishes, I devised a plan for reorganization and reclassification. Books would be arranged by diseases such as typhoid fever, stroke, diabetes, and their cures using Chinese medicine. An English text would appear on the opposite pages. Other prescriptions would be arranged in a similar way. I presented this plan to the foundation. Mary E. Ferguson,[3] the foundation president, said, "It would be better if you could find a Princeton professor to partake in this plan." I soon found Professor Frederick W. Mote, who could speak Chinese and whose wife was Chinese. I complimented him on his reputation and asked him whether he would be interested in joining me in this reorganization plan. He was very pleased and quickly accepted my invitation to help with my work.

The foundation approved my plan but asked another Chinese scholar, Ch'en K'o-hui, to look at it. Ch'en was well known for his research on the Chinese medicine called *Ma-huang* [ephedrine]. From *Ma-huang* he had extracted a remedy that was particularly effective in treating asthma. After he had read my plan, he commented, "It is befitting to ask Ch'en to take charge of this plan because Ch'en has a good knowledge of Chinese medicine."

The first year the foundation appropriated $20,000 for our work, planning to continue the funding in later years. But to my surprise, Mote wanted to remove me so that he could handle this project by himself. Ferguson, however, rejected him outright, saying that the idea was originally mine and that I had devised the plan. In the end, Mote refused to accept his role in this project. He would not even see me when I went to talk it over with him. Later, I asked Tung Shih-kang, curator of the Chinese collection in the Gest Library of Princeton University, to give Mote a message saying that I would be his assistant if he wished to take the project over. But I stipulated that he must do the job seriously and that he should not accept money and do nothing. He did not answer me. So the task of reorganizing and reclassifying the Chinese medical collection failed just as it seemed likely to succeed.

A friend in the legal profession later told me that in the United States everything must be clearly written down beforehand and signed by the parties involved. If that was not done, any project could be easily claimed by an immoral person who only wanted monetary reward. That was not what I had learned as a young student at Pittsburgh.

Columbia University's Oral History Project

I was now without income and found it hard to get by. On the recommendation of my good friend Ho Lien, I was invited to take a job as a senior research fellow at Columbia University. C. Martin Wilbur of the university's Modern History Research Institute was then in charge of a project recording contemporary Chinese history, and my job was to help organize the memoirs of Chinese notables. Ho Lien wanted me to work on my own memoir first. This project was to include such people as H. H. Kung, Li Tsung-jen, Wellington V. K. Ku, Ch'en Kwang-fu, Tseng Chi, Chang Fa-k'uei, Hu Shih, and many other well-known contemporary personalities in Chinese society. My memoir, the first, was to serve as a model to be submitted to the Ford Foundation for funding. The university sent a Chinese historian, Hsia Lien-ying (Julie Lien-Ying Hsia), to my home once a week to record my oral account, and we provided her with lunch. I spoke in Chinese when recording, and she translated that into English. The contract we signed stated that nothing in my memoir would be published without my consent. This work continued for a little over a year. Then, one day, Hsia told me: "You are still young. Would it be all right if I work on the older people in Hong Kong first? It's better that you wait." I agreed.

So Miss Hsia went to Hong Kong to work on the memoirs of other notables for more than two years, thus delaying my memoir. The delay continued, and I put my memoir aside. Although a little was done later, it was not completed. The problem was that Miss Hsia had an excellent command of English but a poor command of Chinese. Only two chapters, about a hundred pages or roughly one-tenth of my memoir, were finished before she went off to be married. Her husband was an overseas Chinese from Thailand, and she ceased work on my memoir after her marriage. Every year Miss Hsia and I exchanged New Year cards, but in 1982 her cards stopped coming. She had passed away! She left my memoir unfinished. Her grandfather was Hsia Jui-fang, a former owner of the famous Commercial Press who had worked for Yüan Shih-k'ai. The failure of the *Shao-ho* Gunboat Uprising of 1915 must be attributed to him [Hsia]. Carrying a huge amount of money, he hurried to persuade another gunboat, the *Ying-jui*, not to participate, and that action caused the uprising to fail. Hsia was later assassinated. But I doubt if Miss Hsia knew about this historic episode.

Eggs, Books, and Confucian Learning

After the Princeton medical collection project failed, a number of friends in Lakewood suggested we begin a business producing traditional Chinese thousand-year eggs, which are simply preserved eggs. Duck eggs are preferred. We already had a recipe for preserved eggs, and we knew there was a good market for Sung-hua preserved eggs [*Sung-hua p'i-tan*] in New York City's Chinatown. Sung-hua preserved egg is an egg wrapped and preserved in pinus lime. It is a very popular, enjoyable, and simple dish found on a Chinese dining table. The preserved eggs we produced indeed looked and tasted very good, and people named them Ch'en Li-fu preserved eggs or *Ch'en Li-fu p'i-tan*.

When the Autumn Festival [August 15, lunar calendar] was approaching, we thought that duck egg yolks would be needed to make moon cakes, so we used twenty thousand duck eggs to produce enough duck egg yolks to meet the market's demand. I want to point out that duck egg yolks were processed only once a year. In those days we did earn some money, but our work was truly very hard. Because our chicken barns were spacious and making preserved eggs did not require much space, I decided to use the room to organize a food production company with the Pao and Shen families. The company expanded to produce *tsung-tzu*, a pyramid-shaped, three-cornered dumpling made of glutinous rice and wrapped in bamboo or reed leaves, to be eaten during the Dragon Boat Festival on the fifth lunar calendar day of the fifth moon. We also produced New Year rice cakes [*nien-k'ao*] for Chinese New Year. We concocted a special peppery chili sauce [*la-chiao*], which was so delicious that it became known as Ch'en Li-fu chili sauce and was marketed as far away as San Francisco. We [Ch'en and his partners] were not yet seventy years of age. Still being physically strong, we could work and earn a profit. While I was living in the United States from 1950 to 1969, on six occasions Chiang asked Ching-kuo to offer me a number of posts, including representative to the United Nations, ambassador to Japan, Spain, Greece, and president of the Examination Yüan. He also wanted me to be ambassador-at-large. But I declined them all.

In addition to work on the chicken farm and making and selling preserved eggs and peppery chili sauce, I concentrated on the study of Confucius's writings, my second most favorite topic, as the first was studying the *Book of Changes* [*I-Ching*]. My writing had been interrupted by my father's passing. But in 1961, I finished a 614-page book entitled *The Confucian Way: A New and Systematic Study of The Four Books* [*Ssu-shu tao-kuan*].

Why my fondness for Confucian teaching? Briefly, it was my mother's influence. In my childhood, everyone had to study *The Four Books*, and many of my generation memorized the Confucian teaching in its entirety. Even today I can still recite long passages. At first, I wanted to systematically rearrange *The Four Books* and annotate them according to modern ideas. I recall Sun Yat-sen's comment that *Ta-hsüeh*, the Great Learning, began with the individual, then the family, then the nation, and finally the world. I found that 95 percent of *The Four Books* could be compiled according to that order. The remaining 5 percent required more thought, but I finally managed to categorize it. Chiang was to celebrate his eightieth birthday on October 30, 1966; Ching-kuo wrote me on April 23, 1966, hoping I would return to Taiwan to live. I brought back with me the first copy of the published work *Ssu-shu tao-kuan* as my birthday present to Chiang. He again offered me a position on the National Security Council. I declined and said I had absolutely no interest in politics.

Many friends had read my book. The historian Ch'ien Mu and others had written reviews. Wu K'ai-hsien, former head of the Kuomintang Shanghai municipal branch and then manager of Taipei's World Book Company [Shih-chieh shu-chü], wanted to publish it. I had no money of my own, so Wu helped me with a loan of 120,000 yuan in new Taiwan currency (the exchange rate was 40 to 1 then) to cover publishing expenses. Most friends suggested that books on Confucian teaching were perhaps out of date and that no market could be found in the Chinese world or elsewhere. They suggested that no more than a thousand copies should be printed and that I should not take the matter so seriously. Yet I took the risk and asked Wu to issue three thousand copies. In 1962, the Cheng Chung Book Company, which I had founded, surprised me by accepting only two hundred copies to sell. But within a month, the three thousand copies were sold out. None were in stock even when the Cheng Chung Book Company was asked for additional copies.

Before I returned to Taiwan in 1966, I had written to Chiang Ching-kuo that, once the book was published, many schools might invite me to lecture. If so, I was prepared to give only ten lectures. After Chiang read my book, he was so appreciative that he invited me to stay overnight in his residence at Tzu Hu and assigned me to lecture on Confucianism at all the military schools. I had thought there were only three or four; little did I know that there were more than a dozen. Once I lectured, more than a hundred schools wanted me to speak. By the time I had given seventy-five lectures in two months, I began to tire. I was overburdened, and one day in the middle of a lecture at the International Lions Club in Taipei I fell ill. I was sent to the Veterans General Hospital and found to have acute hepatitis.

Chiang came to the hospital to see me. Doctors reported to him that my problem was "very serious." Chiang sent for Chang Kwang-pi, a well-known gastroenterologist in Hong Kong, to treat me. Chang examined my chart and said the diagnosis was correct. Although my condition was serious, it was not dangerous. I needed plenty of rest. I took the medicine provided by the hospital, and I also drank soup made of small clam shells. My condition gradually stabilized, and I was finally cured. During this lecture tour, Chiang asked me to remain in Taiwan, and so I finally closed my farm in Lakewood and returned to Taiwan in 1970. Chiang told me at Tzu Hu that he thought my book was well written but that the title was "a bit too abstruse." Later he wrote down on a piece of paper "*The Four Books: The Ways of Consistency*, written by Ch'en Li-fu." He inscribed his name, Chiang Chung-cheng, and told his son Ching-kuo to give it to me with the words "no need to change the title, simply insert this in the book's front page." The book has been translated into English, Japanese, and Korean, and the Chinese-language edition alone sold more than 69,000 copies.

On returning to Taiwan in 1970, Chiang Ching-kuo passed on to me his father's request that I try to revitalize Chinese tradition and culture because I had declined all other party and government posts. The elder Chiang wanted me to be his deputy, vice-president of the Chinese Cultural Renaissance Association [Chung-hua wen-hua fu-hsing yün-tung wei-yuan-hui]. That association was supposed to revitalize ethics, democracy, and science [*Lun-li, min-chu, k'o-hsüeh*]. The first two spheres already had many advocates, but hardly anyone concentrated on science. I began the project of translating Joseph Needham's multivolume work *Science and Civilisation in China* into Chinese.

The reader will recall that Joseph Needham had served as a staff member at the British Information Service in Chungking when I was minister of education. After agreeing to translate his work, I wrote him a letter and he immediately gave his approval.

My preliminary cost estimate was at least US$50,000 to $60,000. Tung

Hao-yun, a wealthy friend in the shipping business, committed $40,000, and Chiang Ming-yu of Chia Hsin Cement assisted with $10,000. Wang Yun-wu of the Commercial Press happily agreed to publish my translations. With this problem almost solved, Chiang, then president of the association, approved and promised he would provide the rest if my funds were not sufficient. I organized a translation committee under the association's control with myself as editor in chief and Liu Tu, former director of the National Institute of Compilation and Translation, as my associate. In 1986, we had published fourteen volumes with about one-fifth unfinished. I used my spare time to compile thirty volumes to complement Needham's work; entitled the History of Chinese Science and Technology series [Chung-kuo k'o-hsüeh ch'i-i tsung-shu], it covers agriculture, irrigation, the salt industry, and silkworms. So far twenty-two volumes have been published.

With Sun Fo, my fellow vice-president of the association, I also organized a committee to reward scientific and technological innovations. Because of the importance of mathematics to science, this committee gave financial awards to top senior, middle, and vocational school students with high grades in mathematics and guaranteed their entry to colleges.

I also worked for the Confucius-Mencius Learning Society [K'ung-men hsüeh-hui], headed by Chiang, and served as his deputy. We published a *Confucius-Mencius Monthly* [*K'ung-meng yüeh-k'an*], sponsored monthly lectures on ethics, democracy, and science, and conducted essay and calligraphy contests at schools of all levels. We encouraged primary school pupils to learn *The Four Books*. We held summer seminars, symposiums for teachers and students and built Confucian temples throughout Taiwan and elsewhere, such as in Germany, the Ryukyu [Liu-ch'iu] Islands, and in many overseas Chinese communities. I have always believed that Confucianism can help us develop values that can cure the social illness connected with modern social change.

The Chinese Medical Institute

My interest in Chinese medicine originated in my early years and had been renewed by my contact with the Chinese medical collection at the Gest Library of Princeton University. With the establishment of the Chinese Medical Institute in Taipei, many obstacles loomed because many people were uninformed about Chinese traditional medicine. Chiang Kai-shek believed that traditional medicine had its own merits and that it must be supported and improved. Internal troubles paralyzed this institute in its early years, and leadership was needed. The Ministry of Education took the lead and sent fifteen people to serve as a board of directors to initiate a reorganization. Because nine of the fifteen were Western-trained physicians, it appeared as though the Western medical experts tried to seize control of the institute. Noisy opposition and struggle emerged. When Chiang heard about this, he summoned me to his office and said I must save the institute. He said that the traditional physicians would welcome me and that the Western-trained physicians would find it difficult to oppose me. I had always praised traditional medicine but promoted science.

At first I declined, but at his insistence I finally consented. I then picked five traditional physicians, five Western-trained physicians, and five persons without medical training but associated with the institute and formed a board of directors with myself as chairman. We registered with the Ministry of Education but could not find a suitable scholar versed in Chinese and Western medicines to become the president of the institute. We therefore selected Cheng Tung-ho, a well-known educator, to become president.

Although we managed an institute of traditional medicine, we could not locate any teachers in Taiwan and had to hire some from Hong Kong. We also had no teaching materials and had to compile those ourselves from scratch. Neither the public nor the private hospitals wanted our graduates. After numerous setbacks and with much effort, we persevered. With the help of Chiang Ching-kuo, who found funds to build a hospital, and with the help from our colleagues, the institute expanded to include departments of all subjects. More than seven hundred students a year are trained, and the hospital has more than seven hundred beds. Its reputation is impeccable. It is China's only hospital in which traditional medicine and Western medicine are practiced side by side. The theoretical foundation of Chinese traditional medicine and the legal status of traditional physicians are combined. Both public and private hospitals now have traditional medicine departments, and traditional medical doctors have the benefit of labor unions and insurance. Our health authorities changed their attitude and now have confidence in the traditional medical profession. These developments took ten years to accomplish.

The Passing of Chiang

Chiang passed away after midnight on April 5, 1975. Early the next day I learned the sad news. I rushed to the Veterans Hospital to offer my condolence. Ching-kuo kneeled down in front of me and sobbed: "I've lost my father. You are my only elder brother. I beg you to do what you can to help me!" I helped him up to his feet and expressed my sympathy: "Of course I will help. Please restrain your grief and take care of yourself to prepare to shoulder your huge responsibility." The whole nation mourned his death.

When the funeral committee met, someone suggested that entertainment be suspended nationwide for a month. As a member of the committee I rose to oppose, declaring that "we are not in the era of a monarchy. We should absolutely not suspend entertainment for such a long period. At most, maybe one week." Most at the meeting agreed with me. During the ceremony to close the coffin, someone suggested that only Christian books such as the Bible be placed with the body. I requested that books representing Chinese culture like *The Four Books*, *The Five Classics*, and Sun Yat-sen's writings also be placed there to eulogize Chiang as founder and president of the Chinese Cultural Renaissance Association, and everyone agreed.

The coffin lay in state in Sun Yat-sen Memorial Hall to allow people to pay their respects. In a matter of a few days, millions went by, day and night, and there was great weeping and crying. When the coffin was being moved to Tzu Hu, to a temporary shelter pending burial, tens of thousands of people lined the road to make offerings to his departed spirit. This demonstration of public grief illustrates how Chiang's noble character had influenced the people.

After Chiang was gone, the Chinese Cultural Renaissance Association was without a leader. Chiang Ching-kuo asked me if I would take over. I said no, because the association's charter says the president must also be the president of the republic, although the constitution did not give clear indication as to whether it must be a current president, so I suggested that former President Yen Chia-kan might be a suitable person. Ching-kuo then sought Yen's agreement, but he replied that only if I consented to remain as vice-president would he agree to take on the job. Ching-kuo again came to me. Mindful of the duty to perform as a public servant, I agreed. So Yen became the president, and I did my best to assist him. To promote more cultural activities, we formed committees on Chinese calligraphy, chess, opera, and the study of traditional and Western medicine. After Yen suffered a stroke, I was delegated to chair our meetings until 1991, when we both resigned and President Lee Teng-hui became the association's president. Its work continues today.

From 1925 to 1950 I devoted twenty-five years of my life to the national revolution with Chiang as my supreme commander. I think that I was very close to him and that few were as close to him as I. I took full responsibility for our defeat on the mainland and resigned from active political life by declining many positions Chiang offered me. Even while I earned my living abroad raising chickens, selling preserved thousand-year eggs, and manufacturing peppery chili sauce, I still maintained a good, respectable relationship with Chiang. It was at his suggestion that I had returned to Taiwan to undertake cultural work.

How do I see Chiang, his successes and failures? I consider Chiang a

With Chiang Kai-shek at his summer residence, Sun Moon Lake, Taichung, Taiwan, in 1970.

great Chinese patriot and a disciple of Sun Yat-sen's who strove to enhance the honor and integrity of the republic that Sun had founded. I also consider Chiang a product of his era, a military-political leader of modern China. His talents were more military than political. Chiang possessed considerable intelligence and courage. Self-educated and highly disciplined, he did not smoke or drink. Chiang was a Confucianist and influenced by the Wang Yang-ming [Wang Shou-jen] philosophy of the unity of knowledge and action [*Chih-hsing ho-i*]. I never doubted his sincerity and unselfishness in serving the country. He did not manifest the "I am always right" attitude, and he was not the despot that the Chinese Communists portrayed him as being. To my recollection, Chiang really never severely punished his subordinates, whether military or civilian. To be sure, some of his tactics might have been wrong. He greatly emphasized political maneuvering, and he skillfully used checks and balances to maintain his power. This method of his created distrust, fear, and suspicion; therefore unity among his subordinates was always in doubt. His firm, strong anticommunist beliefs, however, made him the natural leader of our national revolution.

During his lifelong career, the Chinese Communists were not his only enemy. The forces of opposition and destruction also came from remnants of the Ch'ing court, the warlords who worked on behalf of foreign powers, the Japanese imperialists, and our allies of World War II including Great Britain, the Soviet Union, and the United States. The problem was that none of the above elements truly wanted to see China become a united country. To some extent, Chiang never had the wholehearted support of the general public. His power only reached a few provinces. Yet Chiang was a symbol of resistance. He had a chance to make himself the greatest leader in the history of China since Emperor Chien-lung [of the Ch'ing dynasty]. Although that did not happen, the success of the national revolution was due to his leadership.

Opposition to Chiang from within was even stronger than from without: that opposition included the senior members of the Kuomintang from Kwangtang and Kwangsi provinces such as Wang Ching-wei, Hu Han-min, Sun Fo, later Pai Ch'ung-hsi, and Li Tsung-jen. Each of those I have just mentioned believed he could lead China to unity with the ideological guidance of Sun Yat-sen better than Chiang. In reality, none of them could accomplish such a gigantic task. Chiang's efforts were undermined by this opposition. The loyalty, obedience, discipline, mutual trust, ethics, and morality of the Kuomintang elite were all suspect. Moreover, the Kuomintang's real power never extended beyond a few provinces. Chiang's leadership never had full Kuomintang support. In my opinion, Chiang's power and that of the Kuomintang were never deeply rooted in Chinese soil. The Kuomintang's power was not solid enough for him to become the top leader of the nation. Indeed, Chiang had unbelievable difficulty maintaining his leadership, but with great courage he tried to do so. After Japan's unconditional surrender, Chiang became an entirely different person. He acted alone and made all decisions by himself without any consultations of which I was aware. Chiang might have admitted mistakes to others but never to me.

In the twenty-five years that he was in power before the communist takeover, Chiang really tried to keep the foreigners at bay. Yet he hoped the foreign powers would offer China a helping hand. For selfish reasons, none of them did. Chiang also longed for a peaceful environment to allow him time to work for the common people, but, ironically, there was not a day that he was not involved in some military action. The internal and external pressures were too great. Services provided to social and economic aspects were so limited. How could he fight against such odds and win?

Yet under these impossible circumstances, Chiang still accomplished some remarkable things. He convened China's National People's Convention [Kuo-min hui-i] and the abrogated unequal treaties, as Sun Yat-sen had desired. He assembled the National Congress and brought China into the constitutional era. He briefly united a disunited China to lead the people to defeat Japan. His hard work delayed the communist takeover of China for almost twenty-four years. China was no longer a semicolonial nation; it became a founding member of the United Nations with Big Five Power status. The Chinese language was accepted as one of the five major languages of the contemporary world. Chiang was responsible for the repeal by the U.S. Congress of the Chinese Exclusion Acts of 1882 and 1892. But unfortunately, Chiang must take ultimate responsibility for the loss of the Chinese mainland to the Communists, although all of us who worked with him share that burden. A final note: no one should forget that Chiang saved Taiwan from communist domination. The signing of the Mutual Defense Agreement with the United States in 1954 was a great achievement. The Kuomintang made Sun Yat-sen's Three People's Principles a workable doctrine on Taiwan and its offshore islands. We are now, once again, in a position to greatly influence mainland China. Within a twenty-five-year period, Chiang tasted the sweetness of quick victory and the bitterness of defeat. Everything came too quickly, too soon, and too unexpectedly. Regretfully, he did not live to see the fall of Soviet communism. Nor did he see the recent emphasis on economic growth rather than Marxist doctrine in mainland China, as evidenced at the Fourteenth Chinese Communist Party Congress of 1992.

What are the prospects for the Kuomintang and the Three People's Principles? My answer is that everything depends on the combined efforts of the Kuomintang's members in the future. Our generation tried. The days of my generation, like spring flowers, are numbered. The future of the Three People's Principles depends on the will of the younger generation. Their decisions and choices will reflect the quality of education we elders gave them.

Chiang Ching-kuo

Chiang Ching-kuo's friendship with my brother and me goes back to his boyhood, as clearly written in his letter to me on October 26, 1981, in commemoration of what would have been Kuo-fu's ninetieth birthday. In addition, he was very much concerned about my living conditions, chicken farm, and financial difficulties during my stay in New Jersey from 1959 through 1968. In all the letters he wrote me, twelve of them inquired about my return to Taiwan. The first time he mentioned that his father wanted

An autographed photo of
Chiang Ching-kuo, 1970.

me to end my "exile" in the United States was February 9, 1959, and the
last was August 30, 1968.[4] After I settled in Taiwan in 1970, Chiang Ching-
kuo often visited me to show his respect for an elder brother. Whenever he
received gifts of foods from others, without failing he always shared them
with me. Before making any important government personnel appointments
or any policy decisions of importance, usually he first asked my advice. I
gave him my sincere views, and we were as close as blood brothers.

He briefed me on the plan for ten industrial projects before that idea
was implemented. He even invited seven military advisers of high rank and
me to make on-the-spot inspections as projects were being built. His capacity
to honor elders was similar to that of his father. For that reason, he enjoyed
the support of all Kuomintang members, who only wanted to help him to
succeed. In my opinion, the ten industrial projects were the key factor for
Taiwan's economic miracle. His foresight and great resolve were admirable.
The projects attracted surplus capital as the results of land reform and savings
from civilians. The projects created thousands of jobs, quickened the birth
of a new merchant class, and introduced new technologies from foreign
countries. Taiwan now has high-rise buildings, modern hotels, factories,
bridges, automobiles, fast food, self-employed small businessmen, stock
markets, and cross-island highways, to say nothing of airlines, steel, and
shipbuilding industries. This prosperity made Taiwan stand in sharp contrast

Chiang Ching-kuo (at right) greeting my wife and me in 1970.

to Mao's Cultural Revolution on the mainland. The cessation of U.S. aid in 1965, the withdrawal from the United Nations in 1972, and worldwide inflation did not stop the growth of Taiwan's economy. Chiang Ching-kuo was naturally excited about the prospects of Taiwan's self-sufficiency.

The Kuomintang lost its center of gravity with Chiang's death. It needed reorganization, with Chiang Ching-kuo as the party's leader. We then decided that the title for party leader should be chairman [*Chu-hsi*] and that Ching-kuo should be elected by the plenary session of the Central Executive Committee. The secretary-general of the committee was then Chang Pao-shu, who asked my advice and stated that the entire Standing Committee of the Central Executive Committee would recommend Ching-kuo to be selected as chairman at the plenary session. I told Chang that the recommendation must be jointly signed by all the Central Executive Committee members and that certain senior members of the Central Committee for Deliberation and Consultation [Chung-yang p'ing-i wei-yüan hui] should go to the podium to express praise. Chang followed my suggestion, and three seniors, Chang Chün, Ho Ying-ch'in, and I, spoke at the meeting.

(*above and below*) To celebrate my father's ninetieth birthday (February 28, 1960), Chiang Kai-shek and Chiang Ching-kuo gave a party.

The recommendation passed unanimously, and the Kuomintang's center of gravity was again established.

In 1973 I suggested to Ching-kuo that we should not always react defensively to communist "united front" tactics but should take the initiative and counter them. We had several discussions and he agreed. And when Ching-kuo invited me to speak at the commemoration of Sun Yat-sen's birthday on November 12, 1980, I chose as my topic "The Inevitability of Unifying China under the Banner of the Three People's Principles." My message visibly moved the audience. In my address, I synthesized the teachings of Sun Yat-sen and the Taiwan experience and concluded that the Three People's Principles will eventually replace Chinese communism on mainland China. Lying between capitalism and communism, the guiding principles of *San Min Chu I* would be the best alternative for the entire Chinese nation in the twenty-first century. Once again, I predicted the collapse of communism and communist systems. Soon afterward, the Kuomintang Twelfth National Congress of March–April 1981 made its theme "Unifying China under the Banner of the Three People's Principles." The Chinese Communists reacted by publishing twenty-three articles in its press to attack us. What they published merely allowed the Chinese people to understand better the Three People's Principles without discrediting that doctrine.

Shortly after the Kuomintang Twelfth National Congress, an organization called the San Min Chu I Grand Alliance for the Unification of China [San-min chu-i t'ung-i Chung-kuo ta-t'ung-meng] took form with Ho Ying-ch'in in charge. In the beginning, it was very active. Chiang's counterattack strategy of "70 percent political, 30 percent military" could only succeed if it mobilized overseas Chinese throughout the world to launch psychological warfare on the mainland. If Ho's Grand Alliance confined its activities only to Taiwan, its influence would be minimal. When the revered Ho Ying-ch'in passed away, Chiang Ching-kuo wanted me to manage the Grand Alliance. But I was now too old, already over ninety years of age; I declined. Ma Shu-li stepped in and took charge.

At the second plenary session of the Kuomintang's Thirteenth National Congress, July 7–13, 1988, former Minister of Economics Chao Yao-tung and I, along with thirty-two members of the Central Committee for Deliberation and Consultation, proposed that we use Chinese culture as a basis to build common confidence [Kung-hsien] and appropriate ten billion U.S. dollars to invest in the mainland to pave the way for the eventual reunification of Taiwan with the Chinese Communists.[5] That money might initiate Sun Yat-sen's industrial reconstruction plan, which he vividly wrote about in his *The International Development of China* [Shih-yeh chi-hua]. Chao and I believed that we could nurture peaceful reunification between the two sides of the Taiwan Straits by this gift and that the concept was more suitable than referring to the Three People's Principles. The communist leader Chao Tzu-yang reacted favorably. Our government, however, feared that the Communists lacked sincerity, and our proposal was abandoned. Although public reaction in Taiwan and overseas was mixed about Chao Tzu-yang's final fall from power, I regret that this exciting initiative died.

When Ching-kuo was inaugurated as president, my wife and I congratulated him by sending a painting, mounted on a vertical scroll, of a boat surging forward while riding the wind. The fine calligraphy of the inscription read "Make a roc's flight of 10,000 *li*." Inscribed on the upper corner of the scroll were these words: "Teach loyalty and filial-piety; love country and the people; heaven helps those who help themselves; then you will succeed." Ching-kuo admired the scroll and hung it in his study. In the years of his presidency, he worked day and night, often made inspection tours, and kept close contact with the people. They loved and respected him.

The severe diabetes that afflicted Ching-kuo required him to engage in outdoor activities as one way to control the ailment. When news of international assassinations became more frequent, friends and Kuomintang members of the Legislative Yüan and representatives of the National Assembly urged him to restrict his outings among the people to avoid such dangers. Their good intentions changed his life-style, and his health actually took a turn for the worse. His feet, afflicted with open sores, would not heal, and walking became so difficult that his ailment worsened. Sadly, once Ching-kuo's internal bleeding started, it could not be checked. He bid farewell to the world on January 13, 1990. When the funeral procession arrived at Tao-yüan, people lined the road and wept unabashedly to show their love for him.

How did Chiang Ching-kuo regard the Democratic Progressive party (DPP), the first organized political party to oppose the KMT in Taiwan? He became worried about the DPP running wild without regard to the laws. But he did nothing to check its power because he wanted to promote democracy. It is my personal observation that he saw the DPP as a troublesome headache. To handle the DPP as a political issue, he realized, was a matter of timing. To him, the longer the Kuomintang stayed in Taiwan, unable to influence the mainland, the greater would be the challenge of local opposition. The DPP represented that opposition force. The problem could not, however, be solved by tight and repressive measures such as martial law. Chiang Ching-kuo, however, never opened the issue for discussion within his party; therefore, once he decided to recognize the opposition, many members of the Kuomintang felt that psychological and actual preparation were lacking.

His choice of Lee Teng-hui as successor was a good one. All those concerned about the future of Taiwan felt that if we were to continue in

Taiwan, then, for political stability, we should have a native Taiwanese as president. Lee Teng-hui, a well-educated native Taiwanese with considerable administrative experience, led no faction in the party when he took the presidential oath of office. Above all, he stressed harmony between the Chinese who came to Taiwan before and after 1945. I observed that Chiang Ching-kuo believed that Lee, a member of the Kuomintang, had faith in Sun Yat-sen's Three People's Principles.[6]

I recall that Chiang Ching-kuo left China on October 19, 1925, and returned on April 19, 1937, after an absence of almost twelve years.[7] I had urged that he return to China from the Soviet Union. Ever since his appointment as special administrator in southern Kiangsi Province in the spring of 1938, he had been known as "Chiang the Just" [Chiang ch'ing-tien], and his actions were only for the people's benefit. Hard working, hard driving, a man without vanity, he rose from provincial official to president. When Ching-kuo first took the highest office in the republic, he nominated Hsieh Tung-min as his vice-president, but he informed me ahead of time. In his second presidential term, he nominated Lee Teng-hui as his vice-president. Again he notified me ahead of time. I was completely won over by Ching-kuo's painstaking consideration of personnel matters.

Needless to say I was saddened by the passing of Chiang Ching-kuo. His poor health had always been an impediment to his ambition. I remember that Ching-kuo had been unhealthy ever since childhood. The main cause of his suffering was diabetes, but I believe he did not have enough daily exercise and did not eat properly. He was not even interested in taking a walk every day. He took food so casually. His feet ached. To relieve his pain, I suggested he have a "self-massage" as I have been doing every day, but he only paid lip service to my advice. And he knew very little about medicine. He did not know how to take care of his own body, especially when he had to work under great pressure.

His diabetes eventually produced internal bleeding and finally death. His son, Hsiao-wu, also died of internal bleeding. My lifelong experience taught me that by applying a Chinese herbal medicine called *paiyo*, a kind of white styptic powder produced in Yunnan Province, the internal bleeding will stop. But Ching-kuo had little confidence in Chinese herbal medicine, although the use of *paiyo* was not contraindicated by Western medical personnel. The Taipei press reported that Ching-kuo had loved to go here and there around the island to learn about the problems of ordinary people. These kind of activities were good for his diabetes, but fear of assassination induced people to request that he limit his public appearances.

How did Chiang's health influence his policies as premier and president? When a man is ill, he cannot make right decisions at the right time. I believe his poor health made him indecisive in handling the problem of the Taiwan Independence Movement.

After he died, the Kuomintang named Lee Teng-hui as acting president. According to the constitution, a presidential election must be held within a certain time limit. The Kuomintang again nominated Lee as the candidate, and there did not seem to be any problems. But when the Second National Assembly convened in 1990, some representatives had different ideas and wanted to nominate others as president and vice-president.[8] Those actions threatened to violate the party's decision. Eight senior comrades came out to negotiate, and I was one of them. Fortunately, both the nominees of the opposition, Lin Yang-kang and Chiang Wei-kuo, decided to withdraw from the race. Lee had nominated Li Yüan-tsu as vice-president. Both were over-whelmingly elected by the National Assembly, and that disturbance soon quieted down.

Later, to everyone's surprise, the aged representatives serving in the First National Assembly in 1948 were asked to retire. The Second National Assembly was elected on December 21, 1991, and charged with the task of revising the constitution. In the meantime, those pushing for Taiwan inde-pendence only gave the Chinese Communists a pretext for invading Taiwan. Fortunately, former Premier Hau Pei-tsun stood firm on this matter and opposed a separatist movement for Taiwan independence. As for what happens in the future, we must wait and see.

How did Chiang Ching-kuo feel about the Taiwan Independence Move-ment?[9] He took it with the very greatest pain. The movement was extremely impolite and rude to him. At one point, they even wanted to take his life by violent means. He could only keep his troubles to himself. The endorsement of violence by the movement embarrassed him. I believe, in general, the situation created by the Taiwan Independence Movement was truly hard on him, to say nothing about the other domestic and foreign policy matters he had to confront. Ching-kuo was a filial son, a capable leader of the executive branch, and a good president. The policies he introduced and implemented, like the ten industrial projects and the three-no policy [no direct air and sea link, no direct communication, and no direct exchange of mail] toward mainland China, were influenced by his father. The three-no policy, from my point of view, was correct, for I feared that the Taiwan people were really inexperienced in dealing with the Chinese Communists. For our own safety and security, we must be cautious in expanding ties and promoting relations with the mainland. Yet I agree with those critics that saw the three-no policy as more defensive than offensive.

Because of his father's high expectations, and his long years in the Soviet Union, Ching-kuo worked hard on Chinese language and culture after he returned to China. I would say that Ching-kuo was not as intelligent, decisive, bold, or broad-minded as his father. But he quickly learned and tried to make the right decisions despite great difficulties. He was very reserved and not a talkative person. We must acknowledge that he acted the best way he could, and, most important, he did not make any grave errors.

Sometimes Ching-kuo worried about the education of his children. He probably restricted them too much. Following the teaching of Mencius that "the ancient exchange sons to teach," he occasionally asked me to supervise his sons' activities. Ching-kuo was a very strong anti-Communist, and, according to him, the Russians never treated him well. Perhaps he thought he could never return to China and was in love and so married a Russian woman. His marriage was good, and he had great affection toward his wife. He never knew that I negotiated with Soviet ambassador Bogomoloff to get him back. Chiang Kai-shek truly wanted his son to succeed him, but Ching-kuo did not want any member of his family to be involved in politics or become his successor. I thought that was undemocratic. Complex national affairs might have overburdened him and made him weary of politics, but he should not have prevented his offspring from engaging in politics.

Devoted to Learning

China was weak in the past because China lagged behind in the natural sciences. Sun Yat-sen had been correct when he said, "Effect a radical cure by the root" and "Try head on to catch up." Therefore, when Taiwan Normal University invited me to teach a graduate course in the philosophy of man, I readily accepted. I taught it for ten years. After constant revisions I put all my lectures together into a book called *The Study of the Philosophy of Man* [*Jen-li hsüeh yen-chiu*], later translated into French. Altogether about 150 students worked under my tutelage. I resigned from teaching only when I became old and infirm.

People often think the Chinese language is difficult to learn because its characters do not use a phonetic alphabet. That is true. Eighty percent of Chinese ideographs are pictophonetic characters, with one element of the word indicating meaning and the other sound. By looking at the ideograph, we know what category it belongs in. The element that provides sound makes the word complete. If you know how the word is composed, the Chinese language is not difficult to learn at all. So I invited a few experts to divide the characters into four categories: *t'ien*, or heaven (moon, sun, star, light, wind, rain, etc.), *t'u*, or earth (metal, wood, water, fire, earth, etc.), *jen*, or man (ear, eye, hand, foot, etc.), *shou*, or animal (cow, goat, sheep, pig, etc.). Arranged in order, they were compiled into eight volumes with illustrations, with the title *Learning Chinese Made Easy* [*Chung-wen i-hsüeh*].

I believe that the Chinese Communist party had good intentions when it adopted the simplified Chinese character system to make it easy for common people to learn how to read and write. But if such a system is put into practice for too long a time, young people will not learn the ancient classics and our culture will suffer. In asking experts to research Chinese calligraphy, I aimed to make the writing form simple and quick. If running hand calligraphy can be standardized, it will have the advantages of the simplified character system without its weak points. After a few years of study, in which many opinions were solicited, a final decision was made on standardization. My recommendations were adopted at a meeting of the Chinese Cultural Renaissance Association and approved by the Ministry of Education. After implementation began, we began sending association members to schools to speak and demonstrate. Our communities had no objections. We hope that when the two sides of the Taiwan Straits peacefully unify, we can work together to improve the Chinese language and have a simplified character system.

China differs from other countries because of its family system and the special emphasis placed on ethics and morality. We first teach filial piety and fraternal duty, which begin in the family and then extend outward, as the ancient proverb states: "Filial piety is to serve the emperor (senior officials); fraternal duty is to serve the elder; kindness is to prevail upon all."

Today's education system starts at the kindergarten level, yet children, influenced by what they constantly see and hear at home at an early age, still learn mainly from their parents. Therefore, family education remains the foundation of all education. Hsieh Tung-min, former vice-president of the Republic of China, and I agreed that teaching materials must be developed for family education. We invited experts to compile four textbook volumes for family education, entitled *Happy Family* [*K'uai-lo chia-t'ing*], for the public. We will have to wait for a few years to find out what impact these books have on the public.

I have written a great deal about culture, and, in addition to translations and editing, I have published a total of twenty-four works. In 1973, I edited and annotated *Mencius* and issued a 400-page edition of *The Political Thought of Mencius* [*Meng-tzu chih cheng-chih ssu-hsiang*]. In 1989, a three-volume collection of my writings, roughly from 1927 to 1988, entitled *A Collection of Essays From the Hung-i Study* [*Hung-i-chai wen-chi*], appeared. That 287-article collection is a systematic reflection of my thoughts during the past years. Incidentally, *Hung-i* means liberal-mindness and constant endurance. Many of my friends collected all my writings as a gift for my ninetieth birthday. I believe I stated before that the *I-Ching* had always been my favorite topic, Confucianism second, and then Sun Yat-sen doctrine followed by ethics and morality, Chinese culture, language, medicine, applied sciences, economics, and translations of non–Chinese-language works.

I recall the Kuomintang policy immediately after the purge of 1927 was to accept anyone from the Communist party who offered his or her services to our party. Every day twenty or thirty students had appointments to talk to me. After these discussions I noted some common patterns among their reasons for joining the Chinese Communist party. First, they did not understand their national culture, and more than half of them had very little education. Second, our schools lacked good teachers, and the students had failed to understand that the Three People's Principles was a doctrine more suitable to Chinese circumstances than any other ideology. Finally, many young people had no idea that other ideologies greatly harmed our society and culture, and they were easily seduced by communist ideology and the Communist party. To prevail upon young people to be patriotic, to support the Kuomintang, and to take pride in our history and culture, they first had to understand our history and culture. For this reason, whenever I had the time, I presented my views to them. I have always enjoyed teaching.

I also recall that these youth from the Chinese Communist party showed a great interest in my lectures on Chinese culture and ethics. All nations have their indelible history and culture, and to study Chinese history and culture, one begins with the basics. I stressed that our cultural history had been so long that, after a century of being subjected to semicolonial status, we had nearly forgotten and abandoned our heritage. That was why Sun Yat-sen wanted to rescue China and understand its essence. Our culture was like a mineral resource buried underground for too long, and we needed to explore and extract it in order to use it effectively. I always believed that, because I never applied what I had learned in coal mining, why should I not engage in cultural mining?

I hold the view that the roots of Chinese culture are in the *I-Ching*; Confucian and Taoist ideas have their source in this book. Other ideas such as the Hundred Schools of Thought, their followers of pre-Ch'in [221 B.C.], and the early years of the Han dynasty also can be traced to the *I-Ching*. Our basis for anticommunism is based on Chinese culture. Life is comprised of two elements: the mind and matter, which Sun Yat-sen also introduced and which he referred to as the elements of life [*sheng-yuan*]. Both mind and matter are connected, and the *sheng-yuan* has not only substance but also spirit. *Yin* and *Yang* are also explained in the *I-Ching*. Life exists only when there are both *Yin* and *Yang*, and because "neither *Yin* nor *Yang* can exist alone," then only *Wei-sheng* can exist. With this concept I developed a series of lectures, which were published as a book entitled *On Vitalism* [*Wei-sheng lun*] in 1933. Materialism recognizes that everything in the universe is governed by matter. I thought that idea was wrong. What controls everything is neither matter nor spirit alone but life, which is the union of material and spirit. This book theoretically criticized materialism. With the principle of "life connotes change" in the *I-Ching* and Sun Yat-sen's concept of people's livelihood, we are confident that the latter concept can correct the mistakes of On Idealism [*Wei-hsin lun*] and On Materialism [*Wei-wu lun*].

My thinking then went a step further: under only two circumstances must a man die: first, when his existence affects the existence of many people. For instance, an armed robber intending to kill threatens many people's lives, so he must accept the legal sanction of being put to death, which means death not of his own will. Second, when the country and many people's lives are in danger, an individual must sacrifice himself for the good of the nation. He must, of his own will, give his life to save the lives of many and his country. Except for these two circumstances, even a small insect or an ant would try to safeguard its own life to avoid death. In my 1933 book, *On Vitalism* [*Wei-sheng lun*], I tried to develop a very powerful theory to smash the theory of materialism, which distorted the evolution of our history. The Chinese Communist party went so far as to instruct its members to buy a copy of my book within one year, so they could write articles to attack and criticize my theory. But none of them successfully refuted my original idea. For this reason, the Communists came to hate me even more.

But how did their attacks on me turn out? In their criticisms, not one single piece of evidence they presented really undermined my theory. The more the Communists opposed that theory, the more my book sold. That was the first book I wrote to refute the Chinese Communists.

I was then so busy that I had no spare time to write more books. I never finished the second half of *Wei-sheng lun*. While minister of education, in the ministry I found a young man named Tang Chün-i who was an editor and versed in philosophy. I invited him home, and for half an hour each day I talked and he took notes. From these notes, in 1944 we completed a philosophy book called *The Fundamental Truth of Life* [*Sheng-chih yüan-li*]. This work substituted for that section of *Wei-sheng lun* I never could write. Published in Chungking in 1944, it sold around 120,000 copies, helping to expose the fallacy of communism. In 1948, Roscoe Pound, former dean of Harvard Law School, wrote an introduction to the first edition of the English translation appearing in the United States.

After sixty years of marriage, my diamond wedding celebration in 1986 in Taipei.

My Long Life

In my advanced years, my body is still in good condition, and I have learned how to preserve my health. Ever since childhood, my favorite food has been the brains of chicken, duck, or pig. But I never eat much of these items except once every two weeks or once a month. The reason my eyesight is still good is that I am fond of eating small silver fish [whitebait]. I love eggs scrambled with small silver fish, each time using almost a hundred or two hundred of them. Since ancient times people have reported that good nutrients come only from certain foods. If true, then a hundred or more small silver fish eaten at a time should supply me with nutrients to equal three or four hundred eyes. Over a long period, eyesight should never deteriorate.

I appeal to scientific findings. The inside of a human body does not reflect an agricultural society but rather an industrial society. The inner organs manufacture the material needed by the body; whatever is eaten passes through the digestive system to supply specific substances to the body after chemical decomposition. One need not eat a certain food to acquire a certain nutrient. A young and strong body can be self-sufficient like a person planting his cotton, spinning and weaving his cloth, and making his clothes. But once reaching advanced years, a body can no longer sustain itself and extra care is required, just as a former cloth producer will buy ready-made clothes. Eating the brains of chicken, duck, and pig can nourish an elderly person's brain, and there is evidence for this comparison. But one cannot eat too much of this type of food because it contains considerable cholesterol. In order not to be harmful, the quantity of such food must be carefully measured. Sometimes I buy a pig's heart, but I eat it only once a month. Then, every one or two months I would eat a pig's brain. By adhering to this schedule, my physical checkup report reveals a cholesterol level of 180, so I have no problem eating such food.

Recently, a friend of mine returned from Switzerland and told me that a hospital there had developed a special formula of medical treatment called Cell Therapy based on the principle of "eat certain foods for certain nutrients." The person who invented this formula is the hospital's vice-president. But some people still do not believe in this kind of medical treatment, although it has cured many. Famous people and heads of states such as Queen Elizabeth of Great Britain, Marshal Tito of Yugoslavia, and Prime Minister Adenauer of West Germany have benefited from such treatment. Adenauer's last words on his deathbed make one ponder: "Germany's universities must develop the formula for a medical treatment using cells to replace cells. Without such a treatment to cure my illness, I could not have served my country for another twenty years!"

According to my friend Mr. Hsu, the formula of that Swiss hospital was to use the embryo from a ewe's belly, bake it dry after sterilization, dissect and separate the ear, eye, mouth, nose, and other internal organs and make powder of each, to be used for patient injections. The results have been spectacular. I present a recipe for maintaining good health:

Exercise to maintain physical well-being

Rest to attain mental tranquility

Do not overindulge in food and drink

Keep regular hours in daily life

Eat only well-cooked food

Drink only boiled water

Consume more vegetables and fruits

Consume less meats and fat

Keep your head cool

Keep your feet warm

Be content with your lot and you will always be happy
Exorcise greed and you will find peace

In the past, Westerners have often mocked our feeble nation and weak people and insultingly referred to our country as "the sick man of East Asia." For this reason, Chiang started a New Life Movement just before the war to correct this image and encourage our people to discard old habits, strengthen their bodies, and dedicate themselves to serving our country.

While in America, I read an article in the *China Tribune* written by a Chinese woman in which she briefly explained the benefit of Eight Movements to Health [*Nei-pa tuan-chin*] as a kind of Chinese *kung fu* exercise for strengthening both the body and the mind. This will promote blood circulation. I was most impressed by that article and made a special trip to New York City to call on her. She told me that she had been doing the *Nei-pa tuan-chin* exercise for eight to nine months and had already had benefited in three ways: (1) her appetite had increased; (2) her long-lasting ear disease that produced pus had been cured; (3) the varicose veins in her legs had disappeared.

According to her the *Nei-pa tuan-chin* is practiced as follows:

Start the exercise around the eyes. Rub the hands until they are warm; massage the face from the eyes in a left to right and right to left motion; rub the temples; massage the ears; lightly tap the back of the head with two fingers; rub areas behind the ears; rub the nose; bite the teeth tightly; rub the throat; massage the back of the head to energize the central nervous system; then knead the chest and the belly with two hands; massage the waist; massage both sides of the prostate area; then sit down and knead the knees with one hand and rub the underside of the arch of the feet with the other. Each movement of the exercise described above must be done at least a hundred times. I myself add a stand-up and squat-down exercise at least sixteen times.

After I learned this set of exercises, I performed these diligently each day for thirty-four years. I do the above exercise 35 to 40 minutes every morning on rising at 5:30 A.M. and have continued doing it without a break until today. After exercising, I go to the toilet, then I take a shower, and wash in the general manner, all of this requiring about one hour, and by 6:30 I am ready for breakfast; then I take a walk. At first I did this exercise in bed, but some ten years ago I started going through the exercise while taking a shower, which means that whatever part of the body the water falls on, I would rub that part of the body with my hands. I feel that combining exercising and showering is even more effective because exercising during showering enhances blood circulation. I claim the latter activity as my original idea. Looking back, ever since I began doing this exercise, my aches in the waist, a chronic complaint of mine, have been completely cured. I lead a regular life.

At home, supper begins at 6:30. After supper I watch television news and other programs while eating, but whenever the program is interrupted by commercials, I use that period to take a walk inside the house, from the living room to the kitchen to the bedroom, pacing back and forth. I usually go to bed at 9:30 in the evening, sleeping a total of eight hours. The days I do not go out to attend meetings, I stay home and write and perform chores like organizing my manuscripts. I take a nap for about an hour at noontime. I then rise and continue my work.

I eat very simply. I love vegetables and bean curd and eat little fatty food such as meats. After my gallbladder surgery, greasy foods do not agree with me. I have a slight case of diabetes, which means that if I am a little careless in eating, my blood sugar rises to 170 or 180. The ideal level of blood sugar is 120 degrees, and when it rises above 200 an insulin injection is required. My blood sugar level is now under control, at about 140 degrees, but still almost 20 degrees above the normal. A recent medical theory claims that anyone over sixty years of age will experience a 1-degree rise in blood sugar for each added year. Given my thirty-odd years beyond the age of sixty, my ideal blood sugar level should be between 130 to 150 degrees.

My blood pressure is very good: 100 to 120 [mm Hg, systolic] over 60 to 70 [mm Hg, diastolic]. This figure is very normal. Few people at my age have such normal blood pressure, and I attribute this to my exercise. I have always remembered the advice of an old Buddhist abbot: "Exercise to strengthen physical well-being; rest to attain mental tranquility." When this eminent monk uttered these words he was already more than ninety-four years of age, and he repeated these words to demonstrate to people how a healthy, long life could be attained.

I also benefit by my exercises. Long ago in middle school I enjoyed sports like tennis, basketball, soccer, swimming, ice-skating, high jump, hurdling, and running. I always had a strong interest in sports.

I also fall asleep within three minutes after lying down. I always have a good night's sleep. I adhere to an important principle: if I should promise someone to do something, I will go all out to keep my promise; even if what I do is not the ideal result, at least I have done all I can. As I spare no effort at what I do, at night I peacefully fall asleep without anxiety.

I have another special quality that seems unattainable for most people. I am not distracted when people nearby engage in loud, empty talk; I can still reflect and calmly go on writing.

I keep myself busy. Each day I usually write at least five letters in my own hand. I have many social obligations and fulfill many requests to write inscriptions and forewords for other people's work. I compile material for teaching Chinese culture, and I daily read papers, documents, and correspondence, which flow in an unending stream. But I never tire. I owe this to my ability to improve myself and my year-round exercise.

Final Notes

I have been struggling to complete this *Memoir* for several years. For sentimental reasons, I have stopped many times and then continued. I often write a few lines or even one or two paragraphs. I tried to restrain myself and be accurate. I am not sure when this idea came to me to record my lifelong experiences to inform the younger generations that once upon a time such events actually occurred and such persons made those events possible. I think certain friends made this suggestion to me long ago, and I only can assume the Columbia University Oral History Project in the 1950s was such a beginning. As I finish these final lines, I am approaching ninety-five years of age. Can you imagine, ninety-five years? Indeed, I am a man who has crossed the twentieth century.

When this century began, China was in chaos. The old empire had disintegrated; the economy was rapidly changing; traditional values were being challenged. The Boxer Rebellion had taken place, and the U.S. Open Door policy was emerging. In 1900, Sun Yat-sen, father of the republic, staged his uprising in Hui-chou. His revolutionary activities covered the first twenty-five years of this century, and in those twenty-five years I was born, grew up, and completed my Chinese and Western education. Sun Yat-sen was China's president for only three months, and the republic survived only in name. Just think of all the foreign interventions, civil wars, assassinations, unethical and immoral dealings, murders, opium smoking, foot binding, torture, heavy taxation, and so on. Those were the conditions in China in the first twenty-five years of this century, and it was a noble thing to change those conditions regardless of the costs.

From 1925 to 1950, China came under attack on two fronts by communism and Japanese imperialism, and the Kuomintang party was in the leading position to cope with all the problems facing China. In those twenty-five years, I threw myself into the cauldron of national revolution even though coal mining was my first love. Chiang Kai-shek was China's leader. From 1950 to 1975, we Kuomintang members consolidated our base in Taiwan during the cold war era. It was our last chance to survive, and we had to launch significant reforms. Our safety and security have constantly been threatened, but war never came to the island. We worked hard. The foundation for democraticization was solidly laid. We gradually made the

Three People's Principles a reality on Taiwan. Chiang was in the command-ing position to lead us.

From 1975 to 1990, we experienced economic prosperity, rising living standards, improved education, and the building of a multiparty political life. We Kuomintang members no longer acted as an underground, secretive political organization, and we did not continue to associate with underworld elements as we did in Shanghai with the Green Gang in the 1920s. We again offered the Three People's Principles as an alternative to Chinese Communist party rule on the mainland. What we have achieved in Taiwan has begun to have an enormous impact on China. Communism in the Soviet Union has been buried in the debris of history. As we Kuomintang revolutionaries always predicted, communism cannot work and cannot survive. The Chinese Communist party must take steps to change, and the Three People's Prin-ciples is China's only hope. The predictions I made seven decades ago are now coming true. I am happy I played a very small role in making those changes come about; nothing makes me more happy than that realization.

After I recollected events of the past ninety-four years, I believe I can conclude that there were several turning points in my life. The very first was undoubtedly my Uncle Ch'i-mei's participation in the Shanghai Upris-ing in 1915, assisting Sun Yat-sen in consolidating his revolutionary base in Shanghai. The second turning point was my childhood education, which made me so profoundly interested in Confucian teaching. The third point was Chiang's desire that I should not devote myself to coal mining but rather work for the cause of the national revolution. The fourth turning point was my decision to be in exile in the United States for fifteen years. The fifth point (regarding which, most probably, few will believe) is my effort to arrange Chiang Ching-kuo's return to China from the USSR in March 1937 as his father's successor. I then would transfer to him all the duties his father had assigned me. Let me be factual: From the day Chiang Ching-kuo ac-cepted his first assignment in Kiangsi Province in the spring of 1938 until his death in January 1988 I truly shared in the pride of his success.

I have great faith in China's cultural strength and traditional values. After the downfall of Soviet communism, where will Chinese communism go? Nowhere, absolutely nowhere.[10] Nobody can change my belief that communism is out of tune with Chinese culture.

On September 9, 1992, I was interviewed by five mainland Chinese journalists in Taipei. In response to a question about China's future, I stated that the reunification of China could be achieved through the revitalization of traditional Chinese culture by the mutual efforts of our Kuomintang and the Chinese Communist party.[11]

If China is reunified by returning Chinese culture to China, the nation will be able to play an active role in helping the world economically and culturally during the forthcoming twenty-first century. After forty-five years apart, it is clear that neither communism nor capitalism can suit the needs of the Chinese people. Chinese culture prefers the golden mean, a balance between extremes. Both communism and capitalism are extremes and therefore out of line with the Chinese culture.[12] I am, as always, optimistic about the prospect of unifying China under the banner of Chinese culture. Equally, I profoundly believe what China needs now is Western science and technology. I think total democracy will make China free and independent. I envision a great China in the future. I hope the Kuomintang will always be vigorous, dynamic, zealous, unselfish, having a new, fresh spirit. As Sun Yat-sen wrote, "The work of the revolution has not yet been completed. Let all my comrades continue to work hard." Indeed, let us all work hard and together with tolerance, patience, and persistence. Let all Chinese be united, let us not act as a sheet of sand. Let us march forward. Let us welcome the challenge of the twenty-first century. Let us be fully prepared. Tears fall from my eyes.

Notes

Introduction

1. Angela Partington, ed., *The Oxford Dictionary of Quotations* (New York: Oxford University Press, 1992), p. 513.

2. Some comments on the important connection that Ch'en Ch'i-mei provided for Ch'en Li-fu are in order. Ch'en Ch'i-mei led the Shanghai insurrection in early November 1911, one of many such uprisings that toppled the Ch'ing dynasty. Ch'en Ch'i-mei was also a close friend of Chiang Kai-shek and had recommended to Sun Yat-sen that Chiang serve as his military adviser, an action that launched Chiang Kai-shek's career with Sun. Ch'en Ch'i-mei's revolutionary leadership also helped capture Nanking from the Ch'ing as early as December 4, 1911. The new provisional government in Nanking then elected Huang Hsing as generalissimo, and Huang immediately arranged for Sun Yat-sen's return to China. Ch'en Ch'i-mei also was prominent in the *Shao-ho* Gunboat Uprising in Shanghai in December 1915, and he continued to support Sun even after Huang Hsing had broken with Sun over the issue of reorganizing their revolutionary party in 1914. Ch'en Ch'i-mei's close relations with the Shanghai underworld gangs later proved beneficial to Chiang Kai-shek and Ch'en Li-fu in eliminating the Communists in 1927.

3. Lloyd E. Eastman, *The Abortive Revolution: China under Nationalist Rule, 1927–1937* (Cambridge, Mass: Harvard University Press, 1974), chaps. 1 and 7.

4. John King Fairbank, *China: A New History* (Cambridge, Mass.: Belknap Press of Harvard University Press, 1992), p. 331.

5. See Lloyd E. Eastman, *Seeds of Destruction: Nationalist China in War and Revolution, 1937–1949* (Stanford: Stanford University Press, 1984).

6. Suzanna Pepper, "The KMP-CCP Conflict, 1945–1949," in John King Fairbank and Albert Feuerwerker, eds., *The Cambridge History of China*, vol. 13, *Republican China, 1912–1949*, Part 2 (Cambridge, Eng.: Cambridge University Press, 1986), pp. 723–41.

7. Donald G. Gillin, "Marshall Comes to China: A Chinese Viewpoint," in Committee for the Compilation of Scholarly Essays on the Eighty Years of ROC Nation-Building, *Proceedings of Conference on Eighty Years History of the Republic of China, 1912–1991*, vol. 2 (Taipei: Chin-tai Chung-kuo ch'u-pan-she, 1991), pp. 91–116.

Chapter One
Early Years, 1900–1925

1. For the life of Ch'en Li-fu's mother, see Ch'en Kuo-fu, "Wo-ti mu-ch'ing" (My Mother), in his *Ch'en Kuo-fu hsien-sheng ch'üan-chi* (*Complete works of Mr. Ch'en Kuo-fu*), vol. 5 (Taipei: Cheng-chung shu-chü, 1991), pp. 1–17, 18–19.

2. For the origin and historical background of the revolution of 1911–1912, see Sun Yat-sen, "My Reminiscences," *Strand Magazine* 43, no. 255 (April 12, 1912): 301–7, *Memoirs of a Chinese Revolutionary: a Programme of National Reconstruction for China*, with a frontispiece portrait of the author (London: Hutchinson, 1918, 1927); Leonard S. Hsu, "Tzu Chuan" (Autobiography), *China Tomorrow*, June–December 1929; see also Leonard S. Hsu *Sun Yat-sen: His Political and Social Ideals, a Source Book* (Los Angeles: University of Southern California Press, 1933), pp. 41–84; Harold Z. Schiffrin, *Sun Yat-sen and the Origins of the Chinese Revolution* (Berkeley: University of California Press, 1970).

3. For Ch'en Ch'i-mei's declaration of the indepenence of Shanghai on July 12, 1913, see Jerome Ch'en, *Yüan Shih-k'ai, 1856–1916* (Stanford: Stanford University Press, 1961), pp. 166–67; in the Second Revolution of 1913, Jerome Ch'en concluded that "the most obvious result of the Revolution was the breaking of the Kuomintang's control over six provinces." See also Ch'in Hsiao-yi, ed., *Ch'en Ying-shih hsin-sheng chi-nien-chi* (*Collected Essays in Commemoration of Mr. Ch'en Ying-shih* [Ch'en Ch'i-mei]) (Taipei: Chinese Cultural Serice, 1977); for more about Ch'en Ch'i-mei's role in the Second Revolution of 1913, see Wang Kêng-hsing, *Sun Chung-shan yü Shanghai* (Shanghai: Jen-min ch'u-pan-she, 1991), pp. 94–101, and his opposition to Yüan Shih-k'ai, pp. 102–7.

4. For more on Ch'en Ch'i-mei's friendship with Sun Yat-sen and his earnest support of Sun's revolution, see his "Letter to Huang Hsing [Huang K'e-hsiang], February 4, 1915," English translation in Hsüeh Chun-tu, "Politics in the Early Years of Republican China," *Chinese Studies in History* 7, no. 3 (Spring 1974): 3–18; John C. H. Wu, *Sun Yat-sen: The Man and His Ideas* (Taipei: Commercial Press, 1971), pp. 445–58. For more on Ch'en Ch'i-mei's friendship with Chiang Kai-shek and the two Ch'en brothers' participation in the national revolution, see Owen Lattimore, *China Memoirs: Chiang Kai-shek and the War against Japan*, Fujiko Isono, comp. (Tokyo: University of Tokyo Press, 1990), pp. 146–48; on Ch'en Ch'i-mei's study in Japan and his revolutionary career, see Mary Backus Rankin, *Early Chinese Revolutionaries: Radical Intellectuals in Shanghai and Chekiang, 1902–1911* (Cambridge,

Mass.: Harvard University Press, 1971), pp. 60, 113, 118–19, 149, 191, 193, 205–14, 220.

5. On the death of Ch'en Ch'i-mei, see "Ch'in Ying-shih pei-tz'u an-ch'in kai-yao" (Summary of the Case of the Assassination of Ch'en Ying-shih), in Ch'in Hsiao-yi, ed., *Ch'en Ying-shih hsien-sheng chi-nien-chi (Collected Essays in Commemoration of Mr. Ch'en Ying-shih* [Ch'en Ch'i-mei]) Taipei: Chinese Cultural Service, 1971), pp. 153–56; Ch'en Chieh-yü (Jennie Ch'en), "The Testimony of the Assassin at the Municipal Court of Shanghai," in *Ch'en Chieh-ju hui-i-lu (The Memoirs of Ch'en Chieh-ju),* vol. 1 (Taipei: Biographical Literature, 1992), pp. 122–23 (author is the second wife of Chiang Kai-shek, 1921–1927); see also *Chiang Kai-shek's Secret Past: The Memoir of Ch'en Chieh-ju, His Second Wife,* edited and with an introduction by Lloyd E. Eastman (Boulder, Colo.: Westview Press, 1993).

6. About Peiyang University, see Reneville Clifton Lund, "The Imperial University of Peking" (Ph.D. diss., University of Washington, 1956). Concerning Ch'en Li-fu's learning English at Peiyang University, see Lattimore, *China Memoirs,* p. 147. According to Lattimore, "I might mention here that Ch'en Li-fu was also a student of my father's when my father was teaching at Peiyang University in Tientsin. Ch'en Li-fu studied English under him, and then went to the United States and earned a degree as a mining engineer."

7. There were two Chihli-Fengtien wars in China. The first was fought from April 29 to May 5, 1922. Ten provinces were involved, ending with the defeat of Chang Tso-lin. The second was from September 16 to November 8, 1924, and ended with the defeat of Wu P'ei-fu. The war touched fourteen provinces. Hsi-sheng Ch'i, in his *Warlord Politics in China, 1916–1928* (Stanford: Stanford University Press, 1976), p.168, states that the first war cost Chang Tso-lin approximately US$24 million, and the second cost about US$50–60 million. For more analysis of the war in 1924, see *U.S. Military Intelligence Reports: China 1911–1941,* G-2 Report no. 538, April 18, 1925. The report states that "the Fengtien Army strength was placed at 150,000 maximum. Its allied force under Feng Yü-hsiang at 58,000. The Chihli Army had an immediately available strength of 225,000 and estimated reinforcements of another 200,000."

8. From 1918 to 1924, Ch'en Li-fu's elder brother, Ch'en Kuo-fu, was involved in business operations. He "first specialized in handling cotton stocks and later became assistant manager of a brokerage firm dealing with cotton yarn, gold, and silver." "These financial activities were designed to raise funds for political activities. In a recession in 1922, Ch'en Kuo-fu lost his business but he still managed to send his younger brother Ch'en Li-fu to the United States for further study after he graduated from the Peiyang University in 1923." See "Ch'en Kuo-fu," in Howard L. Boorman, *Biographical Dictionary of China,* vol.1 (New York: Columbia University Press, 1967–1971), pp. 201–6.

9. G. Raymond Fitterer, *A History of the University of Pittsburgh School of Engineering* (Pittsburgh, Penn: University of Pittsburgh School of Engineering, 1991), pp. 18–25.

10. See Sun Yat-sen, *The International Development of China* (*Shih-yeh chi-hua*) (Shanghai: Commercial Press, 1920) pp. 1134–35.

11. *San Min Chu I* (Three People's Principles), Sun Yat-sen's revolutionary ideology, was first officially proposed in October 20, 1905, and in Sun's speech in Tokyo in December 2, 1906. In 1924, Sun presented it in the form of sixteen public lectures in Canton. See Sun Yat-sen, *San Min Chu I, Three People's Principles*, translated into English by Frank W. Price, ed. L. T. Chen (Shanghai: China Committee Institute of Pacific Relations, 1928). On the origins, development, and impact of the Three People's Principles, see Sidney H. Chang and Leonard H. D. Gordon, *All Under Heaven . . . Sun Yat-sen and His Revolutionary Thought* (Stanford: Hoover Instution Press, 1991), pp. 93–122.

Chapter Two
Before the Northern Expedition,
Winter 1925–Summer 1926

1. On May 2, 1924, Sun Yat-sen appointed Chiang Kai-shek as the commandant of Whampoa Military Academy (Huang-p'u chün-hsiao) and the chief of staff of the Kwangtung Army (Yüeh-chün).

2. The Eastern Campaign (or Eastern Expedition) aimed to defeat Ch'en Chiung-ming in Kwangtung. The action began on February 1, 1925, on the basis of the strength of the Whampoa Military Academy cadets. Chiang Kai-shek's victory coincided with the passing of Sun Yat-sen in Peking March 12, 1925. Chiang also suppressed the Yunnan and Kwangtung armies. The victory led to the establishment of the National government (Kuo-min-*cheng-fu*) in Canton on July 1, 1925, and the formation of the National Revolutionary Army on August 26, 1925. The Kuomintang Central Political Committee (Chung-yang cheng-chi hui-i), on September 28, 1925, named Chiang Kai-shek as the commander in chief of the Eastern Route Army (Tung-ch'en chün) and started the Second Eastern Expedition. The episode ended on November 4, 1925, with the occupation of Swatow. Meanwhile, in the North, Feng Yü-hsiang and his National People's Army (Kuominchün) entered the city of Tientsin on December 24, 1925. The Kuomintang Second National Congress was called in Canton on January 1, 1926. See C. Martin Wilbur and Julie Lien-ying How, eds., *Documents on Communism, Nationalism and Soviet Advisers in China* (New York: Columbia University Press, 1956), pp. 157, 162, 170, 212, and 504. See also James Robert Shirley, "Control of the Kuomintang after Sun Yat-sen's Death," *Journal of Asian Studies* 25, no. 1 (November 1965): 69–82; Ch'in Hsiao-yi, ed., *Tsung-t'ung Chiang-kung ta-shih ch'ang-pien ch'u-k'ao* (*Preliminary Draft of the Materials Gathered and Arranged from Various Sources for the Compilation of the Major Events of President Chiang* [Kai-shek]), vol. 1 (Taipei: Kuomintang Central Executive Committee Historical Commission, 1978), leaves 91–114. One major result of Chiang's victories in 1925 was the promotion of Ho Ying-ch'in, who assumed command of the First Army of the National Revolutionary Army on December 10, 1925.

3. Regarding Kissan'ka's mission in China, see "Resolution Relating to the Bol-shevization of China," passed by the seventh plenary session of the Executive Committee of the International Communist party, Moscow, in the first part of 1927. The document was received by the Soviet military attaché on March 28, 1927; in *U.S. Military Intelligence Reports, China 1911–1914*, Document no. 4, G-2 Report 3020, "Soviet Activities in China," 2–2657–1–281–102, signed by John Magruder, Major, General Staff, Military Attaché.

4. Chiang's temper can also be seen from the memoir of his second wife, Ch'en Chieh-ju, *Ch'en Chieh-ju hui-i-lu*, vol. 2, pp. 224–25, 327–29. On the Chiang-Ch'en marriage, see also *Shanghai shih-pao*, September 4, 1927; *Honolulu Star-Bulletin*, September 2, 3, 1927; *San Francisco Chronicle*, September 20, 25, 1927; *San Francisco Examiner*, September 9, 1927; *New York Times*, August 20, 1927; interview by Henry Misselwitz, *New York Times*, September 18, 25, October 1, November 26, December 2, 1927; *Washington Post*, September 26, 1927. Ch'en Chieh-ju was paid $170,000 not to publish her memoir. See *Washington D.C. Examiner*, November 22–26, 1967. The original of this *Memoir* was found in H. H. Chang Papers, Hoover Institution; see Preface by Tong Te-kong, dated May 30, 1992, pp. 1–33. Tong is a professor of history at New York City University. The authenticity of Ch'en Chieh-ju's memoir has been confirmed by Ch'en Li-fu in an oral interview with Sidney H. Chang, coeditor of this volume, on August 9, 1992, in Taipei.

5. About Ch'en Li-fu's account, also see Cheng Tien-fong (Ch'eng T'ien-fang), *A History of Sino-Russian Relations* (Washington, D.C.: Public Affairs Press, 1957), pp. 133–363. Ch'en Kung-po, in his *K'u-hsiao lu*, devoted a chapter to the March 20, 1926, *Chung-shan* Gunboat Incident. He recorded the same fact from a speech given by Ch'en Li-fu in 1928 at the Shanghai Municipal Headquarters of the Kuomintang; Li Tien-min, *Chou En-lai* (Taipei: Institute of International Relations, 1970), pp. 63–64; Chiang Kai-shek, *Soviet Russia in China* (New York: Farrar, Straus and Cudahy, 1951), pp. 37–48. Also see C. Martin Wilbur and Julie Lien-ying How, eds., *Missionaries in Revolutions*, p. 279, note 99. Ch'en Chieh-ju, *Ch'en Chieh-ju hui-i-lu*, vol. 2, pp. 262–63.

6. Han-min Hu, "Wang Ching-wei kou-chieh kung-ch'an-tang chih yun-yuan yü ch'ing-kuo (The Origin and the History of Wang Ching-wei's Illict Connection with Communists), *Chung-yang jih-pao* (*Central Daily News*), Nanking edition, August 18, 1930.

7. In addition to the financial contribution, Ch'en Kuo-fu's dedication to the organizational aspect of the Kuomintang and the building up of the National Revolutionary Army began at the recruitment of new cadets for Whampoa Military Academy; see Donald Jordan, *The Northern Expedition* (Honolulu: University of Hawaii Press, 1976), pp. 18, 21; for reasons for the success of the Northern Expedition, pp. 287–95, and Boorman, *Biographical Dictionary of Republican China*, vol. 1, p. 203. See especially Ch'en Kuo-fu, *Ch'en Kuo-fu ch'üan-chi* (*Complete Works of Ch'en Kuo-fu*), vol. 5, pp. 62–70. He stated that in addition to the recruitment of cadets, Chiang Kai-shek also asked him to recruit able-bodied young men to join the National Revolutionary Army, recommend talented men, provide logistic support, and purchase horses. Ch'en Kuo-fu took the responsibility from September

1924 to the end of 1925. He arrived in Canton in May 1926 to become the chief secretary of the Kuomintang Organization Department, and Chiang Kai-shek was his immediate superior. In July 1926 he succeeded Chiang Kai-shek as the chief of the Kuomintang Organization Department; see Ch'en Kuo-fu, *Ch'en Kuo-fu ch'üan-Chi*, vol. 5, pp. 62–83.

8. There were two Kuomintang Second National Congresses held in 1926. One convened in Canton, January 4–19, 1926 (see Wilbur and How, *Documents on Communism*, pp. 213–15); one was called by the anticommunist Western Hills Conference Group (Hsi-shan hui-i-p'ai) on March 29, 1926. That group had a conference earlier in 1925, from November 23 to December 30, that consisted of fifteen members of the Central Executive Committee and Central Supervisory Committee. The conference was called before Sun Yat-sen's tomb in the Western Hills of Peking. See Wilbur and How, *Documents on Communism*, pp. 209–12.

Chapter Three
The Northern Expedition,
Summer 1926–Summer 1927

1. For the activities of Galen, see C. Martin Wilbur and Julie Lien-ying How, eds., *Documents on Communism, Nationalism, and Soviet Advisers in China, 1918–1927* (New York: Columbia University Press, 1956), pp. 150, 167, 176–80; for his opposition to Chiang Kai-shek's strategy of attacking the Southeast in the direction of Nanking and Shanghai, see pp. 382–83, 395. For Galen's role in Northern Expedition, see C. Martin Wilbur, *The Nationalist Revolution in China, 1923–1928* (Cambridge, Eng.: Cambridge University Press, 1983), pp. 49–50. For an estimation of the strength of various militarists in China on the eve of the Northern Expedition, see Lawrence Impey, *The Chinese Army Considered as a Military Force* (Tientsin: Tientsin Press, Ltd., 1925).

2. Michael Borodin (Mikhail Markovich Gruzenberg), Soviet chief adviser to Sun Yat-sen, was born July 9, 1884. He arrived in Canton on October 6, 1923. He returned to Moscow on October 6, 1928, having failed in his mission to China. Arrested by Stalin in 1949, Borodin died May 29, 1951, in a Siberian camp near Yakutsk. See Wilbur, *Nationalist Revolution in China*, pp. 5, 146; C. Martin Wilbur and Julie Lien-ying How, *Missionaries of Revolution: Soviet Advisers and Nationalist China, 1920–1927* (Cambridge, Mass.: Harvard University Press, 1989), pp. 6, 423, 427. For detailed studies of Michael Borodin, see Chiang Yung-ching, *Po-lo-ting yu wu-han cheng-chuan (Michael Borodin and Wuhan regime)* (Taipei: Kuomintang Central Executive Committee Historical Commission, 1961); Lydia Holubuychy, *Michael Borodin and the Chinese Revolution, 1923–1925* (Ann Arbor, Mich.: Microfilms International, 1979); Daniel Norman Jacobs, *Borodin, Stalin's Man in China* (Cambridge, Mass.: Harvard University Press, 1981); in addition, see Chiang Sung Mei-ling (Madame Chiang Kai-shek), "Conversations with Mikhail Borodin," *China Post*, October 29, 1976, pp. 5–8.

3. On the death of Sun Lu-ch'ing (Mrs. Ch'en Li-fu), see *Shih-chieh jih-pao* (*World Journal*) (San Francisco), September 30, 1992, where Sun Lu-ch'ing was described as "a talented artist from Ch'en's native district of Wu-hsin." See also "Ch'en Li-fu," in Boorman ed., *Biographical Dictionary of Republican China*, p. 211.

4. Ch'en Chieh-ju, *Ch'en Chieh-ju hui-i-lu*, pp. 317–42, revealed Chiang's bitterness toward the Wuhan government's exclusion of him and his attempt at suicide after he found out that he had lost his power; see also "The Revolution in China," *U.S. Military Intelligence Reports: China 1911–1941*, April 2, 1927; "Central Government's Approach to Foreign Powers," G-2 report no. 2019, April 14, 1927.

5. For the role Chang Ching-chiang played in the national revolution, see Ch'en Kuo-fu, *Ch'en Kuo-fu hsien-sheng hui-i-lu*, vol. 5, pp. 84–91 (in commemoration of the passing of Chang Ching-chiang in the United States of America in 1950); Wilbur and How, eds., *Documents on Communism*, pp. 229, 230, 233. Chang Ching-chiang was elected chairman of the Central Executive Committee on May 19, 1926. After Chiang Kai-shek was elected chairman of the Central Executive Committee Standing Committee, Chang served as his deputy during the period of the Northern Expedition.

6. For an examination of Ch'en Pu-lei's career, see Li Ao, *Lun Chiang Chieh-shih* (*On Chiang Chieh-shih* [Chiang Kai-shek]) (Taipei: Ch'üan-neng ch'u-pan-she, 1987), vol. 4, pp. 257–304. Ch'en was born in 1890; as a member of the T'ung-meng hui, he held high positions in the Kuomintang and in the National government. Suffering from the defeat of the Kuomintang on the mainland, he committed suicide on November 13, 1948, at age of fifty-nine. At that time he was the secretary-general of the Central Political Committee. On Ch'en Pu-lei's work, see Chen Pu-lei, *Ch'en Pu-lei hsien-sheng hui-i-lu, 1949, 1962, 1967, 1989*, and *Ch'en Pu-lei hsien-sheng wen-chi* (Taipei: Chinese Culture Service, 1984).

7. For Sun Yat-sen's speech delivered on November 28, 1924, before the members of five Japanese organizations, including the Kobe Chamber of Commerce, see *China Weekly Review* 94, no. 5 (October 5, 1940): 149–52; *New York Times*, December 1, 1924, p.3; W. G. Beasley, "Japan and Pan-Asianism—Problems of Definition," in Janet Hunter, ed., *Aspects of Pan-Asianism* vol. 2 (London: School of Economics and Political Science International Studies, International Centre of Economics and Related Disciplines, 1987), pp. 17–27; for a more recent study, see Li Tai-jing, *Chung-shan hsien-sheng ta-ya-chou chu-i yen-chiu* (*A Study on Mr. Chung-shan* [Sun Yat-sen]'s *Pan-Asianism*), (Taipei: Wen-hsin-chê ch'u-pan-she 1992).

8. For the complete record of the British attitude toward the Nanking Incident of March 24, 1927, see Great Britain, *Parliamentary Publications*, 1927, House of Commons 26, Accounts and Papers 14 (2953), "Papers Relating to the Nanking Incident of 24th and 25th March, 1927," London, 1927; and *Parliamentary Publications*, 1928–1929, House of Commons 23, Accounts and Papers 14 (3188) "Papers Relating to the Settlement of the Nanking Incident of 24th March, 1927." London, 1928–1929. On the anti-British sentiment in China in 1927, see Harold R. Isaacs, *The Tragedy of the Chinese Revolution*, 2d rev. ed. (Stanford: Stanford University Press, 1961), pp. 123–24.

9. On the Green Gang, see Jordan, *The Northern Expedition*, pp. 255–56, and

Donald Jordan,*Chinese Boycotts versus Japanese Bombs* (Honolulu: University of Hawaii Press, 1976), pp. 127–29 (on the involvement of the two Ch'en brothers, pp. 34–36); see also Brian G. Martin, "The Green Gang and the Guomindang Policy in Shanghai, 1927–1937," *Papers on Far Eastern History* (The Australian National University Department of East Asian History), no. 42 (1990): 59–96; see also Brian G. Martin, "The Pact with the Devil: The Relationships between the Green Gang and the French Concession Authorities, 1925–1935," *Papers on Far Eastern History*, no. 39 (1989): 94–125.

10. For the activities of the Green Gang in the British Concession in Shanghai during the period of the Northern Expedition, see *The Shanghai Municipal Police Files, 1894–1944*, records of the Central Intelligence Agency. Record Group 263 has been declassified under project number NND 863055, 1927–1929.

11. For the detailed history of the Kuomintang investigation units under the direction and command of Ch'en Li-fu, see Hsu En-tseng, *The Invisible Conflict* (Hong Kong: 1956, 1958, 1962); see also Hsu En-tseng, *Hsi-shuo chung-tung chün-tung* (*Detailed Discussion on the Central Bureau of Investigation and Military Bureau of Investigation*) (Taipei: Biographical Literature, 1992).

Chapter Four
Working with Chiang,
Spring 1928–Winter 1931

1. The fourth plenary session of the Second Central Executive Committee met in Nanking, February 2–6, 1928. The session adopted resolutions defining the formation of the National Reconstruction Commission and the reorganization of the Kuomintang Central Headquarters, the National government, the Military Committee of the Central Executive Committee, and the Fundamental Plan for the Readjustment of Kuomintang Party Affairs. The session also passed resolutions on party discipline and problems related to the completion of the Northern Expedition. During this session Ch'en Li-fu was nominated as a member of the National Reconstruction Commission.

2. On the effects of the Tsinan Incident of May 3, 1928, see *U.S. Military Intelligence Reports: China 1911–1941*, (hereafter, *U.S. Military Intelligence Reports*) G-2 Report no. 7277, June 18, 1928. See also Kuo Min News Agency account, May 4, 1928. To conclude this incident, a Sino-Japanese agreement was signed by Dr. Cheng-t'ing Wang, minister of foreign affairs of the National government, and Japanese minister Kenkichi Yoshizawa on March 28, 1929. For the complete text in an English translation, see "Sino-Japanese Agreement Settling Tsinan Incident," *U.S. Military Intelligence Reports*, G-2 Report 7485, April 10, 1929.

3. On Huang Fu's role in the Tsinan Incident, see Shen I-yün (Mrs. Huang Fu), "Pei-fa shih-chi" (Period of Northern Expedition), in *I-yün hui-i* (*Memoirs of Shen I-yün*) vol 1 (Taipei: Biographical Literature, 1980), pp. 263–89. After the unpopular Ts'ao K'un resigned his presidency on November 2, 1924, as the result of Feng Yü-

hsiang's control of Peking, Huang Fu became acting head of the Peking government in the North. His regent cabinet lasted until November 24, 1924, a total of twenty-two days. See Li Chien-nung, *The Political History of China, 1840–1928* (Princeton, N.J.: Van Nostrand, 1956), pp. 467–75.

4. On Feng Yü-hsiang's career, his involvement in the national revolution, and his struggle for power in the National government, see James Edward Sheridan, *Chinese Warlord: The Career of Feng Yü-hsiang* (Stanford: Stanford University Press, 1966), pp. 175, 359, 360–62; Sheridan lists twenty-two works of Feng Yü-hsiang. See also Marcus Ch'eng, *Marshall Feng: the Man and His Work* (Shanghai: 1926).

5. For an impression of Yen Hsi-shan, see Assistant Military Attaché C. J. Kanaga's reports from Shansi Province, September 26, 1929, October 25, 1929, in *U.S. Military Intelligence Reports*, 4.1/2055–674; for a recent work about Yen, see Ai Fei, *Yen Hsi-shan* (Shih-chia-chuang shih: Ho-pei jen-min ch'u-pan-she, 1984). For an analytic study of Yen Hsi-shan, see Donald G. Gillin, *Warlord: Yen Hsi-shan in Shansi Province, 1911–1949* (Princeton, N.J.: Princeton University Press, 1967).

6. For Li Tsung-jen's career, see Tong Te-kong and Li Tsung-jen, *The Memoirs of Li Tsung-jen* (Boulder, Colo.: Westview Press, 1979). (This volume is included in the Studies of the East Asian Institute, Columbia University.)

7. For the strength of Feng Yü-hsiang and Yen Hsi-shan during the period of the Northern Expedition and their changing relationship with Chiang, see Jordan, *Northern Expedition* pp. 270–75. In the 1920s Feng's Kuominchün, or People's Army, was considered the best trained army in China. As a result of Chiang Kai-shek's forceful final drive against Feng in September 1930, the Kuominchün was forced to withdraw north of the Yellow River on October 6, 1930, which marked the end of the Chinese civil war. By the end of 1930, the strength of Feng's remnant Kuominchün army was about 50,000; it was reported to be located in southwestern Shansi. See *U.S. Military Intelligence Reports*, 9–2 Report no. 7905, December 16, 1930; on the reorganization of certain Kuominchün troops into National government forces, see *U.S. Military Intelligence Reports*, G-2 Report no. 7890, December 1, 1930. In 1931, civil war in China ended; there was no organized military opposition in the National government; Chiang Kai-shek and Chang Hsüeh-liang maintained a close relationship; and communist activities continued throughout most of China. The defeat of Yen, then of Feng, which resulted in the disintegration of the Kuominchün and the declaration of loyalty to the National government at Nanking by Chang Hsüeh-liang in the Northeast, brought great prestige and power to the Kuomintang and in particular to Chiang Kai-shek. The Fourth National Congress of the Kuomintang was thereafter held from November 12 to 23, 1931.

8. This National government was formed on September 9, 1930, in Peking. Yen Hsi-shan was the chairman of the National government (council). Wang Ching-wei, Feng Yü-hsiang, Chang Hsüeh-liang, and Li Tsung-jen all were members of the council. This strong alliance of forces opposed Chiang Kai-shek's National government in Nanking; see Kuo T'ing-i, *Chung-hua min-kuo shih-shih jih-chih* vol. 2 (Taipei: Institute of Modern History, Academia Sinica, 1979–1985), pp. 619–20.

9. For the best English-language source on Chang Tso-lin, see McCormack

Gavan, *Chang Tso-lin in Northeast China, 1911–1928: China, Japan and the Manchu-rian Idea* (Stanford: Stanford University Press, 1977), especially chapter 6, "Chang's Last Years," pp. 188–249.

10. For an analysis of the negotiations bringing Manchuria voluntarily under the flag of the National government led by Chiang Kai-shek in July 1928, see Military Attaché John Magruder's report to the War Department in *U.S. Military Intelligence Reports*, G-2 Report no. 7306, August 2, 1928, and Report no. 7305. On the strength of Chiang Kai-shek in 1928, see (Major) Joseph W. Stilwell, "Tables of Organization of the Nationalist Revolutionary Army," January 1928.

11. On Chang Hsüeh-liang's attitude toward the National government, see Parker G. Tenney, assistant military attaché, "Interview with Chang Hsüeh-liang," September 30, 1930. Tenney was sent to Mukden to find out the true conditions via personal interviews. In 1921, Tenney visited Mukden with First Sergeant Wilson of the 15th Infantry to demonstrate the Browning automatic rifle and the infantry pack to Chang Hsüeh-liang's father, Marshall Chang Tso-lin. On December 10 and 11, 1930, U.S. military attaché Nelson E. Margetts interviewed William N. Donald, an Australian by birth. Donald had been in China for more than thirty years, during which he advised practically every government since the establishment of the republic. From 1928 to the Sian Incident, Donald was the intimate adviser to Marshall Chang Hsüeh-liang. Donald told Margetts that "the Nanking delegates had approached him with an offer from Chiang Kai-shek of one million dollars for interference on the side of Nanking. When asked what reply he had made to them, he said that if Chiang Kai-shek would give him one hundred million dollars in cash, the provinces of Hopei and Shantung, half the appointments in the cabinet, and remove the Kuomintang from government affairs, he would consider the matter of intervention, and laugh-ingly added that he did not believe Chiang Kai-shek would accept his proposition." In his report Margetts concluded that he "got the impression from Donald that the relationship between Chiang Kai-shek and the young Marshall had become very close, and that so long as these two dominating figures work together there is little danger that the peace of China will be disturbed by civil war"; see *U.S. Military Intelligence Reports*, G-2 Report no. 7902, December 13, 1930.

12. There were two National Reorganization and Disbandment conferences. The first was called January 1–25, 1929, and the second was August 1–6, 1929. The first conference discussed a wide range of topics including the reduction of the size of armies under the command of various military leaders. The conference had the support of Feng Yü-hsiang but not Pai Ch'ung-hsi, Li Tsung-jen, or Yen Hsi-shan. The second conference proposed that the annual military expenditures of China should be no more than eighteen to nineteen million U.S. dollars; see Kuo T'ing-i, *Chung-hua min-kuo shih-shih jih-chih*, vol. 2, pp. 422–29, 480–81; John Magruder, U.S. military attaché in China, reported that the second conference had appointed a committee to carry out its pronouncements, which included the reduction of the army from about 2,225,000 to 800,000 and the payment of some US$30,000,000 in back pay to the soldiers. The first conference in January also aimed at the reduction of the army to 800,000 men a year and also appropriated millions for its purposes, but the 800,000 men were increased to 2,225,000 and no concrete results were

achieved. The second conference also decided to reduce the armies of China, not including Manchuria, to sixty-five divisions of 11,000 men each, or a total of 715,000 men, and about 50 million U.S. dollars were appropriated to bring this reduction into effect; see *U.S. Military Intelligence Reports*, G-2 Report no. 7575, August 14, 1929, also G-2 Report Y.1/2055.66, January 25, 1929, and G-2 Report no. 8005, April 30, 1931.

13. For a complete factual record of the National government during this period, see Min-ch'ien T. Z. Tyau, ed., *Two Years of Nationalist China* (Shanghai: Kelly and Walsh, 1930).

14. For a detailed record of the Kuomintang Third National Congress held in Nanking, March 15–28, 1929, see *U.S. Military Intelligence Reports*, G-2 Report no. 7477, March 27, 1929, by John Magruder, U.S. military attaché; see also "The Third National Congress," *U.S. Military Intelligence Reports*, G-2 Report no. 7478, March 29, 1929, by Parker G. Tenney, assistant military attaché.

15. For a good reference, see Jerome Ch'en, "The Left Wing Kuomintang—A Definition," *Bulletin of the School of Oriental and African Studies* (University of London) 25 (1962): 557–76.

16. For a list of the members and alternate members of the Central Executive Committee and Central Supervisory Committee of the Kuomintang elected at the Third National Congress, March 15–28, 1929, see *U.S. Military Intelligence Reports*, G-2 Report no. 7486, recorded by Major John Magruder (both Ch'en Kuo-fu and Ch'en Li-fu were elected to the Central Executive Committee). For background and highlights of the congress, see "The Third National Congress," *U.S. Military Intelligence Reports*, G-2 Report no. 7478, March 29, 1929: the fourteen articles of the regulations of the congress appear on pp. 3–4; the principles of China's foreign relations, on p.6.

17. From 1927 to 1931 the Kuomintang–National government relationship is best described by Paul A. M. Linebarger in *The China of Chiang Kai-shek: A Political Study* (Boston: World Peace Foundation, 1941), pp. 330–31; chart 1 shows the relationship between the Kuomintang and the National government during 1927–1931; chart 2 shows the internal organization of the Kuomintang between 1927 and 1931.

To lay the foundation of the National government, the Kuomintang Central Executive Committee promulgated the Organic Law of the National Government of China on October 3, 1928, in Nanking. The law was revised and passed by the first plenary session of the Fourth Central Executive Committee and Supervisory Committee on December 26, 1931. For the Chinese text, see *National Government Gazette* (*Kuo-min cheng-fu kung-pao*), no. 964 (December 26, 1931); see also *North China Daily* (*Hua-pei jih-pao*), January 26, 1932. For the English translation, see *U.S. Military Intelligence Reports: China 1911–1941*, G-2 Report no. 8255, April 12, 1932, by Military Attaché Lt.-Colonel W. S. Drysdale; and G-2 Report no. 7938, February 11, 1932, by Captain Parker G. Tenney, assistant military attaché. See also *The Organic Law of the Republic of China: The Final Draft Constitution of the Republic of China* (New York: Rockefeller Center, Chinese News Service, 1936). For contem-

CHART I

KUOMINTANG AND THE NATIONAL GOVERNMENT, 1927–1931

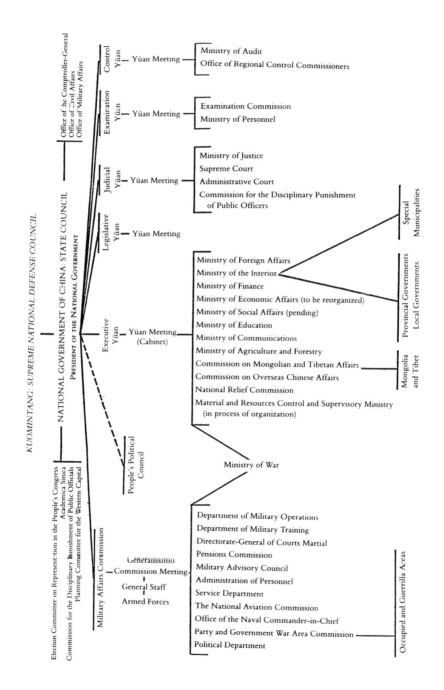

CHART 2
THE KUOMINTANG, 1927–1931

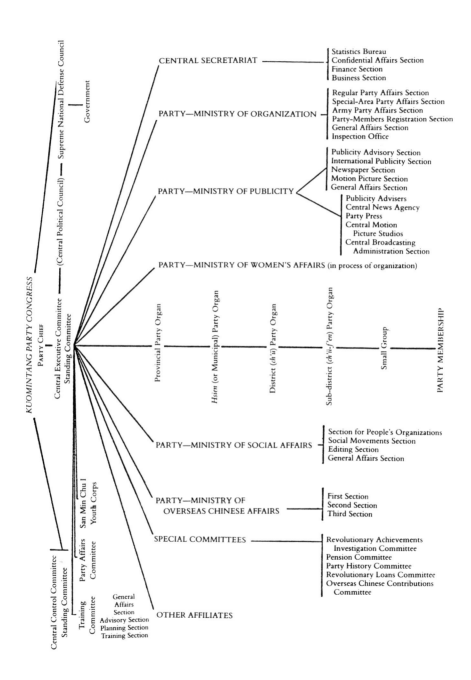

CENTRAL SECRETARIAT
- Statistics Bureau
- Confidential Affairs Section
- Finance Section
- Business Section

PARTY—MINISTRY OF ORGANIZATION
- Regular Party Affairs Section
- Special-Area Party Affairs Section
- Army Party Affairs Section
- Party-Members Registration Section
- General Affairs Section
- Inspection Office

PARTY—MINISTRY OF PUBLICITY
- Publicity Advisory Section
- International Publicity Section
- Newspaper Section
- Motion Picture Section
- General Affairs Section

- Publicity Advisers
- Central News Agency
- Party Press
- Central Motion Picture Studios
- Central Broadcasting Administration Section

PARTY—MINISTRY OF WOMEN'S AFFAIRS (in process of organization)

Provincial Party Organ — Hsien (or Municipal) Party Organ — District (ch'ü) Party Organ — Sub-district (ch'ü-f'en) Party Organ — Small Group — PARTY MEMBERSHIP

PARTY—MINISTRY OF SOCIAL AFFAIRS
- Section for People's Organizations
- Social Movements Section
- Editing Section
- General Affairs Section

PARTY—MINISTRY OF OVERSEAS CHINESE AFFAIRS
- First Section
- Second Section
- Third Section

SPECIAL COMMITTEES
- Revolutionary Achievements Investigation Committee
- Pension Committee
- Party History Committee
- Revolutionary Loans Committee
- Overseas Chinese Contributions Committee

OTHER AFFILIATES

KUOMINTANG PARTY CONGRESS
PARTY CHIEF
Central Executive Committee — (Central Political Council) — Supreme National Defense Council
Standing Committee
Government

Central Control Committee
Standing Committee

Party Affairs Committee
San Min Chu I Youth Corps

Training Committee
General Affairs Section
Advisory Section
Planning Section
Training Section

porary comments on the law, see E. S. Corwin, "Some Observations on the Organic Law," *China Tomorrow* 1, no. 2 (1928): 17–20; in the same issue, Samuel S. Sung, "The Relations of the Kuomintang to the Common People," pp. 23–24. For all the resolutions and personnel changes of the first plenary session of the Fourth Central Executive Committee and Supervisory Committee on December 26, 1931, see *U.S. Military Intelligence Reports*, G-2 Report no. 8179. Ch'en Kuo-fu was elected as a member of the Standing Committee. Ch'en Li-fu was elected to the Organization Committee.

18. As of May 1930, both Ch'en Kuo-fu and Ch'en Li-fu were members of the Central Executive Committee and the Central Political Committee. In addition, Ch'en Kuo-fu was on the nine-member Standing Committee of the Central Executive Committee, headed by Chiang Kai-shek, and a member of the National Reconstruction Committee. Ch'en Li-fu, however, became a member of the Examination and Selection Committee with Tai Ch'i-tao, who was the chairman. In addition, Ch'en Li-fu was appointed as the director of the Political Training Bureau and the secretary-general of the Central Political Committee. See "Personnel of Kuomintang Central Committees and the National Government (as of May 1930)," *U.S. Military Intelligence Reports*, G-2 Report no. 7769, July 7, 1930.

19. For the list of sixteen members of the National government (council) see *U.S. Military Intelligence Reports*, G-2 Report no. 7356, October 24, 1928.

20. To expand Chiang Kai-shek's power, some changes in the Organic Law of the Republic of China were adopted at the fourth plenary session of the Central Executive and Supervisory Committee, November 12–18, 1930. It was on November 18, 1930, that the Central Executive Committee appointed Chiang Kai-shek to serve concurrently as president of the Executive Yüan and ex officio as chairman of the (new) National Council (Kuo-min cheng-fu hui-i). The Ministry of Foreign Affairs immediately announced that the National government had adopted Kuo-min cheng-fu hui-i and Kuo-wu hui-i as official translations for meetings of the National Government Council and the (new) State Council. The National Government Council was the former State Council, and the present designation of State Council replaced the designation of meetings of the Executive Yüan. The Executive Yüan, however, retained its designation as such but in deliberative session was known as the State Council. In its editorial of November 19, 1930, the Kuo Min News Agency in Shanghai remarked that it should be emphasized that the president of the National government, either under the old or the new Organic Law, did not automatically become president of the Executive Yüan. The fact that Chiang Kai-shek had to be appointed by special resolution of the plenary session to serve concurrently as president of the Executive Yüan indicated that the appointment was a matter of temporary expediency due, probably, to the exigencies of the situation. Lt. Colonel Nelson E. Margetts, U.S. military attaché in China, commented that "the change with respect to the Executive Yüan was most confusing. A new organ, the New State Council, had been created. It existed, however, only as meetings of the Executive Yüan. The wording of the change [Article II, revised law], that the President of the Executive Yüan shall be Chairman of the State Council, indicates two separate bodies, yet the composition of each is the same and it is difficult to understand what difference of

power, or authority (presumably intended) is delegated to them. When now reading of any decisions of the State Council, it is important to understand they are really decisions by the Executive Yüan." See *U.S. Military Intelligence Reports*, G-2 Report no. 7938, February 11, 1931. For a further analysis of Chiang's expansion of power, see *U.S. Military Intelligence Reports*, G-2 Report no. 7496, April 4, 1929, pp. 3–4.

21. For Hu Han-min's thoughts on this particular issue, see Chiang Yung-ching, ed., *Hu Han-min hsien-sheng nien-p'u (Chronological Biography of Hu Han-min)* (Taipei: Kuomintang Central Executive Committee Historical Commission, 1978), pp 487–91; Wang Ching-wei's view, October 27, 1930, p. 491; Hu Han-min's debate with Wu Chih-hui and Li Shih-tseng on November 12, 1930, pp. 492–96; Tientsin *Ta Kung Pao's* interview, November 20, 1930, pp. 496–97.

22. The fourth plenary session of the Kuomintang Third Central Executive Committee, held at Nanking November 12–18, 1930, adopted a resolution to call a National People's Convention (Kuo-min hui-i) May 5–17, 1931. For a detailed report, see *U.S. Military Intelligence Reports*, G-2 Report no. 8024, May 23, 1931, background of the convention, G-2 Report no. 7929, January 28, 1931, and G-2 Report no. 7929, 1959. An eighty-nine-article provisional constitution for the period of political tutelage of the Republic of China was adopted on May 12, 1931. For an English translation of the text, see *U.S. Military Intelligence Reports*, G-2 Report no. 8020, dated June 23, 1931, by U.S. military attaché Lt. Colonel Nelson E. Margetts.

23. For Chiang Kai-shek's opposition to Hu on the question of the provisional constitution dispute of 1930, see Chiang's letter to Hu dated February 28, 1930, in Ch'in Hsiao-yi, ed., *Tsung-t'ung Chiang-kung ta-shih ch'ang-pien ch'u-k'ao*, vol. 2 (Taipei: Kuomintang Central Executive Committee Historical Commission, 1978), leaves 91–92, approval of Hu's resignation from the presidency of Legislative Yüan, leaf 93.

24. On May 20, 1918, the Extraordinary Parliament in Canton elected Sun Yat-sen, T'ang Shao-i, Wu T'ing-fang, Ch'en Ch'un-hsüan, Lu Jung-t'ing, T'ang Chi-yao, and Lin Pao-i as the committee members of the Military Government (Council). This was called "seven-director system." See Li Chien-nung, *The Political History of China: 1840–1928* (Princeton, N.J.: Van Nostrand, 1956), pp. 387–88.

25. Hu Han-min, a close associate of Sun Yat-sen's and one of the founding fathers of the republic, was officially taken into custody on March 1, 1931, because of his opposition to Chiang's provisional constitution. He was removed by Chiang to T'ang-shan. On the immediate effects of Chiang's action, see Chiang Yung-ching, *Hu Han-min hsien-sheng nien-p'u*, pp. 505–9. Hu was released on October 13, 1931. On June 8, 1935, Hu left for Italy on the S.S. *Conte Verde* and returned to Hong Kong on January 19, 1936. He passed away on May 12 of the same year. U.S. military attaché Lt. Colonel W. S. Drysdale reported that Hu's departure for Europe was expected to ease the relations between Canton and Nanking and that the prospects of a rapprochement between the two political parties were much brighter than they had been in years. See *U.S. Military Intelligence Reports*, G-2 Report no. 9145, June 21, 1935.

26. For an analysis of the historical background of Canton's opposition to Chiang

Kai-shek, see *U.S. Military Intelligence Reports*, G-2 Report no. 8049, July 8, 1931, G-2 Report no. 8643, August 24, 1933, and G-2 Report no. 8651, September 7, 1933

27. For an analysis of Chiang Kai-shek's failure to reorganize the military and the opposition of the Kwangtung faction that caused his resignation as chairman of the National Government Council, commander in chief of the land, sea, and air forces, and president of the Executive Yüan on December 15, 1931, see *U.S. Military Intelligence Reports*, G-2 report no. 8173, December 22, 1931, by Assistant Military Attaché Captain Parker G. Tenney. The first plenary session of the Fourth Central Executive Committee of the Kuomintang, held from December 22 to 29, 1931, made Chiang Kai-shek chairman of the Military Affairs Committee (Chün-shih wei-yuan-hui), and in effect, if not in theory, his power was substantially enlarged from what it was when he held the position of the commander in chief of the land, sea, and air forces; see *U.S. Military Intelligence Reports*, G-2 Report no. 8266, April 14, 1932. The official appointment of Chiang Kai-shek materialized at the second plenary session of the Fourth Central Executive Committee, March 1-6, 1932, at Loyang; see *U.S. Military Intelligence Reports*, G-2 Report no. 3110.

Chapter Five
Between Two Japanese Attacks,
Spring 1932–Summer 1937

1. The fourth plenary session of the Fourth Central Executive Committee was held January 20-25, 1934. Senior member Lin Shen was reelected as the chairman of the National Government Council. Panchen Lama of Tibet became a new member of the council, and Mongolia petitioned to be self-governed. See Kuo T'ing-i, *Chung-hua min-kuo shih-shih jih-chih*, vol. 3, pp. 336-38.

2. See Ch'en Li-fu, *The Functions of the Commission on Land Research and Planning* (Nanking: International Relations Committee, 1934, 1935; microfilm, Columbia University libraries).

3. It was the sixth plenary session of the Fourth Central Executive Committee, November 1-6, 1935. The Kuomintang Fifth National Congress was convened one week later, from November 12 to 23, 1935.

4. Chiang Kai-shek, in his work *Soviet Russia in China* (New York: Farrar, Straus and Cudahy, 1957), p. 72, stated that "in the autumn and winter of 1935 Ch'en Li-fu reported to me that through a friend's introduction Chou En-lai had approached Tseng Yang-fu, a government representative in Hong Kong. Chou hoped that the government would designate someone to conduct negotiations with the Communists. All Chou reportedly wanted was to stop the fighting at home and to resist Japan together. There were no other conditions. Chou wrote to Ch'en Kuo-fu and Ch'en Li-fu on September 1, reaffirming this position of the Chinese Communists."

5. For Ch'en Li-fu's negotiations with Chinese communist representative Pan Han-nien on behalf of the Kuomintang, see Wu T'ien-wei, *The Sian Incident* (Ann

Arbor: University of Michigan Center for Chinese Studies, 1976), pp. 21–22, and Ch'en's continued negotiation with Chou En-lai, p. 145. For Ch'en's negotiations with Chou En-lai in May 1936, see Kai-yu Hsu, *Chou En-lai: China's Gray Eminence* (Garden City, N.Y.: Doubleday, 1968), pp. 128–35, and Wu, *Sian Incident*, pp. 135–44; Li Tien-min, *Chou En-lai* (Taipei: Institute of International Relations, 1970), pp. 197–202; John McCook Roots, *Chou: An Informal Biography of China's Legendary Chou En-lai* (Garden City, N.Y.: Doubleday, 1978), pp. 81–82.

6. For an English translation of the four points, see Immanuel C. Y. Hsu, *The Rise of Modern China*, 4th ed. (New York: Oxford University Press, 1990), p. 588.

7. On Ch'en Li-fu's secret trip to the Soviet Union, see "Ch'en Li-fu, orig. Ch'en Tsu-Yen," in Boorman, *Biographical Dictionary of Republican China*, vol. 1, pp. 206–11; Cheng Tien-fong (Ch'eng T'ien-fang), *A History of Sino-Russian Relations* (Washington, D.C.: Public Affairs Press, 1957), pp. 190–91.

8. On December 30, 1932, the National government announced that it had approved the appointment of Dimitri Bogomoloff, then counselor of the Soviet embassy in London, to be Soviet ambassador to China; see *U.S. Military Intelligence Reports*, G-2 Report no. 8476, January 5, 1933, by Major S. V. Constant, assistant military attaché. For Bogomoloff's travels in North China, ibid., G-2 Report no. 8638, August 10, 1933, pp. 2–3; the Transocean-Kuomin News Agency reported that his mission was preventing a reconciliation between Japan and National China, ibid., G-2 Report no. 9514, February 8, 1937, p. 7; Domei News Agency reported on the 23d of March 1937 that the USSR had concluded a six-point understanding with National China, ibid., G-2 Report, no. 9536, April 9, 1937, prepared by Captain David D. Barret; Havas News Agency dispatch from Moscow reported that Soviet Far Eastern commander general Vasilii Blyukher, whose mission was concluding an agreement on arms deliveries to the National government, had been denied, ibid., G-2 Report no. 9584, August 8, 1937, p. 4, prepared by Military Attaché Joseph W. Stilwell; Soviet arms were delivered from Turkestan through Hami and Lanchou, October 18, 1937; Stilwell misreported the date of the signing of the nonaggression pact; ibid., G-2 Reports nos. 8696, 8816, and 9589, August 21, 1937.

9. The four-article Soviet-Chinese Nonaggression Treaty was signed on August 21, 1937, but not made known to the public until August 29, 1937. For the complete text in English, see *U.S. Military Intelligence Reports*, G-2 Report no. 8964, September 2, 1937; for the Chinese text with English translation, see *Treaty of Non-Aggression Between the Republic of China and the Union of Soviet Socialist Republics*, Nanking, 1937, issued as White Book, no. 55, Republic of China: Ministry of Foreign Affairs, September 1937; original print in Bibliotheque Municipale de Lyon, France, CH5580. For the Japanese press reaction, see G-2 Report no. 8964, September 2, 1937, pp. 2–3; statement of Chinese ambassador in Tokyo, pp. 3–4. The Japanese press reported in October that a secret mutual assistance agreement had been reached between China and the USSR and that, as a result of this agreement, Soviet policy was to supply China with arms, ammunition, and aircraft in order to strengthen Chinese resistance in the fighting with Japan. The press even speculatively reported that Sun Fo, Chiang Ching-kuo, and Ch'en Li-fu went secretly by plane to Moscow on September 27, 1937. The press reported that Soviet ambassador Bogomoloff returned to Moscow

September 28, 1937, by plane for the purpose of arranging loans, a supply of ammunition, and 260 Soviet planes flown by Soviet pilots to China via Lanchou and Sian. See *U.S. Military Intelligence Reports*, G-2 Report no. 9027, October 13, 1937, by Assistant Military Attaché John Weckerling. Not long after the nonaggression pact was signed, Bogomoloff ended his mission in China. See ibid., G-2 Report no. 9614, November 27, 1937. Moscow announced on November 23, 1937, that (Ivan Trofimovich) Lugmets-Orelsky was to succeed Bogomoloff as the new ambassador to China. He presented his credentials in Chungking on January 23, 1938; see ibid., G-2 Report, no. 9633, February 1, 1938. The Soviet embassy moved from Hankow to Chungking on July 11, 1938, ibid., G-2 Report no. 9676, July 15, 1938. On April 30, 1945, A. A. Petrov succeeded Ivan Trofimovich Lugmets-Orelsky as the third ambassador of the Soviet Union to National China during the World War II period; see *Ta Kung Pao*, Chungking edition, May 1, 1945; English translation in U.S. State Department (confidential) *Central Files: China Internal Affairs, 1945–1949*, Dispatch no. 372, May 8, 1945.

10. Regarding the Japanese-Soviet neutrality pact negotiations, see *U.S. Military Intelligence Reports*, G-2 Report no. 9986, April 18, 1941; Raymond James Sontag and James Stuart Beddie, eds., *Nazi-Soviet Relations 1939–1941: Documents from the Archives of the German Foreign Office*, Publication 3024 (Washington, D.C.: Department of State, 1948), pp. 321–24, very urgent secret cables of the German ambassador (Schulenburg) in the Soviet Union to the German Foreign Office, April 9, 1941, April 10, 1941, April 13, 1941.

11. On April 4, 1938, the Japanese ambassador to Russia protested to the Soviet government against the presence of Russian aviators serving in the Chinese army. One Russian aviator was captured alive; see *U.S. Military Intelligence Reports*, G-2 Report no. 9656, April 6, 1938, prepared by Major David D. Barrett, assistant military attaché.

12. Immanuel C. Hsu, *The Rise of Modern China*, 4th ed. (New York: Oxford University Press, 1990), pp. 599–601; Lend-Lease (Bill H. R. 1776) was approved on March 11, 1941; see Roosevelt's press conference 225 (excerpt) March 11, 1941; in Samuel I. Rosenman, comp., *The Public Papers and Addresses of Franklin D. Roosevelt* (New York: Harper & Brothers Publishers, 1941), pp. 48–51, 449–50. From March 11, 1941, to September 30, 1946, the total Lend-Lease was $50,692,109; China's share was $1,564,698; British Empire, $31,392,361; USSR, $11,297,883; France and possessions, $3,233,859. See Thomas A. Bailey and David M. Kennedy, *The American Pageant: A History of the Republic*, vol. 2, 9th ed. (Lexington, Mass.: D.C. Heath and Company, 1991), p. 830. See also Edward R. Stettinius, Jr., *Lend-Leased: Weapon for Victory* (New York: Macmillan Co., 1944), chap. 10, pp. 109–18, on Lend-Lease agreements with China, see Charles I. Bevans, comp., *Treaties and Other International Agreements of the United States of America, 1776–1949* vol. 6 (Washington, D.C.: Department of State Publication 8549, January 1971), pp. 735–60.

13. The Sian Incident occurred on December 12, 1936. For detailed reports on Chang Hsüeh-liang's demands and the situation in Suiyuan, see *U.S. Military Reports*, G-2 Report no. 9501, December 18, 1936; for Chiang Kai-shek's release on

Christmas Day, the immediate aftereffects, and the response of Yen Hsi-shan, Han Fu-ch'ü, Sung Che-yüan, and Li Tsung-jen, see ibid., Report no. 9510, January 25, 1937; on the general situation in Shensi, Kansu, and Suiyuan from January 26 to February 6, 1937, see ibid., Report no. 9512, February 6, 1937, pp. 1–4, by Joseph W. Stilwell, military attaché. For more analysis, see U.S. ambassador Nelson Trusler Johnson's report to the secretary of state, "The Sian Incident, Detention of Generalissimo Chiang Kai-shek, by General Chang Hsüeh-liang," dated January 12, 1937; see also "Speech made by General Chiang Kai-shek to General Chang Hsüeh-liang and Yang Hu-ch'eng at Sian on December 25th [1936]," English translation; and statement made by Chiang Kai-shek to newspaper representatives on December 26, 1936; see ibid., G-2 Report no. 2657-J-281-146. In addition, see Chiang Mei-ling (Madame Chiang Kai-shek), *Sian: a coup d'état, A Fortnight in Sian: Extracts from a Diary by Chiang Kai-shek* (Shanghai: China Publishing Co., 1937); for more specific studies, see Wu T'ien-wei, *The Sian Incident; A Pivotal Point in Modern Chinese History* (Ann Arbor: University of Michigan Center for Chinese Studies, 1976); Earl Albert Selle, *Donald of China* (New York: Harper, 1948), pp. 253–68, pp. 316–36.

Chapter Six
The War of Resistance against Japan, Autumn 1937–Summer 1945

1. For a detailed analysis of the Japanese attack on July 7, 1937, see *U.S. Military Intelligence Reports*, G-2 Report no. 9583, August 8, 1937, by Infantry Colonel Joseph W. Stilwell; on National Defense Council appointment of July 13, 1936, and account of the incident, see ibid., G-2 Report no. 9579, July 16, 1937; ibid., G-2 Report no. 9441, July 17, 1937, pp. 4–5. Chiang Kai-shek needed the cooperation of the Kwangsi faction including Li Tsung-jen and Pai Ch'ung-hsi for the resistance to Japanese aggression. For a more recent study, see a special issue on the event in the *Journal of Studies of Japanese Aggression Against China*, no. 11 (August 1992).

2. From 1927 to 1938, the Office of U.S. Military Attaché made a series of reports estimating the strength of Chiang Kai-shek through intelligence gathering in China that was as follows:

    A. As of August 1927, The National Revolutionary Army under the command of Chiang Kai-shek in Nanking numbered 278,000; the Wuhan government, including Feng Yü-hsiang's Kuominchün, had 252,000 soldiers. See *U.S. Military Intelligence Reports*, G-2 Report no. 7063, June 6, 1927, no. 7099, August 3, 1927.

    B. As of the end of 1927:

1. Chiang Kai-shek	355,000
2. Feng Yü-hsiang	90,000
3. Yen Hsi-shan	90,000
4. Chang Tso-lin	286,000
5. Chili-Shantung	289,000

6. Sun Ch'üan-fang	440,000
7. Southern Provinces	30,000

(See ibid., G-2 Report no. 7183, December 20, 1927.)

C. As of December 1930:

1.	Chiang Kai-shek	825,600
2.	Old Chiang Divisions	205,000
3.	Pai Ch'ung-hsi	95,000
4.	Lu Chung-lin	244,000
5.	Shansi-Suiyuan Forces	133,000
6.	Shih Yu-san	72,000
7.	Miscellaneous Anti-Chiang Forces	301,500
8.	Northeastern Frontier Forces	418,100

(See ibid., G-2 Report no. 7487, April 10, 1929; no. 7583, August 29, 1929; no.7890, December 3, 1930.)

D. As of April 1935:

Total Chinese Forces	1,750,000
1. Loyal to Chiang	1,186,000
2. Semiloyal to Chiang	435,000
3. Independent of Chiang's control	129,000

(See ibid., G-2 Report no. 9093, April 10, 1935.)

E. As of March 1939:

Total Chinese Forces	200 army divisions
	5 new divisions
	10 reserve divisions

3. Sheng Shih-ts'ai left his governorship in Sinkiang Province on August 29, 1945; concerning his involvement in domestic and foreign affairs, particularly with the USSR during World War II in China, see Tu Chung-yüan, *Sheng Shih-ts'ai yü hsin-hsin-chiang* (*Sheng Shih-ts'ai and New Sinkiang*) (Tihwa, Sinkiang: 1945); Tu was the head of Sinkiang Institute (Hsin-chiang hsüeh-yüan) and head of Sheng Shih-ts'ai's Bureau of Education; see also Martin R. Norins's *Gateway to Asia: Sinkiang* (New York: John Day, 1944); the book was introduced by Owen Lattimore in an essay entitled "Sinkiang's Place in the Future of China." Norins's assertion was that Sheng, in his governance of Sinkiang, was a wily, cunning, cruel, and ruthless man whose only interest was maintaining his personal power and who did not hesitate to use the Soviets for all that he could get out of them. For comment on the book, see *Time*, May 28, 1945; see also U.S. State Department (confidential) *Central Files, China's Internal Affairs, 1945–1949*, no. 127, 893.00/7–545 (Frederick, Md.: University Publications of America, 1984), for the American consul in Tihwa's report to the secretary of state and his no. 8 secret report, "The Practice of Torture in the Prison of Sinkiang," March 15, 1945. For academic works, see Li Tung-fang, "Are the Compatriots in the Province of Sinkiang of the Turkish Race?" *Central Daily News* (Chungking), October 14, 1944; the article was translated into English for Ambassador Hurley; see also Allen S. Whiting and Sheng Shih-ts'ai, *Sinkiang: Pawn or Pivot* (East Lansing: Michigan State University Press, 1958); Owen Lattimore,

Pivot of Asia, Sinkiang and the Inner Asian Frontiers of China and Russia (Boston: Little Brown, 1950).

4. For a detailed analysis on the Kuomintang struggle for power in Sinkiang Province, see "Alleged Relationship of the Political Science Clique [Cheng-hsüeh-hsi] to the Situation in the Northeast," memorandum (secret) of American consulate in Tihwa to the secretary of state, no. 38, March 14, 1946, U.S. State Department (confidential) *Central Files: China's Internal Affairs, 1945–1949*, 839.00/3–1446.

5. From 1927 to 1937, Germany sent five military advisory missions to National China. On the activities of the German advisers in China in 1930, see *U.S. Military Intelligence Reports*, G-2 Report no. 7741, March 20, 1930, by Lt. Colonel Nelson E. Margetts in a narrative form after his interview with Chiang Kai-shek's air adviser Bert Hall. Hall was a U.S. citizen by birth but a naturalized citizen of France. He was a member of the Lafayette Escadrilles during World War I. Hall informed Margetts that (1) the German advisers with the National government enjoyed unusual influence over Chiang; (2) there was evidence that enormous quantities of war supplies were purchased upon their recommendations; (3) the German advisers attempted to persuade Chiang to organize a chemical warfare service and to employ gas against his opponents, but Chiang rejected that advice. Furthermore, Hall quoted a Reuters dispatch, which appeared in the *London Daily Herald*, to the effect that Germany was prepared to send large quantities of munitions to China. In German eyes the idea of the Japanese-German agreement was that Japan should oppose Russian penetration of China and if necessary fight the Soviets but not that Japan should try to conquer and dominate China and liquidate all European interests in China. German diplomacy in 1930 was to convince Chiang Kai-shek that Germany, in China's hour of trouble, was its firmest friend. Dr. Gunther von Wolff, leader of the German citizens in China, declared through the Transocean News Agency that all German nationals in China had the greatest sympathy for China. He made the statement at the Congress of German Foreign Organizations in Stuttgart. See *U.S. Military Intelligence Reports*, G-2 Report no. 9596, September 30, 1937, by Military Attaché Colonel Joseph W. Stilwell; on German influence in China in general, see ibid., G-2 Report no. 8804, April 12, 1934, by Major S. V. Constant, assistant military attaché.

6. On August 16, 1937, Adolf Hitler declared that, in principle, he adhered to the idea of cooperation with Japan. Mainly owing to the signing of the Sino-Soviet Nonaggression Pact on August 21, 1937, Germany gradually shifted its diplomatic efforts from China to Japan. From late October 1937 to mid-January 1938, German ambassador to China Oskar Trautmann attempted to mediate between China and Japan. On Trautmann's mission in China, see Kirby, *Germany and Republican China*, pp. 234–35, 237–42; Thomas Leroy Lauer, "German Attempts at Mediation of the Sino-Japanese War, 1937–1938" (Ph.D. diss., Stanford University, 1973). See also *U.S. Military Intelligence Reports*, G-2 Report no. 9679, August 17, 1938, G-2 Report no. 9922, July 30, 1940. During the first sixteen months of the war of resistance, Germany provided 60,000 tons of munitions to National China each month. For example, in 1936, National China orders amounted to 64–65 million reichsmarks worth of arms; the actual deliveries were 23–24 million reichsmarks. For 1937,

National China orders were 60–61 million reichsmarks; the actual deliveries were 82–83 million reichsmarks. That is to say, in 1937, National China received approximately 37 percent of Germany's total exports of arms that year; German arms trade with Japan during 1937, in contrast, was only 16.8 million reichsmarks, and deliveries were 10.9 million reichsmarks. In 1938, after the military advisory mission was recalled, Germany continued to supply 60,000 tons of war materials via Hong Kong to National China. During this long period of time, National China supplied Germany with wolfram and other high-quality ores vital for rearmament. On April 28, 1938, Hermann Göring prohibited deliveries of war matériel to China, and the German military advisory mission officially ended June 23. Trautmann, however, still argued whether the actual interests of Germany in China should be abandoned in favor of possible advantages with Japan. He suggested that Germany's investment in China was about 400 million reichsmarks. See John P. Fox, *Germany and the Far Eastern Crisis, 1931–1938: A Study in Diplomacy and Ideology* (London: London School of Economics and Political Science, 1982), especially pp. 108, 241, 297, 315–17; see also Beverley D. Causey, "German Policy toward China, 1918–1941" (Ph.D. diss., Harvard University, 1942), pp. 274–76. Causey states that, in 1935, Germany exported 8.1 percent of its total arms production to National China and, in 1936, 28.8 percent. For other references, see Allen Gary Burden, "German Policy toward China and the Chinese Revolution, 1919–1937, with Special Reference to the Beginning of Sino-German Military Cooperation" (Ph.D. diss., University of Alberta, 1972); and Jerry Bernard Seps, "German Military Advisers and Chiang Kai-shek, 1927–1939" (Ph.D. diss., University of California at Berkeley, 1972).

7. On May 23, 1938, reports were circulated in Nanking that all German military advisers were ordered to return to Germany. It was the estimation of the United States that the replacement of German advisers with Soviet advisers was possible, but in view of the purges in the ranks of the Soviet army, it would appear that any particularly outstanding military talent could be employed to good advantage at home. See *U.S. Military Intelligence Reports*, G-2 Report no. 9668, June 25, 1938; on the illness of the Soviet commander in the Far East, General (Vasili) Blyukher, see ibid., G-2 Report no. 9208, p. 4, September 26, 1935; on the removal of General Blyukher from the command of the Soviet Far Eastern Army and the difficult circumstances of forty-three other generals of the Far Eastern Army due to Stalin's purge, see ibid., G-2 Report no. 9687, October 12, 1938, by Assistant Military Attaché David D. Barrett; for more about the German advisers, see Kirby, *Germany and Republican China*, pp. 102–44.

8. T'ang Leang-li, *Wang Ching-wei* (Peiping: China United Press, 1931); Jiu Hwa Lo Upshur, "China under the Kuomintang: The Problems of Unification, 1928–1937" (Ph.D. diss., University of Michigan, 1973); Howard L. Boorman, "Wang Ching-wei; China's Romantic Radical," *Political Science Quarterly* 79, no. 4 (December 1964): 504–25. For more on the World War II Chiang Kai-shek–Wang Ching-wei–Japanese triangle relationship, see Gerald E. Bunker, *The Peace Conspiracy: Wang Ching-wei and the Chinese War* (Cambridge, Mass.: Harvard University Press, 1972); John Hunter Boyles, *China and Japan at War, 1937–1945: The Politics of Collaboration* (Stanford: Stanford University Press, 1972); James R. Shirley, "Political Career of

Wang Ching-wei to 1932" (Ph.D. diss., University of California at Berkeley, 1962); Lin Han-sheng, "Wang Ching-wei and the Japanese Peace Efforts" (Ph.D. diss., University of Pennsylvania, 1967); Gordon A. Craig, *The Germans* (New York: New American Library, 1983), pp. 61–63.

9. For a careful analysis of the attempted assassination of Wang Ching-wei on March 21, 1939, at Hanoi, see *U.S. Military Intelligence Reports*, G-2 Report no. 9754, dated April 6, 1939, by U.S. assistant military attaché Captain F. P. Munson; for the reasons for Wang Ching-Wei's betrayal of the National government, ibid., G-2 Report, no. 9170, January 3, 1939, pp. 3–7.

10. Concerning the Chungking-Japan-Nanking–puppet government relationship, see Ambassador (Patrick J.) Hurley to the secretary of state, top secret document no. 238, "KMT-Communist Negotiations, for the eyes of the Secretary of State alone," 7 P.M., February 17, 1945, page 6: "There are at present approximately 900,000 puppet troops in China including 410,000 regulars and 490,000 local troops. During 1941 Communist forces won over 34,167 puppet soldiers (or approximately 3.8% of the local puppet strength in China) and 20,850 rifles, side arms, mortars, field pieces, et cet. It is estimated that with American financial help the former figure could be increased during 1945 to 90,000 men or 10% of entire puppet force" (U.S. State Department [confidential] *Central Files: China Internal Affairs, 1945–1949*, 893.00/2–1745, DSH-1085.) On January 23, 1945, communist Chu Teh, commander of the 18th Army group, wrote to General Albert C. Wedemeyer requesting that the U.S. Army lend the communist army $20,000,000 (twenty million dollars in U.S. currency) for work among the puppet troops; see ibid.; top secret no. 170, 893.00/ 2-2345, February 23, 1945, George Atcheson, Jr., chargé d'affaires to the secretary of state. See also "The Chinese Tug-of-War: Prospects for Settlements at Chung-king—Kuomintang and Communist Suspicions," editorial page, *Times* (London), January 2, 1946, by a special correspondent. The article says that "after the Japanese surrender the Kuomintang relied largely on the puppets and Japanese. The puppets were made responsible for maintaining order till the arrival of Kuomintang forces." See also "Communism in China: Policy as Expounded by Yenan, an Eastern Form of Marxism," *Times* (London), January 17, 1946.

11. The full text of the letter of March 2, 1924, is in Ch'in Hsiao-yi, ed., *Tsung-t'ung Chiang-kung ta-shih ch'ang-pien ch'u-k'ao* vol. 1 (Taipei: Kuomintang Central Executive Committee Historical Commission, 1978), leaves 67–72.

12. Ch'in Hsiao-yi, ed., *Kuo-fu ch'üan-chi* (*Complete Works of the Father of the Nation* [Sun Yat-sen]) (Taipei: China Cultural Service, 1989), vol. 5, p.540.

13. For an account of Wang Ching-wei's puppet regime in Nanking, see Huang Mei-ch'en and Huang Chang-yüan, eds., *Wang Ching-wei kuo-min-cheng-fu ti ch'eng-li* (*The Founding of Wang Ching-wei's National Government*). (Shanghai: Jen-min ch'u-pen-she, 1987).

14. In January 1945, the U.S. embassy in China estimated the Regular Army of National China in Shanghai to total about 85,000. Chinese communist forces known to be stationed in adjacent areas of Anhwei and Honan provinces numbered about 25,000; see *U.S. Foreign Relations, 1945* vol. 7 (Washington, D.C.: U.S. Govern-

ment Printing Office, 1969), p. 166. Chiang's greatest hope for regaining control of the central and east China area was through future cooperation with the puppets, who had maintained contacts with Nanking and Peking. The Japanese knew of these relationships and approved of them because they did not wish Chiang destroyed. The Japanese believed that Chiang was essential to them; ibid., p. 161; see also *U.S. Foreign Relations, 1947*, vol. 7, pp. 218–19.

15. Wang Ching-wei died at Nagoya, Japan, on November 10, 1944; see Boorman ed., "Wang Ching-wei, orig. Wang Chao-ming," in *Biographical Dictionary of Republican China*, vol. 3, 369–76; see also, in the same volume, "Bibliography: Wang Ching-wei," pp. 374–77.

16. For Wang Ching-wei's view on the Sino-Japanese relationship during World War II, see T'ang Leang-i, ed., *China and Japan: Natural Friends—Unnatural Enemies: A Guide for China's Foreign Policy* (Shanghai: China United Press, 1941).

17. Ch'eng T'ien-fang (Cheng Tien-fong), Chinese ambassador to Germany from 1937 to 1939, in his book *A History of Sino-Russian Relations* (Washington, D.C.: Public Affairs Press, 1957), p. 190, writes that in the latter part of 1935, Chiang was "worried lest Japan might take a sudden thrust against China proper which would nullify his long-range policy. So he also looked to the Soviet Union for help in case of such an emergency. . . . Upon Chiang's instructions Ch'en Li-fu, Director of Organization in the Central headquarters of the Kuomintang approached [Soviet ambassador Dimitri] Bogomoloff for a possible secret alliance. Bogomoloff told Ch'en that he personally favored such an alliance and suggested that Ch'en go to Moscow, as Chiang's personal representative, to negotiate with Stalin."

18. The best source on the Blue Shirts Society (Lan-i-she) and its relationship with the CC Clique during the pre–World War II period is Iwai Eiichi (Hidakusu), *Ranisha ni kansuru chōsa (An Investigation of the Blue Shirts Society)* Research Division of the Foreign Ministry, Japan, 1937, in *U.S. Military Intelligence Reports, 1911–1941*, G-2 Report, War Department, 893.00/3.3045. This highly secret, now unclassified document was translated into English by the U.S. Federal Bureau of Investigation on March 30, 1945, as *The Chinese Lan-i-Society*. The English translation is divided into two parts; see U.S. State Department (confidential) *Central Files, China Internal Affairs, 1945–1949*, 893.00/3–3045: (1) (confidential) *Investigation Pertaining to the Lan-i-she* (as of March 1937), published June 1938 by Section 5 of the Investigation Bureau of the Ministry of Foreign Affairs of Japan, pp. 73–75, "Its Relation to the CC Band." On page 14, the study stated that "in fact, the Lan-i-she is for Chiang a lifeless party, the central support of his political power, and the last line of defense for his political life"; on page 53, it stated that "the American Branch of the Lan-i-she was located in Washington, D.C., comprising three directors, one secretary and 33 members." (2) (confidential) *Rules and Regulations Pertaining to the Lan-i-she*, published February 1938, by Section 3 of the Investigation Bureau of the Ministry of Foreign Affairs of Japan. For an English-language source, see Hsu En-tseng, *The Invisible Conflict* (Hong Kong: Dragonfly Press, 1956). For academic works, see Lloyd E. Eastman, *Seeds of Destruction, Nationalist China in War and Revolution, 1937–1949* (Stanford: Stanford University Press, 1984), pp. 91, 96, 100–102, 213; Eastman, *The Abortive Revolution, China under Nationalist Rule, 1927–1937* (Cam-

bridge, Mass.: Harvard University Press, 1974), pp. 32–36, 56–60; 61–63; Eastman, "Fascism in Kuomintang China: The Blueshirts," *China Quarterly*, no. 49 (January–March 1972): 1–31; and T'ien-wei Wu, "Contending Political Forces during the War of Resistance," in James C. Hsiung and Steven I. Levine, eds., *China's Bitter Victory: The War with Japan* (New York: M.E. Sharpe, 1992), pp. 51–78.

19. On the Whampoa Clique and the Blue Shirts, see William C. Kirby, *Germany and Republican China* (Stanford: Stanford University Press, 1984), pp. 158–69, and Eastman, *Abortive Revolution*, pp. 31, 36, 56.

20. Concerning the CC Clique, see Eastman, *Seeds of Destruction*, pp. 28, 35, 83, 91, 100–102, 109–16. Edgar Snow, *Red Star over China*, 1st revised and enlarged edition (New York: Grove Press, Inc., 1968), p. 384, noted that "the two C's'" were Ch'en Li-fu and Ch'en Kuo-fu, brothers who controlled the Kuomintang apparatus."

21. Kan Kuo-hsün, *Lan-i-she, Fu-hsing-she, Li-hsin-she* (*Lan-i-Society, F'u-hsing Society, Li-hsin Society*) (Taipei: Biographical Literature, 1984); Eastman, *Abortive Revolution*, pp. 61, 329. For the administrative structure and a list of personnel of the three organizations, see *Ch'uan-chi wen-hsüeh* (*Biographical Literature*) 61, no. 6 (December 1992): 127–33; ibid. 62, no. 1 (January 1993): 123–31.

22. For the contribution of the Chinese Engineering Society headed by Ch'en Li-fu during World War II in China, see James Reardon-Anderson, "Science in Wartime China," in Hsiung and Levine, eds., *China's Bitter Victory*, 213–34, especially pp. 216–18.

Chapter Seven
Wartime Education Minister,
January 1938–December 1944

1. Concerning the power of Tai Li, see "Reported Attempt of Tai Li to obtain for himself a unified control over Intelligence Operations," secret report of Edward E. Rice, second secretary of the U.S. embassy to Ambassador Patrick J. Hurley, June 25, 1945, at Sian, Shensi Province. See U.S. State Department (confidential) *Central Files: China Internal Affairs, 1945–1949*, 893.00/0–2545 CS/MAJ.

2. For Ch'en Li-fu's wartime educational policy, see his *Four Years of Chinese Education (1937–1941)* (Chungking: China Information Committee, 1947); "China's Ch'en Li-fu: The Essence of Life Is the Performance of Benevolence," *Time* 49, no. 21 (May 26, 1947); 33–36; "Chinese Education during the War," in *China Handbook* (New York: Macmillan, 1937–1945), p. 399; Thomas Daniel Curran, "Education and Society in Republican China" (Ph.D. diss., Columbia University 1986); Hubert Freyn, *Chinese Education in the War* (New York: Kelly & Walsh, 1940).

3. See *Memoranda Submitted by the Chinese Assessor to the Commission of Enquiry of the League of Nations*, bilingual edition (N.p., April–August, 1932), pp. 207–10.

4. The new local provincial and urban government and a new county (*hsien*) system were set up in the 1930s. The organizational aspects of these two systems can

CHART 3

ORGANIZATION OF THE VARIOUS CLASSIFICATIONS OF *HSIEN*

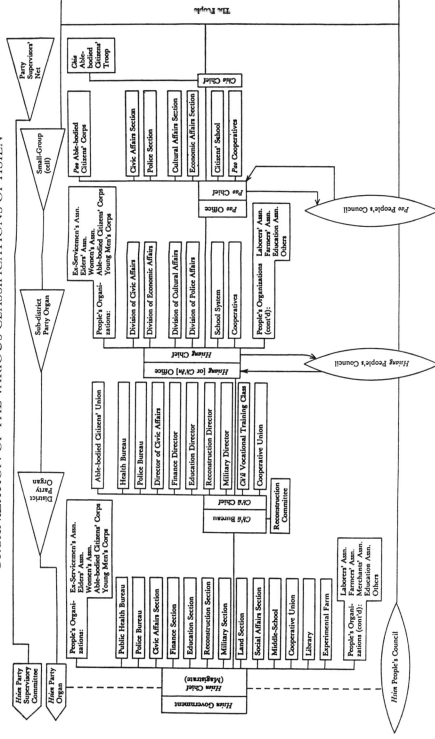

CHART 4
PROVINCIAL AND URBAN GOVERNMENT

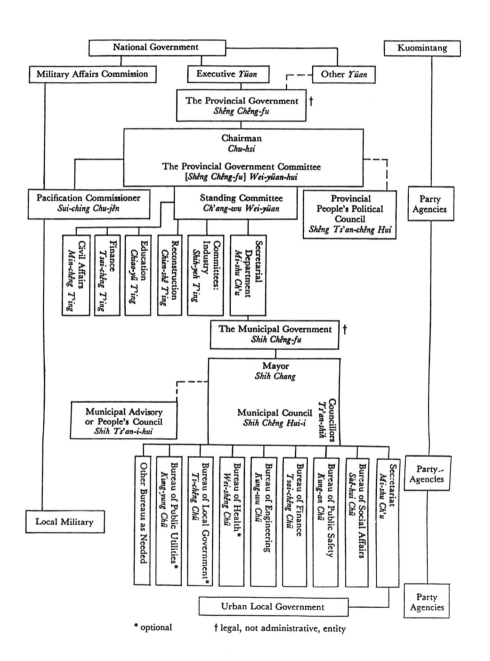

* optional   † legal, not administrative, entity

be seen in charts 3 and 4. See Paul M. A. Linebarger, *The China of Chiang Kai-shek* (Boston: World Peace Foundation, 1941), pp. 98-99, 388-89.

5. On July 8, 1929, the Standing Committee of the Central Executive Committee adopted a resolution introducing twenty-eight days as Revolutionary Memorial Days including (1) March 18, punitive expedition against Yüan Shi-k'ai by the navy led by the gunboat *Shao-ho*, (2) April 12, party purgation movement, (3) May 18, anniversary of the death of martyr Ch'en Ch'i-mei, (4) July 9, launching of the Northern Expedition. The two Ch'en brothers played a significant role in these four events. See *U.S. Military Intelligence Reports*, G-2 Report no. 7562, July 17, 1929, by Assistant Military Attaché Parker G. Tenney.

6. See Proclamation 6182 of September 20, 1990, National Teacher Appreciation Day, 1990, 55 F.R.38971, by the president of the United States of America (signed by George Bush): "In grateful recognition of America's teachers, the Congress, by Senate Joint Resolution 313, has designated October 3, 1990, as 'National Teacher Appreciation Day' and has authorized and requested the President to issue a proclamation in observance of this event."

7. For Fairbank's view on Ch'en Li-fu's request and his policy matters, see Fairbank, *Chinabound*, pp. 198–99, 248; for comment on Ch'en's career, see p. 249. Fairbank had two recorded conversations with Ch'en: one in October 1942 and the other in the evening of November 2, 1943. Both were about the subject of using projectors for educational purposes. Fairbank's unkind words about Ch'en and the CC Clique were printed in his "Memorandum for the Ambassador, November 3, 1943"; see Fairbank, *Chinabound*, pp. 250–51. Fairbank writes that Ch'en "envisaged the installation of 80,000 'reflectorscopes' in the 80,000 villages of China, where the masses could be shown pictures of the world. . . . My strongest impression, from this and earlier conversations with the Minister of Education, is that his interest in and understanding of education is extremely superficial, as though he seldom had found time to contemplate any of the topics which we discussed." Fairbank concluded that "the CC are a type interested in power and regimentation to preserve it. They are not capable of much innovation. . . . To put Ch'en Li-fu in charge of education was a step toward politicizing it and was resented accordingly by the Peking liberal educators, who had seldom been enthusiastic about the KMT in any case." In his trip to Taiwan in 1960, Fairbank wrote that "of the Nationalist ministers I had seen in wartime Chungking, the party organizer Ch'en Li-fu had retired to raise chickens in New Jersey, whereas the more liberal Wang Shih-chieh was still in the cabinet and responsive to my proposals for more academic contact and opening of archives"; Fairbank, *Chinabound*, pp. 379, 384. However, in his *The United States and China* 4th edition (Cambridge, Mass.: Harvard University Press, 1979), p. 255, Fairbank acknowledged that "the revival of Confucianism was most actively promoted by Ch'en Li-fu, whose uncle had been Chiang Kai-shek's patron and who became Chiang's most loyal political organizer. . . . The Ch'en brothers led the CC Clique which dominated the right wing of the Kuomintang. In general Ch'en Li-fu called for the fusion of Western technology and Confucian social values. He [Ch'en Li'fu] urged that the dicta of famous Confucian scholars be systematically arranged and

explained to the people. Confucianism belongs to no specific class, it is actually in keeping with Sun's [Sun Yat-sen] Three Principles."

8. Fairbank's view of Chinese Communists can be seen from his personal letter to John Carter Vincent dated December 6, 1945, wherein he proposed that "our positive program should continue to emphasize economic help in China, while cutting down on support of one party in the civil conflict. This can be done only if some kind of coalition government is attained." See "U.S. Policy in China," Mr. (John Carter) Vincent to Mr. (Dean) Acheson, office memorandum, United States Department of State, January 14, 1946; in U.S. State Department (confidential) *Central Files: China Internal Affairs, 1945–1949*, 893.00/1–1446; see also Carter's statement before the Senate Foreign Relations Committee, March 10, 1966, and the Congressional Quarterly Service, *China and the U.S. Far East Policy: 1945–1966* (Washington, D.C.: Government Printing Office, April 1967), pp. 179–80, 284–87. David Gonzalez, writing for the *New York Times*, September 16, 1991, stated that "three decades later [1960s], Fairbank acknowledged his earlier belief that Communism was 'bad in America but good in China.' . . . Mr. Fairbank entered a prolific period in the 1960s, with his extensive writings and active lecture schedule focused on urging the United States to recognize the People's Republic of China and to bring it into the United Nations and replace Taiwan on the Security Council." David Gonzalez went to state that "some critics charged that he [Fairbank] had ignored the repressive excesses of the Communist dictatorship." For more about Fairbank's academic works, see George H. Stevens, comp., *Fairbank Bibliography*, 1970, mimeograph (mainly articles appearing in the *New York Times*, on or by John K. Fairbank, from December 20, 1946, to December 30, 1966). Marius B. Jansen, "Obituaries: John K. Fairbank (1907–1991)," *Journal of Asian Studies* 51, no. 1 (February 1992): 237–42. John K. Fairbank, Preface to *An Unauthorized Digest of L. A. Bereznii, a Critique of American Bourgeois Historiography on China: Problems of Social Development in the Nineteenth and Early Twentieth Centuries* (Leningrad: Leningrad University, 1968) distributed by the East Asian Research Center, Harvard University.

9. For a U.S. analysis of Chinese education in the border area, see Assistant Military Attaché S. V. Constant's report, "Education in the Frontier Provinces," in *U.S. Military Intelligence Reports*, G-2 Report no. 9051, February 1935. The report covers the area of Tibet, Mongolia, Chahar, Suiyuan, Ninghsia, Chinghai, Kansu, Sinkiang, and Yunnan.

10. For Wilma Fairbank's (wife of John K. Fairbank) harsh criticism of Ch'en Li-fu and her displeasure over National China's education policy during World War II, see Wilma Fairbank, *America's Cultural Experiment in China, 1942–1949* (Washington, D.C.: U.S. Department of State Bureau of Educational and Cultural Affairs, 1976), pp. 121–43. On page 129, she states that "in Chungking Ministry of Education officials earned their pay by controlling the thoughts and deeds of students. It was the normal and expected procedure, presided over by Minister Ch'en Li-fu in the interest of the Kuomintang Party and of his patron, the Generalissimo."

11. Joseph Needham, F.R.S., of the Cambridge Biochemical Laboratory, accepted a mission of cultural and scientific cooperation, on behalf of the British Council, to

China in September 1942; see *Nature* 151, no. 3804 (September 26, 1942): 369. The well-known Chinese newspaper *Ta Kung Pao* in Chungking published a leading article to welcome him; see *Nature* 151, no. 3806 (October 10, 1942): 426. From September 1942 to the end of 1944, Needham published a series of articles in *Nature* reporting various aspects of scientific and technological research conducted at various colleges and universities during World War II in the area of China under the National government's jurisdiction; see *Nature* 153, no. 3920 (December 16, 1944): 763. The titles were "Science in Western Szechuan," *Nature* 152, no. 3856 (September 25, 1943): 343–45, and 152, no. 3857 (October 2, 1943): 372–74; "Fortieth Anniversary of the University of Peiping," *Nature* 152, no. 3844 (July 3, 1943): 23; "Science in South-West China," *Nature* 152, no. 3844 (July 3, 1943): 9–10, 152, no. 3845 (July 10, 1943): 36–37; "Science in Chungking," *Nature* 152, no. 3846 (July 17, 1943): 64–66; "Science and Technology in the North-West of China," *Nature* 153, no. 3878 (February 26, 1944): 238–41; "Chungking Industrial and Mining Exhibition," *Nature* 153, no. 3892 (June 3, 1944): 672–75; "The International Science Co-operative Service," *Nature* 154, no. 3917 (November 25, 1944): 657–60. Needham was elected honorary member of the Science Society of China on July 18, 1944; see *Nature* 153, no. 3877 (February 19, 1944): 228.

12. John T. Flynn, in his book, *The Lattimore Story: The Full Story of the Most Incredible Conspiracy of Our Time* (New York: Devin-Adair, 1953), pp. 40–41, states that there were fourteen "poisonous books" published by the Institute of Pacific Relations during World War II that greatly affected China-U.S. relations. He further states that they were all reviewed by the *New York Times* and the *New York Herald Tribune* and that John K. Fairbank's work, *The United States in China*, was one of them. The fourteen books are as follows:

Unfinished Revolution in China by Israel Epstein
United States and China by John K. Fairbank
Report from Red China by Harrison Forman
Journey from the East by Mark Gayn
Solution in Asia by Owen Lattimore
New Frontiers in Asia by Philip J. Jaffe
Making of Modern China by Owen and Eleanor Lattimore
Situation in Asia by Owen Lattimore
China's Wartime Politics by Lawrence K. Rosinger
China's Crisis by Lawrence K. Rosinger
Battle Hymn of China by Agnes Smedley
Challenge of Red China by Guenther Stein
Chinese Conquer China by Anna Louise Strong
The Phoenix and the Dwarfs, a play by George E. Taylor

13. Beginning in the latter part of 1943, the U.S. Department of State showed its "natural concern" for the press and thought control in China. "Reports said that the Chinese government [National government] restrictions are operating to prevent the press from giving a true and objective picture of affairs in China, and also reports of measures to control the thought of Chinese students, including those sent abroad for study. In November 1943, the Chinese government in Chungking planned to

NOTES TO PAGE 167

send six hundred students to study abroad: 60 percent to study the sciences and 40 percent, the arts. On behalf of the U.S. embassy, Ambassador C. E. Gauss, on November 16, 1943, reported to the secretary of state that the embassy was of the opinion that "a list of regulations governing students proceeding abroad for education" had been used by the Ministry of Education (headed by Ch'en Li-fu) and that "students of known liberal political beliefs or those suspected of a questioning or critical attitude toward the Kuomintang will find it extremely difficult, if not impossible, to obtain the approval of the Ministry of Education for study abroad." Chinese students in the United States would be recalled "if found to be guilty of statements contrary to San Min Chu I." Ambassador Gauss believed that such pronouncements boded "fascist-like practices which are thus to be effective control beyond the borders of China." See *U.S. Foreign Relations, 1943: China* (Washington, D.C.: U.S. Government Printing Office, 1957), pp. 756–58. On February 10, 1943, the State Department's Advisory Committee on Adjustment of Foreign Students passed a resolution evidencing displeasure with the Chinese government's "controls established in the appointment and supervision" of these students who were preparing to study in the United States. On March 14, 1944, the State Department instructed the U.S. embassy in Chungking to inform the Chinese minister of foreign affairs that "the Department would view with disfavor such political surveillance of Chinese students" in the United States as described in the regulations governing students. On April 5, 1944, the *New York Times* published a statement signed by a group of Harvard professors "expressing the hope that the decision to exercise control over the Chinese students abroad would be reconsidered by the Chinese government and rescinded." See *U.S. Foreign Relations, 1944*, vol. 6, *China* (Washington, D.C.: U.S. Government Printing Office, 1967), pp. 1130–34. On April 8, 1944, Secretary of State Hull instructed Ambassador Gauss that the U.S. embassy should defer issuing visas to any Chinese officials coming to the United States in the capacity of suprintendent of students and referred the matter to the State Department. Hull stated that "confidential information received by the Department indicates that the prospective superintendent in the United States may be Z. Y. Kuo, described as a henchman of Ch'en Li-fu and fascist in attitude." See *U.S. Foreign Relations, 1944*, vol. 6 *China*, pp. 1134–35. On April 25, 1944, Ambassador Gauss reported that he had heard that the "Generalissimo has decided that no more Chinese students shall be permitted for the time being to go to the United States or England for study," for "he [the generalissimo] is angry over the 'thought control' criticism in the United States." See *U.S. Foreign Relations, 1944*, vol. 6, *China*, p. 1139. On May 17, 1944, Peck, the special assistant in the Division of Science, Education and Art of the State Department, had a long conversation with Chinese ambassador Wei Tao-ming concerning the "thought control" issue. Wei told Peck that when he was in Chungking he had talked with Minister of Education Ch'en Li-fu about the matter: "The Minister of Education insisted that the regulations did not mean that the Superintendent of Students should try to control the thoughts of Chinese students in the United States since, in the first place, control of thought is obviously impossible in any circumstances, and, in the second place, there will be so many Chinese students in the United States, that it would be impossible for the Superintendent of Students even to attempt any such control." See *U.S. Foreign Relations, 1944*, vol. 6, *China*, pp. 1140 42. For more about the "thought control" issue, see "Cultural Relations Program of the State Department to Provide Technical Assistance to China and to Facilitate Greater Cultural Cooperation between the United States and China," see *U.S. Foreign Relations, 1942, China*, pp. 697–727; *U.S. Foreign Relations, 1943, China*, pp. 732–64; *U.S. Foreign Relations, 1944*, vol. 6, *China*, pp. 1111–56.

14. Regarding the services National China's Youth Army (Ch'ing-nien-chün) rendered to the China-India-Burma theater from the winter of 1944 to the Japanese unconditional surrender, the best and most complete record is Charles F. Romanus and Riley Sanderland, *United States Army in World War II: China-Burma-India Theater, Stilwell's Mission to China* (Washington, D.C.: Department of the Army, Office of the Chief of Military History, reprinted, 1968), and their *Stilwell's Command Problems* (Washington, D.C.: Department of the Army, Office of the Chief of Military History, 1955).

15. The total collection of salt revenue in 1936 was around US$205,433,000; in 1937 it was approximately US$213,000,000; see *U.S. Military Intelligence Reports*, "Collection of the Chinese Salt Administration," Report no. 9650, March 24, 1938, p. 17. The report stated that "all foreign loan obligations [of China] secured on the salt revenue have been fully met." For research on salt production and administration in China, see S. A. M. Adshead, *Salt and Civilization* (New York: St. Martin's Press, 1992), especially "China—Late Imperial, Republican and Early Government," pp. 162–74, and tables of salt revenues in China from 1500 to 1950, pp. 125, 129, 165, 292, 343, 354. For an academic work on the history of the salt industry in Szechuan Province, see Hans Ulrich Vogel, "The Great Well of China," *Scientific American* 268, no. 6 (June 1993): 116–21, and his *Salt Production Techniques in Ancient China* (translated and revised work of Yoshida Tora's *Gendai seien gijutsu shiryō "Gohazu" no kenkyū*) (Leiden: E. J. Brill, 1993).

Chapter Eight
From Victory to Defeat,
Spring 1945–Winter 1949

1. For Stalin's requests, see Chiang Kai-shek, *Soviet Russia in China*, revised, abridged edition (New York: Farrar, Straus and Cudahy, 1965), pp. 101–4. Stalin complimented Chiang Kai-shek as "selfless," "a patriot" and said that "the Soviets in times past had befriended him." For Ambassador Hurley's telegram, April 17, 1945, from Moscow, top secret and urgent for the eyes of the secretary of state only, see U.S. State Department (confidential) *Central Files: China Internal Affairs, 1945–1949*, 893.00/4-1745. In April 1945, Stalin decided to send a new ambassador to Chungking; see "Welcome to Ambassador [A.A.] Petrov, and the future of Sino-Soviet Relations," editorial of *Ta-kung pao* (Chungking), May 1, 1945. *Ta-kung pao* was the most popular and prestigious daily in World War II China. The editors expressed the view that, to meet the challenging new international situation, the

nonaggression pact signed on August 29, 1937, was not sufficient. A new Chinese-Soviet treaty of mutual assistance should be negotiated and signed. For an English translation of the editorial, see dispatch no. 372, May 8, 1945, from the U.S. embassy, Chungking, China. For an analytic study on the National government–Soviet relationship during World War II in general, see Charles B. McLane, *Soviet Policy and the Chinese Communists, 1931–1946* (New York: Columbia University Press, 1958). See also footnote 9, chapter 5, of this work.

2. Whether Outer Mongolia should be returned to China was an issue of debate in the high levels of Soviet Union officialdom. Nichi Nichi (a Tokyo news agency) reported that Bogomoloff favored canceling the independence of Outer Mongolia and returning this territory to China, a move that would make it possible to use the Outer Mongolian Army to attack Manchuria. General Lepin, Soviet military attaché in China, who was not in favor of giving back Outer Mongolia, was of the opinion that Soviet assistance to China should be limited to supplying munitions of war and securing joint action on the part of the powers concerned to restrain the Japanese advance. Stalin said Nichi Nichi had partially acceded to Bogomoloff's recommendations and was considering abrogating the Soviet–Outer Mongolian alliance, recognizing China's suzerainty over Outer Mongolia, and placing the Outer Mongolian Army under the control of the National government for operations on the Mongolian-Manchurian border. See *U.S. Military Intelligence Reports*, G-2 Report no. 9601, October 18, 1937.

3. T. V. Soong resigned from the premiership on March 1, 1947. U.S. assistant commercial attaché in China Boehringer commented that "Dr. Ch'en Li-fu was among those responsible for Dr. Soong's resignation on the charge that his economic policies had failed." Ch'en's proposal for economic reform was adopted by the Central Executive Committee on March 23, 1947, as an economic reform plan, which, since May 25, had been under study by the National Economic Council. The plan was revised and passed by the plenary session of the National Economic Council on July 21, 1947. Boehringer commented that "there are no major changes either in content or in spirit of the original proposals. The plan contains recommendations under 15 headings: Full utilization of manpower; Increase production of goods; Stabilization of the value of the currency; Reform of the banking system; Development of industries, commerce, communications; Reforms of food administration; More reasonable collection of land tax and adoption of a granary system to stablize grain prices; Division of the idle capital; Encouragement of foreign capital; National adjustment of treatment accorded public employees, school teachers and Army personnel; Severe punishment for persons who utilize political influence to benefit private enterprises; Strengthening of the economic organization with over-all planning of the nation's finance and economy." Boehringer, however, did not think "the suggestion is then valid"; see his "Memorandum on Economic Situation in China," Nanking, July 23, 1947, *U.S. Foreign Relations, 1947*, vol. 7, pp. 661–67. Instead, he listed nine unfavorable factors that led to the continued economic deterioration in China including official indecision and ineptness; the continuing heavy unfavorable trade balance; shortage of coal; steady increase in wages; multiplicity of taxes, with discrimination in collection of taxes from foreign concerns; Chinese insistence on

sovereign rights; jockeying for power in the Kuomintang, with the CC Clique emerging as the potentially dominant group in the economic and political science group, with China's ablest administrators in eclipse; hope for loans from the United States; badly administered import trade controls. For a detailed summary from the U.S. embassy about Ch'en Li-fu's plan and comments, see *U.S. Foreign Relations, 1947*, pp. 1099–1103, "The Minister-Counselor of Embassy in China Butterworth to the Secretary of State, April 16, 1947." Butterworth held a similar view, as Brehringer stated in his memorandum of July 23, 1947. Butterworth questioned the motives "which prompted the reactionary CC Clique to sponsor seemingly liberal and much-needed sweeping reforms." An embassy officer had a discussion with Ch'en Li-fu on July 9, 1947. Ch'en stated that the "only defect" of the plan is that it does not take up in detail the question of land problems; see Ambassador Stuart to Secretary of State Marshall, July 12, 1947, *U.S. Foreign Relations, 1947*, pp. 1157–58; for comparisons of the plan of March 23, 1947, and the plan of July 21, 1947, see ibid., pp. 1184–89. As to the post–World War II U.S. aid and T. V. Soong's handling of financial matters, a timely report can be seen in "Insiders Got Rich on Chinese Aid," *U.S. News and World Report*, August 26, 1949, pp. 15–17.

4. Commenting on Chiang Kai-shek's decision March 1, 1945, to call the National Assembly on November 12, John Stewart Service writes to the Department of State that "the National Congress cannot be called while half of the country is cut off or accepted by the enemy and while all parties but the Kuomintang are denied legality. What the situation requires, and the only thing that can save it, is a coalition government. We hope that America will use her influence to achieve it"; *U.S. Foreign Relations*, 1945, vol. 7, pp. 278–79. Actually, on October 10, 1944, Service sent a memorandum to the Department of State from Yenan, wartime capital of the Chinese Communist party, saying that "the United States [1] does not need Kuomintang for military reasons; [2] need not fear Kuomintang surrender or opposition; [3] need not fear the collapse of the Kuomintang Government; [4] need not support the Kuomintang for international political reasons; and [5] need not support Chiang in the belief that he represents pro-American or democratic groups." Service states that the U.S. policy "toward China should be guided by two facts: First, we cannot hope to deal successfully with Chiang without being hard-boiled. Second, we cannot hope to solve China's problems (which are now our problems) without consideration of the opposition forces—communist, provincial and liberal."

5. "Marshall increasingly felt that the chief antagonist to all his efforts in China was a man of whom he often heard but whom he almost never saw—Ch'en Li-fu, who, with his elder brother, headed the ultra-right 'CC Clique,' which was powerful in the Kuomintang." See Forrest C. Pogue, *George Marshall: Statesman 1945–1949* (New York: Viking, 1987), pp. 82–83. U.S. ambassador John Leighton Stuart fully confirmed this view in his book, *Fifty Years in China* (New York: Random House, 1954), p. 164, where he writes that "General Marshall had frequently referred to him [Ch'en Li-fu] as the leader of the reactionary forces which were blocking his efforts." For Stuart's view on Ch'en Li-fu, see Yu-ming Shaw, *An American Missionary in China: John Leighton Stuart and Chinese-American Relations* (Cambridge, Mass.: Harvard University Press, 1993), pp. 155, 190, 202–4.

6. It was in July 1946 that Ch'en Li-fu had two conversations with Ambassador Stuart. Boorman, ed., "Ch'en Li-fu," in *Biographical Dictionary of Republican China*, p. 210, recorded that "after the appointment of John Leighton Stuart as American Ambassador to China in July [11], 1946, Ch'en Li-fu on two occasions called on Stuart to express his point of view regarding the Communist and related problems." He stated Ch'en held that "there was no middle road possible between communism and anti-communism." On April 17, 1947, Ch'en was appointed as the secretary-general of the Kuomintang Political Committee of the Central Executive Committee; see *U.S. Foreign Relations, 1947*, vol. 7, pp. 100–101; Stuart reported to Secretary of State Marshall, who was in Moscow attending a meeting of the Council of Foreign Ministers from March 10 to April 24, 1947, ibid., pp. 102–4. In two telegrams dated April 18 and April 19, Stuart informed Marshall that "it must be borne in mind that the CC Clique while at the moment not in the forefront, is still substantially in the control of the Kuomintang party machinery." For Stuart's two conversations with Ch'en Li-fu and his reports to Marshall about the conversations, see Stuart, *Fifty Years in China*, pp. 164–65. Stuart writes that "Mr. Ch'en Li-fu paid me two visits and talked at length on the Communist and related problems from his point of view. . . . Ch'en Li-fu argues with trenchant sarcasm that, although denounced, especially by Americans, as a reactionary he was in reality more of a pioneer or prophet in that he saw clearly the menace of Communism long before others had come to the same conclusion. I sent General Marshall a message asking whether he wished to hear a report of these interviews."

7. Meetings between Chou En-lai and Marshall might have affected Marshall's attitude toward Ch'en Li-fu. On July 22, 1946, Marshall reported to President Truman that Ch'en Li-fu was "the political leader of the government party [Kuomintang], and the man most opposed to my efforts." See Marshall files, 121.893/7–2246 telegram, Nanking, 22 July, 1946, in *U.S. Foreign Relations, 1946*, vol. 9, pp. 1394–95. Marshall's impression of Ch'en was also affected by T. V. Soong; on August 2, 1946, Marshall reported to President Truman that T. V. Soong was "strongly opposed to the actions, terroristic in my opinion, of Ch'en Li-fu, the political leader of the Kuomintang and the virtual successor of Tai Li, former head of all secret police or plain-clothesmen operations in China"; see *Marshall Mission Files*, Lot 54–D270; telegram, *U.S. Foreign Relations, 1946*, vol. 9, pp. 1439–40, "General Marshall to President Truman, Nanking, August 2, 1946." The issue of requesting Chiang Kai-shek to send Ch'en Li-fu abroad was again pursued by Stuart, on August 19, 1947. Stuart reported to the secretary of state; see *U.S. Foreign Relations, 1947*, vol. 7, no. 945, pp. 254–57: "Last week at the close of an interview with President Chiang I suggested that Dr. Ch'en [Li-fu] be sent to the United States for the observation of our political parties, pointing out that his previous experience there had been in technical and labor matters. He laughed heartily and said that he had himself been thinking of having him make a trip to Europe but that for the immediate present he could not spare him in view of the approaching elections. It was especially because of these that I had hoped to have him out of the country. Since that occasion, however, General Cheng Chieh-min has told me that it might be possible to arrange Dr. Ch'en's departure earlier." On September 12, 1947, Stuart reported to the secretary

of state again about his suggestion of sending Ch'en Li-fu abroad for the study of political party methods in democratic countries; see airgram 893.00/9–1247, *U.S. Foreign Relations, 1947*, vol. 7, pp. 282–83. On December 6, 1947, Stuart called Premier Chang Ch'ün about his concern: "The increasing power of the CC Clique as seen in their control of the government economic and financial institutions [and] its intimidation of liberals through the activities of the Party [Kuomintang] secret police." Chang Ch'ün replied at length "with special reference to the place of the CC Clique as an almost inevitable feature of the process." Thus, Stuart reported that "these brothers [the two Ch'en brothers] are narrow and bigoted but their realization of the communist danger and their courage in meeting it have not been without value to the national cause." As to "the evils" mentioned by him, Stuart "and his colleagues are quite aware of these but the situation is now so critical that any attempt to correct them would precipitate internal disturbances which a tottering edifice could not attend." Stuart reported that "Chen Li-fu has remarked, quoting a phrase from Mencius, that those who are now denounced as reactionaries were true prophets"; *U.S. Foreign Relations, 1947*, vol. 7, pp. 395–96. However, Stuart reported to Marshall that he learned that the "CC Clique was too strong for T. V. Soong to oppose," ibid., p. 294, September 27, 1947, and "also hard for liberals such as Shao Li-tzu to win the CC Clique to their point of view," ibid., September 29, 1947, pp. 295–97. On December 2, 1947, Stuart explained to Marshall that "in a certain sense there is no CC Clique, but rather a permeation of the whole party machinery by the Ch'en brothers whose control of patronage and of the secret police gives them immense power. They are fanatical in their conviction that the Communist Party must be crushed and that its agents, disguised as KMT members or as liberals, are everywhere carrying on subversive activities. There is enough evidence to justify their fears if not their methods." See Stuart to Marshall, December 2, 1947, *U.S. Foreign Relations, 1947*, vol. 7, pp. 382–83. Stuart's response to Chiang Kai-shek's New Year's message of 1949 announcing his intent to retire was favorable. In his report to the secretary of state dated January 3, 1949, Stuart denounced Ch'en Li-fu as "all the evil influence of the KMT [Kuomintang]"; see *U.S. Foreign Relations, 1949*, vol. 8, pp. 1–2. Tang Tsou, in his book *America's Failure in China, 1941–50* (Chicago, Ill.: University of Chicago Press, 1963), states that "the CC Clique and the Whampoa faction were the main obstacles to the pursuit of an effective American policy in China" (p. 377); therefore, to remove and/or send away Ch'en Li-fu, and the leader of Whampoa faction was one of the goals of the U.S. policy in China. The idea was first suggested to the secretary of state in July 1944 by Wm. R. Langdon, U.S. consul general at Kunming. See Langdon's report to the secretary of state, July 14, 1944, *U.S. Foreign Relations, 1944*, pp. 475–77: "One well-placed Kuomintang liberal at Kunming describes the Generalissimo as fundamentally anti-western, Ch'en Li-fu as anti-foreign, and General Ho Ying-ch'in as anti-western and asserts that China cannot embark upon a progressive program of National Reconstruction under such leadership. . . . In the absence of American pressure, he does not see any hope for liberalism and democracy in China." On July 2, 1946, General Marshall cabled acting Secretary of State Dean Acheson asking his "and [John Carter] Vincent's frank and quite informal reactions to present developments and the imperative issues that might soon and suddenly arise." John Carter Vincent was then director of the Office of Far Eastern Affairs; see *U.S. Foreign Affairs, 1946*, vol. 9, pp. 1277–78. In a five-page top-secret confidential telegram, Acheson replied to Marshall on July 4, 1946: "Eyes alone General Marshall," he stated. "We do not believe that Chiang, as some reports indicate, has lost control over reactionary political elements surrounding him or over trigger-happy anti-communists in his army. He is in a dilemma. Neither he nor the Communists want war but he fears the consequences of peaceful agreement. He is closely tied to his reactionary political and military cronies but he is most anxious to avoid responsibility for jeopardizing the success of your mission. Under pressure of expediency we believe he will choose to avoid war but we cannot ignore, as you do not, possibility that he may choose the other course. At this juncture it would be a particularly helpful gesture if Chiang could send Ho Ying-ch'in off on some innocuous tour or mission abroad and give Ch'en Li-fu a similar mission or some diplomatic post." Acheson concluded his statement by saying, "The foregoing are, as you will understand, our informal and personal views. Your own recommendations in the light of actual events would of course be of primary importance in reaching a decision as to this Government's policy and course of action"; see U.S. State Department (confidential) *Central Files, China: Internal Affairs, 1945–1949*, 893.00/7–446. Also see *U.S. Foreign Relations, 1946*, vol. 9, pp. 1295–97. From Acheson (and Vincent's) view, in July 1946, Ch'en Li-fu was an obstacle to Marshall's mission in China and should be sent abroad by Chiang. Chiang eventually sent Ch'en Li-fu abroad in the summer of 1948.

8. Sometimes Chinese Communists presented false reports to General Marshall about Ch'en Li-fu's actual power. For example, Chou wrote to Marshall in Shanghai that "by the personal order from Generalissimo Chiang Kai-shek, all the forces of the Kuomintang Party, Administration, and Army are available at the command of Ch'en Li-fu to suppress opposition forces." Ch'en never commanded "all the forces of the Kuomintang," nor did he command the Kuomintang Army. See Chou's memorandum to Marshall, July 16, 1946, in *U.S. Foreign Relations, 1946*, vol. 9, pp. 1362–63. On the following day, Chou told Marshall in person that Ch'en was in Shanghai to organize secret police work; see ibid., pp. 1371–78, Minutes of Meeting between General Chou En-lai at No. 5, Ning Hai Road, Nanking, July 17, 1946, at 10:45 A.M. On July 26, 1946, Chou En-lai told Marshall that when he "went to Shanghai, Mr. Ch'en Li-fu was at the height of his activities. He authored a blacklist in preparation for violent actions against the liberal minded people. . . . [Chou] therefore felt compelled to reveal his designs publicly . . . that means he [Ch'en Li-fu] is publicly advocating civil war." See Minutes of Meeting between General Marshall and General Chou En-lai at No. 5, Ning Hai Road, Nanking, July 26, 1946, 10:15 A.M., in *U.S. Foreign Relations, 1946*, vol. 9, pp. 1404–10. After some contacts with "liberal and other circles which have been critical of Kuomintang policies," Ambassador Stuart reported to the secretary of state on the same day "they refer to the presence in Shanghai of Ch'en Li-fu, the recent suspension of the liberal newspaper *Wen Hui Pao* for one week, and special police activities including certain arrests as supporting their view." See the ambassador in China (Stuart) to the secretary

of state, July 26, 1946, 893.00/7–2646, telegram, *U.S. Foreign Relations, 1946*, vol. 9, pp. 1414–16

9. Chou En-lai stated to Marshall that Ch'en Li-fu "directed the reactionaries to oppose the Political Consultative Conference (PCC) from behind the scene. . . . The CC Clique are aiming to overturn the decisions of the PCC; they deem that these decisions are to the disadvantage of their own clique. . . . As to the Kuomintang Central Committee meeting, their attempt is to upset all the decisions laid down by the PCC; they are opposing not only the Chinese Communist Party but also all the people within Kuomintang who are for peace, democracy and unification. . . . In the Session of past few days the CC Clique upbraided others almost everyday." See "Statement made by General Chou En-lai to General Marshall regarding Chinese Communist position toward Manchuria, March 10, 1946," in *U.S. Foreign Relations, 1946*, vol. 9, pp. 529–35. See also Ramon H. Myers and Donald G. Gillin eds., *Last Chance in Manchuria* (Stanford: Hoover Institution Press, 1989). Concerning the minor parties, Chou En-lai told Marshall that Ch'en Li-fu's view was that "the minor parties should not wait for the Communists but should participate directly in the Government and break with Communists." Chou reported that Ch'en "openly condemned General Mao Tse-tung as a traitor. He is openly sowing dissensions among the democratic elements and paving the ground for a government organization without Communist participation." Furthermore, Chou stated that the Chinese Communist party "would never pursue the way to civil war to try to overthrow the government." See "Minutes of Meeting between General Marshall, General Chou En-lai, and Dr. Stuart at No. 5, Ning Hai Road, Nanking, August 10, 1946, 10:40 A.M., in *U.S. Foreign Relations, 1946*, vol. 9, pp. 1493–1502.

10. For Chiang's speech of September 12, 1946, see Ch'in Hsiao-yi, ed., *Tsung-tung chiang-kung ta-shih ch'ang-pien ch'u-k'ao*, vol.6 (Taipei: Kuomintang Central Executive Committee Historical Commission, 1978) leaves 251–53. See also speech of Chen Cheng, secretary-general of the San Min Chu I Youth Corps, at the weekly memorial service of October 28, 1946; full text, U.S. embassy to the State Department, 893.00/11–1546; November 15, 1946. See also top-secret report from U.S. embassy to the secretary of state, *U.S. Foreign Relations, 1946*, vol. 10, *China*, November 5, 1946, concerning the factional struggle among T. V. Soong, the CC Clique, the Political Science Clique, and Chen Cheng's Youth Corps. According to the report, "source states Generalissimo has selected General Chen Cheng as his successor and is strengthening General Chen's position." For more about the Kuomintang–San-min-chu-i Youth Corps relationship, see Wang Tung-yuan, *Wang Tung-yuan t'ui-ssu-lu*, pp. 171–73.

11. For full text of Ch'en Li-fu's statement, see *New York Times*, January 14, 15, 1947; see also *U.S. Foreign Relations, 1946*, vol. 10, pp. 699–703; for Ambassador Stuart's comment, pp. 703–4.

12. The close association of Tillman Durdin with General Marshall in 1946 in China attracted the attention of U.S. embassy personnel. See "Situation in China," office memorandum, Mr. Acheson to Mr. Penfield, August 1, 1946; U.S. State Department (confidential) *Central Files: China Internal Affairs, 1945–1949*, 8930.00/8–145; see also Durdin's reports, "Chiang Again Threatened with All-out Civil War,"

New York Times, July 28, 1946; "How Marshall Practices Diplomacy," *New York Times Magazine*, January 20, 1947, pp. 10, 49. For more about Marshall's mission reported as by Durdin, see "General Marshall's Mission," editorial, *The Economist*, April 20, 1946, p. 628, and *China and the World* (New York: Foreign Policy Association, 1953).

13. For a study of Ch'en Li-fu's contributions to the interpretations of the Three People's Principles, see Sidney H. Chang and Leonard H. D. Gordon, *All Under Heaven . . . : Sun Yat-sen and His Revolutionary Thought* (Stanford: Hoover Institution Press, 1991) pp. 125–30; Wang Tien-Shan, *Ch'en Li-fu ch'uan (Biography of Ch'en Li-fu)* (Taipei: Li Ming Cultural Enterprise, 1993); Yeh Yu-fu, *Ch'en Li-fu hsien-sheng t'i che-hsüeh ssu-hsiang yen-chiu (Study of Mr. Ch'en Li-fu's Philosophical Thought)* (Kuo Shiung: Fu-wen Book Co., 1991); Charles Ray Kitts, "An Inside View of the Kuomintang: Ch'en Li-fu, 1926–1949" (Ph.D. diss., St. John's University, 1978); Thomas J. Rasmussen, "The Thought of Ch'en Li-fu: An Ideology of Modernization?" (M.A. thesis, Brown University, 1969). During World War II, Japan highly complimented Ch'en Li-fu's work *Wei-sheng lun (On Vitalism)*: "The Japanese viewed Sun Yat-sen's ideas as only a portion of the Three People's Principles and gave equal credit to the thought of Chiang Kai-shek, based upon Ch'en Li-fu's Vitalism." In addition, "Ch'en Li-fu's Vitalism was understood [by the Japanese] to have built upon Sun's thought but rationalized Chiang Kai-shek's dictatorship"; Chang and Gordon, *All Under Heaven*, pp. 155–57.

14. See also Te-kong Tong and Li Tsung-jen *The Memoirs of Li Tsung-jen* (Boulder, Colo.: Westview Press, 1979), chap. 44, pp. 452–67. Leslie Li, "The Battle for Vice President," in *Bittersweet* (Rutland, Vt.: Charles Tuttle, 1992), chap. 7, pp. 301–15.

15. An estimate of National China's military strength is found in two sources: (1) The Soviet *Pravda* of April 7, 1947, stated that since the surrender of Japan, Americans had trained and equipped 40 Kuomintang divisions, 50,000 Kuomintang police troops and that the U.S. military advisers have established 27 military schools. During the war the United States trained 36 divisions of Chinese troops, numbering less than 400,000 men. Of this total, 6 divisions were trained in India and totally equipped by the United States. The remaining 30 divisions, trained in China and largely equipped by Chinese-manufactured arms, were also partially equipped by the United States. At the time of the article, there were fewer than 36 divisions of these troops owing to mobilization and reorganization of the Chinese army. (2) U.S. general McConnell reported on March 21, 1947, that "the strength of the Chinese Air Force was 342 combat aircraft and 152 transport aircraft, comprising an air force of 494 operational aircraft. There were 430 combat air crews and 186 transport crews. It was estimated that as of January 1948 the Chinese Air Force would be reduced to one-half of its 1947 operational strength, and that by August 1947 it would be totally ineffective except for a few transport aircraft. Ammunition on hand was 13,000,061 rounds of 50 caliber ammunition and 4,000 tons of U.S. bombs. There was ammunition for 10 months of operations and bombs available for 10 months' operations"; see *U.S. Foreign Relations, 1947*, vol. 7, pp. 79–80, 95–96.

16. See note 7, this chapter.

17. For Ch'en Li-fu's visit to the United States and his meeting with Republican presidential candidate Governor Thomas Edmund Dewey of New York, see Tang Tsou, *America's Failure in China* (Chicago: University of Chicago Press, 1963) pp. 118–19, 354, 490. Tsou states that "on returning to China he [Ch'en Li fu] was reported to have said that, if elected, Governor Dewey would take extraordinary measures toward giving military aid to China." Tsou's source was Charles Wertenbacker, "The China Lobby," *Reporter*, part 1, April 15, 1952, pp. 18–19. Wertenbacker quoted from the November 1948 issue of *Sin Wen Tien Ti* (*Hsin-wen t'ien-ti*), a Chinese-language weekly, with the English title *Newsdom*. For Governor Dewey's position on the Chinese civil war, see his various speeches delivered from June 1948 to late October 1948. His position was also clearly stated in his writing; see Thomas Edmund Dewey, "The Red Czar Moves to Conquer Us," *Collier's*, February 10, 1951, pp. 16–17, 60–62, and "Formosa," in *Journey to the Far Pacific* (Garden City, N.Y.: Doubleday, 1952), chap. 4, pp. 97–144.

18. Concerning Ch'en Li-fu's view of the complete removal of the National government from Nanking to Canton, see *U.S. Foreign Relations, 1949*, vol. 3, p. 258, U.S. minister-counselor of embassy Clark's report to the secretary of state, April 21, 1949.

19. On January 13, 1949, Chiang directed Ch'en Li-fu, minister without portfolio, "to seek a direct approach to the Communists," along with Chang Ch'ün, military and political affairs director for southwest China, and Chang Chih-chung, military and political affairs director for northwest China and the government representative during the 1946 negotiations with the Chinese Communist party; see *U.S. Foreign Affairs, 1949*, vol. 8, the ambassador in China (Stuart) to the secretary of state, January 15, 1949, pp. 50–51. On January 20, 1949, Ch'en Li-fu had a conversation with John Leighton Stuart, U.S. ambassador in China, about Senator Sol Bloom, chairman of the Senate Committee on Foreign Relations Committee's public demand of January 17, 1947, for Chiang Kai-shek's removal; see *U.S. Foreign Relations, 1949*, vol. 8, pp. 67–69. For Senator Bloom's statement, see *Congressional Record*, appendix, vol. 95, pt.1 2, p. A272. Ch'en states that "if the United States did not desire a Communist regime in China dominated and directed from Moscow," he felt that "the United States should support any elements in China resisting Communism and hoped the United States would do so." On February 21, 1949, Ch'en inquired whether U.S. China policy remained unchanged. Ch'en states two points: (1) "We non-Communists must stick together, (2) We must find some way to continue the cooperation at present existing between Li Tsung-jen and Sun Fo." See "Ch'en's conversation with U.S. Minister Counselor Clark," at Canton, February 21, 1949, *U.S. Foreign Relations, 1949*, vol. 8, pp. 140–41. On U.S. aid to China from 1948 to 1950, see June M. Grasso, *Truman's Two-China Policy, 1948–1950* (Armonk, N.Y.: M. E. Sharpe, 1987), pp. 35, 132–34; for U.S. ambassador Stuart's and the State Department's position on acting President Li Tsung-jen's request for U.S. aid, see pp. 50–56.

20. For Ch'en Li-fu's view on the situation in Canton, see U.S. minister-counselor Clark to the secretary of state, May 17, 1949, *U.S. Foreign Relations, 1949*, vol. 8, p. 324: "Ch'en thinks neither Li nor Gimo [Chiang Kai-shek] can save the situation

alone and is making strenuous efforts to bring things together. He is suggesting that Gimo come to Canton as party head and that he with Li as head of government would determine policy, Li executing policies." Clark commented, "This of course is just what Li has so far refused flatly to do." For more about Ch'en's views on possible Chiang-Li cooperation, see Clark to the secretary of state, May 23, 1949, ibid., pp. 340–41.

21. For Ch'en Li-fu's role in the Kuomintang elders' plan of inviting Chiang Kai-shek back to Canton from Tainan, May 27, 1949, see Clark to the secretary of state, May 28, 1949, *U.S. Foreign Relations, 1949*, vol. 8, p. 351. On May 26, the letter was carried to Taiwan, where Chiang was located by a group including Yen Hsi-shan, Yu Yü-jen, Wu T'ieh-ch'eng, Ch'en Li-fu, and Chu Chia-hua. The group returned to Canton May 28, 1949; see also Kuo T'ing-i, *Chung-hua min-kuo shih-shih jih-chih*, vol. 4 (Taipei: Institute of Modern History, Academia Sinica, n.d.), p. 874; for more about Chiang's return to Canton and his possible meeting with Li Tsung-jen in July 1949, see Clark to secretary of state, July 8, 1949, *U.S. Foreign Relations, 1949*, vol. 8, pp. 410–12. For Chiang Kai-shek's view on the situation in China in July 1949, see his interview with Scripps-Howard correspondent Clyde Farnsworth, July 4, 1949, full text, ibid., pp. 412–17.

22. In June 1949, Chou En-lai felt that "USA should aid China for reconstruction and he did not favor coalition with elements Ho Ying-Ch'in and Ch'en Li-fu type but felt that without coalition reconstruction might be so delayed that the party [Chinese Communist party] would lose the support of the people." See Consul General Clubb to the secretary of state, June 1, 1949, in *U.S. Foreign Relations, 1949*, vol. 8, pp. 357–60, "The Question of Possible Aid to the New Regime."

23. Chiang Kai-shek returned to Canton from Taiwan on July 14, 1949, and the Chung-yang fei-ch'ang wei-yuan hui (Extraordinary Committee of the Central Executive Committee) was immediately formed. Chiang was elected chairman of the committee, and Li Tsung-jen, vice-chairman; see Kuo T'ing-i, *Chung-hua min-kuo shih-shih jih-chih*, vol. 4, p. 885. On July 22, 1949, Ch'en Li-fu had a two-hour conversation with U.S. minister-counselor Clark: "Ch'en maintained that economic aid must come before military victory." Clark, however, took the other side of the argument: "Although he [Ch'en Li-fu] repeated more than once that he had insisted to the Generalissimo that the Nationalist Government must itself demonstrate its ability to do something before expecting aid from the U.S., he kept coming back with an expression of hope we would in some way reconsider and provide at least stabilization loan or grant." Clark commented that "it was a question of which came first, the chicken or the egg"; see *U.S. Foreign Relations, 1949*, vol 3, pp. 450–51; minister-counselor of embassy in China (Clark) to the secretary of state, July 22, 1949.

24. For a complete list of "war criminals," see the *New York Times*, December 26, 1948, p. 1; see also *Times* (London), December 26, 1948, p. 1.

25. As of September 15, 1993, the three were Madame Chiang Kai-shek, Hsüeh Yüeh, and Ch'en Li-fu.

26. For a detailed study and timely evaluation of the five anticommunist campaigns

of the National government, see Joseph W. Stilwell, "Political Parties and Groups: Present Trend of the Chinese Communist Party," in *U.S. Military Intelligence Reports*, G-2 Report no. 9283, January 29, 1936.

Chapter Nine
The Hopeful Years, 1950–1993

1. Chiang Kai-shek acknowledged his loss of mainland China to the Chinese Communists. Thomas Dewey writes of his visit to Formosa (Taiwan) in the spring of 1951, when Chiang told him that "I will accept full blame for losing the mainland in the struggle against the Communists." See Thomas Dewey, *Journey to the Far Pacific* (Garden City, N.Y.: Doubleday, 1952), p. 132. For Chiang Kai-shek's assessment of the failure in China, see his report of October 16, 1949; text in Ch'en Hsiao-yi, ed., *Tsung-t'ung Chiang-kung ta-shih ch'ang-pien ch'u-k'ao*, vol. 8, (Taipei: Kuomintang Central Executive Committee, n.d.) leaves 392–400. After Chiang's withdrawal to Taiwan, however, one of the most serious problems the National government faced was the ideological crisis. High officials such as Chu Chia-hua, successor to Ch'en Li-fu as the minister of education in 1944, said "the *San Min Chu I* [Three People's Principles] was hopeless as an instrument of political or psychological appeal to the Chinese people." Chiang Mon-lin, former president of Peking University, and K. Y. Yin, head of China Trust, told Robert W. Barnett, who was in Taiwan in late August and early September 1951 on an information-gathering mission, that "the *San Min Chu I* had no dynamic appeal whatever to the Chinese people." Barnett, however, suggested "a [new] ideology, perhaps based upon the Chinese tradition, might serve as an alternative to Communist ideology." See memorandum of Barnett to Assistant Secretary of State for Far Eastern Affairs Rusk, October 3, 1951, in *U.S. Foreign Affairs, 1951*, vol. 7, pp. 1816–27. Barnett's thoughts in 1951 coincided with Ch'en Li-fu's thinking.

2. Hu Shih, "The Gest Oriental Library at Princeton University," a reprint from *The Princeton University Library Chronicle* 15 (Spring 1954), with an introduction by William S. Dix, January 1967. "The Gest Library has premier collection of Chinese rare books outside of the Far East, including many Sung (960–1279) and numerous Ming (1363–1643) editions."

3. The name Mary E. Ferguson is the suggestion of Martin Heijdra, Chinese/East Asian bibliographer of Princeton University Gest Oriental Library and the East Asian collections. In his letter dated October 23, 1992, to Jean Tempesta, interlibrary loan assistant at Henry Madden Library of California State University, Fresno, Heijdra states "the most likely candidate is Mary E. Ferguson." She is the author of *China Medical Board and Peking Union Medical College; a Chronicle of Fruitful Collaboration, 1914–1951* (New York: China Medical Board of New York, 1970).

4. For these letters, see Chiang Ching-kuo, *Chiang Ching-kuo ch'üan-chi (Complete Works of Chiang Chiang-kuo)*, vols. 15 and 16 (Taipei: Bureau of Information, 1991).

5. For the proposal of Ch'en Li-fu and thirty-four senior members of the Kuo-

mintang in July 1988 at the Thirteenth Congress, see Immanuel C. Y. Hsu, *The Rise of Modern China*, 4th ed. (New York: Oxford University Press, 1990), p. 919; Chang and Gordon, *All Under Heaven* pp. 161–62.

6. In his New Year's message of January 1, 1990, Lee stated that he saw "traditional Chinese culture, the achievements of the Taiwan experience, and Sun Yat-sen's principles as the proper guide for reunification." He predicted that China might be reunified within six years; see *China Post*, January 1, 1990; Chang and Gordon, *All Under Heaven*, pp. 165–66. See also, "Lee Sees Communism Dying on Mainland," *China Post*, January 1, 1990; "Lee Sees Reunification of China within Six Years," *China Post*, March 13, 1990. On October 17, 1992, Lee reiterated his opposition to the Taiwan Independence Movement and his insistence that there is only one China; on the Double Tenth Celebration of 1992, Lee told the Chinese citizens that "the struggles of the entire Chinese people for national independence unity, and modernization under the guidance of the Three People's Principles have laid an unmovable foundation for cultural development and national resurgence today." For full text, see *China Post*, September 10, 1992. For more, see CNN Lou Dobbs's interview with Lee on March 26, 1993, *Free China Journal* 10, no. 24 (April 2, 1993).

7. After Chiang Ching-kuo's return to China from the Soviet Union in March 1937, he was first appointed as deputy director of the Peace Preservation Headquarters for the Province of Kiangsi (Kiangsi-sheng pao-an-ch'u fu-ch'u-ch'ang). He took the office on January 5, 1938; see *U.S. Military Intelligence Reports*, Report no. 9623, p. 4, January 12, 1938. For a detailed record of Chiang Ching-kuo's study in the Soviet Union and his return, see Ch'en Chieh-ju, *Ch'en Chieh-ju hui-i-lu*, vol. 2 (Taipei: Biographical Literature, 1992), chap. 21, pp. 239–52, and Chiang Ching-kuo, "Wo-tsai Su-lien ti sheng-ho, December 3, 1925–March 25, 1937" (My Life in the Soviet Union, December 3, 1925–March 25, 1937) in his *Chiang Ching-Kuo Ch'üan-chi (Complete Works of Chiang Ching-Kuo)*, vol. 1 (Taipei: Bureau of Information, n.d.), pp. 1–90.

8. For the election of 1990 in Taiwan, see the *New York Times*, March 8, A10; March 19, A8; March 21, A3; March 23, A2; April 13, A7; editorial comment, March 25, 1990. For U.S. comments, see the Atlantic Council of the United States and the National Committee on United States–China Relations, *United States and China Relations at a Crossroads, Policy Paper*, February 1993, chap. 4: "Taiwan: Developments and Implications," pp. 29–33: "The U.S. government should suggest, and others should state clearly, to the Taiwanese that the automony that is now enjoyed would be jeopardized if the people of Taiwan declared de jure independence."

9. For an excellent study on the U.S. role in the initial stage of the Taiwan Independence Movement, and the U.S. attitude toward the National government in Taiwan, see June M. Grasso, *Truman's Two-China Policy, 1948–1950* (Armonk, N.Y.: M.E. Sharpe, 1987), pp. 45–56.

10. As to the future of Chinese communism, Ch'en's view is similar to the opinion of Robert W. Barnett (see footnote 1, this chapter) and to the view of Ross Terrill in his *China in Our Time: The Epic of the People's Republic of China from the Communist Victory to Tiananmen Square and Beyond* (New York: Simon and Schuster, 1992).

Terrill writes that "in a way it is a good thing that Marxism fails" and that "China is on an open sea before the winds and currents of universal values" (p. 330). He further states that "it is not just that human rights abuses exist in China—the entire system is a fundamental denial of human rights, Communism will end in China." On October 28, 1992, in a news conference at the Democracy for China Foundation in Newton, Massachusetts, Ross Terrill said, "Chinese society is evolving in ways similar to Eastern Europe before the fall of Communism there. . . . Communism is a dead shell, waiting to be swept away." See also *Boston Globe*, October 29, 1992. Donald S. Zagoria, however, argues that "although this dire assessment of China's future could be right, it is not the only possibility. Communism could gradually wither away and be replaced by a looser, more pragmatic but still authoritarian system devoted to economic modernizations. This is what is already happening in southern China"; see *Foreign Affairs*, Fall 1992, p. 216. Robert Scalapino, in contrast, states that "the most likely future for Asian Communism [mainly Chinese Communism] might take a move toward authoritarian pluralism on the model followed by South Korea and Taiwan"; see his *The Last Leninists: The Uncertain Future of Asia's Communist States* (Washington, D.C.: Center for Strategic and International Studies, 1992); see also editorial, "Beginning of the End of Communist Rule in Mainland China," *China Post*, October 19, 1992.

11. "Interview with Ch'en Li-fu," *People's Daily* (Beijing), overseas edition, September 12, 1992; *Shih-chieh jih-pao* (*World Journal*) (San Francisco), September 10, 11, 1992. In an interview on September 6, 1993, in Hong Kong, Ch'en said that the reunification of the people on either side of the Taiwan Straits will be founded on their cultural commonalities, for there is a *tao-t'ung* (a common belief, a mutual trust) in the long history of China that can eliminate those divisions artificially made by men; see *World Journal*, September 7, 1993. Ch'en's words coincide with the view of Samuel P. Huntington, "The Clash of Civilizations?" *Foreign Affairs Quarterly* 72, no. 3 (Summer 1993): 28, that "common culture . . . is closely facilitating the rapid expansion of the economic relations between the People's Republic of China and Hong Kong, Taiwan, Singapore, and the overseas Chinese communities in other Asian countries . . . cultural commonalities increasingly overcome ideological differences, and mainland China and Taiwan move closer together. *China Post*, September 10, 1992; editorial, "Reunify China under the Banner of Chinese Culture," *China Post*, September 14, 1992.

12. See Ch'en Li-fu, *Eastern and Western Cultures: Confrontation or Conciliation* (New York: St. John's University Press, 1972).

Glossary of Names, Organizations, and Place Names

Allen, Leonard G.—U.S. Economic Cooperation Administration

Artzybasheff—Russian artist, painter

Battle of Hsuchou-Pangfu of 1948

Black Dragon Society—Amur Society, Kokuryūkai

Bogomoloff, Dimitri—Soviet ambassador to China, May 1933–November 1937

Borodin, Michael M.—Mikhail Markovich Gruzenberg, appointed by Sun Yat-sen to be the organizational officer (*Tsu-chih chiao-lien-yüan*) of the Kuomintang, 1923–1928

Boxer Indemnity College—Tsinghua University

Buchman, Frank—Leader of the world Moral Rearmament Movement

CC—the two Ch'en brothers, Ch'en Kuo-fu and Ch'en Li-fu

CC Clique—Individual of the Kuomintang associated with the two Ch'en brothers or Kuomintang group led by the two Ch'en brothers, Ch'en Li-fu and Ch'en Kuo-fu, or simply the Ch'en brothers

The Central Club—CC Clique

Central Executive Committee—The organ of final authority in the Kuomintang, excepting only the National Congress of the party, which meets infrequently

Ch'a-ma ssu—Department of Tea and Horses

Ch'ang-hsin Mining Company—Privately owned in Ch'ang-hsin, Chekiang Province

Ch'ang-lu—Noted for salt production, in the Tientsin area

Ch'en Cheng—Ch'en Li-fu's pseudonym in writing

Ch'en Ch'i-ts'ai—Ch'en Ai-shih, third uncle of the two Ch'en brothers

Ch'en Ch'i-mei—Ch'en Ying-shih, second uncle of the two Ch'en brothers; military governor of Shanghai after 1911 revolution and leader of Shao-ho Gunboat Uprising of December 5, 1915, in Shanghai

Ch'en Ch'i-yeh—Ch'en Ch'in-shih, father of the two Ch'en brothers

Ch'en Ch un—Member of the Kuomintang Shanghai municipal branch Executive
Committee and cochair of the Purge Committee with Yang Hu

Ch'en Chiung-ming—Senior member of the Kuomintang, governor of Kwangtung
Province

Ch'en Hsien-fu—Eldest son of Ch'en Ch'i-mei, cousin of Ch'en Li-fu

Ch'en Hsing-shen—S.S. Chern, Shing-shen Chern, noted mathematician at the
University of California at Berkeley

Ch'en K'o-hui—Scholar in Chinese medicine

Ch'en Kung-po—Succeeded Ch'en Kuo-fu as the head of the Organization Department of the Kuomintang, minister of industry, succeeded Wang Ching-wei as the
head of Nanking puppet government and author of early Chinese communist
history, executed on June 3, 1946

Ch'en Kuo-fu—Ch'en Tsu-t'ao, Ch'en Li-fu's elder brother

Ch'en Kwang-fu—K.P. Chen, a noted banker

Ch'en Li-fu—Ch'en Tsu-yen, author of this memoir

Ch'en Pi-chün—Wife of Wang Ch'ing-wei

Ch'en P'o-ta—Chinese communist theoretician

Ch'en Pu-lei—A noted journalist, Chiang Kai-shek's secretary, secretary-general of
the Central Political Committee

Ch'en Shao-kuan—Senior member of Kuomintang, vice-commander of navy

Ch'en Shao-ying—Senior member of Kuomintang, commander of Humen Fort

Ch'en Shih-fu—Member of Ch'en's Moral Rearmament delegation

Ch'en Teh-chen—Member of Kuomintang Shanghai Municipal Executive Committee

Ch'en Tu-hsiu—Cofounding father of the Chinese Communist party, arrested in
1932, sentenced to eight years in prison

Ch'in-shih—An academic degree in the Ch'ing dynasty Chinese examination system

Ch'ing-nien-chün—Youth Army, recruited for China-Burma-India theater, approximately six divisions totally equipped with U.S. arms

Ch'ing-nien chün-jen nien-ho-hui—League of Chinese Military Youth

Ch'ing-nien-tang—Youth party, or Young China party, a minor party in China; it
participates in the National government on a limited basis

Ch'ing-pai-she—Blue-White Society

Ch'ing-pang—Green Gang

Ch'ing-tang wei-yüan-hui—Party (Kuomintang) Purge Committee

Ch'iu Ch'iu-pai—Chinese communist theoretician, secretary of the Chinese Community party, author of *Chung-kuo Latixua tzu-mu* (*Chinese Latinized alphabet*),
captured and executed in 1935

Ch'u Wan-li—Author, professor, and scholar

Ch'ün-shih kung-tso tuan—Military Engineering Corps

Chan-t'i fu-wu t'uan—Corps of Combat Zone Service

Chang Carsun,—Chang Chün-mai, leader of the Social Democratic party

Chang Ch'ün—Governor of Szechuan Province, prime minister of China, and a leader of the moderate Political Science Clique in the Kuomintang. He was closely associated with General Marshall as a member of the Committee of Three, the third member of which was Chou En-lai.

Chang Chung-ning—Magistrate of Hui-t'ung and Hsiang-hsiang counties, head of the Seventh and Eighth Administrative districts, commissioner of Finance and commander of the Provisional Eighth Army in Hunan

Chang Ch'ung—A Russian-language expert of the Kuomintang, alias Kiang Yung-ch'ing

Chang Chi-yun—President of Chekiang University, founder of Chinese Culture University, secretary-general of the Kuomintang

Chang Chih-chung—Chang Wen-pai, Chiang's favorite general, governor of Hunan and Sinkiang, administrator of northwestern region of China, defected to the Chinese Communist party

Chang Ching-chiang—Leader of the Western Hills faction, acting chairman of the Central Committee of Party Affairs, chairman of the Executive Committee of the Reconstruction Committee of National government

Chang Ching-hu—A Green Gang leader in the 1920s in Shanghai

Chang Fa-k'uei—Noted Cantonese military leader, commander of the 12th (Ironside) Division and the Fourth Army

Chang Fei—Noted military leader during the period of Three Kingdoms

Chang Hsiao-lin—A Green Gang leader, key figure in Shanghai purge

Chang Hsien-yun—Communist agent in Ch'en Li-fu's office

Chang Hsüeh-liang—Young marshall of Manchuria, vice-chairman of National government (Council), key figure in the Sian Incident

Chang Kuo-t'ao—Student of Li Ta-chao, founding member of the Chinese Communist party

Chang Kwang-pi—Well-known gastroenterologist

Chang Li-sheng—Vice-premier of National government

Chang Li-yuan—Army commander under Sheng Shih-ts'ai

Chang Ming-yin—Assassin of Wang Ching-wei

Chang P'o-lin—Noted educator, president of Nankai University

Chang Pao-shu—Secretary-general of the Kuomintang

Chang Tao-fan—Ch'en Li-fu's loyal colleague, undersecretary of the Ministries of Transportation and Interior, president of Legislative Yüan

Chang Ting-hsiü—Secretary-general of Honan provincial government, follower of Hu Han-min

Chang Tso-lin—A bandit, commander of An-kuo army, founder of Tung-pei University, noted for his execution of Li Ta-chao, assassinated by the Japanese on June 4, 1928

Chang Tsung-ch'ang—Warlord in the North, Chang Tso-lin's First Army commander, governor of Kiangsu and Shantung provinces, murdered on September 3, 1932

Chang-ti pier—In Canton

Changchun—City, administrative center of Manchuria

Changsha Provisional University—Changsha, Hunan Province

Chao Ti-hua—Head of Ch'en Li-fu's investigation data-gathering team, financial commissioner of Kiangsu Province, noted banker and industrialist

Chao Tzu-yang—Communist leader, purged as the result of Tiananmen Square Incident of 1989

Chao Yao-tung—President of Chinese Steel Corporation, minister of economics

Chen—Small town

Chen Cheng—Ch'en Ch'eng, Ch'en Tz'u-hsiu, commander of the Eighteenth Army, leader and organizer of the San-min chu-i Youth Corps, governor of Taiwan, premier and vice-president of the Republic of China

Chen Chi-t'ang—Military leader in Kwangtung, leader of People's Anti-Japanese National Salvation Army

Chen Ch'ien—Cheng Ch'ien, commander of Sixth Army Group and the Fourth Route Army; governor of Hunan and vice-presidential candidate of the 1948 election; defected to the Chinese Communist party

Chen Ching-yün—Member of the board of *Hua-mei jih-pao*

Chen Hsing—Ancient philosopher, agriculturalist mentioned in *Mencius*

Chen Ju-liang—Ch'en Li-fu's friend

Chen Kung-ju—Ch'en Li-fu's assistant on military affairs in 1935

Chen Min-keng—Editor in chief of *Current Affairs Monthly* (*Shih-shih p'ing-lun yüeh-k'an*), a magazine founded by Ch'en Li-fu

Cheng-chung Book Company—Founded by Ch'en Li-fu

Cheng Kuang-pi—Naval commander during the early years of the republic

Ch'eng T'ien-fang—Cheng Tien-fong, dean of National Chengchi University, Chinese ambassador to Germany, minister of education

Cheng Tung-ho—Undersecretary of the Ministry of Education, author, and professor

Cheng I—Assisted Ch'en brothers to organize the political training corps

Cheng I-tung—Editor of *Political Review* (*Chen-chih p'ing-lun*), monthly founded by Ch'en Li-fu

Cheng-chi hsüan-lien-ch'u—Bureau of Political Training

Cheng-chi p'ing-lun yüeh-kan—*Political Review Monthly*

Cheng-hsüeh-hsi—Political study group, political study clique, faction in the Kuomintang

Chi Chao-ting—Financial expert, worked as a spy for Communists in the National government

Chi Shan-chia—Kissan'ka, General Nikolai Vladmirovich Kuibyshev, Soviet military adviser to the National Revolutionary Army, opposed Northern Expedition plans of Chiang Kai-shek

Chi Shih-ying—Senior member of the Legislative Yüan

Chi-shu yen—Chi-shu Dam, near Shanghai

Chi-yao-k'o—Confidential Materials Section

Chiang ch'ing-tien—Chiang the Just, Chiang Ching-kuo

Chiang Ching-kuo—Eldest son of Chiang Kai-shek, founder of Fu Hsing Kang College, secretary of defense, premier, president of the Republic of China

Chiang Chung-cheng—Chiang Kai-shek, Chiang Chieh-shih, successor of Sun Yat-sen as top leader of Kuomintang, founder of National Revolutionary Army and the National government, president of the Republic of China

Chiang Meng-lin—Chiang Mon-lin, president of Peking University, secretary-general of the Executive Yüan

Chiang Ting-wen—Chiang Ming-san, commander of the Second Division of the First Army Group, governor of Shensi

Chiang Wei-kuo—Wego W. K. Chiang, younger son of Chiang Kai-shek

Chiang-chia t'ien-hsia Ch'en-chia-tang—The country (China) belongs to Chiang's family and the party (Kuomintang) belongs to Ch'en's family

Chiao-ch'ang-kou—An open market place in the city of Chungking, center of student activities, mass meetings, especially 1943–1945

Chien-chiao—Airfield at Hangchou

Chien Hsin-chih—President of Ch'ang-hsing Mining Company

Chien-chiao ho-tso wei-yüan-hui—Committee of Cooperation for Reconstruction and Education

Chien-kuo ta-kang—Fundamentals of National Reconstruction, authored by Sun Yat-sen

Ch'ien Mu—Ch'en P'in-ssu, noted historian, president of New Asia College in Hong Kong

Chih-hsing ho-i—Unity of knowledge and action, Wang Yang-ming School of Learning

Chih-kiang—Name of a city

Chih-tao yüan—Instructor, guiding official, or officer, political commissar

Chih-tung—Name of a warship

Ching-kuo—Chiang Ching-kuo

Chingkangshan—Base of Chinese Communist party before the Long March

Chin Shu-jen—Governor of Sinkiang, a warlord

Chin-chi kai-ko wei-yüan-hui—Committee for Economic Reform

Chin-ling—Nanking

Chin-sheng tsung-t'ung-yüan yun-t'ung—General Spirit Mobilization Campaign

Ching-pao—The *Capital News*, founded by Ch'en Li-fu in April 1928

Ching-shen chung-yü wu-chih—Spirit winning over matter

Chou Chih-yüan—Member of the Kuomintang Shanghai municipal Executive Committee

Chou En-lai—Chou Shao-shan, premier of the People's Republic of China

Chou Fo-hai—Helped to found the Chinese Communist party, Kuomintang theoretician, editor of *New Life Monthly*, puppet premier, received death penalty in 1946

Chou Hung-ching—Noted mathematician

Chou Tso-min—Party worker

Chu Cheng—Chu Chüeh-sheng, member of the Western Hills faction, president of Judicial Yüan, candidate for premier in 1949

Chu Chia-hua—Chu Liu-hsien, German educated, succeeded Ch'en Li-fu as minister of education, vice-president of the Examination Yüan, acting president of the Academia Sinica

Chu Ching-nung—Educator, scholar, president of Kuang-hua University, vice-minister of Education

Chu-i—Ism

Chu Pei-teh—Commander of Third Army Group

Chu Teh—Commander in chief of the Chinese Communist Red Army

Chu-chi-ch'u—General Accounting Office

Chu-hsi—Chairman

Chüeh-kiang—Chüeh River

Chung-yang cheng-chi hsüeh-hsiao—Central Political Institute

Chung-yang chih-hsing wei-yuan-hui cheng-chih hui-i—The Political Conference of the Political Committee of the Central Executive Committee

Chung-yang ta-hsüeh—National Central University, formerly Kiangsu University

Chung-yang yü-lei hsüeh-hsiao—Central Torpedo Training School

Chün-tung—Abbreviation of Chun-shih wei-yüan-hui tiao-cha-chu, Bureau of Investigation and Statistics of the Central Military Committee

Chung-hua Publishing Company—In China, Hong Kong, and Taiwan, founded by Ch'en Li-fu

Chung-hua wen-hua fu-hsing yün-tung wei-yuan-hui—Chinese Cultural Renaissance Association

Chung-kuo chiao-yü tien-ying hsieh-hui—Chinese Educational Film Association

Chung-kuo chih ming-yun—*China Destiny*, book authored by Chiang Kai-shek

Chung-kuo k'o-hsüeh ch'i-i tsung-shu—*History of Chinese Science and Technology Series*, title of a book

Chung-kuo k'o-hsüeh-hua yun-tung—Association for Movement of Chinese Scientification

Chung-kuo kung-pao—*China Gazette*, title of a journal

Chung-kuo kuo-min-tang ko-ming wei-yüan hui—The Revolutionary Committee of China's Kuomintang

Chung-kuo nung-min yin-hang—Farmers' Bank of China

Chung-kuo pen-we wen-hua chien-she yün-tung—Movement for Cultural Construction on a Chinese Basis

Chung-kuo ssu-ta chian-tsu—Four Big Families in China, book authored by communist theoretician Ch'en P'o-ta

Chung-shan Gunboat Incident of March 20, 1926

Chung-tung—Abbreviation of Bureau of Investigation and Statistics of the Central Executive Committee of Chung-kuo kuo-min-tang

Chung-wen i-hsüeh—Learning Chinese Made Easy, title of a book by Ch'en Li-fu

Chung-yang cheng-chih hsüeh-hsiao—Central Political Institute, predecessor of National Chengchi University

Chung-yang chien-ch'a wei-yüan-hui—Central Supervisory Committee

Chung-yang chih-ch'en wei-yuan-hui fei-ch'ang hui-i—Extraordinary Conference of Central Executive and Supervisory Committees

Chung-yang chih-hsing wei-yuan-hui cheng-chih hui-i—Political Committee of the Central Executive Committee

Chung-yang kan-pu hsüeh-hsiao—Central Cadre Training School

Chung-yang lu-chün chün-kuan hsüeh-hsiao—Central Military Officer's Academy

Chung-yang p'ing-i wei-yüan-hui—Central Committee for Deliberation and Consultation

Chung-yang tang-wu hsüeh-hsiao—School of Party (Kuomintang) Affairs

Chung-yang ta-hsüeh—National Central University

Chung-yang t'u-shu-k'uan—National Central Library

Chung-yang yü-lei hsüeh-hsiao—Central Torpedo Training School

Chungking—National China's World War II capital

Control Yüan—The branch of the Chinese government chiefly responsible for investigation of governmental malpractices

DeBary, William Theodore—Noted scholar of Columbia University

Dewey, Thomas—Governor of New York, presidential candidate of the Republican party in 1944, 1948 elections

Durdin, Tillman—Correspondent of the *New York Times*, a newsman of long experience in China

Emperor Ch'ien-lung—Third emperor of Ch'ing dynasty

Emperor Wu of Han—Fifth emperor of Former Han dynasty

Executive Yüan—Executive branch of the National government

Fairbank, John K.—Scholar, author, noted China specialist, head of USIS in Chungking

Fang Chih—Party worker in Anhwei

Fang Chüeh-hui—Director of Political Training of the National Army

Feng Ti—Commissioner of Police Bureau in Changsha, executed in 1938

Feng Yü-hsiang—Feng Chi-san, Feng Hung-chang, "Christian general," commander of Kuominchün, the best trained army in China in the 1920s, burnt to death on September 1, 1948, aboard the Russian ship *Pobeda*

Ferguson, Mary E.—Author, head of Peking Union Medical College Foundation

Five-Stroke Indexing System

Forrestal, James—U.S. secretary of defense

Fu Ching-po—Philip C. Fugh, assistant to U.S. ambassador John Leighton Stuart

Fu Ssu-nien—Supporter of Chen Cheng faction, president of National Taiwan University

Fu-hsing she—Revive China Society

Galen—Galin, Vasilii K. Blyukher, Soviet adviser to the National Revolutionary Army

Gest Library—Princeton University, founded by Guion Moore Gest, a Quaker in religion and an engineer by profession

Gills, I. V.—Author, scholar, naval attaché of the U.S. legation in Peking, cofounder of the Gest Library

Grain, Frederick—*Time* magazine China correspondent

Hami—City in Sinkiang Province noted for melons

Han, Fu-ch'u—Served under Feng Yü-hsiang, commander of the First Army, governor of Shantung and Honan, executed in 1938

Han-chien—Traitorous Chinaman

Hanchung—City in Shensi Province

Hangchou—National capital of Southern Sung dynasty

Hankow—Central China, Hupei Province

Hau Pei-tsun—Chief of the Joint Staff, premier of the Republic of China in Taiwan, vice-chairman of the Kuomintang

Heijdra, Martin—Bibliographer of Princeton University, Gest Oriental Library

Hindenburg, Paul von—Supreme commander of German military forces in World War I, president of Weimar Republic

Ho Hsiang-ning—Wife of Liao Chung-k'ai, first woman to join T'ung-meng-hui, member of Kuomintang Central Executive Committee, defected to the Chinese Communist party

Ho Lien—Columbia University scholar

Ho Lung Ho Yün-ch'ing, responsible for Nanchang uprising of August 1, 1927, noted communist military leader

Ho Pu-kuang—Assassin of Wang Ch'ing-wei

Ho Yao-tsu—Chinese minister to Turkey, special envoy to the USSR, mayor of Chungking

Ho Ying-ch'in—Commander in chief of the National Army, premier of National China

Hoffman, Paul G.—U.S. director of Economic Cooperative Administration

Hsi-nan nien-ta—Southwest Associated University

Hsia Jui-fang—Julie Lien-ying Hsia's father

Hsia Lien-ying—Julie Lien-ying Hsia, Julie Lien-ying How, noted scholar

Hsiang—Village

Hsiang Ting-jung—Leader in New York Chinatown, supporter of Ch'en Li-fu

Hsiao Cheng—Land reformer, supporter of the two Ch'en brothers

Hsiao-hsüeh—*Lesser Learning*, title of a book

Hsiao-wu—Chiang Hsiao-wu, son of Chiang Ching-kuo

Hsieh Tung-min—Governor of Taiwan, vice-president of the Republic of China

Hsieh Tzu—Elder anticommunist Kuomintang leader, member of the Western Hills group

Hsien—County, a district, formerly a subdivision of a prefecture, or *fu*

Hsin ch'ao—*New Tide* or *The Renaissance*, title of a magazine

Hsin-ching jih-pao—*New Capital Times*

Hsin chung-hua—*New China*, title of a magazine

Hsin-hua jih-pao—*New China Daily*, official organ of Chinese Communist party

Hsin-ssu-chün—New Fourth Army

Hsin-ya tung-chi-she—New Asia Mutual Aid Society

Hsin-yen-fa—New Salt Bill

Hsing ch'ing-nien—*New Youth* or *La Jeunesse*, title of a magazine

Hsing-chung-hui—Revive China Society

Hsing-shih su-chien-fa—*How to Locate Surnames [Clan Names] Quickly*, a book authored by Ch'en Li-fu

Hsu Ch'ung-chih—Kwangtung military leader, principal commander of Sun Yat-sen's forces in Kwangtung

Hsu En-ts'eng—President of Chinese Student Association at University of Pittsburgh in 1923–1924, head of investigation, Ch'en Li-fu's close friend

Hsu Hsing—Ancient philosopher, agriculturist mentioned in *Mencius*

Hsu Kan—Minister of food and minister of finance

Hsu Shao-ti—Party worker in Chekiang Province, legislator

Hsuchou—Noted strategic location in Central China

Hsüan-cheng shih-ch'i—Political tutelage period

Hsüan-wu Lake—In Nanking, a tourist spot

Hsüeh Kuang-ch'ien—Dean, St. Johns University

Hsüeh Yüeh—Hsüeh Po-ling, division commander of First Army Group during Northern Expedition, governor of Hunan and Kwantung, noted for his defense of Changsha during World War II, chairman of National Assembly, awarded U.S. Medal of Freedom in 1946

Hsüeh-sheng-hui—Federation of Students

Hsüeh-sheng tsung-hui—Federation of All Students

Hsün-yü kang-yao—Outline of General Ethical Teaching

Hu Chien-chung—Member of Ch'en's Moral Rearmament delegation, publisher of *Central Daily News*

Hu Han-min—Founding member of T'ung-meng-hui and the republic, foreign minister and president of Legislative Yüan, briefly imprisoned in 1931

Hu Kung-mien—Communist conspirator, played a role in *Chungshan* Gunboat Incident

Hu Shih—Noted historian, China ambassador to the United States, president of Peking University and Academia Sinica

Hu Shu-hua—President of Hunan University

Hu Tsung-nan—Chiang's favorite military leader

Hu Yi-sheng—Suspected assassin of Liao Chung-k'ai, Hu Han-min's cousin

Hu-chou t'ung-hsiang-hui—Huchou Association of Fellow Townsmen

Hu-sheng-chiao—Hu-sheng Bridge

Hua-mei jih-pao—*China Tribune*, New York Chinese-language newspaper founded by Ch'en Li-fu

Huang Chin-jung—Green Gang leader, key figure in Shanghai purge

Huang Fu—Huang Ying-pai, Chiang Kai-shek's sworn brother, close associate of Feng Yü-hsing, foreign minister and minister of education and interior, premier, and chairman of the Peiping Political Affairs Council

Huang K'e-ch'iang—Huang Hsing, cofounder of T'ung-meng-hui and the Chinese republic, broke with Sun Yat-sen over party organization in 1914

Huang Li-sung—President of University of Hong Kong

Huang Mu-sung—Teacher of Sheng Shih-ts'ai

Huang Shao-hsiung—Governor of Kwangsi, close associate of Li Tsung-jen

Huang-ku-tun—City where Chang Tso-lin was assassinated

Huang-p'u chün-hsiao, also Huang-p'u chün-kuan hsüeh-hsiao—Huang-p'u Military Officers' Academy, predecessor of Central Military Officers' Academy

Huchou—City also named Wu-hsing in Chekiang Province

Hui Tai-ying—Communist leader, key figure in Shanghai in 1927

Humen Fort

Hunan-Wuhan Battle of 1926

Hung-i-chai wen-chi—Three-volume collection of essays from the Hung-i Study (*Collected Essays of Ch'en Li-fu*)

Hung-pang—Red Gang

Hung-tze-lang—Red Paper Corridor in Nanking

Huo Pao-shu—An economist

Hurley, Patrick J.—World War II U.S. ambassador to China

Ichang—City in Hupei Province

I-Ching—*Book of Changes*

I-tang chih-kuo—Rule the country through the party

Intramural China—China proper, China within the Great Wall

Jen-min jih-pao—*People's Daily*, official organ of Chinese Communist party

Jen-li hsüeh yen-chiu—*Study of Philosophy of Man*, a book authored by Ch'en Li-fu

Joffe, Adolph—Representative of the Comintern, coauthor of the Sun-Joffe Declaration

K'ai-tsao hui-i—Kuomintang Reform Conference of 1949

K'ai-tsao wei-yüan-hui—Reform Committee of the Kuomintang in 1950

K'ang-jih ta-hsüeh—Resisting Japanese University, formed by the Chinese Communist party in Yenan

K'o-hsüeh—Science

K'uai-lo chia-t'ing—Happy Family

K'uo-ta hui-i—Expanded Conference of July 13, 1930, established by Wang Ching-wei, Yen Hsi-shan, and Feng Yü-hsiang

Kai-tsu-p'ai—Reorganizationists, led by Wang Ching-wei

Kaiser Wilhelm II—Of Germany

Kan Nei-kuang—Member of the Wang Ching-wei faction, Kuomintang theoretician

Kang Tse—Chief of Division of Organization of the Youth Corps

Kao Chung-wu—Puppet undersecretary of foreign affairs of Wang Ching-wei

Kao Lin-pai—Secretary of Ch'en Li-fu, in charge of radio equipment

Kao Lu—Thatched hut on high, name of Ch'en Li-fu's residence in Chungking

Kiang I-p'ing—Member of Legislative Yüan, lawyer

Kiang-nan Arsenal

Kiangsu Medical School

King, Galden—Professor, Shanghai Medical College

Kiukiang—City in Kiangsi Province

Ku Chu-t'ung—Kuo Mo-san, commander in chief of the Western Route Army Group, Third War Area, Chinese National Army, minister of defense, governor of Kiangsu, chief of the Joint Staff

Ku Meng-yu—Noted leader of Wang Ching-wei faction, German educated economist, member of the Third Force Movement in Hong Kong

Ku Shun-chang—Communist leader in Shanghai, surrendered to Ch'en Li-fu in 1927

Ku, Wellington V. K.—Ku Wei-chün, premier, foreign minister, Chinese ambassador to France, Great Britain, and the United States, member of the International Court of Justice at The Hague

Ku Yü-hsiu—Dean of Central Political Institute, vice-minister of education

Kuan Tzu—Title of a book, political philosophy of Kuan Tzu during the period of Warring States, 403–221 B.C.

Kuan-yün min-hsiao—Government shipping, civilian selling

Kung-ch'an chu-i—Communism

Kung-chin-hui—Society for Joint Progress

Kung-fu kuo-nan—Together we confront the national crisis

Kung-hsien—Common confidence

Kung-jen chiu-cha-tui—Workers Investigation Brigade

Kung-jen tsung-hui—Federation of All Workers

K'ung-Meng hsüeh-hui—Confucius-Mencius Learning Society

K'ung-Meng yüeh-k'an—*Confucius-Mencius Monthly*

Kung-sheng—Common living

Kung-yeh chien-she chi-hua hui-i—Conference on Industrial Reconstruction Plans

Kung-yeh chien-she kang-ling shih-shih yüan-che—The Fundamentals for Implementation of the Industrial Reconstruction Program

Kung-yeh chien-she kang-ling—A Program for Industrial Reconstruction

K'ung, H. H.—Banker, businessman, minister of finance and industry, premier, responsible for currency reform and founder of Oberlin-Shansi Memorial Schools, Madame Chiang Kai-shek's brother-in-law

K'uo-ta hui-i—Expanded Conference (of 1930)

Kuo Sung-ling—Military leader under Chang Tso-lin

Kuo T'ai-ch'i—Qui Tai-chi, diplomat, involved in Nanking Incident negotiation, ambassador to Great Britain and Brazil, delegate to the League of Nations

Kuo-chün pien-ch'ien hui-i—National Military Reorganization and Disbandment Conference January 1-25, 1929

Kuo-fu shih-yeh chi-hua yen-chiu-hui—Learning Society for the Study of Sun Yat-sen's International Development of China

Kuo-fu—Father of the Republic, Sun Yat-sen

Kuo-li pien-i-kuan—National Bureau of Editing and Translation

Kuo-min cheng-fu—Officially translated as National government, resolution adopted by the Central Executive Committee, October 11, 1928

Kuo-min cheng-fu chu-hsi—Chairman of the National Government Council

Kuo-min ko-ming-chün tsung-cheng-chih-pu—General Political Department of the National Revolutionary Army

Kuo-min-cheng-fu chien-she wei-yuan-hui—Executive Committee of the Reconstruction Commission of the National Government

Kuo-min hui-i—National People's Convention, 1931

Kuo-min ts'an-cheng-hui—National State Council, Wang Ching-wei's proposal

Kuomintang Shanghai Municipal Branch

Kwangtung Provincial College of Arts and Sciences

Kwantung Army—Japanese army stationed in Manchuria during World War II

La-chiao—Peppery chili sauce

Lai Lien—Party worker in Kuomintang, editor of *Chung-yang jih-pao*, president of Northwest University

Lai Shih-tu—Ch'en Li-fu's colleague

Lan-i-she—Blue Shirts Society

Lee Teng-hui—Mayor of Taipei, governor of Taiwan, vice-president, president of the Republic of China in Taiwan

Legislative Yüan—Principal legislative organ of the National government

Li Chen-lung—Mayor of puppet Shanghai muncipal government

Li Cheng-tao—Chinese physicist, Nobel Prize winner

Li Chi-shen—Kwangtung military leader, director of military affairs

Li Chih-lung—Captain of *Chungshan* Gunboat, a communist

Li Chün-lung—Puppet mayor of Shanghai

Li Fan-i—Director, Chinese Radio Manufacturing Company

Li Fu-cheng—Ch'en Li-fu's pseudonym, used for trip to the USSR in 1935

Li Fu-lin—Commander of Fifth Army Group

Li-hsing—Practice

Li Huan—President of National Chung-shan University, minister of education, secretary-general of Kuomintang, premier

Li Shih-tseng—Senior member of Kuomintang

Li Shu-hua—Supporter of Ch'en Li-fu

Li Shu-t'ien—Engineer, scholar, Ch'en Li-fu's classmate

Li Ta-chao—Librarian of Peking University, cofounder of the Chinese Communist party, also named Li Shou-ch'ang, executed in 1927

Li Tsung-huang—Senior member of the Kuomintang

Li Tsung-jen—Commanding officer of the Seventh Army Group, vice-president and acting president of the Republic of China

Li Wei-kuo—Deputy director of Chinese Information Service in Chungking

Li I-chih—Water conservation engineer

Li Yuan-zu—Li Yüan-tsu, vice-president of the Republic of China on Taiwan

Li—Ceremonial, ritual, property

Liang Lung—Chinese ambassador to Hungary and Czechoslovakia

Liang T'ing-ming—Artist, cartoonist

Liao Cheng-chih—Son of Liao Chung-k'ai, senior member of Chinese Communist party

Liao Chung-k'ai—Enthusiastic supporter of Sun Yat-sen, president of Chinese Students Association in Japan, minister of finance, Kuomintang representative at Whampoa Military Academy, assassinated in 1925

Lien-o yung-kung—Alliance with Russia Accommodation of Communists

Lin Ch'i-han—Secretary-general of Shanghai Party Purification Committee

Lin Chao-hsi—Principal of Nanyang Railway and Mining School

Lin Chih-fu—Member of the Preparatory Committee of the National People's Convention, 1931

Lin Shen—Lin Sen, Lin Tzu-ch'ao, leader of the anticommunist Western Hills faction, chairman of the National government (Council)

Lin Tsu-han—Senior member of the Chinese Communist party

Lin Yang-kang—Governor of Taiwan, president of Judicial Yüan of the Republic of China

Ling-shih ch'üan-kuo tai-piao ta-hui—Extraordinary National Congress

Liu Chen-huan—Kwantung military leader

Liu Chien-ch'ün—Senior member of the Kuomintang, vice-president of Legislative Yüan

Liu Chih—Commander of the Eastern Route Army

Liu Fei—Member of National Military Council of the Board of Military Operations, vice-minister of the Ministry of Defense, a communist agent, executed in 1952

Liu Lu-ying—Party worker

Liu Pei-ming—Editor, writer

Liu Shih—Commander of the First Division of the First Army group, governor of Honan, commander of National Army in the Battle of Hsiuchou-Pangfu, 1948

Liu Shih-shun—Diplomat, ambassador to Canada, member of U.N. delegation

Liu Tu—Editor, writer of National Institute of Compilation and Translation

Liu Wen-hui—Chairman of the Sinkiang provincial government

Liu Wen-tao—Director of the Political Department of the Eighth Army Group, mayor of Hankow, ambassador to Italy

Liuho—River

Lo Chia-lun, Lo Chih-hsi—President of Tsinghua University, ambassador to India

Lo Shih-shih—Party worker in Kiangsi, member of Ch'en's Moral Rearmament delegation, director of Kuomintang Historical Commission

Lu Han—Lu Yung-heng, governor of Yunnan

Lu Ti-ping—Lu Yung-an, senior member of the Kuomintang, deputy commander of Second Army Group, governor of Hunan, Kiangsi, and Chekiang

Lu Tzu-tung—Water conservation engineer, graduate of Colorado School of Mines

Lu-feng—City in Kwangtung Province

Lü-tao—Green Island, designated for criminals and political prisoners, an offshore island of Taiwan

Luce, Henry—Founder of *Time* magazine

Lugmets-Orelsky, Ivan Trofimovich—Soviet ambassador to China (January 1938–May 1945) who succeeded Dimitri Bogomoloff

Lun-li—Ethics

Lung Yün—Lung Teng-yün, governor of Yunnan from 1928 to 1945

Lushan—Lu Mountain

Ma Chao-chun—Senior member of the Kuomintang in opposition to Wang Ch'ing-wei

Ma Hung-k'uei—Governor of Ninghsia Province

Ma Shu-li—Secretary-general of Kuomintang, Taiwan representative to Japan

Ma-huang—Ephedrine

Ma-lu nien-ho-hui—Association of Streets and Neighborhoods

Man-tou—Steamed dumplings, northern Chinese food

Mao Ching-hsiang—Military code specialist, secretary of Military Commission

Mao Tse-tung—Chairman of the Central Committee of the Chinese Communist party, founder of the Chinese Red Army and the People's Republic of China

Marco Polo Bridge Incident of July 7, 1937

Marshall, George C.—President Truman's special envoy to China, U.S. secretary of state

Mei I-ch'i—President of Tsinghua University, minister of education

Meng-tzu chih cheng-chih ssu-hsiang—The Political Thought of Mencius, title of a book authored by Ch'en Li-fu

Min-ch'iung ts'ai-chin—People impoverished, wealth drained

Min-chu she-hui-tang—Democratic Socialist party

Min-ch'üan chu-i—Principle of Democracy

Min-chan kuan-shou—Civilian producing, government purchasing

Min-tsu chu-i—Principle of Nationalism

Moral Rearmament (MRA) movement

Mote, Frederick W.—Fulbright scholar in China and professor of Princeton University

Nan-wen-ch'üan—South Hot Springs, located in outskirts of Chungking

Nanking Incident, March 24, 25, 1927

Nanking-Shanghai Railroad

Nanyang lu-k'uang hsüeh-hsiao—Nanyang Railway and Mining School

National Institute of Tung-huang

Needham, Joseph—Scholar, author, head of British Cultural Office in Chungking

Nei-pa tuan-chin—Eight Movements to Health

Nichi Nichi—Newspaper agency in Tokyo

Nien-kao—New Year rice cake

Niu Yung-chien—Principal commander of Sun Yat-sen's revolutionary forces in 1911

Nung-jen tsung-hui—Federation of All Peasants

Nung-min hsieh-hui—Association of Peasants

Ouyang Ke—Key figure in *Chungshan* Gunboat Incident, deputy commandant of Naval Academy, executed in 1926

P'i-yun Temple—In Peking, temporary burial place of Sun Yat-sen

Pai Ch'ung-hsi—P'ai Chien-sheng, noted leader of Kwangsi faction, chief of the General Staff of National Revolutionary Army, minister of defense

Pai P'ing-ch'i—Scholar, author

Paiyo—White styptic powdered medicine

Pan Han-nien—Communist leader, representative of the Third International

Pan Kung-chan—Noted newspaperman

Pan Yi-chih—High official of the Eastern Route Army

Pao-pao—Precious baby

Pao-wei-t'uan—Defense Brigade

Pei-fa—Northern Expedition

Pei-ta—Peking University

Peiyang University—Imperial University of Peking

Peng Chi-ch'ün—Alternate member of the Presidium of National People's Convention, 1931

Peng-pai—Communist leader, key figure in Nanchang Uprising, 1927

Petrov, A. A.—Soviet ambassador to China (May 1945–September 1949) who succeeded Ivan Trofimovich Lugmets-Orelsky

Pi Shu-cheng—Legislator

Piao-chun ts'ao-shu—Standard Free-style Calligraphy, title of a book

PPC—People's Political Council, a quasi-representative body having advisory powers under the Central Government

Pu Meng-chiu—Member of the Kuomintang Central Investigative Bureau

Pu-ti-k'ang chiang-chün—Nonresistant general

Radhakrishnan, Sarvetalli—President of India

Sa Pen-tung—Professor, Peking University

San-min chu-i ti ching-chi cheng-ts'e yen-kai tse-mo-yung—How Should the Economic Policy of *San Min Chu I* Be?

San Min Chu I—Three People's Principles, authored by Sun Yat-sen

San-kuo yen-i—Romance of Three Kingdoms, a classical novel

San-min Publishing House

San-min chu-i ch'ing-nien-t'uan—San-min chu-i Youth Corps

San-min chu-i ta-t'ung-meng—San Min Chu I Grand Alliance

San-min-chu-i t'ung-i Chung-kuo ta-tung-meng—San Min Chu I Grand Alliance for Unification of China

Shanghai shang-hui—Shanghai Chamber of Commerce

Shanghai shih-pao—Shanghai Times

Shao Hua—Senior member of the Kuomintang

Shao Li-tzu—Shao Chung-hui, governor of Shensi, ambassador to the USSR, defected to the Chinese Communist party

Shao-ho Gunboat Insurrection—December 5, 1915, led by Ch'en Ch'i-mei

Shao-nien Chung-kuo ch'en-pao—Young China Morning News, a Chinese-language daily in San Francisco founded by Sun Yat-sen

Shapingpa—Location, outskirts of Chungking, left bank of Chia-lin River, center of Chinese student movement during World War II

Shen Chieh-sheng—Ch'en Li-fu's English-language tutor

Shen Jo-chen—Ch'en Li-fu's childhood tutor

Shen Pai-hsien—Engineer, Ch'en Li-fu's brother-in-law

Shen Shih-hua—Ch'en Li-fu's close friend in New Jersey

Shen-kuang t'ung-hsien-she—Morning Light News Agency

Shen Pao—Newspaper in Shanghai

Sheng Shih-tsai—Governor of Sinkiang

Sheng-chih yüan-li—*The Fundamental Truth of Life*, title of a book authored by Ch'en Li-fu

Sheng-yuan—Element of life

Shih Hsing-chia—Publisher of the *New Capital Times, Hsin-ching jih-pao*

Shih Man-liu—Pilot

Shih Yu-san—Military leader in the North, a key figure in the Mutiny of 1930

Shih-chieh shu-chü—World Book Company

Shih-chien-she—The Practice Society or Action Society

Shih-shih yüeh-pao—*Current Affairs Monthly*

Shih-yeh chi-hua—*The International Development of China*, by Sun Yat-sen

Shimbu Gakko—Japanese military officers' school

Shuan—Instant boiled mutton, a special food of the people in Chinghai Province

Sian Incident—December 12, 1936

Social Democrats—Members of a moderate third party that participates in the National government on a limited basis

Soong T.V.—Tze-wen Sung, Tse Vung Soong, brother-in-law of Sun Yat-sen and Chiang Kai-shek, minister of foreign affairs and premier

Ssu-shu tao-kuan—title of a book authored by Ch'en Li-fu, *The Confucian Way: A New and Systematic Study of The Four Books*

Steele, A.T.—Correspondent for the *New York Herald-Tribune*, one of the best and most experienced newsmen in China and the Far East

Stuart, J. Leighton—Noted missionary, president of Yenching University, U.S. ambassador to China

Suchou—Strategic railway center north of Shanghai

Sun Ch'üan-fang—Warlord in Central China, commander in chief of southeastern alliances in the Upper Yangtze Valley including Kiangsu, Kiangsi, Chekiang, Anhwei, and Fukien provinces, assassinated in 1935

Sun Feng-ming—Newsman involved in the assassination of Wang Ching-wei in 1935

Sun Fo, Sun Foo, Sun K'o—Son of Sun Yat-sen, premier of National China, Soviet expert, president of Legislative Yüan and Executive Yüan

Sun Jung-kiang—Ch'en Li-fu's father-in-law

Sun Lu-ching—Wife of Ch'en Li-fu

Sun Yat-sen—Cofounder of Hsing-chung-hui and T'ung-meng-hui, father of the republic, author of *San Min Chu I*

Sun-wen chu-i hsüeh-hui—Society for the study of Sun Wenism (Sun Yat-senism)

Sung-hua p'i-tan—Sung-hua preserved eggs, an egg wrapped and preserved in pinus lime

T'ai-p'ing Rebellion—T'ai-p'ing tien-kuo

T'an Yen-k'ai—Supporter of Chiang Kai-shek, governor of Hunan, chairman of National Government Council

T'ang Chün-i—Philosopher, writer

T'ang Po-kung—Columnist, newsman

T'ang Shao-i—T'ang Shao-ch'uan, premier of Yüan Shih-k'ai, allied with Sun Yat-sen but opposed to Chiang Kai-shek, assassinated in 1938

T'ang Sheng-chih—Military leader in Hunan, commander of the Eighth Army Group, key figure in Nanking-Wuhan split

T'ang Yu-jen—Puppet undersecretary of foreign affairs under Wang Ching-wei

T'ao-yüan-chün tsung-ssü-ling—Commander in chief of the (Shanghai) Anti-Yüan Army

T'ien—Heaven

T'ung-ting Lake—Hunan Province

Ta-hsüeh—Great learning

Ta-tao k'ung-chia-tien—Down with Confucius

Tai Ch'uan-hsien—Tai Chi-t'ao, Kuomintang theoretician, president of Examination Yüan

Tai Li—Head of military investigation and statistics, top spy of National government during World War II, died in plane crash in 1946

Tan P'ing-shan—Influential Communist in the Kuomintang hierarchy from 1924 to 1926

Tang chün—Kuomintang Army, National Revolutionary Army

Tang kao-yü cheng, cheng kao-yü chün—Party above government, Government above military

Tang-ch'üan chih-shang—Party power above all

Tang-chia-chuang—Name of a village

Tang-hua chiao-yü—Kuomintangization of education

Tao-t'ung—A traditional virtue, a principle of legitimacy that came to mean that the most virtuous men were entitled to rule

Teng Hsi-hou—Szechuan warlord, governor of Szechuan

Teng Yen-ta—Teng Tse-sheng, procommunist military leader, dean of Whampoa Military Academy, executed in 1931

Tien-lei hsüeh-hsiao—School of Submarine Warfare

Tien-yin chiao-yüeh hsieh-hui—Association for Film Education, formed by Ch'en Li-fu

TIM—Taiwan Independence Movement

Ting Mo-tsun—Head of Third Division of Ch'en Li-fu's Investigation Department and head of Wang Ching-wei's secret service in Nanking, executed in 1947

Ting Wei-fen—Key person in Kuomintang in Shantung and North China, vice-president of Control Yüan

Ting-ssu Bridge—Hupei Province, where the Battle of Hunan-Wuhan of August 30, 1926, was fought

Tingchou—City in Hopei Province

Toyama Mitsuru—Leader of the Japanese Black Dragon Society

Trautmann, Oskar P.—German ambassador to China

Ts'ai Kung-shih—Special representative of the Ministry of Foreign Affairs, murdered by the Japanese on May 3, 1928, in Tsinan

Ts'ai Meng-chien—Chief of Ch'en Li-fu's investigation team in Wuhan

Ts'ai Yüan-p'ei—Hanlin scholar, minister of education, founder of Academia Sinica, president of Peking University

Ts'ao K'un—Commander of the Third Division of Peiyang Army, governor of Chihli, head of Chihli Clique, president of the Republic of China, author of Ts'ao Kun constitution; on June 18, 1938, the National government made him a full general, first class, in honor of his refusal to collaborate with the Japanese during World War II

Tseng Chi—Cofounder of the Youth party, member of the State Council

Tseng Chung-ming—Wang Ching-wei's secretary, assassinated in Haiphong in 1939

Tseng Yang-fu—Ch'en Li-fu's classmate, head of the Kuomintang Central Bureau of Investigation

Tsinan Incident—May 3, 1928

Tso-p'ai—Leftist faction

Tsung tzu—Dumplings of millet or glutinous rice flour, filled with meat or sweet stuff, a delicacy for Dragon Festival Celebration

Tsung-Kung hui—Federation of trade unions in Shanghai

Tsung-ssü-ling—Commander in chief

Tsung-ts'ai—Party leader, director-general of Kuomintang, a special title for Chiang Kai-shek

T'u-ti cheng-ts'e kang-ling—Outlines of land policy of 1934

Tu Tung-sun—Senior member of the Kuomintang, legislator

Tu Yüeh-sheng—Banker, industrialist, leader of the Green Gang, key figure in Shanghai Purge, supporter of National government

Tuan Hsi-p'eng—Leader of the May Fourth Movement, vice-minister of education, devoted party worker

Tung Hao-yun—Wealthy shipping businessman

Tung Kuan-hsien—President of Legislative Yüan

Tung Shih-kang—Curator of Chinese Collection at Princeton University

Tung-fang tsa-chih—Eastern Miscellany, a magazine

Tung-lu-chün tsung-chih-hui-pu—Headquarters of the Eastern Route Army

Tupan—Governor-general

Tzu Hu—Temporary burial place of Chiang Kai-shek in central Taiwan

Walker, Richard L.—Scholar, professor, U.S. ambassador to South Korea

Wan-shih pu-ch'iu-jen—Self-help for Everything, title of a book

Wang Ch'ung-hui—President of Judicial Yüan

Wang Ching-wei—Wang Chao-ming, intimate associate of Sun Yat-sen, revolutionary, Kuomintang elder statesman, leader of Wuhan regime, foreign minister, premier, chairman of National Government Council, leader of the Nanking Puppet regime, died at Nagoya on November 10, 1941

Wang Lu-p'ing—Kuomintang party worker in North China, close to Wang Ching-wei

Wang P'o-ling—Military commander of National Army

Wang Shih-chieh—wartime foreign minister who signed the Thirty-Year Non-aggression Pact with the USSR in 1945, president of Academia Sinica

Wang Shou-hua—President of Shanghai Federation of Labor Unions

Wang Tien-shan—Philosopher, historian, and poet, leader of Chinese community in the San Francisco Bay Area

Wang Tsuan-hsü—Military leader of Szechuan National Army

Wang, Tung-Yüan—Close associate of Chen Cheng, deputy director of Central Training Corps, governor of Hunan, ambassador to South Korea

Wang Yun-wu—Scholar, founder and publisher of Commercial Press

Wei-hsin lun—On Idealism

Wei-sheng lun—On Vitalism, title of a book authored by Ch'en Li-fu

Wei-wu lun—On Materialism

Wen Chien-kang—Director of Bureau of Public Security in Nanking

Whampoa Military Academy—Huang-p'u chün-hsiao

Wilbur, Clarence Martin—Scholar, author

Wu Ch'ao-shu—C.C. Wu, Sun Yat-sen's foreign minister, son of Wu T'ing-fang, minister to the United States, Chinese delegate to the League of Nations

Wu Chih-hui—Senior member of Kuomintang

Wu Chun-sheng—Chairman, Department of Education, Fudan University

Wu I-tsang—Acting director of the Kuomintang Canton municipal headquarters

Wu K'ai-hsien—Head of the Kuomintang Shanghai municipal branch

Wu P'ei-fu—Leader of Chihli Clique, inspector general of Chihli-Shantung-Honan, power expanded to Honan-Hupei-Hunan area, murdered by the Japanese in 1939

Wu T'ieh-ch'eng—Public security director of Canton, mayor of Shanghai, secretary-general of Kuomintang Central Executive Committee, and vice-president of Legislative Yüan

Wu Ta-chün—Deputy of Ch'en Li-fu's investigation data-gathering team, cofounder of Cheng-chung Publishing Company in 1930

Wu-ch'ang Uprising (Double Tenth Uprising)—October 10, 1911

Wu-p'i chien-tzu fa t'i yüan-li chi ying-yung—The Principle and Practice of Five-Stroke Indexing System for Chinese Characters, by Ch'en Li-fu

Wu-tao hsing-i—My Way Prevails

Yang Chen-ning—Noted scientist, Chinese physicist, Nobel Prize winner

Yang Hsi-min—Militarist in Kwangtung who opposed Sun Yat-sen

Yang Hu—Senior member of Kuomintang from Anhwei Province, key figure in *Shao-ho* Gunboat Insurrection of December 5, 1915

Yang Hu-ch'eng—Military leader in Sian Incident, executed in 1949

Yang Sheng—Governor of Szechuan

Yang Teng-ying—Member of Kuomintang Central Investigation Bureau

Yang Yü-ting—Manchurian militarist executed by Chang Hsüeh-liang on January 11, 1929

Yang Yung-t'ai—Leader of political study group

Yaolo, Doctor—Sinkiang representative of the National Assembly, supporter of the Kuomintang

Yeh Chu-tsang—Acting secretary-general of Kuomintang, member of Standing Committee

Yeh Hsiü-feng—Director of the Kuomintang Central Bureau of Investigation

Yeh Ting—Communist military leader in Nanchang uprising of August 1, 1927, commander of the New Fourth Army, captured on January 12, 1941

Yen Chia-kan—Governor of Taiwan, premier, vice-president, and president of the Republic ofChina

Yen Hsi-shan—Chairman of the Shansi provincial government, governor of Shansi, premier of the Republic of China

Yenan—Town in north Shensi in which the headquarters of the Chinese Communist party were located for ten years, captured by National government forces March 19, 1947

Yen-t'ieh Lun—Discourses in Salt and Iron

Ying-jui—Name of a gunboat

Yin-an—System designed to protect the salt workers' livelihood and their industry

Yu Ching-tang—Minister of interior, vice-premier of the Republic of China

Yu Chun-hsien—Right-hand man of Chen Cheng, a Youth Corps man

Yu Kuo-hua—Governor of Central Bank, premier

Yu Yü-jen—Senior member of the Kuomintang, president of Control Yüan

Yu-hsüeh—*Young Learning*, title of a book

Yüan Shih-k'ai—Last Chinese governor in Korea, last premier of Ch'ing dynasty, president of the Republic of China

Yuan Shou-chien—Senior member of the Kuomintang, member of Chen Cheng faction, Youth Corps Deputy secretary-general

Selected Bibliography

Part 1: Documentary Sources

The Atlantic Council of the United States and National Committee on United States–China Relations, *United States and China Relations at a Crossroads*, February 1993. This policy paper examines the current state of relations between the United States and the People's Republic of China, Taiwan, and Hong Kong.

C.C. dan ni kansuru chōsa (*An Investigation of the CC Clique*). Prepared by the Special Investigation Section at Shanghai of the Japanese Ministry in China, 1939. Microfilm. Analytic study on CC Clique, 1927–1936.

C.C. Tokumu Kōsaku no enkaku (*The development of the CC Clique's special service work*), 1940. Microfilm. A top secret Japanese government report about CC activities.

Chang, Li-sheng, *Chung-kuo kuo-min-tang cheng-kang chi chüeh-i*, Chungking, Kuomintang, 1942. The platforms, policies, and resolutions of the Kuomintang.

Ch'ing-tang shih-lu (*A true record of party purifications*) (Nanking or Shanghai?) n.p., n.d. Microfilm. Stanford University Libraries, 1965, 1 reel.

Clyde, Paul Hibbert, ed. *United States Policy toward China: Diplomatic and Public Documents, 1839–1939*. Durham, N.C.: Duke University Press, 1940, 1964.

Congressional Quarterly Service. *China and U.S. Far East Policy, 1945–1966*, April 1967. *China and U.S. Foreign Policy*, 2d edition, 1973. *China: U.S. Policy since 1945*, 1980.

Eudin, Xenia Joukoff, and Robert C. North. *Soviet Russia and the East, 1920–1927: A Documentary Survey*. Stanford: Stanford University Press, 1957, 1964.

Great Britain. *Parliamentary Publications*, 1927. House of Commons 26, Accounts and Papers 14 (2953) "Papers Relating to the Nanking Incident of 24th and 25th March, 1927." London, 1927.

——. *Parliamentary Publications*, 1928–1929. House of Commons 23, Accounts and Papers 14 (3188) "Papers Relating to the Settlement of the Nanking Incident of 24th March, 1927." London, 1928 1929.

Hatano ken'ichi, ed. *Hsien tai chih-na chih chi-lu* (or *Gendai shina no kiroku*) (*A Complete Record of Modern China*), July 1924–1932. Microfilm. Stanford University, Hoover Institution, East Asian Collection, 1965, 23 reels.
Reels used for reference:
Reel 1—July–October 1924
Reel 2—November–February 1925
Reel 3—March–June 1925
Reel 4—July–October 1925
Reel 5—November 1925–February 1926
Reel 6—March–June 1926
Reel 7—July–October 1926
Reel 8—November 1926–February 1927
Reel 9—March–June, 1927
Reel 10—July–October, 1927
Reel 11—November 1927–February 1928
Reel 12—March–June 1928
Reel 13—July–October 1928
Reel 14—November 1928–February 1929

Kawamura, Masaru. "Samminshugi no rekishiteki hatten to sono hihan toku ni Shō Kaisheki no dokusai riron to shite no yuiseiron shisō no hihan" ("Criticism on the historical development of the *San Min Chu I*, especially concerning the criticism on the thought of *Wei-sheng lun* [*On Vitalism*] authored by Ch'en Li-fu in the dictatorial theories of Chiang Kai-shek"), marked "Ken renrakuin hikkei Dai-4" ("Number 4 [document] must be carried by a county-level information officer"), mimeographed by Kanan-shō kosho komonbu (Advisory Department of the Honan Provincial Office) (Shōwa 14 1939). Private collection of Yamaguchi Ichirō, Son Chūsan kinenkan (Sun Chung-shan [Sun Yat-sen] Memorial Center), Kobe, Japan.

Li, Min-jun, ed. *Ch'ih-se tang-an* (*Red Documents*). Microfilm. University of Malaya, 1965, 1 reel.

Library of Congress. China / Circular no. 2, *Pre-1949 Kuomintang Party Organs and Nationalist Government Gazettes*. Microfilm Collections on Asia (in Chinese), 7 reels.

Lo, Chia-lun, ed. *Ko-ming wen-hsien* ([Collection of] *Revolutionary documents*) vol. 31. Taipei: Kuomintang Historical Commission, 1953– .
Volumes used for reference.
Vol. 6. The second revolution, 1913–1914
Vols. 10–11. The organization of the National Revolutionary Army and the unification of Liang-Kwang (Kwangtung and Kwangsi provinces)
Vol. 12. Occupation of Changsha
Vol. 13. Occupation of Wuhan and the advance to the coastal area
Vol. 14. Nanking incident and the Shanghai strike

Vol. 15. Russian advisers, Soviet–Feng Yü-hsiang and Soviet–Yen Hsi-shan relations

Vol. 16. The Nanking-Wuhan split and the Wuhan party purifications

Vol. 17. Canton uprising, the Nanking-Wuhan cooperation

Vol. 18. Diplomacy before the Northern Expedition

Vol. 19. Tsinan incident of May 3, 1928

Vol. 20. The establishment of the Canton National government, 1925

Vol. 21. Northern Expedition

Vol. 22. The establishment of the Nanking Nationalist government, 1927, and Tsinan incident

Vol. 23. Tsinan incident of May 3, 1928

Memoranda submitted by the Chinese Assessor to the Commission of Enquiry of the League of Nations. Bilingual edition. April–August, 1932, pp. 207–10.

Mitarevsky, N. *World Wide Soviet Plots, As Disclosed by hitherto Unpublished Documents Seized at the U.S.S.R. Embassy in Peking.* Tientsin: Tientsin Press, 1927.

National Archives and Records Service, General Services Administration. *Records of the Department of State Relating to Internal Affairs of China, 1910–1920,* reels 58, 59, 60, 77, 85, 91, 122, 127, 182, 221.

Oral interviews with Ch'en Li-fu (Tapes) by Sidney H. Chang

November 13, 1991 (morning)

November 13, 1991 (afternoon)

December 3, 1991 (morning)

December 9, 1991 (morning)

December 9, 1991 (afternoon)

December 11, 1991 (morning)

December 11, 1991 (afternoon)

December 17, 1991 (morning)

August 8, 1992 (morning)

August 9, 1992 (afternoon)

People's Republic of China. *The Taiwan Question and the Reunification of China.* Beijing: Taiwan Affairs Office and Information Office, State Council, August 1993. A white paper in English, French, Japanese, German, Spanish, Korean, and Chinese reaffirming China's position and policy on Taiwan. For complete Chinese text, see *Chung-yang jih-pao (Central Daily News* [Taipei]), September 2, 1993, p. 8.

Proclamation 6182 of September 20, 1990: National Teacher Appreciation Day, 1990. 55 F.R. 38971. By the president of the United States of America (George Bush).

Shieh, Milton J. *The Kuomintang: Selected Historical Documents, 1849–1969.* New York: St. John's University Press, 1970.

Sontag, Raymond James and James Stuart Beddie, ed. *Nazi-Soviet Relations, 1939–1941: Documents from the Archives of the German Foreign Office.* Washington, D.C.: Department of State Publication 3023, 1948.

Taiwan Relations Act. An act to help maintain peace, security, and stability in the Western Pacific and to promote the foreign policy of the United States by authorizing the continuation of commercial, cultural, and other relations between the people of the United States and the people on Taiwan, and for other purposes. Washington, D.C.. U.S. Government Printing Office, 1979 Public Law 96-8 approved April 10, 1979.

The Shanghai Municipal Police Files, 1894–1944: Records of the Central Intelligence Agency, Record Group 263, have been declassified under project number NND 863055. Washington, D.C.: Scholarly Resources, 1990. Microfilm. Files represent a large portion of the archives of the British-run municipal police force based in Shanghai's former International Settlement. Reels used for reference: reel 1, D1– D106; reel 2, D107–D655; reel 3, D655 continued; 1929. University of California Southern Regional Library Facility. Activities of gangs and Chinese Communists, White Russians.

"The Soviet in China Unmasked: Documents Revealing Bolshevistic Plans and Methods, Seized in the U.S.S.R. Embassy." *North China Daily News and Herald,* April 6, 1927.

U.S. Congress. House, Committee on Foreign Affairs. *China-Taiwan: United States Policy: Hearing before the Committee on Foreign Affairs, House of Representatives.* 97th Cong., 2d sess., August 18, 1982. Washington, D.C. 1982. Monograph, 1017–A, 1017–B (Microfiche).

U.S. Congress. House, Committee on Foreign Affairs. *Taiwan Legislation: Hearings Before the Committee on Foreign Affairs, House of Representatives.* 96th Cong., 1st. sess. Washington, D.C.: U.S. Government Printing Office, 1979. Monograph.

U.S. Congress. House, Committee on Foreign Affairs. *To Recognize the Canton Government as the Government of the Republic of China.* House Resolution 328. 69th Cong., 2d sess., 1927.

U.S. Congress. House. *Relations with Taiwan: Message from the President* (Carter) *of the United States.* 96th Cong., 1st sess. Washington, D.C.: U.S. Government Printing Office, 1979. House Document, no. 96–45, January 29, 1979.

U.S. Congress. House Subcommittee on Asian and Pacific Affairs of the Committee on Foreign Affairs. *Implementation of the Taiwan Relations Act: Hearings Before the Subcommittee on Asian and Pacific Affairs of the Committee on Foreign Affairs, House of Representatives.* 96th Cong., 2d sess., June 11, 17 and July 30, 1980. Washington, D.C.: U.S. Government Printing Office, 1981. Monograph.

U.S. Congress. Joint Economic Committee. *China Under the Four Modernizations: Selected Papers Submitted to Joint Economic Committee, Congress of the United States.* 97th Cong., 2d sess. Washington, D.C.: U.S. Government Printing Office, 1982. (August 13, 1982, part 1; Part 2, 1985).

U.S. Congress. Senate Committee on Foreign Relations. *Taiwan: Hearings Before the Committee on Foreign Relations.* 96th Cong., 1st sess. on S.245. Washington, D.C.: U.S. Government Printing Office, 1979. Hearings held February 5–22, 1979. Monograph.

U.S. Congress. Senate Committee on Foreign Relations. *The Taiwan Enabling Act: Report of the Committee on Foreign Relations, United States Senate, Together with Additional Views on S.245.* 96th Cong., 1st sess. Washington, D.C.: U.S. Government Printing Office, 1979. Senate Report no. 96–7, corrected print, March 1, 1979. Monograph.

U.S. Congress. Senate Committee on Judiciary. *Institute of Pacific Relations*, Senate Report no. 2050. 82d Cong., 2d sess. Washington, D.C.: U.S. Government Printing Office, 1952.

U.S. Congress. Senate Committee on the Judiciary. Subcommittee on Internal Security. *Hearing on the Institute of Pacific Relations*. 15 vols. 82d Cong., 2d sess., 1951–1952. Pagination consecutive.

U.S. Congress. Senate Committee on the Judiciary. Subcommittee on Internal Security. *The Amerasia Papers: A Clue to the Catastrophe of China.* 91st Cong., 1st sess. vol. 2, 1970. See especially "Introduction," pp. 1–113.

U.S. Congress. Senate Committee on Agriculture, Nutrition, and Forestry. Subcommittee on Foreign Agricultural Policy. *Agricultural Trade with the People's Republic of China and Taiwan: Hearing Before the Subcommittee on Foreign Agricultural Policy of the Committee on Agriculture, Nutrition, and Forestry.* 96th Cong., 1st sess., Tuesday, March 13, 1979. Washington, D.C.: U.S. Government Printing Office, 1979.

U.S. Department of State. Bureau of Far Eastern Affairs. *China Since the Revolution of 1911; Prepared from Reports and Memoranda of Various American Foreign Service Officers.* Washington, D.C.: U.S. Government Publications Office, 1926.

U.S. Department of State. Bureau of Public Affairs. "Economic and Commercial Relations with Taiwan." *Department of State Bulletin* 79, no. 2023 (February 1979): 27–28.

U.S. Department of State. Bureau of Public Affairs. "No Sale of Advanced Aircraft to Taiwan." *Department of State Bulletin* 82, no. 2059, (February 1982): 39.

U.S. Department of State. Central Files (confidential). *China's Internal Affairs and Foreign Affairs: 1930–1939, 1940–1944, 1945–1949.* Frederick, Md.: University Publications of America, 1984. Microfilms, 75 reels in total. Reels used for reference: 1–15. Significant events involving Ch'en Li-fu are recorded. Restricted, secret, and confidential reports, dispatches, and memorandum from the U.S. embassy in China to the Department of State, especially "The Cultural Control of the Kuomintang" in 1943.

U.S. Department of State. *Papers Relating to the Foreign Relations of the United States, 1926.* vol. 1, 1927; vol. 2, 1928. Washington, D.C: U.S. Government Printing Office, 1941, 1942, 1943.

U.S. Department of State. *Records of the State Department Relating to the United States with China, 1910–1929.* Washington, D.C.: National Archives, 1960. National Archives Microfilm published micro copy no. 339. Lists of documents: 711.93/14–711, 935/7, 2 reels.

U.S. Department of State. *United States Foreign Relations.* Washington, D.C.: U.S. Government Printing Office (annual), 1937–1949, especially 1943–1949.

U.S. Department of State. *United States Relations with China: with Special Reference to the Period 1944–1949.* 2 vols. Stanford: Stanford University Press, 1967.

U.S. Military Intelligence Reports (confidential). *China: 1911–1941.* Frederick, Md.: University Publications of America, n.d. Microfilms, reels used for reference: 1–15. Detailed confidential reports on the Chinese troop movements, analysis of warlords' relationship, plenary sessions of the Kuomintang Central Executive Committee, Kuomintang Congresses, border problems of China, and Chinese Communist activities.

Van Slyke, Lyman P., ed. *The Chinese Communist Movement: A Report of the United States War Department, July 1945.* Stanford: Stanford University Press, 1968.

Van Slyke, Lyman P. *Marshall's Mission to China, December 1945–January 1947: The Report and Appended Documents.* 2 vols. Arlington, Va: University Publications of America, 1976. vol. 1, *The Report*; vol. 2, *Appended Documents.*

Wilbur, C. Martin, and Julie Lien-ying How. *Missionaries of Revolution, Soviet Advisers and Nationalist China, 1920–1927.* Cambridge, Mass.: Harvard University Press, 1989.

Wilbur, C. Martin, and Julie Lien-ying How. *Documents on Communism, Nationalism, and Soviet Advisers in China 1918–1927; Papers Seized in the Peking Raid.* New York: Columbia University Press, 1956.

Part 2: Newspapers

China Post (Taipei). 1990 1991, 1992.

Chün-shih wei-yüan-hui cheng-chih yüeh-k'an (Political Monthly of the Military Committee of the Central Executive Committee), Canton edition. The monthly issued under the auspices of Wang Ching-wei totaled twenty-one issues, from January 1926 to May 1928. Taipei Central Library has
No. 1, January 1926–no. 4, April 1926 (four issues)
No. 5, July 1926–no. 8, October 1926 (four issues)
No. 9, February 1927–no. 10, March 1927 (two issues)
No. 11, no date (one issue)
No. 12, September 1927 (one issue)

Chung-yang jih-pao (Central Daily News). Shanghai edition, June, October, December 1928, 1945, 1946. Nanking edition, January–July 1946; August–December 1947; July, November 1948. Chungking edition, August–September 1939; January 1942; April, July, October 1944. Canton edition, March–September 1944. Taipei edition, March 1949–December 1951 (in Tapiei Central Library).

Ho-p'ing jih-pao. Chungking edition, 1942, 1944, 1945, 1946. Taiwan edition, August 1947–February 1948.

Hsin-wen-pao. Shanghai edition, September–December 1938, 1939, 1947.

Hsin-wen t'ien-t'i (weekly, with English title *Newsdom*), Shanghai and Hong Kong editions, 1946, 1947, 1948, 1949, 1950. Detailed record of Ch'en Li-fu's activities.

Hua-hsin jih-pao (Western China Daily). October 1944, January–February 1945. Chengtu, Taipei Central Library.

Journal of Studies of Japanese Agression Against China (Carbondale, Ill.). 1991, 1992.

Library of Congress. China / circular no. 5, *Chung-yang jih-pao* (*Central Daily News*) 1928–1990, Microfilm *Collections on East Asia* (in Chinese), 198 reels.

New York Times. 1945, 1946, 1947, 1948, 1949, 1990, 1991.

Ning-po jih-pao (*Ningpo Daily*). March 1946–April 1949. Ningpo, Chekiang Province.

San-min sheng-pao (*San Min Morning News*) (San Francisco Chinese–language daily. August–September, 1947; January 1948–1968.

Sheng Pao. Shanghai edition, 1938, 1941, 1944, 1945, 1946, 1947, 1948.

Ta Kung Pao. Chungking edition, 1941, 1942, 1945. Hankou edition, April–May 1938; Hong Kong edition, September 1938–April 1940. Shanghai edition, November 1945; January–December 1946; January–October 1950. Taiwan airmail edition, July 1, 1946–May 19, 1949.

Taiwan jih-jih-hsin pao (*Taiwan Daily New News*). May 1898–March 1944.

Tang-chün jih-pao (*Party* [Kuomintang] *Army Daily*). October–December, 1943; January–August, November, December 1944; March–July 1945.

Part 3: Writings of Ch'en Li-fu

Ch'en, Li-fu. *Ch'en Li-fu yen-chiang chi* (*Collection of Ch'en Li-fu's speeches*). Chungking, 1943, 1944. Columbia University Libraries.

——. "Chinese-American Relations as Affected by Communist conspiracy in Recent Years." Response to the U.S. State Department's interview, August 15, 1964, at the Sheraton Hotel in New York. Mimeograph. Ch'en's private collection.

——. *Chung-hua i-yao chuan-chi* (*Special collection of Chinese Medicine*). 5th printing. Taipei: Chung-hua jih-pao she, 1983–.

——. *Chung-hua wen-hua kai-shu* (*An Introduction to Chinese Culture*). Taipei: Council of the Chinese Cultural Renaissance, 1977.

——. *Chung-kuo tien-ying shih-yeh* (*The Chinese Film Industry*). Shanghai, 1937. Columbia University Libraries. Microfilm.

——. *Chung-kuo wen-hua kai-lun* (*A General Discussion on Chinese Culture*). Translated by Sean L. E. Gilbert. Taipei: Cheng-chung shu-chü, 1987, 1989.

——. *Cultura y educacion de china en armas . . . ic con prea'ambulo del Ti-tsun Li.* New York: Transpacific News Service, 1941.

——. "Dr. Sun Yat-sen's Thoughts on Enlightened Government." *China Forum* 1, no. 1 (January 1974): 76–95.

——. *Eastern and Western Cultures: Confrontation or Conciliation.* New York: St. John's University Press, 1972.

——. *Four Years of Chinese Education (1937–1941).* Chungking: China Information Committee, 1947. Ministry of Education, 1943. Microfilm, Ann Arbor, Michigan, University Microfilms, 19–. Washington, D.C.: Association of Research Libraries, 1969.

————. *The Function of the Commission on Land Research and Planning.* Nanking: International Relations Committee, 1934, 1935. Microfilm, Columbia University Libraries.

————. *Hsin sheng-ho yü min-sheng shih-kuan* (*The New Life Movement and the Historical Overview of "Collective existence"*). Nanking, 1934. Columbia University Libraries.

————. *Hsin-sheng-ho yün-tung chih li-lun chi-chü* (*An Analytical Study of the Theoretical Aspect of the New Life Movement*). Shanghai: Shih-shih yüeh-pao she, 1935.

————. *Hung-i-chai wen-chi* (*A Collection of Essays from Hung-i Study*). Vol. 1, 81 essays; Vol. 2, 84 essays; Vol. 3, 121 essays. Collection of Ch'en Li-fu's writings and speeches from 1969 to the end of 1989. Taipei: Li Ming Cultural Enterprise, 1989.

————. *I-hsüeh ying-yang chih yen-chiu* (*A Study of the Applications of I-Ching* [*Book of Changes*]). Taipei: Chung-hua Book Co., 1975, 1986.

————. *Jen-wen chiao-yü shih-erh-chiang* (*Twelve Lectures on Humanistic Education*). Taipei: San Min Book Co., 1987.

————. *Ko-min che-hsüeh* (*Revolutionary Philosophy*). Chungking: Chung-yang hsüan-lien-t'uan, 1944. Collection of three lectures.

————. *Kung-tzu hsüeh-shuo tui shih-chieh chih ying-hsiang* (*The Aftereffects of Confucian Learning on the World*). Vol. 2. Taipei: Fu-hsiang shu-chü, 1971–72.

————. *Kuo-chi hsieh-shih* (*Present International Situations*). Chekiang: Chekiang-sheng ti-fang hsing-cheng kan-pu hsün-lien t'uan, 1940. Columbia University Libraries. An extensive analysis of China's place in the international community; addressed to the local cadres training corps of Chekiang Province..

————. *Kuo-fu tao-te yen-lun lei-chi* (*Collected and Categorized Public Orations on Ethics and Morality of the Father of the Nation* [Sun Yat-sen]). Taipei: Ta-tung Book Co., 1981.

————. *Meng-tzu chih cheng-chih ssu-hsiang* (*The Political Thought of Mencius*). Taipei: Chung-hua Book Co., 1973.

————. *Meng-tzu chih tao-te ssu-hsiang* (*The Moral and Ethical Thought of Mencius*). Taipei: Cheng-chung Book Co., 1986.

————. *Min-tsu sheng-ts'un ti yüan-tung li-lun* (*Theory of National Survival Movement*). Nanking: Chu-han shu-chü, 1937.

————. *Sheng-chih yüan-li* (*The Fundamental Truth of Life*). Chungking: Cheng-chung shu-chü, 1944. Translated into English by Jen Tai as *Philosophy of Life*, with a foreword by Roscoe Pound, dean of Harvard Law School. New York: Philosophical Library, 1948.

————, *Shih-yen chi-hua chih tsung-ho yen-chiu: Cheng-chih fang-mien te k'ao-ch'a* (*General Conclusion of the Analytical Study of The International Development of China: A Political Evaluation*). 1943. Columbia University Libraries.

————. *Ssu-shu tao-kuan* (*The Confucian Way: Systematic Study of the "Four Books"*). Taipei: Shih-chieh shu-chü, 1965, 1961, 1967, 1974. Translated into English by Shih-shun Liu, foreword by Joseph Needham. Taipei: Commercial Press, 1964, 1966, 1972; London: Routledge and Kegan Paul, 1986, 1987.

———. *Ts'ung kên chiu-chi (Started from the Grassroots)*. Taipei: San-min Book Co., 1974.

———. "The Way of Heaven, The Way of Man and the Chinese Moral Ethos." Translated by Andrew Morton, *Asian Culture Quarterly* 27, no. 1 (Spring 1989). Taipei, Asian-Pacific Culture Center, pp. 1–13.

———. *Wei-sheng lun (On Vitalism)*. Nanking: Cheng-chung shu-chü, 1934. Chungking, 1944. Shanghai, 1947. Taipei, 1982.

———. *Why Confucius Has Been Reverenced as the Model Teacher of All Ages*. Asian Philosophical Studies no. 7. New York: St. John's University Press, 1976.

———. *Wo-shih Chung-kuo-jen (I Am a Chinese)*. Taipei: Cheng-chung shu-chü, 1982.

———. *Wo-ti ch'uang-tsao ch'ang-chien yü fu-wu (My Innovations, Initiations, and Services)*. Taipei: Ta-tung Book Co., 1989. In commemoration of Ch'en's 90th birthday.

———. *Wu-pi chien-tzu-fa chih yüan-li chi ying-yung (The Theory and Application of the Five-Stroke Index System)*. Shanghai: Chung-hua shu-chü, 1928. Microfilm, Stanford University Libraries. New York: Columbia University Libraries, 1 reel.

———. Comp. *Wu-pi chien-tzu hsüeh-sheng tzu-tien (Dictionary of Five-Stroke Index System)*. Shanghai: Chung-hua shu-chü, 1934. Microfilm, Columbia University Libraries.

———. Ed. *Chin-chi, yüan-tsui, pei-chü, hsin-sheng-tai k'an erh-erh-pa shih-chien (Taboo, Original Sin, Tragedy: The Overview of New Generation [in Taiwan] on February 28 [1947] Incident*. Taipei: Tao-hsiang chü-pan-she, 1990.

———. Ed. *Chung-hua wen-hua chih k'o-hsüeh chieh-hsi (Scientific Analysis of Chinese Civilization)*. Taipei: Chinese Cultural Service, 1984.

———. Ed. *Chung-kuo wen-tzu yü Chung-kuo wen-hua lun-wen chi (Collection of Essays on [the study of] Chinese Character and Chinese Civilization)*. Taipei: Confucius-Mencius Learning Society, 1985.

———. Tr. and comp. *Chung-kuo chih k'o-hsüeh yü wen-ming* (translation of *Science and Civilization in China* by Joseph Needham). Taipei: Commercial Press, 1971; revised edition, 1977.

Ch'en Li-fu and Chi-ming Hou. "Confucianism, Education and Economic Development in Taiwan." Conference on Confucianism and Economic Development in East Asia, May 29–31, 1989. Reprinted by Chung-hua Institution for Economic Research, Taipei, 1989, pp. 365–400.

Ch'en, Li-fu's letter of resignation to Chiang Kai-shek August 18, 1950. Ch'en's private collection.

Ch'en Li-fu's letter to Dr. W. W. Rostow. March 23, 1964. Rostow's reply to Ch'en, March 24, 1964. Memorandum to Dr. W. W. Rostow after interview, April 1, 1964. Ch'en's private collection.

Chiang Kai-shek's letter to Ch'en Li-fu, May 30 (1955? original undated) on the establishment of Anti-Communist League. Ch'en's private collection.

Chung-kuo Kuo-min-tang chung-yang wei-yüan-hui tang-shih wei-yüan-hui

(Committee for the compilation of historical materials of party history of the Central Executive Committee of Chung-kuo Kuomintang). *Chan-shih chiao-yü fang-tseng* (Policy of Wartime [World War II] Education). 1976. Microfilm.

Letter of Chou En-lai to Ch'en Kuo-fu and Ch'en Li-fu. September 1, 1935. Chou En-lai's handwriting, original. Ch'en's private collection.

Part 4: Books and Journal Articles

Acheson, Dean Gooderham. *Present at the Creation: My Years in the State Department.* New York: Norton, 1969.

Adshead, S. A. M. *Salt and Civilization.* New York: St. Martin's Press, 1992.

Ai, Fei. *Yen Hsi-shan.* Shih-chai-chuang shih: Ho-pei jen-min ch'u-pan-she, 1984.

Allen, Gary Burden. "German Policy toward China and the Chinese Revolution, 1919–1937, with special reference to the *Beginning of Sino-German Military Cooperation.*" Ph.D. dissertation, University of Alberta, 1972.

"Asia: Chiang's War." *Time* 33, no. 26, (1939): 29–32.

Barnett, A. Doak. *China on the Eve of Communist Takeover.* New York: Praeger, 1963.

Bartlett, R. M. "Intellectual Leaders of the Chinese Revolution." *Current History* 28 (October 1927): 55–61.

Bate, Don. *Wang Ching-wei: Puppet or Patriot?* Chicago: R. F. Seymour, 1941.

Bates, M. S., and Price, F. W. "Kuomintang," in Edwin R. A. Seligman and Alvin Johnson, eds., *Encylopedia of the Social Sciences*, vol. 8. New York: Macmillan, 1937, pp. 610–614.

Becker, Carl Heinrich. *The Reorganization of Education in China.* Paris: League of Nations, Institute of International Cooperation, 1932. The author was the League of Nation's Mission of Education expert.

Bedeski, Robert E. *State-Building in Modern China: The Kuomintang in the Prewar Period.* China Research Monograph no. 18. Berkeley: University of California Center for Chinese Studies, 1981.

Billingsley, Philip Richard. "Banditry in China, 1911–1928, with Particular Reference to Henan [Honan] Province." Ph.D. dissertation, Leeds University, 1974.

Bingham, Hiram. "New China's Political Bible." *Foreign Affairs* 6, nos. 1–4, (October 1927–July 1928): 203–16.

Bisson, Thomas A. *America's Far Eastern Policy.* New York: International Secretariat, Institute of Pacific Relations, 1945; AMS Press, 1978.

———. *American Policy in the Far East, 1931–1940.* New York: International Secretariat, Institute of Pacific Relations, 1940, 1941.

Blakeslee, George H. "The Foreign Stake in China." *Foreign Affairs* 10, no. 1, (October 1931): 81–91.

Boorman, Howard L. "Wang Ching-wei: China's Romantic Radical." *Political Science Quarterly* 79, no. 4 (December 1964): 504–25.

Boorman, Horward L., and Richard C. Howard. eds. *Biographical Dictionary of Republican China.* 5 vols., New York: Columbia University Press, 1967–1971.

Borg, Dorothy. *American Policy and the Chinese Revolution, 1925–1928.* New York: American Institute of Pacific Relations, Macmillan, 1947.

Borkenau F. *World Communism, a History of the Communist International.* New introduction by Raymond Aron. Ann Arbor: University of Michigan Press, 1962, 1963. Chapters 18 and 19 are devoted to the National Revolution of 1927. (First published in 1938 as *The Communist International.*)

Boyles, John Hunter. *China and Japan at War, 1937–1945: The Politics of Collaboration.* Stanford: Stanford University Press, 1972.

Brinkley, Douglas. *Dean Acheson: The Cold War Years, 1953–71.* New Haven, Conn.: Yale University Press, 1992.

Bunker, Gerald E. *The Peace Conspiracy: Wang Ching-wei and the China War.* Cambridge, Mass.: Havard University Press, 1972.

Carlson, Evans Fordyce. *The Chinese Army, Its Organization and Military Efficiency.* Westport, Conn.: Hyperion Press, 1975. Reprint of 1940 edition issued by the Institute of Pacific Relations.

Causey, Beverly Douglas. "German Policy toward China, 1918–1941." Ph.D. dissertation, Harvard University, 1942.

Ch'en, Chieh-ju (Jennie Chen, wife of Chiang Kai-shek from 1921–1927). *Ch'en Chieh-ju hui-i-lu (Memoir of Ch'en Chieh-yü).* 2 vols. Translated from English. Taipei: Biographical Literature, 1992.

———. *Chiang Kai-shek's Secret Past: the Memoir of Ch'en Chieh-ju, His Second Wife.* Edited and with an introduction by Lloyd E. Eastman. Boulder, Colo.: Westview Press, 1993.

Ch'en, Jerome. "Defining Chinese Warlords and Their Factions." *Bulletin of the School of Oriental and African Studies*, no. 31, part 3 (1968): 563–600.

———. "The Left Wing Kuomintang—A Definition." *Bulletin of the School of Oriental and African Studies* (University of London) 25 (1962): 556–77.

———. *Yüan Shih-k'ai, 1859–1916; Brutus Assumes the Purple.* Stanford: Stanford University Press, 1961.

Ch'en Kung-fu. *Chung-hua min-kuo tsui-chin san-shih-nien shih (The Recent Thirty Years' History of the Republic of China).* Shanghai: Commercial Press, 1928.

Ch'en Kuo-fu jih-chi (Ch'en Kuo-fu Diary). Original, Ch'en's private collection. Also appears in *Chung-yang jih-pao (Central Daily News)*, Taipei edition, November 1, 1991–.

Ch'en, Kung-chu. *Lai-i-she nên-mu (Inside Lan-i Society).* Shanghai, 1924; 5th printing, 1945.

Ch'en, Kung-po. *Ch'en kung-po tzu-chuan (Biography of Ch'en Kung-po).* Hong Kong: Nan-kuo Ch'u-pan-she, 1957.

Ch'en, Kuo-fu. *Ch'en Kuo-fu hsien-sheng ch'üan-chi (Complete Works of Mr. Ch'en Kuo-fu)*. Taipei, Cheng-chung shu chü, 1952, 1991, 10 vols.

————. *Ch'en Kuo-fu hsien-sheng i-chu chü-pen erh-shih chung (Collection of Twenty Published Posthumous Works of Mr. Ch'en Kuo-fu)*. Taipei, 1976.

Ch'en, Pu-lei. *Ch'en Pu-lei hsien-sheng hui-i-lu (Memoirs of Mr. Ch'en Pu-lei)*, 1949, 1962, 1967, 1977, 1989.

————. *Ch'en Pu-lei hsien-sheng wen-chi (Collected Essays of Ch'en P'u-lei)*. Edited by Chung-kuo kuo-min-tang chung-yang wei-yüan-hui tang-shih wei-yüan-hui. Taipei: Chinese Cultural Service, 1984.

Ch'en Pu-lei, ed. *Kuo-min ko-ming-chün chan-shih ch'u-kao (The Draft Military History of the National Revolutionary Army)*. 6 ch'uan in 2 ch'i. Taipei: Wen-hsin Book Co., 1962.

Ch'en, Po-ta. *Chung-kuo ssu-ta chia-tsu (China's Four Big Families)*. Hong Kong, 1946, 1947; Peking, 1955; Taipei, 1991.

Ch'en, Tu-hsiu. "Lun Kuo-min cheng-fu pei-fa" (On the Northern Expedition of the Nationalist Government). *Hsing-tao chou-pao (Guide Weekly)*. chi 169, July 7, 1926.

Ch'en, Walter Hanming. "The New Life Movement." *Information Bulletin* (Council of International Relations), Nanking 2, no. 2, (December 31, 1936): 189–230.

Ch'eng, Marcus. *Marshall Feng: The Man and His Work*. Rev. ed. Shanghai: Kelly & Walsh, 1926.

Ch'i, Hsi-sheng. *Warlord Politics in China, 1916–1928*. Stanford: Stanford University Press, 1976.

Chiang-chia t'ien-hsia Ch'en-chia-tang (The Country Belongs to Chiang's Family, The Party Belongs to Ch'en's Family). Hong Kong, Chung-Hüan Book Co., 1989. East Asian Collection, Hoover Institution.

Ch'in, Hsiao-yi, ed. *Ch'en Ying-shih hsien-sheng chi-nien-chi (Collected Essays in Commemoration of Mr. Ch'en Ying-shih [Ch'en Ch'i-mei])*. Taipei: Chinese Cultural Service, 1977.

Ch'in, Hsiao-yi, editor-in-chief. *Tsung-t'ung Chiang-kung ta-shih ch'ang-pien ch'u-k'ao (Preliminary Draft of the Materials Gathered and Arranged from Various Sources for the Compilation of the Major Events of President Chiang)*. 8 ch'uan, in 4 ch'i. Taipei: Kuomintang Central Executive Committee Historical Commission, 1978. *Ch'uan* (1). 1887–1928; *ch'uan* (2). 1929–1933; *ch'uan* (3). 1934–1936; *ch'uan* (4). 1. 1937–1939, 2. 1940–1941; *ch'uan* (5). 1. 1942–1943, 2. 1944–1945; *ch'uan* (6). 1. 1946, 2. 1947; *ch'uan* (7). 1. 1948, 2. 1949; *ch'uan* (8). Index, historical table of dates and events, 1950–1974.

Ch'in Hsiao-yi, ed. *Chung-kuo hsien-tai-shih tz'ü-tien. (Dictionary of Modern Chinese History)*. Vol. 1. *Notable Personalities*, 1985; Vol. 2. *Historical Events*, (Part I), 1987; Vol. 3. *Historical Events* (Part V), 1987. Taipei, Chinese Cultural Service, 1988.

"Ch'ing-tang chuan-hao" (Special issue for the party purification). In *Hai-wai chou-k'an (Overseas Weekly)*, Nanking, 1927. Microfilm, Stanford University Libraries, 1965, 1 reel.

Ch'u, Ch'iu-pai. *Chung-kuo ko-ming yü kung-ch'an-tang.* (*Chinese Revolution and the Communist Party*). Nanchang, 1928.

Chan, F. Gilbert, and Thomas H. Etzold, eds. *China in the 1920s: Nationalism and Revolution.* New York, Viewpoints, 1976.

Chan, Fook-lan Gilbert. *A Chinese Revolutionary: the Career of Liao Chung-k'ai, 1875–1925.* Ann Arbor, Michigan, 1974.

Chang, Carsun (Chang Chün-mai). *The Third Force in China.* New York: Bookman Associates, 1952.

Chang, Jen-chi. *Pre-Communist China's Rural School and Community.* Boston: Christopher Publishing House, 1960.

Chang, Kuo-hsin. *Kuo-min-tang hsin-chün-fa hun-chan shih-liao* (*History of the Chaotic Wars Fought among the New Warlords of the Kuomintang*). Harbin: Heilunkiang jen-min chü-pan-she, 1982.

Chang, Sidney H., and Leonard H. D. Gordon. *All Under Heaven: Sun Yat-sen and His Revolutionary Thought.* Stanford: Hoover Institution Press, 1991.

————. *Bibliography of Sun Yat-sen in China's Republican Revolution, 1883–1925.* Lanham, Md.: University Press of America, 1990.

Chang, Wen-t'ien. *Chung-kuo hsin-tai ko-ming yun-tung shih* (*History of China's Modern Revolutionary Movement*). Yenan, 1933; Beijing, 1991.

Chapman, H. Owen. *The Chinese Revolution 1926–1927: A Record of the Period under Communist Control as Seen from the Nationalist Capital, Hankow.* London: Constable & Co., 1928; Westport, Conn.: Hyperion, 1977.

Chassin, Lionel May. *The Communist Conquest of China: A History of the Civil War, 1945–1949.* Translated by Timothy Osato and Louis Gelas. Cambridge, Mass.: Harvard University Press, 1965, 1966; London: Weidenfeld and Nicolson, 1966. Original French edition, *La Conquête de la Chine par Mao Tse'-tung, 1945–1949.* Paris: Payot, 1952.

Chen, Jie. *Ideology in U.S. Foreign Policy: Case Studies in U.S. China Policy.* Westport, Conn.: Praeger, 1992.

Cheng, Ronald Yu Soong. *The Financing of Public Education in China: A Factual Analysis of Its Major Problems of Reconstruction.* Shanghai: Commercial Press, 1935.

Cheng Tien-fong (Ch'eng T'ien-fang). *A History of Sino-Russian Relations.* Washington, D.C.: Public Affairs Press, 1957, 1971, 1973.

Chennault, Claire L. "If Red China Strikes." *Collier's*, November 18, 1950.

Chi, Kao-yü. *Chiang Ching-kuo ti i-sheng* (*The Life of Chiang Ching-kuo*). Taipei: Biographical Literature, 1987. Includes chronological biography, pp. 294–301.

Chiang, Ching-kuo. *Chiang Ching-kuo ch'üan-chi* (*Complete Works of Chiang Ching-kuo*). Taipei: Bureau of Information, 1991, 25 vols.

Chiang, Kai-shek. *China's Destiny.* Authorized translation by Wang Chung-hui, with an introduction by Lin Yutang. New York: Macmillan Co., 1947.

————. *The New Life Movement.* Peiping: The Peiping Chronicle, (China Chronicle no. 3), June 1934.

————. *Resistance and Reconstruction; Messages During China's Six Years of War, 1937–1943*. New York. Harper & Brothers, 1943

————. *Soviet Russia in China, A Summing-up at Seventy*. New York: Farrar, Straus and Cudahy, 1957; revised abridged edition, 1965.

Chiang, Mei-ling (Madame Chiang Kai-shek). *Sian: A Coup d'Etat. A Fortnight in Sian: Extracts from a Diary by Chiang Kai-shek*. Shanghai: China Publishing Co., 1937.

————. "Conversations with Mikhail Markovich Borodin." *China Post*, October 29, 1976, pp. 5–8.

Chiang, Yung-ching. *Hu Han-min hsien-sheng nien-p'u (Chronological Biography of Hu Han-min)*. Taipei: Kuomintang Central Executive Committee Historical Commission, 1978.

————. *Po-lo-ting yü Wu-han cheng-chüan (Michael Borodin and Wuhan Regime)*. Taipei: Chung-hua Book Co., 1961, 1963, 1966, 1967.

China Yearbook. Tientsin and Shanghai editions, 1928–1936. Shanghai, 1936–1937. New York: Macmillan, 1937–1943; publication suspended 1947–1949. Continued annually in Taipei, 1950–.

"China's Ch'en Li-fu: The Essence of Life is the Performance of Benevolence." *Time* 49, no. 21 (May 26, 1947): 33–36.

Chou, Ts'ê-tsung. *The May Fourth Movement, Intellectual Revolution in Modern China*. Cambridge, Mass.: Harvard University Press, 1960.

Chu, Samuel C. "The New Life Movement, 1933–1937." In John E. Lane, ed. *Researches in the Social Sciences on China*. Microfilm, New York, Columbia University East Asian Institute Studies, no. 3, 1957. Essays and abstracts by graduates of the East Asian Institute, Columbia University.

Chung-kuo Kuo-min-tang chung-yang wei-yüan-hui tang-shih shih-liao pien-tsuan wei-yüan-hui (Committee for the compilation of historical materials of the party history of the Central Executive Committee of Chung-kuo Kuo-min-tang), ed. *Chung-kuo Kuo-min-tang ch'i-shih-nien ta-shih nien-piao (Historical Table of Dates and Major Events of Chung-kuo Kuomintang for the Past Seventy Years* [November 24, 1894–October 24, 1964]). Taipei, November 24, 1964.

————. *Pa-shih-nien ta-shih nien-piao (Historical Table of Dates and Major Events of Chung-kuo Kuomintang for the Past Eighty Years* [October 27, 1894–June 30, 1974]). Taipei, August 31, 1974.

————. *Chiu-shih-nien ta-shih nien-piao (Historical Table of Dates and Major Events of Chung-kuo Kuomintang for the Past Ninety Years* [January 30, 1895–June 30, 1984]). Taipei, November 24, 1984

Chung-kuo Kuo-min-tang chung-yang wei-yüan-hui tang-shih wei-yüan-hui (Committee for the Compilation of historical materials of the Central Executive Committee of Chung-kuo Kuo-min-tang), ed. *Ch'en Kuo-fu hsien-sheng pei-nien ta-ch'en chi-nien chi (Collected Essays in Commemoration of the Centenary of the Birth of Mr. Ch'en Kuo-fu)*. Taipei: China Cultural Service, 1991. Fifty-nine essays in total, chronological biography, pp. 399–439.

Chung-yang lu-chün chün-kuan hsüeh-hsiao shih-kao (Draft History of the Central Military Officers' School), vol. 10, Nanking, 1936; reprinted as *Huang-p'u chün-hsiao shih-kao (Draft History of Huang-p'u Military School)*, vol. 12, Beijing, Tang-an ch'u-pan she, 1989. Ch'en Kuo-fu's contributions recorded.

Coble, Parks M. *Facing Japan: Chinese Politics and Japanese Imperialism, 1931–1937.* Boston, Mass.: Council on East Asian Studies, Harvard University, 1991.

"Communists Name Chiang a Criminal." *New York Times*, December 26, 1948.

Copper, John F. "Taiwan: A Nation in Transition." *Current History*, April 1989.

Corwin, E. S. "Some Observations on the Organic Law." *China Tomorrow* 1, no. 2, (1928): 17–20.

Crozier, Brian. *The Man Who Lost China: The First Full Biography of Chiang Kai-shek*, with the collaboration of Eric Chou. New York: Charles Scribner's Sons. 1976.

Curran, Thomas Daniel. "Educational and Society in Republican China" Ph.D. dissertation, Columbia University, 1986; Ann Arbor, University Microfilms International, 1986.

DeBary, Wm. Theodore. *Sources of Chinese Tradition*. New York: Columbia University Press, 1961.

Dewey, Thomas Edmund. "The Red Czar Moves to Conquer Us." *Collier's*, February 10, 1951.

———. *Journey to the Far Pacific*. Garden City, N.Y.: Doubleday 1952.

Dirlik, Arif. "The Ideological Foundations of the New Life Movement: A Study in Counterrevolution." *Journal of Asian Studies* 34, no. 4, (August 1975): 945–80.

———. *The Origins of Chinese Communism*. New York: Oxford University Press, 1989.

Dull, Paul S. "The Assassination of Chang Tso-lin." *Far Eastern Quarterly*, 11, no. 4, (August 1952): 453–63.

Durdin, Tillman. *China and the World*. New York: Foreign Policy Association, 1953. (Second part of the book: *The Rebirth of Formosa*, by Robert Aura Smith).

Eastman, Lloyd E. *The Abortive Revolution, China under Nationalist Rule, 1927–1937*. Cambridge Mass.: Harvard University Press, 1974.

———. *Seeds of Destruction, Nationalist China in War and Revolution, 1937–1949*. Stanford: Stanford University Press, 1984.

Esherick, Joseph, ed. *Last Chance in China: The World War II Despatches of John Stewart*. New York: Random House, 1974, 1975, 1984.

Eudin, Xenia Joukoff, and North, Robert C. *Soviet Russia and The East, 1920–1927: A Documentary Survey*. Stanford: Stanford University Press, 1964.

Fairbank, John K. *China: A New History*. Cambridge, Mass.: The Belknap Press of Harvard University Press, 1992.

———. *Chinabound: a Fifty Year Memoir*. New York: Harper and Row, 1982: Chinese translation, 1992.

———. Personal letter to John Carter Vincent, December 6, 1945 (confidential) *U.S.*

State Department Central Files: China Internal Affairs, 1945–1949, 893.00/1–446, 1P.

———. Preface to *An Unauthorized Digest of L.A. Bereznii, a Critique of American Bourgeois Historiography on China: Problems of Social Development in the Nineteenth and Early Twentieth Centuries*. Leningrad: Leningrad University, 1968, distributed by the East Asian Research Center, Harvard University.

———. *The United States and China*. Cambridge, Mass.: Harvard University Press, 1979.

Fairbank, John K. and Albert Feuerwerker, eds. *Republican China 1912–1949*, vols. 12 and 13 of Denis Twitchet and John K. Fairbank, eds. *The Cambridge History of China*. New York: Cambridge University Press, 1978–1986.

Fairbank, Wilma. *America's Cultural Experiment in China, 1942–1949*. Cultural Relations Programs of the U.S. Department of State, Publication 8839, Historical Studies no. 1. Washington, D.C.: U.S. Department of State Bureau of Educational and Cultural Affairs 108, 1976.

Fang, Chin-yen. "The Sian Incident: A Republic in the Coming of the Sino-Japanese War, 1937–1945 in China." Ph.D. dissertation, American University, 1977; microfilm, Ann Arbor, Michigan, University Microfilms, 1983.

Feldman, Harvey J. "Taiwan and Future Sino-American Relations." In William T. Tow, ed. *Building Sino-American Relations: An Analysis for the 1990s*. New York: Paragon House, 1991.

"Fifteen Years of U.S.-Chinese Relations (Events in the Far East, July 1937–March 1952)." *The Reporter*, August 15, 1952.

Fitterer, G. Raymond. *A History of the University of Pittsburgh School of Engineering*. Pittsburgh, Pa.: University of Pittsburgh School of Engineering. 1991.

Flynn, John Thomas. *The Lattimore Story: The Full Story of the Most Incredible Conspiracy of Our Time*. New York, Devin-Adair, 1953, 1962.

Foreign Policy Association. "The Rise of the Kuomintang." *Information Service* 4 (1928–1929): 156–86.

Fox, John P. *Germany and The Far Eastern Crisis, 1931–1938, A Study in Diplomacy and Ideology*. New York: Oxford University Press, 1982.

Freyn, Hubert. *Chinese Education in the War*. New York, Kelly & Walsh, 1940; reprinted, Taipei, 1974.

Fung, Edmund, S.T. "Anti-imperialism and the Left Guomindang." *Modern China*, 11, no. 1 (1985).

Galliechio, Marc S. *The Cold War Begins in Asia: American East Asian Policy and the Fall of the Japanese Empire*. New York: Columbia University Press, 1988.

Gillin, Donald G. *Warlord: Yen Hsi-shan in Shansi Province, 1911–1949*. Princeton, N.J.: Princeton University Press, 1967.

Gonzalez, David. "John K. Fairbank, China Scholar of Wide Influence." *New York Times*. September 16, 1991, B11.

———. "John K. Fairbank, Leading China scholar." Times News Service, September 16, 1991.

Gordon, Leonard H. D. "Japan's Abortive Colonial Venture in Taiwan, 1874." *Journal of Modern History* 37, no. 2 (June 1965): 171–85.

———. "American Planning for Taiwan: 1942–1945." *Pacific Historical Review* 37, no. 2 (May 1968): 201–28.

———. "The Lesson of Taiwan: A Second Look." *Pacific Historical Review* 50, no. 4 (November 1976): 539–67.

———. "United States Opposition to Use of Force in the Taiwan Strait, 1954–1962." *Journal of American History* 73, no. 3 (December 1985): 637–60.

———. "Taiwan and the Limits of British Power, 1868." *Modern Asian Studies* 22, no. 2 (May 1988): 225–35.

Gordon, Leonard H. D., and Sidney H. Chang. "John K. Fairbank and His Critics in the Republic of China." *Journal of Asian Studies* 30, no. 1. (November 1970): 137–49.

Grasso, June M. *Truman's Two-China Policy, 1948–1950.* New York: M.E. Sharpe, 1987.

Hao-men nên-mu (Inside Powerful Families). Shanghai: Hsiao-lü-Sung Book Co., 1947. East Asian Collection, Hoover Institution.

Hartgen, Stephen Anthony. "The Interpretation of the Chinese Communist Revolution, 1945–1949 by Four American Daily Newspapers." Ph.D. dissertation, University of Minnesota, 1976; microfilm, Ann Arbor, Mich.: University Microfilms, 1976.

Heale, M.J. *American Anti-communism: Combating the Enemy Within, 1830–1970.* Baltimore: Johns Hopkins University Press, 1990.

Ho, Chung-hsiao. *Ch'en Ying-shih (Ch'i-mei) hsien-sheng nien-p'u (Chronological Biography of Mr. Ch'en Ying-shih [Ch'en Ch'i-mei]).* Taipei: Wen-hai chü-pan-she, 1975.

———. *Ch'en Ying-shih hsien-sheng chi-nien chüan-chi (Complete Collected Works in Commemoration of Mr. Ch'en Ying-shih).* Vol. 2. Taipei: Wen-hai chü-pan she, 1970, 1971.

Ho, Jui-yao. *Feng-yün jen-wu hsiao-chih* (Brief Notes on the Men of Our Time). Taipei: Wen-hai chü-pan she, 1973. Orginally published as *Fu-hsing-kuan hsia jen-wu hsiao-chih (Brief Notes on the Men of Our Time at Fu-hsing-kuan* [in Chungking]), 1947.

Ho, Ying-ch'in. *Ho Ying-ch'in chiang-chün chiu-wu chi-shih chiang-pien (Commemorative Essays Gathered and Arranged from Various Sources for the 95th Birthday of General Ho Ying-ch'in).* 2 vols. Taipei: Li-ming Cultural Enterprise, 1984.

Hobart, Alice Tisdale (Nourse). *Within the Walls of Nanking.* New York: Macmillan, 1929.

Holubuychy, Lydia. *Michael Borodin and the Chinese Revolution, 1923–1925.* Ann Arbor, Mich.: Microfilms International, 1979.

Hou, Fu-wu (Franklin W. Houn). *Central Government of China, 1912–1928: an Institutional Study.* Madison: University of Wisconsin Press, 1957; Westport, Conn., Greenwood Press, 1957, 1974.

Hsieh, Winston. *The Ideas and Ideals of a Warlord: Ch'en Chiung-ming (1878–1933).* Papers in China, no. 16. East Asian Center, Harvard University, 1962.

Hsiung, James C., and Steven I. Levine, eds. *China's Bitter Victory: The War with Japan, 1937–1945.* Armonk, N.Y.: M.E. Sharpe, 1992.

Hsiung, James C., ed. *Congress, the Presidency, and the Taiwan Relations Act.* New York: Praeger, 1985.

Hsu, En-tseng. *The Invisible Conflict.* Hong Kong: Dragonfly Books, 1956, 1962; Hong Kong: China Viewpoints, 1958.

———. *Hsi-shuo chung-t'ung chün-t'ung (Detailed Discussion on the Central Bureau of Investigation and Military Bureau of Investigation).* Taipei: Biographical Literature, 1992. Partially based on the oral interviews of Ch'en Li-fu.

Hsu, Immanuel C. Y. *China after Mao: The Search for a New Order.* 2d ed. New York: Oxford University Press, 1990.

———. *The Rise of Modern China.* 4th ed. New York: Oxford University Press, 1990.

Hsu, Kai-yü. *Chou En-lai, China's Gray Eminence.* Garden City, N.Y.: Doubleday, 1968.

———. Wen-I-to. Boston: Twayne Publishers, 1980.

Hu, Han-min. "Wang Ching-wei kuo-chieh kung-ch'an-tang chih yun-yuan yü ch'ing-kuo" (*The Origin and the History of Wang Ching-wei's Illicit Connection with Communists*). *Chung-yang jih-pao* (Central Daily News), Nanking edition, August 18, 1930.

Hu, Shih. "The Gest Oriental Library at Princeton University." Reprinted from *The Princeton University Library Chronicle* 15 (Spring 1954), with an introduction by William S. Dix, January 1967.

Huang, Hsü-ch'u. "Kuang-hsi yü chung-yang nien-yü-nien-lai p'ei-huan li-ho i-shu" (*Reminiscences of the Vicissitudes of Relations between Kwangsi and the Central Government during the Past Twenty-odd Years*). *Ch'un-chiu tsa-chih (Ch'un-chiu Magazine)* (Hong Kong) 123–27 (August 16–October 16, 1962).

Huang, Mei-ch'en, and Huang Chang-yüan, eds. *Wang Ching-wei kuo-min cheng-fu ch'êng-li (The Founding of Wang Ching-wei's National Government).* Shanghai: Jen-min ch'u-pen-she, 1987.

Huntington, Samuel P. "The Clash of Civilizations?" *Foreign Affairs Quarterly* 72, no. 3 (Summer 1993): 22–49.

Impey, Lawrence. *The Chinese Army Considered as a Military Force.* Tientsin: Tientsin Press Ltd., 1925.

Isaacs, Harold Robert. *The Tragedy of the Chinese Revolution.* 2d rev. ed. Stanford: Stanford University Press, 1961.

———. "Documents on the Comintern and the Chinese Revolution." *China Quarterly*, no. 45 (January–March, 1971): 100–115.

Iwai, Eiichi (Hidakusu) (Japanese vice-consul in Shanghai). (Secret Report), *Ranisha ni kansuru chōsa (An Investigation of the Blue Shirts Society)*. Research Division of the Foreign Ministry, Japan, 1937. Translated into English by John Edgar Hoover, director, U.S. Federal Bureau of Investigation on March 30, 1945, with the approval of assistant chief of state as *The Chinese Lan-i Society*. With (1) (confidential) *Investigation Pertaining to the Lan-i-she* (as of March 1938), published by Section 5 of the Investigation Bureau of the Ministry of Foreign Affairs of Japan, "Its Relation to the C.C. Band," pp. 73–77, and (2) (confidential) *Rules and Regulations Pertaining to the Lan-i-she* (Blue Shirts Society), published February 1938, by Section 3, Investigation Bureau (Department) of Ministry of Foreign Affairs of Japan. *U.S. Military Intelligence Reports, China 1911–1941*; G-2 Report, War Department, 893.00/3–3045.

Jacobs, Daniel Norman. *Borodin: Stalin's Man in China*. Cambridge, Mass.: Harvard University Press, 1981.

Jansen, Marius B. "Obituaries: John K. Fairbank (1907–1991)." *Journal of Asian Studies* 51, no. 1 (February 1992): 237–42.

Japan, Rikugunsho, Daijin Kambo, Chōsahan. *Chūgoku kokumintō no rinkaku (The Profile of Chung-kuo Kuomintang)*. Shōwa 8, 1933.

Jordan, Donald. *The Northern Expedition: China's National Revolution of 1926–1928*. Honolulu: University of Hawaii Press, 1976.

Judd, Walter Henry, "The Who Lost China Debate" (sound recording). In November 1949 Congressman Walter Judd discusses the question of American policy in China and the fall of the Nationalist Chinese in 1949.

———. *The U.S. and China's Civil War: John K. Fairbank and Walter Judd Discuss U.S. Policy*, November 1948. 3 cassettes. North Hollywood, Calif.: Center for Cassettes Studies, 1972.

Kan, Kuo-hsün. *Lan-i-she, Fu-hsing-she, Li-hsin-she (Lan-i Society, Fu-hsing Society, Li-hsin Society)*. Taipei, Biographical Literature, 1984.

Kaplan, E. David. *Fires of the Dragon: Politics, Murder, and the Kuomintang*. New York: Atheneum, 1992.

Kapp, Robert A. "Szechwanese Provisional Militarism and Central Power in Republican China." Ph.D. dissertation, Yale University, 1970.

———. *Szechwan and the Chinese Republic: Provisional Militarism and Central Power, 1911–1938. (Ssu-ch'üan chün-fa yü kuo-min cheng-fu.)* New Haven, Conn.: Yale University Press, 1973.

Kirby, William C. *Germany and Republican China*. Stanford, California: Stanford University Press, 1984.

Kitts, Charles Ray. "An Inside View of the Kuomintang: Chen Li-fu, 1926–1949." Ph.D. dissertation, Saint John's University, 1978.

Koen, Ross Y. *The China Lobby in American Politics*. Edited and with an introduction by Richard C. Kagan. New York: Macmillan, 1960, 1967, 1970; Harper & Row, 1974; Octagon Books, 1974.

Kubek, Anthony. *How the Far East Was Lost: American Policy and the Creation of Communist China, 1941–1949.* Chicago: H. Regency Co., 1963.

Kung-chi Ch'en kuo-fu hsien-sheng chi-nien tse (Collection of Funeral Orations and Elegiac Addresses in Commemoration of Mr. Ch'en Kuo-fu). Taipei, 1951.

Kuo, T'ing-i. *Chung-hua min-kuo shih-shih jih-chih (A Daily Chronology of the Republic of China).* Taipei: Institute of Modern History, Academia Sinica, 1979–1985. 4 vols. Vol. 1, 1912–1925; Vol. 2, 1926–1930; Vol. 3, 1931–1937; Vol. 4, 1938–1949.

Lai, Tse-han, Ramon H. Myers, and Wei Wou. *A Tragic Beginning: The Taiwan Uprising of February 28, 1947.* Stanford: Stanford University Press, 1991.

Lary, Diana. *Region and Nation: The Kwangsi Clique in Chinese Politics, 1925–1937.* New York: Cambridge University Press, 1974.

Lattimore, Owen. *China Memoirs: Chiang Kai-shek and the War against Japan.* Compiled by Fujiko Isono. Tokyo: University of Tokyo Press, 1990.

———. *Inner Asian Frontiers.* New York: Capital Publishing Co., 1951.

———. *Pivot of Asia, Sinkiang and the Inner Asian Frontiers of China and Russia.* Boston: Little, Brown, 1950.

Lauer, Thomas Leroy. "German Attempts at Mediation of Sino-Japanese War, 1937–1938." Ph.D. dissertation, Stanford University, 1973.

Lautenschlager, Ray S. "The Triumph of Nationalists in China." *Current History,* 29, no. 4 (January 1929): 650–55.

Lei, Hsiao-ts'en. *San-shih-nien tung-luan Chung-kuo (The Turbulent Thirty Years of China).* Hong Kong: Ya-chou ch'u-pan-she, 1955, 2 vols.

Levenson, Joseph R. "Western Powers and Chinese Revolutions: The Pattern of Intervention." *Pacific Affairs* 26, no. 3 (September 1953): 230–36.

Levich, Eugene William. *The Kwangsi Way in Kuomintang China, 1931–1939.* Armonk, N.Y.: M.E. Sharpe, 1993.

Li, Chien-nung. *The Political History of China, 1840–1928.* Translated and edited by Ssu-Yu Teng and Jeremy Ingalls. Princeton, N.J.: Van Nostrand, 1956.

Li, Leslie. *Bittersweet.* Rutland, VT.: Charles Tuttle Company, 1992.

Li, Tien-min. *Chou En-lai.* Taipei: Institute of International Relations, 1970.

Li, Tung-fang. "Are the Compatriots in the Province of Sinkiang of the Turkish Race?" *Central News* (Chungking), October 14, 1944. Translated by T. M. Chu/RSW, with the approval of Robert L. Smyth, counselor of the embassy for the ambassador (Hurley) to China (confidential) *U.S. State Department Central Files: China Internal Affairs 1945–1949.* Stanford Libraries Film, 3989.

Li, Yun-han. *Tsung jung-kang tao ch'ing-tang (From the Accommodations of Communists to the Purifications of the Party).* Taipei: Commercial Press, 1966. 2 vols.

Liao Chung-k'ai. *Liao Chung-k'ai chi (Collection of Liao Chung-k'ai's Works).* Beijing: Chung-hua shu-ch'u, 1963, 1983.

Lin, Han-sheng. "Wang Ching-wei and the Japanese Peace Efforts." Ph.D. dissertation, University of Pennsylvania, 1967.

Liu, Chi-tseng. *Wu-han kuo-min cheng-fu shih (History of the Wuhan National Government)*. Wuhan: Hupei jen-min ch'u-pen-she, 1980.

Liu, F. F. (Frederick Liu). *A Military History of China, 1924–1949*, Princeton, N.J.: Princeton University Press, 1956.

Lo, Kuan-chung. *Three Kingdoms, China's Epic Drama*. Translated and edited by Moss Roberts. New York: Pantheon Books, 1976.

Loh, Pichon Pei Yung, ed. *The Kuomintang Debacle of 1949: Collapse or Conquest?* Boston: D.C. Heath, 1965.

———. "The Politics of Chiang Kai-shek, A Reappraisal." *Journal of Asian Studies* 25, no. 3 (May 1966): 431–52.

Lund, Renville Clifton. "The Imperial University of Peking." Ph.D. dissertation, University of Washington, 1956; microfilm, Ann Arbor, Mich., University Microfilms International, 1990.

Mandel, William. *The Soviet Far East and Central Asia*. New York, Institutional Secretariat, Institute of Pacific Relations, 1942, 1944; microfilm, Dial Press, 1944.

Martin, Brian G. "The Pact With the Devil: The Relationship Between the Green Gang and the French Concession Authorities, 1925–1935." *Papers on Far Eastern History*, no. 39 (1989): 94–125.

———. "The Green Gang and the Guomindang Policy in Shanghai, 1927–1937." *Papers on Far Eastern History* (Australian National University Department of East Asian History), no. 42 (1990): 59–96.

Martin, Edwin W. *Divided Counsel: The Anglo-American Response to Communist Victory in China*. Lexington: University Press of Kentucky, 1986.

McAleavy, Henry. "China Under the Warlords." *History Today* 12 (April 4, 1962): 227–33; 12, no. 5, (May 1962): 303–11.

McCormack, Gaven. *Chang Tso-lin in Northeast China, 1911–1928: China, Japan, and the Manchurian Idea*. Stanford: Stanford University Press, 1977.

McLane, Charles B. *Soviet Policy and the Chinese Communists, 1931–1946*. New York: Columbia University Press, 1958.

Mendel, Douglas Heusted. *The Politics of Formosan Nationalism*. Berkeley: University of California, 1970.

Myers, Ramon Hawley, ed. *Two Societies in Opposition: The Republic of China and The People's Republic of China after Forty Years*. Stanford: Hoover Institution Press, 1991.

Myers, Ramon Hawley, and Donald G. Gillin, eds. *Last Chance in Manchuria: The Diary of Chiang Kia-ngau*. Stanford: Hoover Institution Press, 1989.

Myers, Ramon H., and Ts'ai Ling. "Surviving the Rough-and-Tumble of Presidential Politics in an Emerging Democracy: The 1990 Elections in the Republic of China in Taiwan." *China Quarterly*, no. 129, (March 1992): 123–48.

New World News (a magazine of world moral re-armament) 4, no. 7 (July 1948): 5.

New York Chinese News Service (tr.). *The Organic Law of the Republic of China: The Final Draft Constitution of the Republic of China*, 1936.

Norins, Martin R. *Gateway to Asia: Sinkiang, Frontier of the Chinese Far East.* Introduction by Owen Lattimore. New York: John Day, 1944.

Odnai, Akira. "Wang Ching-wei and the Fall of the Chinese Republic, 1905–1935." Ph.D. dissertation, Brown University, 1975; microfilm, Ann Arbor, Mich.: University Microfilms, 1978.

Pai, Ch'ung-hsi. *P'ai Chung-hsi hsien-sheng fang-wen chi-lu. (The Reminiscences of General P'ai Ch'ung-hsi).* Oral History Series no. 4. 2 vols. Nanking, Taipei: Academic Sinica Institute of Modern History, 1984, 1985, 1987, 1989. Transcript of 53 oral interviews.

Pepper, Suzanna. *Civil War in China, 1945–1949.* Berkeley: University of California Press, 1980.

Pogue, Forrest C. *George C. Marshall: Statesman: 1945–1949.* Foreword by Drew Middleton. New York: Viking, 1987.

Price, Maurice T. "Communist Policy and the Chinese Nationalist Revolution." *Annals of the American Academy of Political Science Review* 152 (November 1930): 229–40.

Pye, Lucien W. *Warlord Politics: Conflicts and Coalition in the Modernization of Republican China.* New York: Praeger, 1971.

Quigley, Harold S. "Foreign Concessions in Chinese Hands." *Foreign Affairs* 7, no. 1 (October 1928): 150–56.

Rankin, Karl Lott. *China Assignment.* Seattle: University of Washington Press, 1964.

Rankin, Mary Backers. *Early Chinese Revolutionaries: Radical Intellectuals in Shanghai and Chekiang, 1902–1911.* Cambridge, Mass.: Harvard University Press, 1971.

Rasmussen, Thomas J. "The Thought of Ch'en Li-fu: An Ideology of Modernization?" M.A. thesis, Brown University, 1969.

Ristaino, Marcia Reynders. "The Chinese Communist Movement 1927–1928: Organization, Strategies, and Tactics for Making Revolutions." Ph.D. dissertation, Georgetown University, 1977; microfilm, Ann Arbor, Mich.: Xerox University Microfilms, 1978.

Rosinger, Lawrence. *China's Wartime Politics, 1937–1944.* Princeton, N.J.: Princeton University Press, 1944; microfilm, 1987.

Roy, H. T. "Confucian Thought in China in the Nineteen Thirties: Ch'en Li-fu's Theory of the Universe and of the Significance of Man." *Chung Chi Journal* (Hong Kong), Part 1, 7, no. 1 (November 1967): 73–89; Part 2, "Application of His Theory to Social, Cultural, and Political Questions," 8, no. 1 (November 1968): 63–92.

Rozek, Edward J. *Walter H. Judd, Chronicles of a Statesman.* Denver, Colo.: Grier, 1980.

Scalapino, Robert A. *The Last Leninists, The Uncertain Future of Asia's Communist States.* Washington, D.C.: Center for Strategic and International Studies, 1992.

Schaller, Michael. *The U.S. Crusade in China, 1938–1945.* New York: Columbia University Press, 1978.

Selle, Earl Albert. *Donald of China.* New York: Harper & Brothers Publishers, 1948.

Seps, Jerry Bernard. "German Military Advisers and Chiang Kai-shek, 1927–1939." Ph.D. dissertation, University of California at Berkeley, 1972.

Seton-Watson, Hugh. "The Russian and Chinese Revolution." *China Quarterly,* no. 2 (April-June, 1962): 149–65.

Seymour, James P. *China's Satellite Parties.* Armonk, N.Y.: N.p., 1987.

Shaw, Yu-ming. *An American Missionary in China: John Leighton Stuart and Chinese American Relations.* Cambridge, Mass.: Harvard University Press, 1993.

Shen, I-yün. *I-yün hui-i (Memoirs of Shen I-yün).* 2 vols. Taipei, Biographical Litera-ture, 1980. Author of this book is the late wife of the late Huang Fu. Introduction by Chiang Kai-shek.

Sheridan, James Edward. *Chinese Warlord: The Career of Feng Yü-hsiang.* Stanford: Stanford University Press, 1966.

Shirley, James Robert. "Control of the Kuomintang After Sun Yat-sen's Death." *Journal of Asian Studies* 25, no. 1 (November 1965): 69–82.

———. "Political Conflict in the Kuomintang: The Career of Wang Ching-wei to 1932." Ph.D. dissertation, University of California at Berkeley, 1962; microfilm, Ann Arbor, Mich.: University Microfilms International, 1978.

Smedley, Agnes. *Battle Hymn of China.* New York: Alfred A. Knopf, 1943, 1944, 1972, 1975, 1984; Peking: Hsin-hua shu-tien, 1985.

Snow, Edgar. *Red Star over China.* First revised and enlarged edition. New York: Grove Press, 1968. Thirty-one total printings.

Sokolsky, Goerge E. "The Kuomintang." In *China Yearbook* (Tientsen: Tientsin Press, 1927–1929), chaps. 26 and 28.

Stolper, Thomas E. *China, Taiwan, and the Offshore Islands: Together with an Impli-cation for Outer Mongolia and Sino-Soviet Relations.* New York: M.E. Sharpe, 1985.

Stuart, John Leighton. *Fifty Years in China; The Memoirs of John Leighton Stuart, Missionary and Ambassador.* New York: Random House, 1954.

Suleski, Ronald Stanley. "Manchuria under Chang Tso-lin." Ph.D. dissertation, University of Michigan, 1974.

Sun Yat-sen. *The International Development of China.* New York: G. P. Putnam's Sons, The Knickerbocker Press, 1922. With sixteen maps in the text and a folding map at end.

Sung, Samuel S. "The Relation of the Kuomintang to the Common People." *China Tomorrow* 1, no. 2 (Peiping: December 20, 1928) 23–24.

Suzuki, Teiichi. "Hokubatsu to Shō-Tanaka mitsuyaku" (*The Northern Expedition and the Secret Agreement of Chiang Kai-shek and Tanaka*). Bessatsu *Chisei* (special issue of *Chisei*), No. 5, (1956).

———. *Himerareta Shōwashi (Neglected Shōwa History).* Tokyo: N.p., n.d., pp. 20–25.

T'ang, Leang-li. *The Inner History of the Chinese Revolution.* London, George Rout-ledge & Sons, 1930; New York, E.P. Dutton & Co., 1930, 1975, 1977, 1978.

————. "A Revolution of the Revolution." *China Weekly Review*, June 15, 1929; also in *U.S. Military Intelligence Reports: China 1911–1941*, G-2 Report 7551, June 20, 1929.

————. *Wang Ching-wei, a Political Biography*. Peiping: China United Press, 1931.

T'ang, Peter S. H. "Stalin's Role in the Communist Victory in China." *American Slavic and East European Review* 13 (March, 1954): 375–88.

Taft, Robert Alphonso. *A Foreign Policy for Americans*. Garden City, N.Y.: Doubleday, 1951.

Tan, Qingshan. *The Making of U.S. China Policy: From Normalization to the Post-Cold War Era*. Boulder, Colo.: Lynne Rienner Publishers, 1992.

Terrill, Ross. *China in Our Time: The Epic of the People's Republic from the Communist Victory to Tiananmen Square and Beyond*. New York: Simon & Schuster, 1992.

Tien, Hung-mao. *The Great Transition: Political and Social Change in the Republic of China*. Stanford: Hoover Institution Press, 1989.

Titles of Publications of Academicians and Research Staffs of the Academia Sinica. (In commemoration of the sixtieth anniversary year of the Republic of China). Nankang, Taipei: 1977.

Tong, Hollington K. *Chiang Kai-shek*. 2 vols. London: Hurst and Blackett, 1938.

Tong, Te-kong and Li Tsing-jen. *The Memoirs of Li Tsung-jen*. Boulder, Colo.: Westview Press, 1979.

Tsou, Tang. *America's Failure in China, 1941–50*. Chicago, Ill.: University of Chicago Press, 1963.

Tu, Chung-yüan. *Sheng Shih-tsai yü hsin-hsin-chiang (Sheng Shih-tsai and the New Singkiang)*. Tihwa, 1945.

Turnley, David, Peter Turnley, and Melinda Liu. *Beijing Spring*. Introduction by Orville Schell. New York: Stewart, Tabori and Chang, 1989.

Tyau, Min-ch'ien T. Z., ed. *Two Years of Nationalist China*. Shanghai: Kelly and Walsh, 1930.

Upshur, Jiu Hwa Lo. "China under the Kuomintang: The Problem of Unification, 1928–1937." Ph.D. dissertation, University of Michigan, 1972; microfilm, Ann Arbor, Mich.: 1973.

Wales, Nyn [Helen Foster Snow, pseud.]. *Notes On The Sian Incident, 1936*. Typescript, Madison, Conn., 1960.

————. *Historical Notes in China*. N.p., 1961.

————. *My Yenan Note Book*. N.p. 1961.

Wallace, Henry Agard. *Tribute to Russia*. Foreword by Corliss Lamont. New York: Congress of American-Soviet Friendship, 1942?

————. *Soviet Asia Mission*. With the collaboration of Andrew J. Steiger. New York: Reynal and Hitchcock, 1946.

Wang, Ke-wen. "The Kuomintang in Transition: Ideology and Factionalism in the National Revolution." Ph.D. dissertation, Stanford University, 1985; microfilm, Ann Arbor, Mich.: University Microfilms International, 1985.

Wang, Keng-hsiung. *Sun Chung-shan yü Shang-hai* (*Sun Chung-shan* [Sun Yat-sen] *and Shanghai*). Shanghai: Jen-min ch'u-pen-she, 1991.

Wang, Tien-shan. *The Chinese Mind: As Seen from Confucianism*. San Francisco, Calif.: San Francisco Confucian Society, 1992.

Wang, Tung-yüan. *Wang Tung-yüan t'ui-ssu-lu* (*Reminiscences of Wang Tung-yuan*). Taipei: Cheng-chung shu-chü, 1992.

Weale, B. L. Putnam (Bertram Lennox Simpson). *Chang Tso-lin's Struggle against the Communist Menace*. Shanghai: Kelly and Walsh, 1927.

Wei, Wou. *Capitalism: A Chinese Version*. Columbus, Ohio: Asian Studies Center, Ohio State University, 1992. Text of the Land-to-the-Tiller Act of National Government, January 20, 1953, pp. 198–208.

Wertenbaker, Charles. "Washington's Darkest Mystery: The Chinese Lobby. *The Reporter* 6, no. 8 (April 15, 1952), Part 1: 4–24; 6, no. 9 (April 29, 1952); Part 2: 4–22. With an introduction by Max Ascoli, editor and publisher of the magazine. Ch'en Li-fu's visit to Dewey in the summer of 1948, Part 1, pp. 18–19.

White, Theodore H., and Annalee Jacoby. *Thunder out of China*. New York: William Sloane Associate, 1946; London, Gollancz, 1947; New York, Da Capo Press, 1980.

Whitfield, Stephen J. *The Culture of the Cold War*. Baltimore, Md.: N.p., 1991.

Whiting, Allen Suess. *Soviet Policies in China, 1917–1924*. New York: Columbia University Press, 1954.

Whiting, Allen Suess, and Sheng Shih-ts'ai. *Sinkiang: Pawn or Pivot?* East Lansing: Michigan State University Press, 1958.

Wilbur, C[larence] Martin. *The Nationalist Revolution in China, 1923–1928*. Cambridge, Eng.: Cambridge University Press, 1983.

Wright, Mary F. "From Revolution to Restoration: The Transformation of KMT Ideology." *Far Eastern Quarterly* 14, no. 3 (August 1955): 515–32.

Wu, T'ien-wei. *The Sian Incident: A Pivotal Point in Modern Chinese History*. Ann Arbor: University of Michigan Center for Chinese Studies, 1976.

"Why Russia Can't Be Trusted: Here's the Record." *Collier's*, January 27, 1951, pp. 22–23.

Yang, Kwang-sheng. "China Abrogating Unfair Treaties with the Powers." *Current History* 25, no. 5 (February 1927): 697–703.

Yang, Shubiao. *Chiang Chieh-shih ch'uan* (*Biography of Chiang Kai-shek*). Hangzhou: T'uan-chieh ch'u-pan-she, 1989,

Yang, Winston L. Y. "Taiwan Since 1988: Democratization, Foreign Policy, and Relations With Peking." *American Asian Review* 10, no. 1 (Spring 1992): 42–61.

Yao, Ping Wang. "The Nanking Incident, March 24, 1927." Master's thesis, University of Wisconsin, 1958

Yeh, Yu-fu. *Ch'en Li-fu hsien-sheng ti che-hsüeh ssu-hsiang yen-chiu* (*Study of Ch'en Li-fu's Philosophical Thought*). Kaoshiung: Fu-wen Book Co., 1991.

Yoshihasi, Takehiko. *Conspiracy at Mukden: The Rise of the Japanese Military*. New Haven, Yale University Press, 1963.

Yu, George T. *Party Politics in Republican China: The Kuomintang, 1912–1924.* Berkeley: University of California Press, 1966.

Part 5: Documentary Videofilms

Sun Yat-sen and the Three Principles of the Revolution. Princeton, N.J.: Films for the Humanities and Archives, GM-2555, 1991, 17 minutes.

The Chinese Revolution. Princeton, N.J.: Films for the Humanities and Archives, GM-2596, 1991, 25 minutes.

Index

NOTE: Chinese names are alphabetized syllable by syllable. When conflicts arise, words beginning with voiced consonants (or consonant blends) precede corresponding syllables that begin with unvoiced consonants (or blends); for example, Cheng Tung-ho precedes Ch'eng tien-fang

STUDIES IN ECONOMIC, SOCIAL, AND POLITICAL CHANGE:
THE REPUBLIC OF CHINA
Ramon H. Myers, Series Editor